Reconciling Ancient and Modern Philosophies of History

Trends in Classics – Pathways of Reception

General Editors
Franco Montanari and Antonios Rengakos

Editorial Board
Lorna Hardwick, Craig Kallendorf, Fiona Macintosh, Miltos Pechlivanos

Associate Editors
Anastasia Bakogianni and Rosanna Lauriola

Volume 3

Reconciling Ancient and Modern Philosophies of History

Edited by
Aaron Turner

DE GRUYTER

ISBN 978-3-11-099590-9
e-ISBN (PDF) 978-3-11-062730-5
e-ISBN (EPUB) 978-3-11-062746-6
ISSN 2629-2556

Library of Congress Control Number: 2020944898

Bibliographic information published by the Deutsche Nationalbibliothek
The Deutsche Nationalbibliothek lists this publication in the Deutsche Nationalbibliografie;
detailed bibliographic data are available on the Internet at http://dnb.dnb.de.

© 2022 Walter de Gruyter GmbH, Berlin/Boston
This volume is text- and page-identical with the hardback published in 2020.
Cover image: Paul Klee, Hauptweg und Nebenwege
Printing and binding: CPI books GmbH, Leck

www.degruyter.com

Contents

Aaron Turner
Introduction: Reconciling Ancient and Modern Philosophies of History —— 1

Part I: Awakening Ancient Historical Consciousness

François Hartog
The Territory of the Historian in Antiquity —— 11

Laurence Paul Hemming
Just Forces: Heidegger, Arendt and Antiquity —— 25

Duncan F. Kennedy
On not Being Modern: Exploring Historical Ontology with Bruno Latour —— 43

Alexander Meeus
Truth, Method and the Historian's Character: The Epistemic Virtues of Greek and Roman Historians —— 83

Jonas Grethlein
The Universal in the Particular: A Core Dilemma of Historicism in Antiquity —— 123

Part II: Transcending Representation and Reality

Aske Damtoft Poulsen
Teleology with a Human Face: 'Side-shadowing' and its Effects in Tacitus' Treatment of Germanicus (*Annals* 1–2) —— 149

Katherine Clarke
Minding the Gap: Mimetic Imperfection and the Historiographical Enterprise —— 183

Inger N.I. Kuin
The Life of the Biographer: Plutarch's Presence in *Sulla*, *Antony* and *Otho* —— 207

Ahuvia Kahane
Demos, Democracy and Method: Political Trust and the Science of Suspicion —— 231

Part III: Antiquating Modernity

Salvatore Tufano
Walter Benjamin and Greek Historiography —— 263

Jerry Toner
When Augustus met Adorno: Class, Mimesis and Restoring the Past —— 291

David Carr
Teleology and the Experience of History —— 311

Aaron Turner
The Limits of Progress and the Modern Problem of Historical Meaning —— 327

Neville Morley
Thucydides and the Historiography of the Future —— 355

List of Contributors —— 369
Index —— 371

Aaron Turner
Introduction: Reconciling Ancient and Modern Philosophies of History

The transition from antiquity to modernity is typically characterised as progress. The tendency in the progress of knowledge is toward greater and greater specialisation. The specialisation of history as a professional discipline in the 19th Century through Wilhelm van Humboldt, Barthold Georg Niebuhr, and, most significantly, Leopold von Ranke concretised historical enquiry as a mode of documentary criticism and textual analysis. Modern historical consciousness emerged from out of the concept of culture that characterised the Enlightenment of the 18th Century. In part, embedded within historical consciousness is the conflict between modern and ancient ideals of politics, ethics, and aesthetics. For Immanuel Kant, Johann Gottfried Herder, and Georg Friedrich Hegel, among others, historical consciousness pertains to an understanding of modernity as the perfection of humanity whereby historical development proceeds from a provenance of constraint toward a state of freedom. Ranke rejected the Hegelian metaphysical comprehension of historical development and instead recognised through the diversity of particular epochs and the nation-states that constituted them a coherence of history driven by divine will. For Ranke, the task of historical enquiry is the revealing of the dominant tendencies that characterise a particular epoch through exhaustive archival research and philological documentary analysis.

The rapid growth of the natural sciences in the mid-19th Century shook the foundations of historicism that had developed principally through Herder and Ranke earlier that century. Despite the emergence of the historical sciences under the likes of Wilhelm Dilthey, Wilhelm Windelband, Heinrich Rickert, and Friedrich Meinecke, whose efforts to radicalise historicism through the broadening of Kant's three Critiques were ultimately futile, the machinery of positivism overwhelmed and subjected historical enquiry to absolute standards of truth. By the mid-20th Century, through Carl Hempel's seminal work on scientific history, the historical particular had been reduced to nothing more than providing the means to produce 'explanation sketches' through which universal, law-like behaviour could be observed in historical processes.

The overturning of positivism within the philosophy of history occurred largely in response to the radicalisation of the historical sciences effected by Hempel. The development of the philosophy of language initiated principally by Martin Heidegger and Ludwig Wittgenstein (though its genesis can be traced back to Gottlob Frege and Ferdinand de Saussure at the beginning of the 20th Century) heralded a new mode of historiographical consideration. The so-called 'linguistic turn' in Western thought reconfigured the notion of language not as an instrument of human thought but as its ground. It was appropriated by the philosophy of history through Hayden White's seminal work, *Metahistory* (1973). White, contending against the views of Hegel, Nietzsche, and Croce that history functions differently to literature, arguing that historiography amounts to "a verbal structure in the form of a narrative prose discourse that purports to be a model, or icon, of past structures and processes in the interest of explaining what they were by representing them".[1] The elevation of the linguistic structure of historiography above the substantive relation of historiography to past reality severed historical enquiry from its engagement with history *wie es eigentlich gewesen*. Historiography, pertaining to classification, emplotment, aesthetic tropes, complexity, and narrative, fell under the auspices of literary theory. The inception of narrativism, conceived by White, continued its legacy under the likes of Frank Ankersmit, Arthur Danto, and Richard Rorty.

It was perhaps inevitable that the study of ancient historiography would approximate itself to this new trend. The linguistic turn facilitated new literary techniques such as narratology to be developed through Tzvetan Todorov, Roland Barthes, and Gérard Genette. The application of narratology to ancient literature was conducted through major studies by the likes of Irene de Jong, Simon Hornblower, and Tim Rood. Eventually, the truth-conditions underlying ancient historiography were brought into question and summarily disbanded. According to Anthony Woodman's *Rhetoric in Classical Historiography* (1988) – a study extending from Thucydides to Tacitus – ancient historiography amounted to nothing more than a branch of rhetoric, wherein poetic tropes were employed for the purpose of persuasion. Where ancient historiographical truth had already begun to be queried by the likes of Moses Finley and G.E.M. de Ste. Croix, Woodman, echoing T.P. Wiseman's *Clio's Cosmetics* (1979), argued that rhetorical education had always been prioritised over truth and accuracy by the ancient historians.

While Woodman and Wiseman epitomised the general stance of the philosophy of history as a form of narrativism toward the end of the 20th Century, J.E. Lendon's retaliatory invective against the encroachment of literary theory upon ancient historiography mirrored the revitalisation of scientific historiography in the 1990s. Lendon was not engaging with these new trends but remonstrated against Woodman and Wiseman, arguing that through White's "fashionable re-

---

[1] White 1973, 2.

duction of history to a function of literature... young classicists [following Wiseman and Woodman] saw in the literary study of historians a road to lofty elevation".[2] Lendon's assault on the radical relativisation of truth that the philosophy of history had engineered through its engagement with literary theory could be substantiated by the philosophy of scientific historiography that has been developing over the past thirty years. Prominent philosophers, such as Peter Kosso, Aviezer Tucker, Yemima Ben-Menahem, among many others, have appealed for history's recourse to the methodologies of the sciences. Through the revision of the sciences since the mid-20th Century as the specialisation of the physical and theoretical sciences, the philosophy of science has particularised its mode of study toward individualised complex systems. The reintegration of abstract concepts of causality, such as necessity and contingency, as well as teleology and progress, into historical discourse underlies rise of the philosophy of scientific historiography.

The conflict between historicism and positivism at the end of the 19th Century has been reignited at the beginning of the 21st Century as neo-historicism under the guise of narrativism and neo-positivism forged through the philosophy of history's appropriation of complex systems theory plunge history into another identity crisis. The aim of this book is not to engage directly with the debate between neo-historicism and neo-positivism but rather to prepare the way for a revaluation of the essence of history through a reconsideration of the genesis of historical thought in antiquity. Each of the fourteen essays that constitute this volume aim in some way to recover an originary understanding of historicality that has been lost through history's constant approximation to other disciplines. The marginalisation of ancient historiography according to the dictates of 'progress' and 'modernity' within the modern philosophy of history is owed to the perpetual revaluation of historical values whereby ancient thought is considered primitive and redundant. By reconsidering the awakening of the ancient historical consciousness, the modes and means by which ancient historians mediated between historical reflection and historiographical consideration, and the essential character of ancient historicity within the context of modernity, this book demonstrates the manifold possibilities that a comprehensive reappraisal of the ancient philosophy of history offers to modern historical thought.

---

2 Lendon 2002, 56–57.

Part 1 – Awakening the Ancient Historical Consciousness

What constitutes historical consciousness? In modernity, consciousness of historicality resulted from a reflective consciousness cultivated through the emergence of the concept of culture. Historical consciousness designated the awareness and acknowledgement of a progressive value. History aspired toward the perfection of humanity. The awakening of historical consciousness in antiquity occurred in conjunction with the self-identification of Greekness as distinct from barbarism. The rise of the *polis* facilitated the delineation of Greek from Greek. The diversity of Greek *poleis* and their particular mythical foundations led to the first known historian, Hecataeus of Miletus, developing a genealogical systematisation of the Greeks stretching back to the heroic age. Greek historiography of the fifth century represents the apex of the ancient historical consciousness. The first section of the book is devoted to the manner in which ancient writers themselves conceived of history. That is, what they understood 'doing' history to be and how they set about its enterprise. The essays that constitute this section consider the emergence of an ancient historical consciousness *on its own terms* and the development of ancient historical thought through antiquity.

This, first and foremost, requires that we put aside our modern, preconceived notions of historical method and locate, as **François Hartog** here suggests, 'the territory of the historian', wherein the essence of the ancient historical project lies stripped of its retrospectively applied concepts and procedures. The development of Greek historical thought inevitably establishes for itself its own schema that subsequent works of historiography could be compelled to follow. Hartog's chapter traces the emergence of historical consciousness through the standardisation of Greek terms that signify the growing understanding of history itself as it seeks to differentiate itself from epic poetry. Such differentiation is marked most significantly by the degree of truth with which historiography in contrast to epic poetry proclaims to comply. For **Laurence Paul Hemming**, the emergence of an ancient historical consciousness is precisely the ground for the awakening of a political consciousness centred around the *polis*. Through an interpretation of Aristotle's *Politics* channelled through modern readings of Martin Heidegger and Hannah Arendt, Hemming attempts to identify the 'essence' of the 'political' within the historical relation of 'man' and '*polis*'. Only through a comprehension of this relation is historical self-understanding – the essential foundation of historical consciousness – possible.

Duncan Kennedy explores the awakening of an ancient historical consciousness by elucidating historical ontology in action through readings of Herodotus and Plato. Kennedy's chapter embraces Bruno Latour's ontological turn and his famous dictum, 'we have never been modern', in order to question the fundamental assumption of modernity's authority over antiquity. Kennedy's rendering of an ancient historical ontology subverts modern comprehensions of a paradigm shift between ancient and modern modes of self- and world-understanding. **Alexander Meeus'** chapter interrogates precisely the nature of truth that characterises ancient historical thought in comparison to its modern equivalent. Meeus attempts to identify the parameters of the ancient concept of historical truth through its various obstacles, such as patriotism, bias, and partisanship. Such accusations, so often levied against the ancient historiographical tradition, serve only to substantiate the claim of epistemological superiority that modern historiography exercises over its ancient counterpart. For Meeus, though, a thorough examination of the epistemic virtues expressed across a broad spectrum of ancient histories reveals a far greater adherence to truth than is often credited. Finally in this section, **Jonas Grethlein** attempts to elucidate the prehistory of the tension between the universal and the particular which has dominated modern historical and philosophical discourse since the Renaissance. Grethlein's paper shows through both Thucydides and Aristotle the primordial foundation of this tension and how, through a reading of the *History* and the *Poetics*, ancient thought can mend the modern tension. For Grethlein, a new range of perspectives on the relationship been the universal and the particular can be established in Thucydides and Aristotle and, ultimately, how narrative can function as a paradigmatic mode of thinking.

Part 2 – Transcending the Distinction of Representation and Reality

The second section concerns the fundamental relation of representation and reality that traditionally distinguishes history as a historiographical exercise and the past itself. The problem of the distinction between historiographical representation and past reality extends back to antiquity but it rose to prominence following Ranke's determination of historical writing as a conveying of the past 'as it really happened' (*wie es eigentlich gewesen*). Such an obligation served only to highlight the inadequacies of historiography as a mode of producing knowledge, especially in light of the more rigorous exactitudes the natural sciences demanded of their subject material. The impossible demand of historiography to produce true propositional statements of the past grounded in a coherent narrative demonstrating cause and effect instigated history's turn to the methodologies and practices of literary studies. The narrativism of White and Ankersmit offered historical narrative an alternative means of extracting historical meaning from texts but in doing so it severed historical enquiry from past reality itself. The chapters that constitute this section explore authorial modes of overcoming the distinction between representation and reality by positing the significance of the author – the writer of history – as a mediating factor between reader and the reality of the past.

The experiential character of the ancient historical narrative is explored by **Aske Damtoft Poulsen**, whose chapter identifies moments of experientiality and 'side-shadowing' devices that restore the possibility of possibility within the narrative. The deployment of such devices to simulate historical open-endedness enables the historian to mitigate the teleology of past events and their inevitability in the narrative. Damtoft Poulsen elucidates such practices within Tacitus' *Annals* and argues that Tacitus laid alternative historical paths in order to challenge the prevailing notion of the Principate as inevitable. In **Katherine Clarke's** chapter, it is precisely the contradistinction between representation and reality that must be overcome. For Clarke, the 'gap' between the historical re-presentation of the past and past reality itself is not a void that must either be overlooked or filled through an experiential orientation to the event in question. By examining the narratives of Herodotus, Diodorus Siculus, Tacitus, and others, the 'gap' is identified as the dwelling of the various layers of meaning and truth that form the essential relationship between author and reader. For Plutarch, the gap between the Greek and Roman historical figures depicted appositionally in the *Parallel Lives* is one he himself fills through the relation of common characteristics and virtues. **Inger Kuin**, though, recognises that the biographer employs more unconventional means in order to bridge the 'gap' between the reader and the representation of character: Plutarch himself. Kuin's chapter explores the rare instances of Plutarch's self-inclusion – his 'intrusions' – within the *Lives* of Sulla, Anthony, and Otho, and asks, ultimately, what do such instances reveal of Plutarch's overall methodology?

Ahuvia Kahane's chapter looks toward transcending the distinction between historiographical representation and the past itself by considering the *logos* of democracy as it is presented by Thucydides in Pericles' Funeral Oration. Kahane, through divergent interpretations of the Oration by A.W Gomme, Josiah Ober, and Jacques Ranciére, attempts to identify important 'isomorphic' principles of politics, philology and philosophy which can guide our understanding of historical perspective and the relation between the classical past, ideological positions and modernity. Like Kuin's Plutarch, Kahane's Thucydides is an intrinsic element of his own work. Ultimately, the unity of thought between Thucydides and Pericles is itself embedded within the historicity of history and essentially dependent on the mediation of historiography.

Part 3 – Antiquating Modernity

Where the foundations of the 18th Century Enlightenment developed out of a modern historical consciousness that distinguished itself from antiquity, and where teleological notions of historical progress characterised the major philosophical debates of the 19th Century, and where the concept of modernity was crystallised in the 20th Century, the roots of antiquity nonetheless occupy, often in significant ways, the minds of modern historical thinkers. This section begins with essays dedicated to the reception of ancient philosophies of history within the development of modern modes of historical understanding. This section then considers the progressive line that modern philosophies of history can take by embracing ancient ideas of historicality. **Salvatore Tufano's** treatment of Walter Benjamin's historical thought offers an insight into the reconcilability of ancient and modern philosophies of history, Benjamin, who, as Tufano shows, was greatly influenced by his reading of the classics, particularly Herodotus and Thucydides. For Tufano, it is only through reading Benjamin through the ancient historical tradition that the profundity of Benjamin's own philosophy of history emerges. For **Jerry Toner**, the relation of ancient and modern modes of historical thought is not limited continuities and discontinuities of historiographical *praxes*. Rather, Toner, in his chapter, identifies a reciprocity between ancient *praxis* on the one hand, in the form of Augustus' political activities as Roman Emperor and, on the other hand, modern philosophical *theoria* in the context of Theodor Adorno's concept of political mimesis. Through this reciprocal interpretation Toner suggests that we're able to identify both an anticipation of Adorno's *theoria* and a new appreciation of Augustus' historical accomplishments. **David Carr** interrogates the fundamental distinction between the philosophical representation of history and the actual experience of history itself. Carr's chapter grounds an understanding of historicity within the phenomenological experience of time in order to ask an important question: Is there a direct experience of history, a distinctively historical experience that differs from other experience? And if so, how might such an understanding legitimate ancient philosophies of history? For **Aaron Turner**, the very concepts of 'progress' and 'modernity' and the various modes of historical enquiry that have developed since the Enlightenment have served only to conceal the ancient understanding of history. Turner's chapter charts the radical steps that modern philosophers of history, from Giambattista Vico to Aviezer Tucker, have taken to bury the essence of history beneath the manifold methodologies that scientific and linguistic theories impose upon historical enquiry. For Thucydides, rather, historical truth emerges through the historicity of human Being, and it is toward such historicity that genuine historical enquiry must proceed. Finally, **Neville Morley** develops a dialogue between

Thucydides and Friedrich Nietzsche in order to establish possible meanings of the past that will serve the future development of historiography. Morley's chapter contrasts Thucydides' philosophy of historiography with the modes of historical writing that Nietzsche criticises in the modern era. Through Nietzsche's indictment of modern historiography and his obvious admiration for Thucydides, Morley poses the question: how can knowledge of the past be made useful or productive?

Ultimately, the fourteen essays that constitute this book serve to demonstrate not simply the immeasurable profundity of ancient historical thought, nor even simply to advocate its enduring relevance to the problems that modern philosophies of history face. Rather, this volume aims at preparing the way for a comprehensive rehabilitation of ancient historical thought within the ongoing discourses that continue to plunge history deeper and deeper into an identity crisis that is already over four hundred years old.

Part I: **Awakening Ancient Historical Consciousness**

François Hartog
The Territory of the Historian in Antiquity

In which sites did history take up residence and what places did ancient historians claim for themselves? To repeat a once well-known expression: what has been the historian's territory?[1] Did history manage in the beginning to carve a space for itself? Can we say, seven centuries last, during the Imperial era, that it "secured" its domain, as a craft or as a discipline? I will limit my remarks to a few highlights, lingering at the sites where the framing device had far-reaching implications for the status of history and the figure of the historian: beyond the ancient world, as it was the case with the intervention of Aristotle in the *Poetics*.[2] These sites had firstly proper names.

1 The Initiators

Our first foray places us during the gradual, inaugural upheaval occurring between Homer and Herodotus, on which I have dwelt on several occasions. On the one hand, we must contend with the disappearance of a forum for speech and narrative form orientated towards the elevated accomplishments of heroes: the epic. On the other hand, we can observe the emergence of a form of story-telling addressing above all 'what men have done'. At the core of the mechanism of epic narration was the dynamic which it presupposed between the muse and bard as her interpreter. It is the undermining of this mechanism, the loss of faith in this inspired speech, which cleared the space in which the discourse of Herodotus establishes itself, allowing for the emergence of its characteristic form and lexicon.

Everything is present from the very first phrase, thereafter the subject of tireless scrutiny and commentary: a name, which is also a declaration of method – *historiē*; a proper name (his own); an objective, which is to counteract the forgetfulness which menaces all with erasure by recounting the great deeds of Greeks and barbarians; a subject: the war they had waged and, 'withal', why they entered into war (in terms of reasons and causes to be identified and responsibility to be apportioned). By thus taking the floor in his own proper name, Herodotus

---
[1] It is the title of a book by Ladurie 1973.
[2] See Hartog 2013, 109–152 where I investigate the use of Aristotle up to Hayden White, on one side, and Carlo Ginzburg, on the other side.

addresses several questions of contemporary concern: 'What must be accomplished before authorizing oneself to say 'I'? 'Where must the one who leads this enquiry (*historei*) stake out his position'? No longer having access to the omniscience of the muse, he can only have recourse to *historiê* and undertake a procedure of enquiry, the first stage of the historiographical operation. Yet serving initially as a substitute, *historiê* ultimately enters into a relationship of affinity with the muse, who for her part knew everything because she was present in everything. Acting as his own source of authority, the narrator-historian aspires to 'drive forward his narrative by calling to memory in equal measure (*homoiôs*) the great and the small among the cities of men'.

If *historiê* both calls to mind the knowledge of the bard and breaks with it, there is another gesture of commencement which brings the figure of the diviner to the fore and invokes the field of divination. Herodotus *historei*, yet he *sêmainei* also: he names, reveals, signifies. Right from the prologue, at the very same moment when for the first time he takes the floor by saying 'I', he *sêmainei*. He reveals, names, for example, the one who first engaged in offensive acts against the Greeks, which is to say Croesus the king of Lydia. Through this seeking and assigning of responsibility, Herodotus does not present himself as or seek to play the role of seer, although he does appeal anew, on the basis of the self-assurance of his own knowledge, to a style of authority of the oracular type. Thus invested, *historein* and *sêmainein* mark the crossroads at which ancient and contemporary knowledge meet and intersect. They constitute two operators for 'seeing clearly' and further into the distance, beyond the visible in space and time; two gestures which give the practice of the first historian its particular character and intimate its possible territory: neither bard nor seer, yet between bard and seer.[3]

Writing some decades later, what is Thucydides' own understanding of what he does? Carefully avoiding *historiê*, *historein*, yet also *semainein*, he determines the nature of his intervention by employing a verb of action of an almost technical character: *sungraphei*.[4] 'Thucydides of Athènes has consigned to writing the war ... how they waged war' (*sungraphei ton polemos, hôs epolemesan*). *Sungraphein* and *sungrapheus* will subsequently become standard terms for designating the writing of history and the historian. From this moment onwards, two paths open for history: one for the historian understood as investigator, the other for the histo-

---

3 Hartog 2007, 72–73.
4 *Suggraphein*: take note, consign to writing, compose a project of law, a contract. The prefix *sun-* also indicates that it is a question of committing to words the war in its entirety and taken as a whole, to bring together all the episodes to make of this a singular totality: the war.

rian understood as author. *Historia* (in Greek and in Latin) was accordingly subject to generalization across the following centuries, even though the former understanding waned in prominence while the latter waxed.

Unlike *historein*, which indicates a method and posture (and which can be traced back to the Archaic and Homeric *histôr*), *sungraphein*, which only relates to the later stages of the historiographical operation, the *mise en forme*, says nothing about method. It is in these terms that Thucydides frames it in subsequent chapters, not directly through any exposé, rather through an extraordinary demonstration of his method in action. In effect, while searching for certainty in the past of Greece, he traces the limits of historical knowledge: to be precise, the touchstone for the acquisition of such knowledge is autopsy; yet this is an autopsy which, to be valid, requires a rigorous critique of witnesses. This demand has the consequence of limiting the truth of history to the confines of the present. For past times we must undertake to 'find' the facts. How? By collecting the *semeia* (signs) and the *tekmeria* (evidence); all so many clues which require sifting through with a view to attaining a knowledge which does not exceed the order of *pistis*. The end result is a form of knowledge with affinities to that of the judge, who by the end of the trial has forged for himself a steadfast conviction.

Leaving the figures of narrator and diviner far behind, the historian of Thucydides locates his system, with all its demands, between the gaze of the doctor (autopsy) and the practice of the judge (*pistis*). He aspires thus to definitively break with all those who he designates and denigrates as *logographoi*, 'storytellers', starting with Herodotus (who is not named). The latter, by aiming to seduce those who listen to them, live in the pleasure of the instant and bask in their own ostentation, whereas Thucydides aims for that which alone has real value. While indeed he signs this '*sungraphie*' with his own proper name, he is economical with the 'I' of the first person.

Nevertheless, Thucydides recognizes along with Herodotus the requirement of embracing both sides of the conflict: the Greeks *and* the Barbarians; the Athenians *and* the Lacedaemonians. This imperative is inherited directly from Homer and the epic. From high on Mt Olympus Zeus sees simultaneously the Achaeans and the Trojans. How are we to maintain this demand when we can no longer assume the position of an all-seeing divinity? To recount all that which is great among the accomplishments of the Greeks and Barbarians, Herodotus makes use of inquiry, which is to say concretely of his voyages: of the exile which he experienced; of his life, not *apolis* certainly but divided between two cites (Halicarnassus and Thourioi, in Greater Greece). Thucydides declares expressly that it is his exile of twenty years which has enabled him to 'see things from both sides' (*Thuc.* 5.26).

These are the positions which have been staked out by the end of the fifth century. Xenophon, who follows immediately after, does not further our understanding of the activity of the historian. On the contrary, his intervention is rather indicative of a loss of bearings for such activity and a clouding over of its horizon. I remarked that the *Hellenica*, the history which follows on from Thucydides, opens and closes with a formula of extreme laconism: 'after that ... (*meta de tauta*). Its first appearance serves to create a link to the closing phrases of the *Peloponnesian War*, whereas the second invites a future successor. Between the two, a man who left Athens after 403, commits all the confusion of his era to writing. There is nothing in the way of a preface, conclusion, or exposé of method; no proper name to delineate a project, to delimit an ambition or clarify expectations. Must we infer that that the reader of the book knew, from the very first words, what was to be made of it? That Xenophon could take for granted that the genre was sufficiently recognizable? Or that it sufficed merely to follow in the footsteps of Thucydides, who himself had followed Herodotus? For his part, Xenophon in the Anabasis is insistent in his use the third person to speak of his own actions, and goes as far indeed as to attribute the work to a certain Themistogenes of Syracuse. Why this recourse to a pseudonym? To praise himself thereby all the more effectively, if we are to believe Plutarch! Through this remark, Plutarch testifies to the emergence of an issue which will subsequently take on much importance: that, namely, of the relation between eulogy and history. Polybius will later wrestle with it, although when Xenophon is writing, the discourse of eulogy, the creation of which Isocrates takes for himself the honors, is still at its beginnings. By appealing to this process, he aspires in any case to a position of exteriority: the historian cannot be the direct protagonist of what is reported. This position of detachment is pursued to the point of effacing the narrator: he is no longer present, he is another. We will later rediscover this temptation.

2 An Outsider

Through his contributions, infrequent yet of great consequence, Aristotle proceeds almost without intending to a process of ordering. This takes the form initially of a questioning of the pretentions of the historian, whose territory is reduced in size and divided up. In the list of those I name the outsiders of history, he represents, in effect, one of the most imposing figures. As proof we could cite the recent appeals to Aristotle of Paul Ricœur and Carlo Ginzburg in the context of their reflections on the contemporary status of history. This might indeed lead us to forget that history was never Aristotle's central problematic. Taking a wider perspective, we can observe a repetition or prolongation of the paradox over the course of the centuries that, in the consideration of what is, what is not or what should not be history, numerous are the appeals to outsiders. It is a paradox which can be traced back to the vacuum left by the demise of the epic, which places us before the advent of history; yet Homer, who occupies the position of an outsider, is no less for that orientated towards the emergence of *historia*. Later we have the *oukase* of Aristotle (polemicizing, in fact, against Plato on the status of poetry), then Cicero (who toyed for a longtime with the idea of writing a history, primarily his own) followed in the 2nd century by Lucian of Samosate, who is anything but a historian.

For Aristotle, history, let us recall, does not arise from *poiêsis* or have access to *mimêsis*; nor can it aspire to *epistemê*. It does not, moreover, have a place of its own within the three (and only three) genres of discourse listed in the *Rhetoric*: the deliberative, judiciary and epidictic. The task of the historian is only to 'say what happened' (*ta genomena legein*), and not what could or should happen. Unlike tragic poetry, history does not give access to the register of the necessary, plausible or possible. Yet while Aristotle clearly sets out what history is not, he barely concerns himself with presenting in a minimally organized or systematic way what it might be.

We in fact find only scattered and indirect notes. As a form of narrative, it has for its domain above all the particular. When we pass to the realm of the deliberation of assemblies, it can take on value as an aide to the political decision-making process. This would involve an understanding of *historia* as the accumulation of examples and useful data, as providing the supplement of *empeiria*. In this subordinate position it supplies material for arguments, which is to say informed premises for the formulation of the syllogism characteristic of rhetoric: the enthymeme. In this somewhat subservient role, *historia*, as compilation and the drawing up of lists, culminates in what we will later call antiquary research, the beginnings of which Arnaldo Momigliano sees in the sophist Hippias. For Aristotle, *historia*, taken in this restricted sense, does not arise from rhetoric; yet it is the 'affair of politics' (*Rhet*. 1360 a37) and with little thought for the past as such it serves the end of immediate utility. Let us finish by noting that Aristotle knows and employs in the *Poetics* the name *historikos* to designate the practitioner of *historia*.

3 A Historian's Response

While reading the first pages of Polybius, we receive the impression of a history sure of its own correctness and a historian confident in his role. He indeed boldly proposes a new history for the new world brought about by Roman domination. As a hostage in Rome he 'saw' global history and understands Rome as its instrument. His organizing concept is *sumplokê* (interconnectedness). Before the year 220, the occurrence of events in the world had the character of being 'disseminated', which is to say 'lacking as much a unity of conception and execution as a unity of place'. Yet following the second Punic war, history 'began to take on the form of an organic whole and its events a woven fabric, the threads lacing together' under the aegis of Fortune which 'has constrained all human affairs to orientate themselves towards a single and same goal' (Pol. *Hist*. I, 3, 3–4). It follows that *autopsie* no longer suffices for the new historian who must accordingly appeal to a new notion, borrowed from philosophy, to express the grasping of the totality: *sunopsis*.

The historian must attain for himself this vision of the whole, this general view of things which corresponds to the perspective of Fortune. He must see it *as* Fortune, strive to assume its position and reconstitute its point of view for the reader, thereby enabling the later to glimpse the universal character of history, which Polybius names 'general' history. *Sunopsis* is two-fold: it has both an epistemological and narrative dimension.

How are we to situate the writing of Polybius? We should note first of all that he is both writing in Rome and in the wake of Roman domination. Yet it is from within the Greek intellectual tradition that he will find the instruments rendering his intellectual undertaking possible. Nevertheless, he makes his own the reflections of Aristotle on tragic poetry and history in order to turn them towards new ends. With and against Aristotle, he elaborates the conceptual framework of a new history yet to be written. The new course taken by history, since Rome has made its presence felt in the Mediterranean, allows him to affirm with assurance the superiority of history over tragedy: of history as real tragedy (Pol. *Hist*. 2.56.11–12). History can be equally described according to the terms of Aristotle's definition of *muthos*, as a 'system of facts': it forms a whole, it has a beginning, a middle and an end. Far from being confined to an isolated particular, it gives access to the general. Yet the 'general' of Polybius is not that of Aristotle: by general we must understand the 'all', the totality which has constituted history since 220 and which we must grasp from a synoptic perspective. General history sets itself apart from partial history (*kata meros*) and can be ultimately understood in a spatial sense as 'catholic history' (*historia katholike*) (Pol. *Hist.* 2.65.11–12).⁵

For Polybius, the place of the historian is not the library, but the field. What counts above all is 'the experience acquired through action and by ordeal'. This is why he sees in Odysseus an ideal for the historian: he who has travelled far and wide, lived and endured much. By ordeal, we must understand the difficulties experienced and risks run in order to enquire, to travel and see places, and to interrogate witnesses. Yet we must also understand by it exile. Polybius knew something of the latter, having spent 17 years in Rome. He does not hesitate to appeal to Plato in advocating the position of the historian. Just as society will only prosper when kings will be philosophers or philosophers kings, history will only prosper once statesmen realize that writing is the highest and most necessary of tasks, or conversely when future historians understand that political training is indispensable. This remains true for as long as we do not separate making and writing history: so believes Polybius, who perhaps converted to history only because he could no longer participate in the sphere of action. Yet these fine proclamations must not have made much of an impression, for history had already lost out to philosophy and in Rome was ousted from the field of serious affairs.

4 A Second Outsider

From Polybius to Cicero, we remain at Rome to trace a sequence of the highest significance, since what is at stake is the determination of who controls the territory of history. Does history enjoy a measure of autonomy, or does it constitute no more than a sub-domain within rhetoric? To be precise, Cicero formulates a paradox, destined to enjoy a long life, which can be summarized in terms of the two following propositions: history does not emerge from within rhetoric; yet its writing falls above all within the domain of competence of the orator. Given such a paradox, how are we to conceptualize the place or "territory" of history? How can we deny that the historian is an orator, and yet affirm that the orator is, by virtue of his position, the best historian?

If we dwell on the principals of rhetoric as outlined by Cicero, we notice that Aristotle's three genres of discourse are still present. Three and three only; yet in reality, they are two plus one. This is because the key divide is between *negotium* and *otium*. The preserve of *otium* is the forum: in other words, the space of the

---
5 Hartog 2007, 130.

judicial, the deliberative and the political, therefore of rhetoric whose central personage is the orator embodied by Cicero himself. All remaining discourses belong to the sphere of *otium* and therefore fall under the category of the third genre: the epidictic. History, which constitutes part of this remainder, belongs thus unmistakably to the latter genre. It is indeed striking to notice that, when Antonius considers the epidictic, he speaks only of history. Certainly, he does not neglect Herodotus or Thucydides or Polybius. Yet such Greek intellectuals, however talented, are to be read merely for the relaxation and feeling of pleasure (*delectationis causa*) they allow. History does not amount to a serious activity. It is placed in the camp of pleasure from where Thucydides had wanted to extract it; excluded from the forum and consigned to the sphere of *otium*, if we follow Cicero. History registers primarily, if not exclusively, in terms of the pleasure taken in stylistic flourish alone.

Might history at least draw comfort from having escaped from rhetoric? Not even this is true, and this is the second proposition. To the extent that the epidictic is the 'cradle' (*nutrix*) of eloquence, as borne out by the formidable discourse of Isocrates, to the extent also that the epidictic emerges from within the sphere of rhetoric (as a third genre according to Aristotle), the orator also believes himself in a position to assert his authority over the epidictic, and therefore ultimately on history. For the orator, in his acquisition of the mastery of speech, the epidictic genre plays an analogous role to the *palaestra* in the preparation for combat. Yet following the end of the Republic and the establishing of the *Principate* the clashes in the forum resonated ever more emptily, while the epidictic for its part occupied ever more territory, to the point indeed of becoming the milieu from within which 'literature' is born. Faced with the expansion of the epidictic, which risked absorbing history by reducing it to a variant of eulogy, historians strove ceaselessly to create distance, to install barriers, by insisting on the unique character of their method, its difficulties and the usefulness of its results.

A century later, Quintilian, who inherited from Vespasian the first chair of rhetoric, reaffirms the traditional distinction between what belongs to the *forum* and all that remains outside it. His subject is the training of future orators, and he is thus concerned with explaining what is to be gained from reading history: 'from history (in similar fashion to poetry) the orator may procure a certain pleasant and abundant sap', he tells us, 'yet we must read it . . . in such a way that we know that most of its qualities are to be avoided by the orator. In effect, in very similar terms to poetry, it is to be regarded as something akin to a poem in prose (*carmen solutum*) and is written for the purposes of storytelling (*ad narrandum*), not to provide proof (*ad probandum*). What is more, the work as a whole does not set out to accomplish anything, neither is it designed for the purposes of immediate verbal combat: its primary goal is to recall facts for the memory of posterity and to spread the renown of the talent (of the historian)[6]. Nothing in this is really new, except Quintilien's way of dotting of the 'i's. Withdrawn from the debating arena, he tells us, it has the need neither to prove (*probare*) nor move (*movere*). It is not animated by concern, nor is it driven by the search for objective proof, which would involve the mobilization of the parts of the defense speech which are the *confirmatio* and the *refutation*. Nor for that matter is it driven by the search for subjective proof, which is to say the appeal while, coming to a conclusion, to emotion and passion (*peroratio*). We can measure the considerable distance taken here from the *Poetics*, by noting that Quintilien, without batting an eye, presents history as a kind of poetry in prose form, whereas for Aristotle the *Histories* of Herodotus, even in verse, would have remained history. Poetry is accordingly from now on the affair of meter and image, and the Aristotelian moment of the poetic has retreated so far into the distance that he now cuts the figure of *hapax*. The boundaries between the genres have been permanently reconfigured. The status of history, however, which never succeeded in making itself recognized as a genre in its own right, remains very much in question, at least until the modern era and the emergence of the modern concept of History (let's say with Ranke).

5 A Third Outsider

Lucian is himself also, if I dare say it, a *hapax* in his genre. His *How to Write History* is the only classical treaty on history which has come down to us.[7] It is assuredly not the work of a historian, but of a man of letters known for his caustic spirit, his acerbic critiques and his parodical style which had so entranced the humanists from Erasmus onwards. Syrian by origin, Greek by culture, having lived in Athens, he served in the imperial administration under Commode. Indis-

---

6 Quintilien, *Institution oratoire*, 10, 31, transl. M. Casevitz. He adds a little later, 10, 34: "Another benefit can be drawn from history – indeed the principal once, yet it does not concern the present question –, it concerns the knowledge of facts and examples on which above all the orator must remained informed". We rediscover here Aristotle and the ancillary function of *historia*.
7 Lucian of Samosata, Volume VI. *How to Write History*.

putably an outsider, he will nevertheless pass for an insider, since his treaty (written in 166), and passed down to us via the *Artes historicae*, echoed loudly throughout the ages from the Renaissance until the 19th century.

His work is decisively marked by the sequence Cicero-Quintilian, which results in his adopting the paradoxical position of presenting history as both outside the field of rhetoric and under its jurisdiction: in other words, both having and not having its own territory. He is cognizant likewise that history can no longer escape the gaze of the prince. The pretext of his treaty is indeed the recounting of the recent Parthian war, conducted under the theoretical command of Lucius Verus (who took it as an opportunity to get his hands on the title *Maximus*). Yet, at the same time, and contradictorily, he draws a portrait of the historian as a Thucydides *redivivus*. On the one hand, he codifies the writing of history in such a way that it appears as if it emerged only from the sphere of leisure and the epidictic. On the other, he reaffirms strongly the need for utility, therefore for the truth of history and the necessity of standing at a distance from both the epidictic and poetry. Thus he insists that between history and the epidictic we must erect a veritable 'wall' (Lucian. *Hist. conscr.* 7). He clearly articulates, in other words, what amounts to the principal risk of their confusion.

He believes he is reactivating through such injunctions the famous distinction of Thucydides between the narrative of the *logographoi*, who seek only the pleasure of the instant, and his own which, seeking only the useful, maintains its value for always. Yet almost seven centuries have passed since its formulation by Thucydides and thousands of histories have been written! If Lucian enables us to come to a decision as to what history should and should not be, as to what the historian should and should not do, he equally leads us to an impossible place and, above all, an untenable position. The historian should be 'a foreigner in his own writings', he should not write for his contemporaries and should be, as sincerely as possible, *apolis* (Lucian. *Hist. conscr.* 41). We are presented, in other words, with an extreme form of self-abnegation on the behalf of the historian, abnegation to the point of negation: he is no-one and nowhere. In fact Lucian thereby situates himself in close proximity to Xenophon, with the caveat that the latter is concerned with recounting the immediate past. Might say that such extreme formulations, especially when put forward by Lucian, cannot be taken at face value?

However we answer this question, the *aporia* remains no less inescapable. History as it is written is ridiculous; history as it should be written is impossible. Lucian sees this ridiculousness exemplified by the historians of the Parthian war, who he takes much delight in denouncing at the beginning of his treatise. He brands those, namely, who consider themselves the new Herodotus, Thucydides, not say Homer, with hypertrophy of the *ego*, castigating their high flown declarations of autopsy even through it is evident that they never witnessed what they are narrating. What ruins their credibility from the outset is the pretension to reclaim *historia*- enquiry, while they have never taken a step outside their own home. They usurp a certain place, and flout the contract constitutive of such narratives.

We could end our observations on Lucian here; yet he has not said his last word on history. In another treatise, *True History*, which should be read in conjunction with *How to Write History*, seems in effect to have as its principal goal to ridicule the pretensions of history and of historians. Lucian presents us with a narrator who says 'I' and carries the name of Lucian: both author and character at the same time. The complete opposite of Xenophon! He makes his position clear from the start in the following terms: 'as I have never lived through anything interesting, I have decided to write on the subject of what I have never seen nor experienced, nor learned from any other and, in addition, on what does not in any way exist and absolutely cannot exist'. Therefore, you must not believe me. What follows are adventures which are parodical exaggerations of well-known authors, beginning with Homer, Herodotus, Ctesias, Iamboulos and a host of others. The 'I am lying' is thus entirely fabricated from the lies of others, with the sole difference that these others had aspired to speak the truth. He assumes his dramatis personae, in other words, to undermine such pretensions. We are to believe that between these authors and the ridiculous 'historians' of the Parthian war, themselves also imitators, there is fundamentally no difference. From the beginning to the end we must cut a path through a play of textual references from which it seems impossible to escape.

Nevertheless, while thus lambasting history, Lucian simultaneously takes up the entirely contrary position, that of the defense of history: a history as exemplified by the writings of the one who for him embodies both law and prophet – Thucydides; a history which has for its aim the truth, a truth for which Thucydides is the spokesperson. It follows that history was possible since, on at least once occasion, it did correspond to this ideal. Thucydides serves as proof of its possibility, which entails of course that the truth depends thereby on the reliability of the historian as its sole guarantee, a quality which can be neither learned nor codified. Thus, through the intercession of Thucydides, Lucian reclaims truth and utility for a historical discourse which has henceforth no trouble distinguishing itself from eulogy and keeping poetry at bay; a discourse which, in seeking to best express 'how things happened', results in a kind of non-rhetorical rhetoric.

Yet what would Thucydides have wished? To 'commit the war to writing', which is to say 'how they made war with each other (*sungraphei ton polemon, hôs epolemesan*). These are his first words, or in a variant phrasing: 'declare in order what came to pass/as it came to pass each summer and winter' (*gegraptai hexês hôs ekasta egigneto kata theros kai cheimôna*, 2.1); or again 'write from point to point, by summers and winters, how/as everything came to pass' (*graphein hexês hôs ekasta egeneto*, 5,26). Lucian sought to fully reenact Thucydides' imperative; yet after Aristotle, Cicero and Quintilian the conditions of its fulfillment had been modified. It is by Lucian's time understood that the 'facts' are present, the historian does not have to 'find' them. Unlike the orator, he does not have to look for *what* to say because, taking care of what has already taken place, he need only concern himself with *how* to say it (no longer *hôs*, but *hopôs*) (Lucian. *Hist. conscr.* 51). He is not a *poiètes*, as Lucian (echoing Aristotle) phrases it; he is a mere 'exhibitor', a 'revealer' of facts, and must strive to act like a limpid mirror. This 'how' (*hopôs*) limits the sphere of the scriptural mission of the historian and it is here, and here alone, that Lucian's prescriptions taken on their particular value.

Believing once more that he is following in the footsteps of Thucydides, Lucian insists that the historian must turn his back on the present and write for posterity. This is yet another way of marking the necessary divide between the discourse of eulogy and history. It serves as a way of escaping the need for sycophancy, yet also of the (extremely real) dangers of not giving sufficient praise to the powerful. We have at work here another form of renouncing or asceticism: the historian should put a cross through the present. Yet posterity has never nourished anyone, and in this appeal to Thucydides can be detected a distancing and a creative misunderstanding: alas, how true it is that too much fidelity can lead to infidelity! The core value of Thucydides' analysis was his concern for accuracy and precision, his aspiration towards the highest measure of truth to be grasped from the present situation ('as that which happened'). It is indeed this rigor which holds open the possibility of its utility in the future, if or when a comparable crisis arises. Otherwise put, there is no question of turning away from the present. On the contrary, only by residing in closest possible proximity to the present can the history of the Peloponnesian War be of future use. This was no meager ambition; and we should remember that at no stage did Thucydides call himself 'historian'. By 'writing the war', he in fact aspired to forge something approaching a political science, indeed perhaps political science as such: one Pericles for always. In sum, therefore, Lucian in his treatise attempts to bring together two heterogeneous visions of history, one pre- the other post-Aristotelian. Despite his best efforts, he does not succeed in bridging the divide, one which will periodically resurface and trouble historians for a long time to come, with Thucydides called on again and again to play the role of great intercessor.

Thus despite the intervening 17 centuries, in the two famous Rankean mottos ('simply say/show how it happened') can be found an echo of the formula of Lucian. The adversary of Ranke is no longer the discourse of eulogy but the historical novel. While we cannot of course understand Ranke as offering here a mere gloss on Lucian, we may understand from their proximity that the dilemma of how to stake out a position for history in the face of the relentless expansion of the epidictic genre has remained a primary preoccupation over the centuries. This would be a position of necessity located both within and without this genre, in search of a non-rhetorical rhetoric to say 'how things took place' (*hôs eprachthe*) (Lucian. *Hist. conscr.* 39): for a rhetoric, that is, which presents itself as a refusal of all rhetoric. Ranke rejects as much the history which judges as the history which would seek to teach lessons.

Thus, the only treatise from the ancient world on history leaves us at an *aporia*: the juxtaposition of a hyper-Thucydidean epistemology with a set of rules arising from the tempered rhetoric of the genre of eulogy. In sum, what emerges from the reconstruction of this Greco-Roman sequence is that there was never a well-defined territory of the ancient historian. The negotiations over the place of history in the order of knowledge, and the historian in public space, have never ceased. Historians have been tireless in finding makeshift solutions, but they remained far away from the *ktêma* forever and from a continuous expansion. From its heady beginnings with Herodotus, discoverer of a new country, we pass to the austerity of Thucydides' dream of firmly establishing his '*sungraphie*' (if possible 'for evermore'), by forging for it a method, but also clear limits. Yet this conquering and self-assured science did not escape the defeat of Athens unscathed, and Xenophon's writing bears its scars in a double sense: in the obscuring of the horizon of the historian, and in the ascendency of philosophy. Political science, as we are wont to imagine, is not the affair of the historian but of the philosopher.

To escape the position of the simple storyteller, or reduction to the subservient role of supplier of examples to decision makers, the historian must strive to present history as a true 'mastery of life'. It must be seen to take on value, that is, as practical moral philosophy. Yet in this ambition it is thwarted by a fundamental weakness: having never gained recognition as a genre of discourse in its own right, history is obliged to constantly struggle to avoid falling into the enormous churn of epidictic discourse or under the yoke of rhetoric. Of course, it can struggle effectively or simply seem to struggle (rhetorically), this is an ambiguity which remains at the heart of the discipline; yet for the historian to settle for anything less would be to abandon any claim to be taken seriously.

Bibliography

Hartog, François (2007), *Évidence de l'histoire*, Paris.
Hartog, François (2013), *Croire en l'histoire*, Paris.
Ladurie, Emmanuel Le Roy (1973), *Le territoire de l'historien*, Paris.

Laurence Paul Hemming
Just Forces: Heidegger, Arendt and Antiquity

We speak now, and often, of "the political".[1] There are books, articles, and talks on "Heidegger and the Political", and "Arendt on the Political", identifying "the political" as an immediately self-evident region, while defining in advance how it is to be entered. We begin, therefore, with a warning – a warning announced by Heidegger in the context of lectures he gave on Freidrich Hölderlin. Heidegger tells us "the πόλις does not admit of being determined politically".[2] What Heidegger means by this, and how we might at least glimpse an understanding of it, I hope to do in what is here merely, and no more than, a sketch for a future thinking.

We may find the first, formal, attempt to secure the meaning of "the political" in Aristotle's *Politics*. Aristotle says "and therefore by nature the πόλις is prior to the household and to each of us considered as individual" (Arist. *Pol.* 1253a19).[3] This is because the whole, the totality, is of necessity prior to its parts. This declaration arises on the basis of two things: one, that "the human being is by nature the living being that is political"; and second, because speech is what the human being, "alone of all living beings, possesses". The human being is the political living being because it is the living being possessed of speech (Arist. *Pol.* 1253a2–3, 9–10).[4]

In this short passage – one which shaped the whole history of the enquiry into "the political" in the West – a decision has already been made: the πόλις is first among those things that enable us to understand whatever is "by nature", κατὰ φύσει. "The political" is the means by which we understand our being with one another. "The political" is therefore a region that stands already as having been opened for us: one which we not so much enter, but to which we are already, and firmly, bound, "by nature". Yet this decision tells us very little: *how* we are bound is left obscure. Contemporary "political" discourse is everywhere at the present time – across the West and beyond it – marked by a confusion as to *how*

---

[1] An earlier version of this paper was offered to the CDEA (DAAD Porto Alegre) conference *M. Heidegger – H. Arendt no seu tempo* at the Catholic University (PUC) in Porto Alegre, Brazil, on October 29th and 30th, 2018, and published as 'Forças justas', translated by Théo Amon in *Martin Heidegger e Hannah Arendt no seu tempo – e no nosso*, edited by Kathrin Rosenfield and Felipe Gonçalves Silva (Porta Alegre 2019), 65–83.
[2] Heidegger 1996, 99. "*Die πόλις läßt sich nicht politisch bestimmen*" (Heidegger's italics).
[3] καὶ πρότερον δὲ τῇ φύσει πόλις ἢ οἰκία καὶ ἕκαστος ἡμῶν ἐστιν.
[4] ὁ ἄνθρωπος φύσει πολιτικὸν ζῷον ... λόγον δὲ μόνον ἄνθρωπος ἔχει τῶν ζῴων.

"the political" is to be secured, because, we presume, it is something that we already understand. How else would we speak so easily of it, if its meaning were not so self-evident to us? We are left with the mere presence of "the political" as such, and with the cities and nations that stand up and out before us, the entire sphere of "the social" and "society" as such, whose presence, whose formations and institutions, all testify that there is "the political".

The nineteenth and twentieth centuries were characterised by repeated attempts at "philosophies" of "the political", often driven by goals of, let us say, overcoming the immiseration of the masses, or protecting individual liberty, or achieving a universalised equality (often without much definition of such equality *is*), establishing "meritocracy", and so forth, resulted in extreme and terrifying experiments involving the fates and lives of millions: whole nations, whole peoples across entire swathes of the globe. In the wars and upheavals that ensued, tens of millions were uprooted from their homes, even exterminated, and hundreds of millions were subjected to daily humiliations at the hands of tyrannical and totalitarian regimes. The ceaseless struggle to define "the human essence", and guarantee its freedom has been both without end, and without outcome. So much faith has been invested in the inevitability of progress, and the capacity of a technologically driven mobilisation of life to guarantee it, that in every case where the stated goals of that progress have failed or found to be wanting, the solution has – without a moment's further thought – been the pursuit of *more*, of *further*, even *better* progress. In the course of all this upheaval, we have submitted ourselves and the world we inhabit to a continuous degradation in the name, continuously stated and claimed, of building a better and more universal future: a better world. The renewed interest in figures like Thomas Hobbes and his *Leviathan* illustrate the extent to which contemporary "philosophy" has been unable to think through for itself the object it has identified as one most proper for it, but has pitched and yawed and been tossed about in the uneven search for that for which it can find no ground.

"The political" has increasingly been constituted by what can be planned in advance to secure it, what can be demanded *of* it, for a future hope. This thought, too, is, in a certain way, already present in Aristotle. For Aristotle argues that the πόλις is at once the reason for the existence of every other κοινωνία, "common life" (many translations have "partnership"), and it has a τέλος, a "purpose", and an "end". This end, Aristotle tells us, is the highest, best, or most proper (βέλτιστον) purpose and end for common life (Cf. Arist. *Pol.* 1252b30–33). We do not have time here to consider how it is, or why, the whole of "the political", as the self-evident region I have identified, has now come to be understood through an imperative mode, a mode of progress that – to simplify – we would need to understand as the mode of "becoming" as such. Every contemporary political theory, from Hegel, Mill and Marx, to the contemporary obsessions over the "politics of identity", operates now, not through what *is*, the πόλις as it *now* is, but rather by pointing up how it *ought* to be. This *ought* is constantly realised as a planning and re-arranging, as a constant mobilising, for what is not yet here, but *must*, and imperatively so, be accomplished. The plan is to be achieved because it can already be conceived: as that which is understood in advance of every occurrence of its being effected, it conforms to what Aristotle himself called τέχνη. Τέχνη is the mode of truth of "the plan". This conception of "the political" is marked, above all, by "the successive", by the constant demand for transformation into an opposite, which, through its constant over-stepping of itself and becoming other, resolves and annihilates every prior difference into itself. This is what Hegel called *Aufhebung*. At once cancellation of what was, for the sake of accomplishing what is (more highly) to become.

Hannah Arendt's thinking the "essence" of "the political" returns us to that region of thinking that prompted above all Hegel's investigations: historical development. For what runs in advance of the political is, she says, that from whence it came. Or, as she puts it, the *polis* emerged because of the "development" of a distinction, "between the public and private realms, between the sphere of the *polis* and the sphere of household and family".[5] Arendt constructs an entirely artificial opposition between household and *polis* in order to ground a notion of freedom (which she contrasts with the "necessity" that arises within and characterises the family), which she proposes as an historical development because "the *polis* was distinguished from the household in that it knew only 'equals', whereas the household was the centre of the strictest inequality".[6] This idealised account of historical development is falsified by history itself: many were the Greek city states in thrall either to the cities that founded them (and so knew no freedom over their own affairs, and knew equality only through a shared and equal servitude); or to those that had vanquished and mastered them by some means or after some war; or were in thrall to "political" tyrannies of their own making. The word tyranny does not always signify an evil regime: tyrants were often simply kings. Arendt, even with her turn to the historical, offers a purely anthropological and historical account that would have been recognisable to Hegel – indeed she places her account firmly within the understanding of progress that Hegel described – where the alterity of the other – the difference of the different – is to be understood entirely through "the successive", as that which

---

5 Arendt 1998, 30.
6 Arendt 1998, 32.

proceeds toward the "goal", the "end" (τέλος) of "the political" as such, as "primitive" forms of human life overcomes their backwardness and progress toward modernity and its accomplishment of freedom.

Hegel's understanding of "the political", indeed all contemporary foundations of "the political", depend on the successive, as what, in a series of dialectical oppositions, attains to the reaching of the "goal", the purpose and end, of "the political", and as what subsumes under a new resolution what previously pertained, resolving it as something higher. This essentially constructive understanding sits at the basis of, and provides the metaphysical explanation for "the political", as it is to be found from Hegel's early "Jena System-Sketches", right up until the publication of the *Rechtsphilosophie*, the work of political thinking published towards the end of his life. There is one feature of this concept of the successive that should not be overlooked. Because we *already* know the goal toward which we are intended (the "best", the "highest" possible expression of "the political"), although the end is not yet attained, the end that we have in view decides *in advance* the value and meaning of everything that tends towards it. This is a peculiar feature of every understanding of "progress", every process of "dialectic", every notion of "social construction": the future goal, "the political", *decides*. It is the decisive ground through which the present is to be re-arranged (for the sake of a better future) and by means of which the past is to be judged. Indeed, this certainty of knowledge, of that place toward which we are headed, provides us with the basis and ground for disposing of, and rejecting, everything that fails to take us where we know already we are headed. It is that against which we measure ourselves and our progress. "The political" is marked by the constant mobilisation of the present for a future whose imperative and meaning we already recognise is some way (the future we have posited for ourselves is already present as an imperative).

Miguel de Beistegui's now well-established book, *Heidegger and the Political*, opens with a quotation from Heidegger's *Being and Time* in John Macquarrie's and Edward Robinson's translation that says the following:

> Dasein's ways of behaviour, its capacities, powers, possibilities, and vicissitudes, have been studied with varying extent in philosophical psychology, in anthropology, ethics, and 'political science' [...] But the question remains whether these interpretations of Dasein

have been carried through with an originary existentiality comparable to whatever existentiell primordiality they may have possessed.⁷

De Beistegui proceeds, on the basis of how he interprets this quotation, to seek the "originary" (modified from Macquarrie and Robinson's "primordial") existentiality that co-ordinates his enquiry to the "existential primordiality" the quotation seems to be speaking of. Because *Being and Time* represents a "fundamental ontology", de Beistegui translates this into what he finds to be Heidegger's belief in the "ontological precedence of philosophy over politics", one that (he argues) allows *Being and Time*, in a sense, he argues, to be "pre-political". This leads de Beistegui to suggest that Heidegger is "wanting always to hand the essence of politics over to something which would not be political (namely: being, presence)".⁸ Is there an "essence of politics"? Is there a "pre-political" ground for thinking that allows us to bring "the political" into view? Isn't Heidegger's very argument that finding ourselves always and already *being* with one another (*in via*, as Augustine would have said – in German, *unterwegs*, but just as much "in the street", we would say, or "in the public square", as North Americans have it, and so in within the πόλις) is the ground and possibility itself for understanding being at all?

Not so: politics, de Beistegui claims, is founded, not in being "with one another", but on justice, a justice derived through Aristotle's thinking: "politics is born from this indelible [justice] which enjoins us to think *away from being* ... the difference through which everyone comes to be related to an Other. Politics is only the expression of this differential relation which is always a relation of power and desire".⁹ We need note only in passing that the "thinking away from being" is precisely the thinking *into* the imperative that we have already identified as the marker of every contemporary expression of "the political". It is the constant demand to reconstruct the πόλις as the *better*, the "beyond (the) being" that it *presently is*. How else are we to begin to understand presence, if not firstly

---

7 De Beistegui 1998, 8. De Beistegui makes only one, significant change to the original translation. See Heidegger 1977, 22. "Weil nun aber zum Dasein nicht nur Seinsverständnis gehört, sondern dieses sich mit der jeweiligen Seinsart des Daseins selbst ausbildet oder zerfällt, kann es über eine reiche Ausgelegtheit verfügen. Philosophische Psychologie, Anthropologie, Ethik, »Politik«, Dichtung, Biographie und Geschichtsschreibung sind auf je verschiedenen Wegen und in wechselndem Ausmaß den Verhaltungen, Vermögen, Kräften, Möglichkeiten und Geschicken des Daseins nachgegangen. Die Frage bleibt aber, ob diese Auslegungen ebenso ursprünglich existenzial durchgeführt wurden, wie sie vielleicht existenziell ursprünglich waren".
8 De Beistegui 1998, 160.
9 De Beistegui 1998, 160 (my emphasis).

and foremostly through that which presently is? Yet for de Beistegui, the πόλις must constantly *become*, in order to become more just. Here, in essence, is the understanding of "the political" that marks the modern age: the relations of power that presently pertain are exactly those over which we are required to *take power*, to organise to become other, in order to guarantee a "better" future: the future of "the political" as such. This is how *becoming* orients itself: as a "toward which", through which I overleap myself (and everything else besides), in order to become most fully what I ought to be (and so really "I am", and what *I* was always supposed to be).

That de Beistegui understands politics in this way is visible from the translation he takes over of the passage of *Being and Time*. The "justice" of which he speaks is derived from the fundamentally and inconcussibly constituted structure of metaphysics: sameness, constituted through difference: every "other" (that is already other to each other) that appears is both alike to what it is other to, and other to it at the same time. Put another way, every other is other to each and all of the others (and can take itself to be as such) in the *same* way. We are all the same because we are – at the same – also different, other, so-constituted through relations only ("always") of "power and desire", which structure, constitute and arrange difference as such. Or rather, the identity of sameness is constituted through the alterity of the other: de Beistegui even emphasises this by capitalising the word "Other". Understood like this even *I*, or rather *every* "I", "I-ness (*Ich-heit*)" as such, is constituted through otherness to itself: it is both same/other to every other, and same/other *as* "an" "itself". How do we know this? The translation speaks of "Dasein's ways of behaviour, *its*...". Elsewhere de Beistegui speaks of "Dasein's ability to relate to *its* own historical situation and to other Daseins".[10] The word "Dasein" functions in de Beistegui's understanding of "the political" as an "it": for him, *Dasein* is the name for the individual, the universally constituted self-hood of the self: the subjectivity of the subject: that mode of being that, as subject, is at the same time object, for itself.

But surely the translation only tells us what the German says? In Heidegger's German there is no "it", no *es*: the German speaks of "der jeweiligen Seinsart [singular] des Daseins" – "the respective mode of being of *Dasein* [as such]": the German indicates that the manner of being (*Seinsart*) – Macquarrie has, not "manner of being", but "behaviour" – of Dasein is singular, and so there aren't many "Daseins", just "Dasein" itself and as such. The German speaks of the particular manner of being of *Dasein* – as such – which takes respective forms in (to use the translation's words) "capacities, powers, possibilities, and vicissitudes", each of

---

10 De Beistegui 1998, 20 (my emphasis).

which is possible within *Dasein* as a whole. It is only within the differing "capacities, powers, possibilities, and vicissitudes" that anything like individuality and anything resembling individuals appear. Macquarrie has subtly shifted the emphasis of Heidegger's meaning, away from *Dasein* as a description of the meaning of being, toward *Dasein* as a name for individuation, which leads de Beistegui to interpret this passage in a very particular way, a way not supported by the original German. Is this accidental? *No!* It is the hardest thing in thinking for us to understand that individuality is *taken off* from our already being-with-one-another: the whole burden of the philosophy of subjectivity has worked in the reverse direction – seeing "us" as a "heap", a collectivity, of individuals, rather than an already present generality *from out of which* individuality is something extracted, individuated, particularised.[11]

De Beistegui's understanding of "the political" as originating in "power and desire", a power and desire constituting the character of what passes between individuals, between subjects, is actually unremarkable:[12] it is the condition under which nearly all thinking of "the political" is now understood (however loosely), as what is always to be taken for granted in advance of any constitution of "the political" in contemporary discourse. The concept of justice at work here

---

[11] Even the most cursory examination of the method of doubt, of the accomplishment of Kant's thought of the "I am" that accompanies our every thought *in advance of every thought*, should reveal to us that the individuation of the "I am" is taken off from an already existent unity of world, and is not the disclosure of an individuality that is already from the outset separate from world.

[12] This analysis owes its origins to Foucault, Deleuze, and Guattari. See Foucault (2011, 186), where he speaks of the "champ du pouvoir et du désir" ("field of power and desire"). Both here and elsewhere Foucault expressly associates this definition of "the political" with his thoughts about Oedipus, and with Deleuze and Guattari's construction of desire. Foucault concludes "Si complexe d'Œdipe il y a, il ne se soue pas au niveau individuel, mais collectif ... à propos du pouvoir et du savoir", this at the level of "the political". Michel Foucault, 'La vérité et les formes juridiques (A verdade e as formas jurídicas)' in *Dits et écrits*, vol. 1, p. 1423. ("If there is an Oedipus complex, it underpins not at the level of the individual, but the collective ... with respect to power and knowledge"). That Foucault understands this within a thinking of subjectivity is revealed by his use of the strange construction "se soue", what underpins, or places itself beneath (*sub-iectum*). Desire does not disappear in this construction – but becomes machinic: it is what every subject involuntarily does in order to become a willing subject, hence Foucault's reference to Deleuze and Guattari. The *social*, and so political, subject is that which appears alongside the not psychic, but machinic representation of desire, which can only be resolved between subjects through, and as, power itself. Deleuze/Guattari 1972, 50 "la machine désirante ... qui produit un sujet à côté de la machine" ("the desiring machine ... which produces a subject alongside the machine").

is not Aristotle's δίκη, but Nietzsche's *Gerechtigkeit*: every subject secures its difference to every other subject through a justification which is the positing of a "highest". Justice is secured on the basis of the highest and strongest drive. In his first investigation into justice, Nietzsche tells us "truly, no-one lays claim to a higher level of veneration than the one in possession of the drive and strength for justice. For the highest and rarest virtues are united and concealed in justice as in an unfathomable sea".[13] The demand for justice is itself the *production* and construction of truth, and of new truths. "The political" necessarily involves an "over-against", a relation of opposition *between* subjects, that both differentiates them one from another, and then sets them into an order of difference, starting at the level of the highest, and ranks them downward according to the scale it produces and establishes. We should note that it is not the one with the claim *on* justice who establishes and founds this claim, but the one capable of establishing justice for the claimant. Power and desire, to be held (rather than challenged and relinquished) must at the same time be *justified*. This production is undertaken from a place of valuation, thus beyond and outside what is valued. What is to be valued may be unaware of the value it has been ascribed. You may not really know, or recognise, yourself in the justice which is to be established for you – according to this scale of values. The place of power is occupied by the one undertaking the valuation, *not* the one being valued, whose power is only derived from the valuation, and so the height of justice is the establishment of the power (the right) to value of the one doing the valuing.[14]

That one alone who is capable of establishing justice is the one who, seeing there is justice to be done, fulfils it, and thereby establishes themselves as the one who establishes the heights and the depths of justice. This is how I (whoever *I* claims to be) can "speak for all who …", can speak on behalf of and in the *name of* all. This is how straight men can become the "allies" of lesbians, and white folk can become the best advocates for the rights of people of colour. This is how the justified can identify the self-hatred of those who need justice but refuse it for themselves. When I understand, and recognise, difference as it *should* be thought, I can even know what's best for you – by this means I can know you better, perhaps, than you know yourself.

---

[13] Freidrich Nietzsche, 'Unzeitmäße Betrachtungen' (KSA1), 286. "Wahrlich, niemand hat in höherem Grade einen Anspruch auf unsre Verehrung als der, welcher den Trieb und die Kraft zur Gerechtigkeit besitzt. Denn in ihr vereinigen und verbergen sich die höchsten und seltensten Tugenden wie in einem unergründlichen Meere".
[14] This is exactly how the "politics of identity" works, and is the most extreme form of Hegel's maxim: "Das Anerkanntseyn ist das Daseyn". See Hegel 1976, 208.

* * * * *

So far, we have left unanswered our two central questions: Is there an "essence of politics"? And is there a "pre-political" ground for thinking that allows us to bring "the political" into view? To answer these questions will mean returning to the lines of Aristotle that I have quoted from the *Politics*, and it will mean returning to the lines of *Sein und Zeit* quoted earlier, whose translation I suggested was inadequate, but which I left, in a certain way, undecided. Above all else, it will mean reaching back into the very question of what philosophy, of what thinking itself, is capable *for*. We need therefore to ask a third question: does thinking *decide*? Does "philosophy" clarify *in advance* the being of whatever is? If it does not clarify "in advance", what, or rather how, can thinking in fact think?

We are to a certain extent dazzled by Aristotle. What dazzles us is his "reason for being" of the πόλις. Aristotle tells us καὶ πρότερον δὲ τῇ φύσει ἐστίν: "and therefore [the πόλις] is prior by nature". From now on, it seems, we are to consider the πόλις because is it *first*. But the text does not say it is first – it says: *because of something else already said*, "and therefore" *it is first*. What was already said? What was already said was that the human being is the ζῷον πολιτικόν. This is normally translated as "the political animal". The πόλις is "first" because the human being is the political living being, rather than the "living being for the household (οἰκίον)" or "the living being for him- or herself (αὐτός) alone". These are the two alternatives that Aristotle suggests as possible rivals to the primacy of the πόλις. Is the πόλις first because the human being is the political living animal, or is it the human being's "politicality" that makes the πόλις first? Clearly it is the latter, since Aristotle sets them in a certain sequence, and tells us "and therefore", because the human being is the living being that is political, the πόλις is first. The πόλις is what is extant and present, and so is what lies before us as the indication of the human being's politicality. We need, therefore, to become concerned with the being of the πόλις, and not be preoccupied with the (individual) being of the human being. And indeed, this is what Aristotle's *Politics* is about: the being of the πόλις. We ask ourselves again, therefore: is "the political" that which pertains to the πόλις, or is it that which belongs to the human being?

Here we must let the *history* of the πόλις free us. For (and despite the anthropological, sociological generalisations of Hegel, Feuerbach, Weber, Marx, Arendt and so forth) there is no "ideal" form of "the πόλις" as such. Every "city", "city state", "nation", "state", as such in one sense stands for itself, and in another sense traces its history to here or there, to such-and-such a founding. But is there is no formal pure "being", no ideal, of "the πόλις" as such? In each case, and for each generation, how the πόλις is to *be* needs to be worked out, all over again, and continually. The πόλις is only prior in that it lets a certain aspect of the living being that is the human being come to view and be understood. So is "being political" the essence of the human being? Is this what Aristotle means when he says πρότερον, "first", τῇ φύσει – "according to nature"?

In fact, Aristotle says, the human is the political living being because something else is already clear: he says it is δῆλον, "shown", "shown to be *thus*". The human being is the political living being because the human being is the living being λόγον ἔχον – "in possession of, and possessed by, speaking". Even more than this, the human being is "alone ... of all living beings" (μόνον ... τῶν ζῴων), the one with speech (Arist. *Pol.* 1253 a 5–10).

Have we now found the "ground" of "the political", the "essence" of the political? Is this what lies behind "the political", and so is the "pre-political" this "speaking", *language*, itself? Perhaps, and perhaps not. For neither the dictionary nor the grammar-book could ever function as a manual of constitutional law. For the aspect of the living being in question that Aristotle brings before us, but which we have so far not addressed, is what Aristotle names when he says τῇ φύσει – "according to nature".

Here a very great deal could be said. What matters, however, is only what Aristotle does *not* say. So far we have translated according to what the dictionaries themselves say: φύσις speaks of what we speak of when we say "nature". "Nature" is, however, only the average translation of the word φύσις. Aristotle names the πόλις with respect to "the whole", τὸ ὅλον. The whole, he told us, is prior with respect to its parts. Whole, therefore of what? Aristotle does not say: the πόλις is the prior form of all the forms of the being of the human being, of which the others are "the household" and the "each", as the individual. Rather, the meaning of the latter two (the household, the individual) is taken off from what is prior, which is the πόλις. The πόλις is therefore that which first allows the possibility of the *whole being* of the human being to be seen: it is what shows up the visibility of this living being in its standing and lasting presence, "as a whole", from which its respective parts can be taken, or read, off.

Strictly speaking, Aristotle knows nothing of "nature" as we have come to know it: as that which is distinguished from the artificial and the made, for instance, in the thinking of the eighteenth and nineteenth centuries, or of that realm of "the natural" that names that part of God's creation that stands over against the human world in the Christian conceptions of the Middle Ages. Here, what is named in φύσις is also in a sense, a "whole", the whole that is everything that is proper to the human being. But everything that is proper to the human being is already contained in the πόλις. The whole that is named with φύσις, therefore, is *that* whole that lies prior even to the πόλις, namely what lets the human being bring the πόλις about. "Prior" does not mean in any causal way: this priority is not temporal, nor legal, nor some "efficient cause". Strictly speaking it is not "prior" at all, but simply what is "always also present", not as an actual presence (the "presence of the πόλις"), but as what lets the presence of the presence come to be: we would say: the "being" of the presence. Is φύσις then, the "being" of the πόλις?

But did we not say that "language", "speaking" is what lies "prior" to "the πόλις"? Shouldn't we be thinking of language and speaking as the "being", as what "lets-into" being the presence, the present reality, of "the πόλις"? Which is it to be? How are we to know?

What is the most fundamental aspect of speaking and language? Speaking and language *names* and so brings "to being" what is "here". Speaking and language grants the "meaning" of the being that presences. As this granting, naming and speaking dis-closes what would otherwise lay hidden. Speaking, as naming, allows what is "here", what is presencing, to be understood, to lie-open before us: it lets what is "here" be here. Speaking is a bringing-to-presence. Not in this passage of the *Politics*, but elsewhere, Aristotle calls this speaking-as-naming: ἀληθεύειν. In Greek "truth" is ἀ-λήθεια, dis-closing, un-covering (ἀ-) from hiddenness (λήθη). The verb ἀληθεύειν names the disclosing of "bringing to light" and "showing", "letting-lie-forth-and shine", the true: the presencing of the present.

What, then, does naming name – what does speaking speak *of*? In the matter of "the πόλις", naming names the πόλις, it brings it to visibility. This is not trivial. We could say that the whole of Aristotle's *Politics*, and much more besides, does precisely this. It names the relation to other states, the laws and customs, the history, the relation to the gods, the standing of the institutions – all of this, and naming names this as the ways of being of the "political" living being. Thus it names this being *in* its being, the being "of" this being, τὸ ὄντως ὄν. What else does naming name, when we speak? Does speaking only ever speak from out of the being of what lies before us?

In 1946 Martin Heidegger wrote to Jean Beaufret, making a claim that at the time it would have been impossible to clarify or substantiate. It is now possible to understand exactly of what Heidegger thought himself to be speaking. Heidegger explains to Beaufret that the "only question" concerns "being itself" which means "the openness and clearing of being (not of what is present)". Heidegger than adds:

> In *Being and Time* the question has to do exclusively with the truth of being and not with the being of beings.[15]

Heidegger refers to "the truth of being", by which he means what he speaks of throughout his vast *Nachlaß* as "Wahrheit des Seyns", the spelling of *das Seyn* Heidegger used privately from about 1934 onwards. The "clearing" (*die Lichtung*) in question is the "here", the *Da* of *Da-sein*. Speaking and naming, *when* it names, also names the clearing, the "here" of "here-being".

This is why the *Dasein* of Heidegger's original quotation is singular, not plural. *Dasein* itself names how the clearing comes to be cleared, how being itself lets whatever is be known in its truth. For now, we can only in the briefest of ways understand what has been disclosed here. At other points Heidegger explains that "Da-*sein* … is itself the being of the *here* … the openness of whatever is (*das Seiende*) as such as a whole". More properly for us, and in the light of my interpretation of Aristotle, Heidegger adds "Da-sein is the properly self-grounding ground of the ἀλήθεια of φύσις".[16] The term Heidegger uses in connection with the *Da* of Da-*sein* is *Wesung*, essencing, occurring, unfolding: "Da-sein … is an essencing of that openness, which alone opens out the self-concealing (the essence of beyng, *das Seyn*), and thus which is the truth of beyng itself".[17] We can see from this that there is no "essence" of the political: the πόλις is itself an essencing (occurring) in being.

Such an understanding of "the political" – if we can even really continue to call it that – cannot decide in advance the way in which everything appears, either historically, or in the future. Such an understanding has to address the things that appear – the persons, the institutions, the modes and ways of being that unfold within *Da-sein* and within present being as a whole (*das Seiende im Ganzem*), by first bringing to light how they may be spoken of and *named*. Such a naming does not begin as a "theory" of "the political", nor as a "demand", that justice be done. On the contrary, such a turning toward the πόλις would require a willingness to undertake those things necessary to allow justice to come to light and unfold. How would this be?

---

15 Heidegger 2012, 2. "Die einzige Frage … ist … nach dem Sein selbst … d.h. zugleich nach der Offenheit und Lichtung des Seins (nicht des Seienden)". "Die Frage in *Sein und Zeit* geht einzig nach der Wahrheit des Seins, nicht nach dem Sein des Seienden".
16 Heidegger 2012, 296. "Das Da-sein ist nicht die Wirklichkeitsweise von jeglichem Seienden, sondern ist selbst das Sein des Da. Das Da aber ist die Offenheit des Seienden als solchen im Ganzen … Das Da-sein ist der eigen sich gründende Grund der αλήθεια der φύσις".
17 Heidegger 2012, 296. "Das Da-sein ist […] die Wesung jener Offenheit, die erst das Sichverbergen (das Wesen des Seyns) eröffnet und die so die Wahrheit des Seyns selbst ist".

Nietzsche names justice as an "unfathomable sea" (*unergründliche Meer*). There is one other figure who made an essential connection between justice and the sea, and one far different from Nietzsche's. Hannah Arendt suggests that in the emergence of "the political" as the establishment of the *polis*'s priority over the household, "one may see the turning-point in Solon's legislation".[18] I propose to pursue that turning-point, but in a way quite different from anything she envisages. For Solon was that one who ended the enslavement of one section of the city by another, through not only cancelling the debts that enslaved them, but by means of a legal reform that, if it did not establish the Athenian democracy as such, laid the basis for it. The most important historical account we have of Solon's reforms was written some seven centuries later, by Plutarch in one of his *Lives*. The accuracy of Plutarch's account – especially in what was said, to whom, and when, is difficult to ascertain, but we can be much more certain of the outline of the reform itself, not least because we have a description of its outline in Solon's own words:

> To the inhabitants of the city-districts (δήμῳ) I gave as much autonomy as is enough, Neither robbing them of worth nor adding to it. To those with power and envied for their wealth, I saw to it they suffered no harm. I stood with a mighty shield round both sides and suffered neither to have an unjust victory.[19]

Whatever – and this means whoever – arises in the πόλις and dwells there, already has a belonging there. We cannot decide in advance that this one or that group or caste must be punished or cast out except in the case of actual crime. It is neither a crime to have enviable wealth, nor to be a (relatively poor) inhabitant of the city-districts. It *is* a crime so to organise the πόλις that one group or faction or caste can violate the freedom of another. None can be allowed to be victor over another: each is worthy of protection and honour. Justice is neither robbery nor false redistribution. What word for justice does Solon employ here? The Greek word we ordinarily translate as Justice is δίκη, a word that is also the name of a goddess.

Heidegger translated the term δίκη as "jointure" (*Fug*) and "ordinance" (*Verfügung*). In a note appended to his scripts for a lecture-course of 1935, when thinking of δίκη, Heidegger says: "right-making – ruling – reaching-through and taking-hold ≠ balance – setting-aside of strife – *coming-into* [?]". He adds "for

---

18 Arendt 1998, 29 n.16.
19 Solon, fr. 5 (Bergk). δήμῳ μὲν γὰρ ἔδωκα τόσον γέρας ὅσσον ἀπαρκεῖν τιμῆς οὔτ' ἀφελὼν οὔτ' ἐπορεξάμενος· οἳ δ' εἶχον δύναμιν καὶ χρήμασιν ἦσαν ἀγητοί, καὶ τοῖς ἐφρασάμην μηδὲν ἀεικὲς ἔχειν. ἔστην δ' ἀμφιβαλὼν κρατερὸν σάκος ἀμφοτέροισι, νικᾶν δ' οὐκ εἴασ' οὐδετέρους ἀδίκως.

example Solon – θάλαττα".²⁰ The reference to Solon cites the Boeotian dialect word for θάλασσα, "maritime", which tells us all too little about δίκη. Heidegger is in fact citing a fragment of Solon's poetry, which reads:

ἐξ ἀνέμων δὲ θάλασσα ταράσσεται· ἢν δέ τις αὐτὴν μὴ κινῇ, πάντων ἐστὶ δικαιοτάτη

The sea is disturbed by winds, but if none moves it, it is, of all things δικαιοτάτη.²¹

Heidegger discusses his arrival at the translation of δίκη as *der Fug* not here, but in connection with his reading of Friedrich Hölderlin. Heidegger is reported as saying of Hölderlin that he had already "gone through and broken the speculative dialectic – just when Hegel was himself preparing to establish it".²² The successive, as the primary element of speculative dialectic, of modern politics, of the dialectic of self-same and other, is not what δίκη names, and has nothing to do with justice. Δίκη is that one who is most present (δικαιοτάτη) when the sea itself, the sea of life in the πόλις, the sea that holds within it all different things (and nourishes them) is protected from winds, from the violent forces of disturbance. This is a true *Verfügung*, a holding-together within itself, of itself, and of opposites.

In his translations of Sophokles and Pindar, Hölderlin ordinarily, but rarely, translates the word δίκη as *Recht*, law (or right) or *Gerechtigkeit*, justice. Although in his translation of often-cited lines of a fragment of Pindar's well known saying "Law, of all things, king".²³ Hölderlin does translate δικαιῶν as *das gerechteste Recht*, the most justified law. In a significant commentary he qualifies the translation. Δίκη concerns that kind of self-ordering and discipline, *Zucht*, wherein humanity and god encounter each other: δίκη is the letting-encounter, but the letting-encounter is not a personal experience, as if by some faith or through personal discipline or even "grace". Hölderlin is not speaking of δίκη as if it were a gift, or exchange of χάρις on the personal level, but the encounter of *ein Volk*, a *people*, that is, of the πόλις itself, entire, in an encounter with a god. It is the poet

---

20 Heidegger, *Der Anfang der Abendländischen Philosophie* (GA35), 209. "Der Fug – *und zwar im Sinne der Verfügung.* Recht-schaffen – herrschen – durch- und angreifen ≠ *Ausgleich* – Beseitigung des Streites – *hineinkommen*!? ... Vgl. Solon – θάλαττα! [?]"
21 Solon, fr. 12 (Bergk).
22 Heidegger, 'Seminar in Le Thor 1968 (Vier Seminare)' (GA15), 287. "[Hölderlin hat] den spekulativen Idealismus durchgemacht und durchbrochen, – während Hegel sich anschickt, ihn zu begründen".
23 Pindar, Fragment 169a: Νόμος ὁ πάντων βασιλεύς ... ἄγει δικαιῶν τὸ βιαιότατον. The fragment is best known from Plato's *Gorgias*, 484 b 4, but see also: Herodotus III, 38:20; Aristotle, *Politics* 1278 a 3 among frequent other citations.

who can let this encounter occur. Solon, we should recall, may have been a law-giver, but before that he is first a renowned and skilled poet.

Δίκη is that which is governing, but governing only in the sense of "lifting to the highest", of us all. These things that lift us up are, Hölderlin says, the church and law of the state and those things which give shape to the historical self-understanding of a people – "the holiness of God, and for man, the possibility of a recognition, an explanation" of himself. We should understand the references to the church and the law not in any conventional way, but as attempts to name the place of sacred custom (νόμος) and the gods (χάρις) as they manifest recognisably to Hölderlin's immediate audience. Hölderlin concludes that ὁ βασιλεύς, "king", indicates here the superlative. The superlative king is the sign for the highest ground of understanding, and so, Hölderlin says, "not for the highest power".[24]

Power is not what such a king wields: thus *not* might, *not* force, *not* the politics of domination, of overcoming and revenge (all of which demand a justice, an equalisation of an imbalance). The king, the poet says, lets-in, lets occur, a self-understanding. The self-understanding of the πόλις takes place and makes itself manifest in, and as, δίκη. Δίκη demands an understanding equal to what it proffers. One capable for understanding at the level of a king, ὁ βασιλεύς, highest of rulers (the sex of the ruler is irrelevant, a queen with such understanding would be the equal of any king) is required for δίκη to prevail. The name of the king is only a figure. Such a ruling figure could arise in a democracy. Such a one would be ὁ πολιτικός, the statesman (stateswoman), the antithesis of the tyrant. In such an understanding, "democracy" is therefore not the exercise of a *generalised* or universalised will, an equalised will levelled out from among all. On the contrary this noble figure represents success in the quest *within the πόλις entire*, for the *one* capable for highest understanding. This *one* is the one whose argument prevails (because it names and brings to light what is demanded of it), one who therefore lets into understanding the highest thought, and makes it available to, and for, all.

We are reminded, once again, not of the dictator-figure who so marks the politics of the modern period, brought to a culmination in those figures who, even

---

24 See Hölderlin 1952, 285: "Das gerechteste Recht mit allerhöchster Hand".... "Die Zucht, so fern sie die Gestalt ist, worin der Mensch sich und der Gott begegnet, der Kirche und des Staats Gesetz und anererbte Satzungen, (die Heiligkeit des Gottes, und für die Menschen die Möglichkeit einer Erkenntnis, einer Erklärung) ... 'König' bedeutet hier den Superlativ, der nur das Zeichen ist für den höchsten Erkenntnisgrund, nicht für die höchste Macht".

in our own day, are sometimes given to claim a quasi-divine origin,[25] but the figure of Solon. Plutarch reports that Solon, having succeeded in advancing a notion of "political" equality that was attractive to both rich and poor parties alike in the Athenian πόλις (each, however, interpreting equality, τὸ ἴσον, to their own advantage), was urged by both to seize the opportunity to establish a tyranny in the city over which he was already effectively master (Plut. *Sol.* 14.3).[26] Plutarch reports that even an oracle of Apollo urged him to occupy the place of helmsman "amidships", but with the clear suggestion of "equally between the two [parties]".[27] Plutarch concludes with Solon's reported response: "tyranny may indeed be an attractive place, but it has no way back" (Plut. *Sol.* 14.5).[28]

If justice, Δίκη, is to rule, even when sufficiently "political", she is perhaps no politician at all. Perhaps, most of all, she is a poet, and not Aristotle, but Solon, should be her first consort, politically, poetically, speaking.

Bibliography

Arendt, Hannah (1998 [1958]), *The Human Condition*, Chicago, IL.
Beistegui, Miguel de (1998), *Heidegger and the Political: Dystopias*, London.
Deleuze, Gilles and Guattari, Felix (1972), *Capitalisme et schizophrénie 1: l'Anti-Œdipe*, Paris.
Foucault, Michel (1980–1994), *Dits et écrits* (edited by Daniel Defert/François Ewald), Paris.
Foucault, Michel (1994), *Essential Works of Foucault 1954–1984*, London.
Foucault, Michel (2011), *Leçons sur la volonté de savoir: Cours au Collège de France, 1970–1971*, Paris.
Hegel, Georg Wilhelm Friedrich (1957-), *Gesammelte Werke* (Hegel-Kommission and Hegel-Archiv edition), Hamburg.
Hegel, Georg Wilhelm Friedrich (1976), *Jenaer Systementwürfe III: Naturphilosophie und Philosophie des Geistes* (edited by Rolf-Peter Horstmann/Johann Heinrich Trede), Hamburg.
Heidegger, Martin (1976-), *Gesamtausgabe* (102 vols.) (edited by Friedrich-Wilhelm von-Herrmann), Frankfurt.
Heidegger, Martin [1927] (1977) *Sein und Zeit*, edited by Friedrich-Wilhelm von Herrmann, translated by John Macquarrie/Edward Robinson (1980) as *Being and Time*, Oxford.

---

25 The Kim family of North Korea claiming to spring from the "Mount Paektu bloodline", after the mountain sacred to Korean history would be the most obvious and most kitsch example, but this claim takes many forms.
26 ὅθεν ἐπ' ἐλπίδος μεγάλης ἑκατέρων γενομένων οἱ προϊστάμενοι προσέκειντο τῷ Σόλωνι τυραννίδα προξενοῦντες καὶ ἀναπείθοντες εὐτολμότερον ἅψασθαι τῆς πόλεως ἐγκρατῆ γενόμενον.
27 The veracity of Plutarch's report of the oracle is perhaps borne out by Solon's maritime reference to δικὴ.
28 καλὸν μὲν εἶναι τὴν τυραννίδα χωρίον, οὐκ ἔχειν δὲ ἀπόβασιν.

Heidegger, Martin [1973] (2003), *Four Seminars* (Trans. Andrew Mitchell/François Raffoul), Bloomington, IN.
Heidegger, Martin (1996), *Hölderlins Hymne 'Der Ister'* (Trans. William McNeill/Julia Davis), Bloomington, IN.
Heidegger, Martin (2012), *Beiträge zur Philosophie (Vom Ereignis)* (Trans. Richard Rojcewicz/ Daniela Vallega-Neu), Bloomington, IN.
Heidegger, Martin (1986), "Die Grundfrage nach dem Sein selbst (1946)", *Heidegger Studies* 2, 1–3.
Hölderlin, Friedrich (2004), *Sämtliche Werke, Briefe und Dokumente in zeitlicher Folge (Bremer Ausgabe)* (edited by Dietrich Sattler), Munich.
Hölderlin, Friedrich (1943–1985), *Sämtliche Werke* (Grosse Stuttgarter Ausgabe) (edited by Friedrich Beissner, 14 vols), Stuttgart.
Hölderlin, Friedrich (1952), *Übersetzungen* (edited by Friedrich Beissner), Stuttgart.
Nietzsche, Friedrich [1967] (1999), *Nietzsche: Kritische Studienausgabe* (edited by Giorgio Colli and Mazzino Montinari), Berlin.
Nietzsche, Friedrich (1997), *Die Geburt der Tragödie: Unzeitgemäße Betrachtungen* (Trans R.J. Hollingdale/edited by Daniel Breazeale as *Untimely Meditations*), Cambridge.

Duncan F. Kennedy
On not Being Modern: Exploring Historical Ontology with Bruno Latour

Bruno Latour's name is not generally associated with the philosophy of history, and this essay does not set out to offer anything as grand as a systematic exposition of his 'theory of history'. But his work over the past forty years has brought philosophy and history into a productively thought-provoking tension (equally irritating to historians and philosophers), in particular through his abiding interest in ontology and his critique of modernity, concerns that are now beginning to have an impact on the study of the classical world. Greg Anderson's recent book *The Realness of Things Past: Ancient Greece and Ontological History*,[1] which presents its 'ontological turn' as a 'paradigm shift' in the study of Athenian democracy, acknowledges a debt to Latour, though Anderson, for all his remarkable willingness to engage in wide-ranging theoretical argument, does not discuss his work in detail. One reason for this is that Anderson's avowed theme is *ontological history*: he seeks to track what were the ontological assumptions of Athenians in the fifth and fourth centuries BC about the world they inhabited and the 'things' that made up the 'reality' they experienced, but without 'translating' those things into, and subordinating them to, the metaphysical assumptions of a 'modern' interpretative schema that has become dominant in historical studies. Thus 'gods' were 'real' for many in this period and permeated their ways of being in their world, but to discuss this in terms of *religion* (e.g. issues of belief, or of a distinction between a sacred realm and a secular realm) is to impose an analytical category that has developed within a 'modern' viewpoint.[2]

The focus of this essay will be subtly, but importantly, different: *historical ontology* shares many of the concerns of ontological history, not least its desire to render visible the assumptions of a 'modern' paradigm of interpretation, but the emphasis here is on the emergence of distinctively 'ontological' modes of thinking in the very period Anderson studies. Its focus, then, will be precisely on the emergence, as 'things', of 'history', 'philosophy', 'theory' and 'the study of being' in such a way as to resist treating that emergence and its subsequent development as necessary or inevitable, or as taken for granted as having the universal

---
[1] Anderson 2018.
[2] Cf. Anderson 2018, 19–21 with 42–43.

https://doi.org/10.1515/9783110627305-004

pretensions the 'modern' paradigm often lays claim to. Latour's continuing interest in exploring the interaction of philosophy and history can help us in this task.[3] 'We have never been modern' is his favourite catchphrase, which I am tempted to re-cast as: 'we need not inevitably be modern'. If there is one lesson we should learn from Latour, it is to take nothing, no 'thing' whatsoever, for granted, not now, not in the past, not in the future. In particular, Latour's exploration of what he calls 'modes of existence' helpfully draws attention to powerful, and often unexamined, metaphysical assumptions.

This essay will fall into two parts. Latour's thinking will help to bind together my argument in both sections, though I will not hesitate to bring in other figures, such as Ian Hacking, Thomas Nail, Hans Ulrich Gumbrecht, Raymond Tallis or Rodolphe Gasché where their work can be helpful. In §1, I shall explore some of the factors that drive the study of what has become (fairly recently) known as **historical ontology** and the implications of that study, and then, in §2, I shall seek to show historical ontology in action, using the texts of Herodotus and Plato to explore the emergence of **history, philosophy, theory** and **the study of being**. This will become more or less a historical ontology *of* ontology. A typographical pointer: when I want to focus on the ontological emergence (and, as it might be, the passing away) of a particular 'thing', I shall, as in this paragraph, use bold. Italics will be conventionally used for emphasis.

1 Historical Ontology after Latour

1.1 Latour's Ontological Turn

Latour's work is extraordinarily wide-ranging, covering science studies, politics and sociology, religion, law, metaphysics, ecology and much else, and we need to get an appreciation of its scope and coherence in order to grasp the significance of his engagement with ontological thinking.[4] He established his reputation by

---

[3] I will only note in passing here Latour's explicit and polemical engagement with Plato, notably the *Gorgias* (Latour 1999, 216–265) and the Cave in the *Republic* (Latour 2004, 10–18 and 2016, 12–17); for the latter cf. Kennedy 2020b, 268–269. The reasons for Latour's antipathy to Plato should emerge in the course of this essay.
[4] As a guide to his career and thinking, De Vries 2016 can be recommended. Schmidgen 2015, 9–24 is helpful on Latour's early training in theology and anthropology which has been so important in shaping his intellectual development.

studying 'laboratory life' and 'science in action',[5] tracking in scrupulous detail what scientists do, as against what they think or say they are doing. Conventionally, science had been viewed in terms its end product, knowledge, and in *epistemological* terms: scientific knowledge has been the gold standard, its extraordinary authority the object of intense philosophical enquiry in the twentieth century and beyond. Latour's approach is rather different. He himself was trained in anthropology and not in the scientific disciplines he encountered. His observations of the activities of the neuroendocrinologists working in the Salk Institute in La Jolla, California, viewed the object of his study as a culture to be observed through the lens of ethnomethodology. Science in action, the processes involved in the production of knowledge, he came to see increasingly in *ontological* terms: the activities of scientists (raising funding, designing and maintaining equipment, record-keeping, experiments, peer review, publishing papers, academic rivalries and so on) have the function, he suggests, of *instituting entities*. In the case of the scientists he was studying at the Salk Institute, this was the emergence of a new object, *'named after what it does'*, somatostatin, 'something that inhibits the release of growth hormone.'[6] Once the existence of a scientific entity and its agency are established to the satisfaction of the exacting protocols of the network of scientists and their practices, and they are in a position to say 'there it *is* and this is what it *does*', the often haphazard and messy processes that have led to this remarkable outcome tend to be elided and forgotten.[7]

In an early book, he applied the methods he used to study contemporary science to an instance from the nineteenth century, Pasteur's discovery of microbes.[8] The existence of microbes is now taken for granted, but Latour's account suggests a prolonged struggle to institute them as entities – with all that implies. Microbes were 'discovered' by Pasteur (this verb implies they were there all along, had we but known it), but the extraordinary efforts this required demands a narrative involving not simply Pasteur but thousands of historical agents (not least the elusive and recalcitrant microbes themselves) who brought about what Latour, playfully but in all seriousness, calls *The Pasteurization of France*. As the blurb to the English edition puts it: 'Although every town in France has a street named for Pasteur, was he alone able to stop people from spitting, persuade them to dig drains, influence them to undergo vaccination? Pasteur's success depended on a whole network of forces, including the public hygiene movement,

---

5 These are the titles of Latour/Woolgar 1979 and of Latour 1987 respectively.
6 Latour 1987, 87; emphasis Latour's. On this see Kennedy 2002, 73–75.
7 Latour's emphasis on the *agency* of non-human entities caused controversy at the time.
8 Latour 1988 [1984].

the medical profession (both military physicians and private practitioners) and colonial interests.' So complex is this narrative that he suggests in the opening pages that we need something of the scope and reflective ambition of 'that treatise on political philosophy which Tolstoy wrote under the name of *War and Peace*'.[9] The institution of entities transforms not only our society but our very manner of being in the world. Not only do we accept the existence of microbes, but that *makes* us all wash our hands after going, doesn't it? It has become 'second nature', part of our way of being in the world. But even within such a grand narrative, there is much, much more we take for granted as well.

1.2 History and Ontology

In a couple of essays written some years later, Latour returned to focus on the historical and philosophical issues this study of Pasteur raised. In 'The Historicity of Things', he posed the question: 'Where were microbes before Pasteur?'[10] In a more playful companion piece, 'On the Partial Existence of Existing *and* Nonexisting Objects',[11] he recalled how traces of Koch's bacillus (first isolated in 1882) had been found in 1976 in the mummified remains of the pharaoh Ramses II. Latour teasingly asked: 'Did Ramses II die of tuberculosis?'[12] His interest in the death of Ramses is not diagnostic; rather he uses the diagnosis to pose a challenge that is at once both historical *and* ontological. The accepted existence of an entity in the here-and-now can allow its presence to be projected into the past ('Ramses died of tuberculosis', and, yes, from a present viewpoint he did) – but in a way that overwrites whatever was the perspective and experience of those at the time (for whom the diagnosis would have been meaningless). Their way of seeing the circumstances in which they were involved is definitively superseded by a 'modern' view underpinned by the authority of science. Commenting on Latour's essay, John Durham Peters remarks:

> After Pasteur discovered microbes, we forgot that they didn't exist before. Pasteur's feat was not only epistemological but historical: the past suddenly had to accommodate microbes where none were before. Discovery makes ontological ripples in history itself. What seems

---

[9] Latour 1988, 13. The original 1984 French version of *The Pasteurization of France* went under the title *Les microbes: guerre et paix suivi de irréductions*. More on 'irreductions' below.
[10] Latour 1999, 145.
[11] Latour 2000. The title is paradoxical, but is an early attempt on Latour's part to capture his sense of the existential *incompleteness* of everything.
[12] Latour 2000, 247.

like common sense – that microbes were always there – turns out to be the deepest kind of idealism about the hidden constancy of unperceived things.[13]

The past is re-viewed and re-vised from the high ground of the present, and the discovery of entities proven to exist re-configures the past. Latour himself asks: 'Is this not an extreme case of "whiggish" history, transplanting into the past the hidden or potential existence of the future?'[14] Such historical accounts subtend a particular manner of being in the world for those who profess them, freighted as they are with powerful notions of 'progress' and (Latour's particular *bête noir*) 'modernity'. At its most critically unreflective, being 'modern' dismisses (whatever was) the worldview of Ramses and his contemporaries as 'primitive', definitively *superseded* by the 'modern' view. It directs towards the past an impulse that in the present would manifest itself as the imperialism of 'advanced' societies, a process of colonization or globalization[15] that would impose modernity on the 'backward'. 'We have never been modern', he famously asserted, in his challenge to confront this particularly powerful and often unexamined historical manner of being in the world.[16]

For all that he enjoys posing as a maverick, Latour is by no means an intellectual outlier. The essay on Ramses appeared in a collection of essays edited by Lorraine Daston entitled *Biographies of Scientific Objects*. She draws together a range of studies across the natural and social sciences under the rubric of what she calls 'applied metaphysics', how 'whole domains of phenomena – dreams, atoms, monsters, culture, mortality, centers of gravity, value, cytoplasmic particles, the self, tuberculosis – come into being and pass away as objects of scientific inquiry'.[17] She explicitly draws attention to Aristotle's *On Generation and Corruption* (1.3, 317b34) in describing applied metaphysics as 'a sublunary metaphysics

---

13 Peters 2015, 41.
14 Latour 2000, 248.
15 Anderson 2018, 102 puts this general point trenchantly from a postcolonial perspective: 'Far from being an enlightened exercise in preserving objective truths about humanity's many extinct worlds, our conventional practice authorizes us to engage in a kind of retrospective political violence, a historicist imperialism that would forcefully impose the realities of our liberal capitalist present upon peoples who can no longer speak for themselves.' For Latour's critique of globalization cf. Latour 2018.
16 Latour 1993.
17 Daston 2000, 1.

of change, of the "perpetuity of coming-to-be".' A separation of 'worlds' characteristic (even constitutive) of what has come to be called 'metaphysical' thinking[18] is invoked in familiar terms to suggest the distinctive viewpoint she advances: 'If pure metaphysics treats the ethereal of what is always and everywhere from a God's-eye-viewpoint, then applied metaphysics studies the dynamic world of what emerges and disappears from the horizon of working scientists.' The philosopher Ian Hacking remarks: 'the comings, in comings into being, are historical', and in surveying associated fields of study and their philosophical affinities, he suggests 'the catchphrase "historical ontology" helps us to think of these diverse inquiries as forming part of a family'.[19]

A prominent member of this family (though Hacking does not mention him) is Reinhart Koselleck, who is particularly associated with the study of what he has called *Begriffsgeschichte* (conceptual history), 'a methodology of historical studies that focuses on the invention and development of the fundamental concepts underlying and informing a distinctively historical *manner of being in the world*' (my emphasis). 'Progress', 'decline', 'modernity' and 'emancipation' are amongst the concepts whose history he discusses.[20] These are not simply analytical terms or inert descriptors of a process, but insofar as they are the objects of (sometimes temporary) ontological investment – a belief that they do, indeed, exist – become modalities of experience and historical action that serve to make human beings what they are at any moment in history and do what they do. Take the example of **revolution**. A term that once was used to invoke a recurrence, a periodically returning cycle, comes to be used of a radical and irreversible reordering; Steven Shapin suggests that **revolution** in this sense was first applied systematically to events in the sciences and only later to events in politics.[21] As François Furet has argued of the events in France in 1789, the historical actors of the time used the term in this latter sense to understand what was happening to them and to shape their actions[22] – thus what Koselleck calls 'a distinctively his-

---

18 This term post-dates Aristotle, perhaps by a couple of centuries (cf. Lear 1988, 248 n. 63), for all that he wrote a series of texts that now go under the familiar title *Metaphysics*. However, the style of thinking described here was developed by Plato, as we shall see in §2 below.
19 Hacking 2002, 4–5.
20 Kosselleck 2002.
21 Cf. Shapin 1996, 3.
22 Furet 1981. Latour, in arguing that the concept of 'modernity' has come into being (and, if he has anything to do with it, should pass away), draws explicitly on the work of Furet: Latour 1993, 40.

torical manner of being in the world'. Hacking calls this 'the looping effect of human kinds':[23] human beings create these conceptual schemata, often as hypothetical ideas, but as ontological investment in them becomes more intense, and these ideas become embedded in human belief and practice, human beings become subject to them as part of their experience, even to the extent of a pathology: in his own work Hacking explores such 'looping effects' in relation to recently emergent and (in Latour's sense) *instituted* entities as 'recovered memory syndrome', 'trauma' and 'child development'.[24] What it is to *be* a human being is a historical variable. From a philosophical perspective that he calls 'neo-existentialism', Markus Gabriel remarks: 'Some of the things human beings do can be accounted for only with adequate reference to the fact that they do them in the light of an historically variable conception of what it is for them to be human. Humans live their lives in the light of a conception of what a human being is. This conception does not pick out a natural kind.'[25] Thucydides would not have agreed: recall his famous statement (1.22.4) that study of the past is useful because the events of the past (*tōn genomenōn*) will at some stage and in much the same ways happen again in the future (*tōn mellontōn*) *kata to anthrōpinon*, which precisely seems to pick out 'the human' as, in Gabriel's philosophese, 'a natural kind', and reduces a multiplicity of human ways of being to just one. Thucydides executes a proto-ontological turn, of enormous consequence for its 'looping effects' on thinking about the past and the future, a key moment in the emergence of the discourse we have come to call **history**.

1.3 Historical Ontology in Theory

'Comings into being' (and 'passings out of being') pose challenges to historical thinking that applied studies of historical ontology such as Koselleck's or Hacking's seek to explore in practice. In discussing historical ontology in a more theoretical vein, Thomas Nail succinctly unfolds some of those challenges (my emphases):

> [T]he past is not an objective set of fixed events. Depending on the conditions of the present, different aspects or dimensions of the past will *appear* and *disappear*. New lines of development between the past and the present can be put forward on the basis of new social, scientific, and aesthetic discoveries or events that emerge in the present... As the present

---

23 Hacking 1994.
24 Hacking 1995 and 2002, 1–26.
25 Gabriel 2018, 39.

changes, however, so do the lines of the past that lead to it. This does not mean that history is illusory and false but rather that it is composed of multiple real coexisting and divergent historical series. There is no other starting point outside of the present from which to begin. Luckily the present is divergent enough to accommodate many lines.[26]

To use Latour's example, the discovery of Koch's bacillus and its agency appears to be true not only for 'our' present but for the past as 'we' know it; new aspects of the past appear, in effect overwriting others. But no line that connects past and present is definitive. Nail goes on to observe that lines of development that connect present to past in this way tend to attribute necessity, causality and finality to such developments.[27] Now, **necessity**, **causality** and **finality** have become familiar features of many historical (and other) narratives, but we should guard against fetishizing them, turning them into entities that are themselves objects of unreflective ontological investment, for, from the perspective of historical ontology, they too (and, of course, **history** and **ontology** as well) have their histories.

Take **causality**: the period since about 1830 has seen an explosion of causal explanations in geology, medicine, endocrinology, sociology, economics, physics, amongst many more disciplines.[28] **Causality** has unquestionably become an entity for 'us', but recall Latour's warning against transplanting into the past the hidden or potential existence of the future, and consider a time before a concept of **causality**, before systematic thinking about causes emerges, and these ways of understanding are just coming into view. The text of Herodotus is an extraordinary accumulation of stories in which (amongst much else) received (from e.g. Homeric stories) and contemporary usage of *aitios* and its cognates[29] attempt to distribute and attribute guilt and responsibility in relation to the specific narratives of the past he fashions – narratives that serve to extend and enrich the sense of what it might mean for a human to be *aitios*, responsible in whole or in part for

---

26 Nail 2019, 14.
27 Nail 2019, 14, who gives his own examples: 'once Newton discovered the inverse square law of gravity, this appeared to be true not only for his present, but also for the entire past as he and others knew it. Newton and others then told a retroactive evolutionary story about the development of this truth, just as Hegel told a similar story about the development of human sociality into its highest present form: the nation-state.'
28 Cf. Kern 2004, who writes a fascinating cultural history of causality by exploring these burgeoning aetiologies through the lens of murder in fiction.
29 E.g. from the lawcourts, medicine and the investigation of natural phenomena by the practitioners of *historiē*, research enquiry in its broadest sense: cf. Bakker 2002, 13–14; Fowler 2006, 31; Thomas 2006, 66.

an event or a series of events.[30] At length, these precipitate a remarkable shorthand in his preface in which Herodotus suggests that his *historiēs apodexis*, the presentation of his research, puts forward 'through what *aitiē* the Greeks and Persians fought against each other'. This is, arguably, not (or at least not quite yet) **history**, not quite yet **historical causality** (though this is a profoundly significant stage in their coming into being), but is part of an explosion in highly elaborate types of discourse, every bit as remarkable as that which has taken place in the two centuries before now, which ask the question 'who or what is responsible for…' and precipitate their different sorts of *aitiē* for the events they describe in the study of nature, of illness, of the past, as it may be. Appeal to an *aitiē* becomes a kind of shortcut that *condenses* complex and extended descriptions or narratives into what comes to be thought of as an explanation.

This is emphatically not to see explanations as illusory. Recall how Latour sought to characterize the process of discovery in the sciences: such descriptive and narrative condensations (recall 'somatostatin') can work to precipitate entities, to characterize the sense of agency associated with them, and to change the perspectives from which we view the past, sending their 'ontological ripples' backwards from the present. Recall what Nail said:

> New lines of development between the past and the present can be put forward on the basis of new social, scientific, and aesthetic discoveries or events that emerge in the present… As the present changes, however, so do the lines of the past that lead to it.

These 'lines of development' take on a form that becomes characteristic of causal/historical thinking, the identification of 'firsts' in the past that arise from present concerns and interests. Hannah Arendt has spoken of 'illuminating events' that reveal 'a beginning in the past that had previously been hidden'.[31] Two brief examples from different discourses to illustrate this. First, in exploring the relationship of the Greeks and barbarians, after dismissing the tit-for-tat abductions that are the stuff of the kinds of stories he distances himself from, Herodotus puts forward the argument (1.6.2) that Croesus was 'the first of the barbarians (*barbarōn prōtos*) of whom we know (*tōn hēmeis idmen*) who rendered the Greeks subject to the exaction of tribute (*es phorou apagōgēn*)', an observation seemingly prompted by his experience of something in his contemporary

---

30 Cf. Hernández Garcés 2018 for a subtle and extended discussion of the ways in which the *attribution* and *apportionment* of responsibility emerge in the stories Herodotus tells.
31 Arendt 1994, 319.

world: '*phoros* was the official term for "tribute" in the Athenian empire in Herodotus' time.'[32] Second, Aristotle in the first book of the *Metaphysics* (983b21–2), as he reviews early thinkers about 'material causes', is happy to make of Thales 'the originator of this kind of philosophy' (*ho tēs toiautēs archēgos philosophias*). Aristotle's search for 'firsts' is *both* historical *and* ontological as he seeks out originary moments for interests that concern him. The point of *inter-est* between the present and the past *is* what makes a link or connection *between* them. From this point of view, conceptual entities ('tribute'; 'material causes'; 'philosophy'), rather than existing *per se* in some timeless realm, *mediate* across time and space – though the degrees of reciprocity can vary. Would – could – Thales have recognized himself in Aristotle's description, any more than the Egyptians of the time have seen Ramses as a victim of Koch's bacillus?

1.4 From Symmetrical Anthropology to Modes of Existence

Interests may generate a line that links past and present, but this crucially does not result in a symmetry of perspectives.[33] Latour is particularly sensitive to this issue. His training as an ethnographer has led him to a methodology sometimes called 'symmetrical anthropology', which resists the impulse to describe other cultures unreflectively in 'our' terms in such a way as to subject them to a worldview that, however much it may believe that it is universal, feels (as it does for Anderson and the modern paradigm) ever more historically local and contingent. By studying other cultures and looking at their ontologies, we might be in a better position to assess our own. The major impulse towards this comes from ethnography, but is not limited to it.[34] Those other cultures may be remote in time as well as space (the past, we might say, is a foreign country; they have different ways of being there and different things exist for them). This does not mean that, ontologically, anything goes. As Patrice Maniglier has put it in his analysis of Latour's approach: 'It is not a question of accepting that whatever someone or other declares exists does, indeed, exist, but of better understanding what exactly exists

---

[32] Asheri/Lloyd/Corcella 2007, 78; for more on Herodotus and *phoros* cf. Ruffing 2018, 152.
[33] In Kennedy 2013, 86, I explored this theme with reference to Bakhtin's notion of the 'surplus of knowledge' the present enjoys over the past. Here I develop a complementary perspective with the help of Latour that shifts the emphasis from epistemology to ontology.
[34] Again, this is an outlook that is not peculiar to Latour, and feels increasingly pressing: cf. especially Descola 2013 and Viveiros de Castro 2014. In classical studies this approach is most clearly exemplified in the work of Geoffrey Lloyd: for a summary of his intellectual affiliations cf. Lloyd 2015, 1–9.

in *our* world by *contrast [différence]* with what exists in others.'[35] Latour's reflections across his career resulted in his *magnum opus* of 2013, *An Inquiry into Modes of Existence*, significantly subtitled *An Anthropology of the Moderns*. This explores not *what* exists (for a remarkable plurality of things exists, or has existed, for 'someone or other') but 'modes of existence', the *ways* (the plural is vital to this approach) in which what exists exists – and may cease to exist. Maniglier once more: '"To be" does not mean the same thing for a Higgs boson as it does for the Argentinian peso, but both equally *are*, and the task of the metaphysician is to exhibit that equality and diversity.'[36] Latour proposes fifteen (at least) such variously intersecting modes in accordance with which entities come into being, subsist, and can, importantly, pass out of existence.[37]

This is metaphysics, but not in the way that is familiar from the Platonic-Aristotelian tradition. There are different ways of instituting entities (for example, the contracts, courts, judges, plaintiffs and so on instituted by the mode of existence Latour calls **Law**). The modes of existence of a Higgs boson are not the same as those of the Argentinian peso, and, crucially, there is no master mode to which the other modes can be 'reduced' – a recurrent concern in Latour's work since his extended philosophical meditations on 'irreductions' in *The Pasteurization of France*.[38] In resisting reduction to a single mode of existence (or realm such as 'nature') his position could not be further removed from the reductive physicalism or naturalism that is almost the default metaphysical outlook across many of the sciences at the moment, and has powerful advocates in the humanities.[39] These modes are, importantly, proposed for the sake of argument, and are not to be regarded as in any way universal or definitive. In many respects they obviously reflect Latour's own outlook, interests and historically situated manner of being

---

35 Maniglier 2014, 38; original emphases.
36 Maniglier 2014, 42.
37 Latour's modes of existence (summarized in Latour 2013a, 488–489): Reproduction; Metamorphosis; Habit; Technology; Fiction; Reference; Politics; Law; Religion; Attachment; Organization; Morality; Network; Preposition; Double Click. When referring specifically to one of Latour's modes, I will cite it with a capital letter and in the bold font as used in the next paragraph.
38 Latour 1988, 153–236. Thus Latour rejects any kind of fundamentalism, be it scientific, religious, economic, or any other.
39 Cf. e.g. Ladyman/Ross 2007 (whose title, *Everything Must Go*, suggests a closing-down sale), where the mode of existence to which all is reduced (including, presumably, Ladyman and Ross themselves) is that of quantum mechanics; cf. more briefly Ladyman 2017. **Nature** is often the shorthand invoked; cf. Hadot 2006, 17–28 for a historical account of how *physis* develops both a relative and an absolute use, a realm of things coming-to-be (plural, processual, temporal) and a realm of being *per se* (single, static, atemporal).

in the world: this is very much his *Inquiry*.[40] This is the 'world', the particular time and place, into which (to use Heidegger's notion) he has been 'thrown'. Being 'thrown' into our respective worlds doesn't mean we can do nothing about it: we can by our efforts seek to acquire a different viewpoint on where we find ourselves. Latour's *Inquiry* is not prescriptive, and emphatically not a system, rather an encouragement to view ourselves, and our ontologies, continually as if through the eyes of others.

This is not the place for a detailed exposition of Latour's modes, but for present purposes, the mode of existence Latour calls **Attachment** is particularly salient. *Nothing* exists *per se*: 'There is no better definition of any existent whatsoever beyond the list of *the other beings* through which it must, it can, it seeks to pass'.[41] He distinguishes between being-as-being and being-as-other. The former 'seeks its support in a *substance* that will ensure its continuity by shifting with a leap into the foundation that will undergird this assurance.'[42] Aristotle's *ousia* is a case in point, and in the word 'leap', Latour references the notion of *transcendence* that, in the Platonic-Aristotelian tradition, frees *substance* from the constraints of time. Being-as-other posits a much more fragile mode of existence: entities 'can but rely on a *subsistence* that they have to seek out at their own risk.'[43] He suggests that we should not think of human beings as if they existed in and of themselves – thus distancing himself from the autonomous individual of some philosophical schools and social theories. 'We are what we are attached to', he

---

40 Thus his characterization of the mode he calls **Religion** is evidently coloured by his own Catholic beliefs (though he is no sense an orthodox Catholic; cf. Latour 2013b).
41 Latour 2013a, 425; original emphasis.
42 Latour 2013a, 162.
43 Latour 2013a, 162. The contrast with Aristotle is emphatic, and is worth pursuing here. Aristotle's central concern in the texts that now go under the title *Metaphysics* was what he called *philosophia prōtē* ('first philosophy'). In *Metaphysics* 1.982b9–10, he says of what he has called the highest or 'sovereign' (*archikōtatē*) branch of knowledge that it 'has to be the theoretical [knowledge] of the first principles and causes' (*dei gar tautēn [epistēmēn] tōn prōtōn kai aitiōn einai theōrētikēn*). Elsewhere he suggests that this kind of knowledge deals not with the being of a specific realm of things, for example living things (biology) or human societies (politics), but with being as such (4.1003a21): 'There is a branch of knowledge (*epistēmē tis*) which studies (*theōrei*) that which is (*to on*) qua being (*hēi on*)' It is *this* study that merits the special distinction conferred by calling it 'first' (*Metaphysics* 4.2.1004a2–4): 'And there are just as many divisions of philosophy as there are kinds of substance; so that there must be a philosophy that is first and embraces them'. For Latour, there is no 'master' discourse in this sense, and if he is to be described as a metaphysician, it will have to be as a 'sublunary' one, in Daston's sense. Latour distances himself from the study (cf. *theōria*) of being(s) qua being, the contemplation of being *per se*, in favour of inquiring into the historical practices of ontological description.

says on several occasions. To be human is to be *distributed* across a multitude of attachments.[44] Some of these attachments we may be explicitly aware of (friends, forms of nutrition, books, ideas), but many, arguably even most, we are not (recall Ramses). For us, here and now, our lives may involve attachments of which we are wholly unaware, though observers of us in times-to-come may (or may not) 'discover' them, or come to describe them in ontological terms that are unimaginable to us. The entities we are attached to are, he says, anthropogenic – they make us what we are. Fresh attachments may change what we are, and may also unmake us (recall Ramses once more). Agency is not only distributed but attributed to non-humans (e.g. microbes, ideas, social media algorithms *make things happen*). The self, distributed over countless entities, is never wholly present to itself. Moreover, no other entity is ever fully realized for us, never wholly 'present' to us, never fully known 'in itself', since the **Network** of attachments that make it what it is may change, or even pass away.[45] Historical ontology involves a turn away from the comforts of **finality** towards acknowledging the existential incompleteness of things. Existential incompleteness can be felt particularly acutely in the case of texts, where meaning is never fully realized at any point. If we see human beings as distributed selves rather than atomized individuals, we cannot treat them 'as if they were always points of emission and reception of scripts'.[46]

1.5 Historical Ontology and Temporal Perspectives

What Latour calls 'scripts' (in which we can include texts, both written and oral, and cultural practices and techniques more generally) cannot anticipate what will be made of them. This is to re-iterate his caution about transplanting into the past the hidden or potential existence of the future. To further emphasize the significance of this, consider what Latour says in an admiring review of Reviel Netz's book, *The Shaping of Deduction in Greek Mathematics: A Study in Cognitive History* (Netz 1999), which seeks to discuss the emergence of geometrical thinking and formalism in the fifth and early fourth centuries BC without reference to Plato's

---

[44] Cf. Anderson 2018, 76–9, who speaks of 'dividual personhood' in contrast to the notion of the fully autonomous *individual*, existing *per se*.
[45] Recall what Daston (2000, 1) said of 'the "perpetuity" of coming-to-be'. Contrariwise, from the perspective of applied metaphysics, ontologies, however secure and stable they may seem, are not to be regarded as final. Thus, if anti-vaxxers had their way, they might even succeed in abolishing the *being* of microbes – while, tragically, facilitating their *agency*.
[46] Latour 2013a, 422.

appropriation of them for his metaphysical agenda. What Netz does, according to Latour, is 'to transport us back in time to when there was no geometry, no apodeictic reasoning, no deduction, and to when each of those practices had to be devised from scratch without relying on any precedent'.[47] That is to say, Latour sees Netz as studying the emergence of geometrical thinking from the perspective of those who were not in a position to know about the ways in which subsequent thinkers would use their ideas – just as the 'land-measurers' (geo-meters) of earlier generations were not in a position to anticipate the ways in which the inventors of formal deduction would draw upon and elaborate their practices.

This may seem an elementary observation, but it is theoretically central to the practical demands of historical ontology or applied metaphysics. The discourses of the sixth and fifth centuries BC are subject to very distinctive receptions of which their authors could have known little or nothing, subject to the ontological ripples of heavily invested entities that were yet to come into being. Transplanting into the past the hidden or potential existence of the future creates the vectors that become the vehicles for a sense of inevitability or finality in the present. Thus Sophocles in the fifth century writes a meticulously crafted tragic dramatization of Oedipus which in the fourth century in the hands of Aristotle in the *Poetics* is figured as 'about' his own particular interests, in particular the tricky question of how an event that comes *after* (*meta*) an earlier one is to be distinguished from an event that comes *because of* (*dia*) an earlier one. Filtered through the concerns of the emergent discourse of **philosophy**, the *Oedipus Tyrannus* becomes 'about' necessity, and, further along the line, about free will and determinism.[48] And it is this philosophical discourse that 'ontologizes' **causality** or **necessity**, seeking a generality or abstraction, a systematic *logos* that transcends particular discursive manifestations. So, in addition to a historical ontology of entities such as these, we need also a historical ontology of **history**, **philosophy** – and of **ontology**. This will be pursued in §2. But for the moment, the practice of historical ontology suggests that ontologies be treated as continually emergent, with no definitive beginnings and, importantly, no *final* moment when they are, simply, *there*, once and for all.

---

[47] Latour 2008, 443; I have attempted to analyze Netz's argument and Latour's response to it in detail in Kennedy 2020c.

[48] Explored in detail in Kennedy 2013, 84–118; especially 112–115. For explicitly philosophical readings of the Oedipus plays of Sophocles, see the essays in Woodruff 2018; however, these offer little in the way of reflection upon their accommodation of dramatic texts to philosophical discourse. For a greater self-awareness, cf. Critchley 2019.

How we think about time and the temporal points of view we inhabit are themselves the effect of the emergence of distinctively ontological modes of thinking. What we call the 'past', the 'present' and the 'future' have become ontologically inflected (as the Latin etymology suggests: the present is that which *is in front* of us, the future that which *is about-to-be*). The terms we use of time colour any study of being and time.[49] Thus for Latour the 'present' is not a point in (chronological) time: 'Time is not a general framework but a provisional result of the connection between entities'.[50] It is the systematic ordering of entities, some of which may be 'very old', some 'new', that constitutes *a* 'present';[51] and it is the replacement of some entities by others that gives the sensation of time *having passed*.[52]

What of the future? Are we, like Ramses, the unwitting pawns of entities that only the future will 'discover' and historicize us accordingly? The point is, we don't know, we will have to wait and see. Nail remarks: 'The future is that which is not yet. As such it bears no necessary resemblance to the present nor the past'.[53] That certain entities in the present will be there in the future is not necessary but contingent. The desire to know what will happen in the way (we think) we know what has happened drives the behaviour of the characters in the *Oedipus Tyrannus* of Sophocles, and their interest in particular modes of talking about what has not yet happened, oracles and prophecy. The gradual emergence of what we,

---

49 Consider the terminology Heidegger developed to defamiliarize received notions of time. Heidegger's preferred term for the 'past' is *Gewesenheit*, 'having been-ness' rather than *Vergangenheit*, 'having gone away-ness', to emphasize (a) the experience of time as ontologically inflected and (b) the relationship of past and present. Cf. Kennedy 2013, 147 (original emphasis) for *Gewesenheit* as 'the *past that is relevant to the choices that "makes" a moment feel "present"*. To see the past as *vergangen*, "gone away" is to regard it as irrevocable, not subject to being called back for re-interpretation, and so under the shadow of necessity, an imposition we can only submit to; to see it as *gewesen*, "having been", is to regard it as open to our interpretation and decision'.
50 Latour 1993, 74; for Latour on time cf. Latour 1993, 67–76.
51 In composing the 'present' (i.e. *this*) article, I have used pen and paper, books, the texts of Herodotus, Plato and Latour, a networked computer etc. – entities that have been around for different passages of time.
52 Cf. Latour 1993, 72 on the temporality of 'modernity' (my emphasis): 'The impression of [time] passing *irreversibly* is generated only when we bind together the cohort of elements that make up our day-to-day universe. It is their systematic cohesion, and the replacement of those entities by others rendered just as coherent in the subsequent period, which gives us the impression of time that passes, of a continuous flow going from the future to the past... Entities have to be made contemporary by moving in step and have to be replaced by other things equally well aligned if time is to become a flow'.
53 Nail 2019, 15.

with our surplus of knowledge, might term 'ontological' modes of thinking in the fifth century (cf. *to anthrōpinon* in Thucydides 1.22) facilitates a fresh way of addressing uncertainty in relation to what will happen (for which Thucydides uses the term *ta mellonta*) by reference to what has happened (*ta genomena*). The projection into the future as well as into the past of **necessity** is a feature of some historical narratives. The desire for a future, an about-to-be, that will be (as one might say 'in all essentials') an extension of the present (what Derrida called 'a predictable, calculable, programmable tomorrow'[54]) is a powerful one that has generated consoling – or disturbing – metaphysical narratives that have themselves looped back into historical experience.[55] Against a programmable future, Derrida suggested an alternative notion of *l'avenir*, a contingent, unforeseen, future that 'arrives' unexpectedly (whether bringing destruction or salvation), and nullifies any sense of necessity encoded in predictive discourses.[56]

Still, as Thomas Nail emphasized, it is the present that is the key to theoretical thinking about historical ontology. Derrida's salutary deconstruction of the ways in which the 'metaphysics' of presence has been configured in the Western philosophical tradition has deterred many from considering the role of *presence* in human ways of being and in ontological thinking; critical thinking has been dominated in recent decades by the question of interpretation and how *meaning* is produced. Before we turn to consider historical ontology in practice in §2, let us cautiously revisit *presence*, shifting the emphasis in its connotations from the (a)temporality of ontological things in the direction of the spatial.

1.6 Meaning, Presence and Embodied Moments of Truth

In his book *Production of Presence: What Meaning Cannot Convey*, Hans Ulrich Gumbrecht has argued 'against the systematic bracketing of presence, and

---

54 Derrida 1995, 386–387. Cf. Derrida and Ferraris 2001, 20: 'Teleology is, at bottom, a negation of the future, a way of knowing beforehand the form that will have to be taken by what is still to come.'

55 Virgil's narrative in the *Aeneid* of 'empire/dominion without limit of time or space' – an extreme version of a desire for an omniscience that embraces past, present and future – and Francis Fukuyama's portrayal of liberal democracy as 'the end of history' (Fukuyama 1992) are two examples of such metaphysical narratives. For detailed analysis see Kennedy 2013, 43–83. We are currently confronted by an extreme example of a 'programmable' future in the form of the algorithms of the social media companies which use unprecedented amounts of 'data' (what Latour would call 'attachments', many of which we are unaware) to predict and guide future behaviour (cf. Zuboff 2019).

56 On Derrida's notion of *l'avenir* cf. Kennedy 2013, 60.

against the uncontested centrality of interpretation, in the academic disciplines that we call "the humanities and arts".'[57] 'Meaning effects' have driven out 'presence effects', and his aim is to restore a balance between the two.[58] This is how he explains what he is getting at:

> The word 'presence' does not refer (at least does not mainly refer) to a temporal but to a spatial relationship to the world and its objects. Something that is 'present' is supposed to be tangible for human hands, which implies that, conversely, it can have an immediate impact on human bodies. 'Production', then, is used according to the meaning of its etymological root (i.e. Latin *producere*) that refers to the act of 'bringing forth' an object in space.[59]

Latour would concur with this, but might be moved to point out that many objects cannot be seen or touched in (or by!) any conventional sense, for example, microbes or the Higgs boson. And that is before we even start thinking about things like **philosophy**! Latour's take on this is the mode of existence he calls **Reference**, the function of which is to 'reach remote entities'.[60] Modes of existence are also modes of veridiction, which do not tell truths in an absolute sense, but are ways of, as Latour puts it, speaking well of the entities they treat. What comes to appearance, such as the Higgs boson, does so through the interaction of 'assemblies' of 'actors', both human and non-human, in accordance with one or modes of existence. Remote entities are reached through mediation, chains of reference. The mode of **Technology** intersects with that of **Reference**, giving us an expanding range of tools to overcome the obstacles to instituting and maintaining those chains of reference that allow us to 'reach remote entities'. The Large Hadron Collider is not simply a particle accelerator, but a device for producing inscriptions that the scientists at CERN must interpret in their quest to institute the Higgs boson as an entity. Experiments – interventions – are carefully designed to make visible what is invisible. Movements of energy in the quantum field are precipitated so as to create a chain reaction of movements at larger scales until something happens that can be photographically recorded, and interpreted as confirming (or refuting) the hypothesis of the experiment – a meaning effect. We will never 'see' or 'feel' a Higgs boson (such language makes little sense at so microscopic a level), but its existence is mediated and warranted in the process of generating what Latour habitually calls 'equipped and rectified knowledge'.

---

57 Gumbrecht 2004, xv.
58 In many respects this reflects the privileging of epistemology over ontology that Latour resisted in his studies of science.
59 Gumbrecht 2004, xiii.
60 Cf. Latour 2013a, 489.

Knowledge is never absolutely complete: it is corrigible (in accordance with its mode of veridiction) and open to supplementation in ways that cannot be wholly anticipated.[61] Being-as-other means that hitherto unsuspected attachments may be revealed, and send out their ontological ripples.

Equipped and rectified *knowledge* is never entirely disembodied or abstract (or 'pure'), never entirely divorced from the experience of *presence*. One does not use the same modes of veridiction to speak of, say, the things of the sciences and the things of law: a Large Hadron Collider would not 'fit' in a courtroom. But the technology most associated with the mode of existence and veridiction Latour calls **Reference** is so common, so humdrum as to easily escape attention, though he habitually reminds us of *its* presence: pieces of paper on which can be inscribed words, graphs, images etc. Entities may be remote in space or time as well as scale, and the researcher may be an anthropologist, historian, or lawyer rather than a scientist. But the *scene* of veridiction Latour carefully explicates[62] is that of an assembly of enquirers, in the field, in the laboratory, in court, or in the seminar room, gathering around a sheet of paper (or a Powerpoint presentation) which is the end result of a complex chain of references, while one of them points at something on it to indicate that *this* what they have been looking for – when meaning effects and presence effects interact to produce a moment of truth. Gestures, pointing above all, are part of this process of *realization*, not optional add-ons.[63] A moment of truth has a performative dimension.

Presence is an effect, felt in the body and performed through the body's movements, though the Western philosophical tradition has downplayed this in its discussions of ontology. Gumbrecht looks back to the Cartesian *cogito*, 'which made the ontology of human existence depend exclusively on the movements of the human mind',[64] though he could have traced the downgrading of embodied existence as far back as Plato, as we shall see. However, 'against the Cartesian paradigm, Heidegger re-affirmed the bodily substantiality and the spatial dimension of human existence – "being-in-the-world"'.[65] Gumbrecht observes that for Heidegger, 'Being is *not* something conceptual. Heidegger is indeed concerned with redefining truth – but Being does not simply substitute truth. Rather,

---

61 Cf. Gabriel 2018, 37, who speaks of 'maximally modally robust facts'.
62 Cf. Latour 1999, 24–79.
63 Cf. Kendon 2004, who offers a historical and cross-cultural account of the significance of gesture; on pointing cf. 2004, 199–224. The philosophical significance of pointing will be considered in §2.
64 Gumbrecht 2004, 17.
65 Gumbrecht 2004, 46.

Heidegger talks about truth as something that happens (*ein Geschehen*)'.[66] Latour's commitment to ontological plurality and modes of existence makes him eschew talk of Being, but he is happy to speak of truths (plural), and, like Heidegger, sees them as events. While he privileges subsistence over substance, a sense of the substantiality of things is also 'something that happens', realized in performative activity. **Religion** is the mode of existence where he concentrates his thinking about this amalgam of meaning effects and presence effects.[67] The emergence of the many things that have *being* for us in this way *in mediation* has resonances with process theology (which was the subject of Latour's doctoral dissertation):[68] God is not a transcendent figure who exists 'outside' the world, beyond space and time, but a being revealed when one exegesis is resumed by another.[69] But what Latour argues of scripture is applicable to reading and study more generally, and, indeed, as Gumbrecht argues, to the quest for intensity in aesthetic experience. What is scholarship other than the repeated resumption of exegesis in pursuit of intense moments of realization?

2 Historical Ontology in Action: being; theory; history; philosophy

2.1 A Brief History (or two) of the Question of Being

Aristotle, as we have seen, speaks in *Metaphysics* 4.1003a21 of 'a branch of knowledge (*epistēmē tis*) which studies (*theōrei*) that which is (*to on*) *qua* being (*hēi on*)' – and calls it an *epistēmē theōrētikē*, a 'theoretical knowledge' (*Met.* 1.982b9–10). This is heady stuff – but also, as I shall go on to argue, 'body' stuff. **Theory** has become a manner of being in the world that remains part of human experience in twenty-first century Western intellectual life, so heavily invested in as to resist critical scrutiny. The issue of being had emerged a generation earlier as a central concern in the dialogues of Plato. In the *Sophist* (244a) the Stranger asks Theaetetus to 'tell us plainly what you mean when you use the expression "being". For it is clear that you have long known this, but we, who used to think

---

66 Gumbrecht 2004, 67; original emphasis.
67 Cf. Latour 2013a, 295–325. He sees its role as 'engendering persons', working to sustain the fragile subsistence of human beings.
68 Latour 2010 offers his own account of his education and intellectual development.
69 Cf. Maniglier 2014, 38. On the role of biblical exegesis in Latour's thought, cf. Schmidgen 2015, 9–24 and de Vries 2016, 17–20.

we knew, have become perplexed'. The Stranger had earlier referred to needing to test the *logos* of 'father Parmenides' (241d).⁷⁰ That *logos* we encounter in the surviving fragments of Parmenides of Elea's poem, probably no later than the mid-fifth century, which sets up a sharp distinction between the 'Way of Truth' and the 'Way of Opinion'. In the prologue to the poem, a young initiate travels on a chariot from the world of daily life to the place where day meets night. There he is instructed by an unnamed goddess that thought must have something to think about: 'it must be the case that what can be talked about and thought about exists; for it is possible for that to exist, but it is not possible for nothing to' (*khrē to legein te noein t'eon emmenai; esti gar einai | mēden d'ouk estin*, B 6.1–2). This assumption, taken to be fundamental, is expressed by the word *esti*; on the other hand, 'you cannot say or think that it is not' (*ou gar phaton oude noēton | estin hopōs ouk esti*, B 8.8–9). On this basis she deduces that whatever can be talked about must be 'without birth or death, whole, the only one of its kind, motionless and complete, nor was it, nor will it be, since now it is, all together, one, continuous' (*hōs agenēton eon kai anōlethron estin, | esti gar oulomeles te kai atremes ēd'ateleston; | oude pot'ēn oude estai, epei nun estin homou pan | hen, sunekhes*, B 8.3–6). That is to say, any talk of temporal change, of coming into being and passing away, of plurality, contrasts and qualitative change, or of non-existence violates this assumption. *esti* is presented as a monolithic simplicity

Historically, the perplexity of which the Stranger speaks has persisted. Heidegger opens *Being and Time* with that quotation from Plato's *Sophist* 244a. Heidegger himself then asks: 'Do we in our time have an answer to the question of what we really mean by the word "being"? Not at all. So it is fitting that we should raise anew *the question of the meaning of Being*.'⁷¹ One line that connects present to past in metaphysical thinking could be seen as the attempt to re-introduce into the question of being the very elements Parmenides and the Platonic-Aristotelian tradition sought to exclude: time (notably Heidegger and those influenced by him in the phenomenological tradition); motion (Nail); plurality (e.g. Latour, Gabriel); coming into being and passing away (those Hacking groups as 'historical ontologists'). But I have been writing 'history' here, of sorts, moreover a history *shaped* by a surplus of knowledge of what-was-to-be not available in the fifth century, and at odds with the parameters and demands of historical ontology sketched out in §1. It also presents what Barbara Cassin calls 'a single path': 'That single, dominant path of ontology goes from Parmenides to Plato via a certain reading of Aristotle up to Heidegger.' In her work, she offers an alternative line

---

70 For Parmenides as a 'father-figure' here cf. Blondell 2002, 320 and 349–350.
71 Heidegger 1962 [1927], 1; original emphasis.

(to recall the word used by Nail),[72] and a neologism, logology, which she characterizes as the 'sophistic history of philosophy…a history of neglected and repressed traditions, of alternative paths', populated by figures such as Gorgias and Protagoras who are marginalized in the 'single, dominant path of ontology'.[73] Thus Gorgias wrote *On Non-Being*, perhaps in response to Parmenides,[74] and Protagoras became famous for his dictum 'man is the measure of all things, of the things that are, that they are, of the things that are not, that they are not' (*pantōn khrēmatōn metron estin anthrōpos, tōn men ontōn hōs estin, tōn de ouk ontōn hōs ouk estin*).[75] While indebted to Cassin's revisionary spirit, my strategy will be rather different from hers. What if we shift our perspective – channelling what Latour said of Netz and the geometers – to a period when there was no Plato, before there was **theory**, before a question of **being**, indeed before **philosophy** or **history** in the senses that are now (all too) familiar? When the subsequent 'developments' I have briefly described were yet to happen and even unimaginable?

2.2 *Theōria*

The emergence of *theōria* as a key element in Plato's philosophical vocabulary has been the subject of Andrea Nightingale's stimulating foray into the conceptual history of this term, to which we shall shortly turn.[76] But first let us think about it how it is being used before Plato. *Theōria* is associated with the verb *theaomai*, to look or gaze at. It is found in the fifth century BC of an act of looking, but usually with a connotation of the fresh knowledge that can accrue from it. According to the intriguing (though probably apocryphal)[77] story in Herodotus, when Solon left Athens for ten years and visited Egypt and then the Lydian king Croesus, he did so not simply to allow his reforms to bed down in his absence but, 'for the sake of *theōria*, so he said' (*kata theōriēs prophasin*, 1.29.1). Croesus gets his servants to lead Solon around his treasures, and Herodotus describes him as both 'looking' (*theēsamenon*) and 'considering' (*skepsamenon*). Croesus then

---

72 Cf. Nail 2019, 14: 'As the present changes, however, so do the lines of the past that lead to it.'
73 Cassin 2014, 1. One need only recall the conspicuous absence of Gorgias and Protagoras from a standard textbook, *The Presocratic Philosophers* of Kirk, Raven and Schofield 1984. Cassin's alternative history was developed at length in Cassin 1995.
74 Cf. Cassin 1995, 23–26 and 122–129.
75 As quoted in Sextus Empiricus *Adv. Math.* 7.60, though it owes much of its fame or notoriety to the discussion in Plato's *Theaetetus* (cf. below §2.4).
76 Nightingale 2004.
77 Cf. Asheri/Lloyd/Corcella 2007, 99.

seizes the moment and asks him, as one who 'by reason of your wisdom and your wanderings, as one who has travelled far and wide seeking wisdom (*philosopheōn*) for the sake of looking (*theōriēs heineken*), if you did ever see one who was the happiest of all men' (1.30.1). According to Herodotus' most recent commentator, 'the verb [*philosopheōn*] appears in Herodotus only here, and is apparently unattested in earlier Greek literature'.[78] The passage prompts many thoughts, which are probably best expressed as questions. Is Herodotus retrojecting on to Solon some notions or buzzwords that were doing the rounds in his own time? Solon does not give the answer Croesus is so obviously angling for, but rather 'tells it *as it is*' (*tōi eonti khrēsamenos legei*). Or should we translate this extraordinary phrase 'he speaks, using the *to eon* argument'? Charles H. Kahn, the doyen of studies of the verb 'to be' in ancient Greek, suggests that at this period the verb was used to suggest that something was the case, or so, and remarks:

> The free use of the participle in this sense also occurs in Attic, but it is most characteristic of Ionic prose... The fullest evidence is in Herodotus, where Powell's *Lexicon* lists ten instances of the idiom. For example, when Croesus asks Solon who is the happiest of mortals, the wise Athenian refuses to flatter the king but τῶι ἐόντι χρησάμενος 'using verity' – sticking to the truth – he answers: Tellus of Athens (Hdt. 1.30.3).[79]

We may still wonder about *khrēsamenos*: does it suggest that the idiom *to (e)on* is itself becoming an explicit object of reflection, as *esti* was for Parmenides? Is Solon (at least as portrayed by Herodotus over a century later) already a 'philosopher' in possession of 'theoretical knowledge'? Not according to Nightingale who suggests that it is only in the fourth century, and especially through the influence of Plato, that **theory** starts to take on the distinctive sense we are familiar

---

[78] Cf. Asheri/Lloyd/Corcella 2007, 100. The dates of Herodotus's travels and the composition of his work are impossible to ascertain with any precision (cf. Asheri, Lloyd and Corcella 2007, 6–7); the second half of the fifth century BC will have to do. His work shows traces of the period of the Peloponnesian War. Elizabeth Irwin is an outlier; she argues he was aware of its conclusion (Irwin 2018).

[79] Cf. Kahn 2009, 24. Kahn is very concerned to keep later 'philosophical' interpretation out of such instances. Thus he argues against retrojecting the (nineteenth-century) distinction between predicative and existential uses of the verb to be on to Parmenides, and suggests the doctrine of Parmenides 'is first and foremost a doctrine concerning reality as *what is the case*' (2009, 24; original emphasis). But for similar reasons, I would be cautious about translating *to (e)on* and similar phrases from this period by the philosophically inflected terms 'verity', 'truth' and 'reality'.

with and with it a new and distinctive discourse, **philosophy**,[80] comes into being. Her argument is largely persuasive, but deserves another look.

Of particular importance for Plato, she suggests, was the cultural practice of *theōria*, a form of official state pilgrimage in which an individual journeyed abroad to witness sacred festivals,[81] and then returned home to report on what he had seen: *theōria* is not complete without the report back. A number of fifth-century figures, whom she repeatedly characterizes as 'sophists', 'intellectuals' and 'early Greek thinkers' (pointedly not 'philosophers')[82] were inveterate travellers in search of knowledge, as was Herodotus himself.[83] Nightingale remarks: 'Of course the practice of *historiē per se* does not make a thinker a *theōros*.'[84] That philosopheme *per se* is a bit problematical in the case of Herodotus, at least. He himself characterized his writings in his preface as *historiēs apodexis*, 'a setting forth' or 'publication' of his 'inquiries'.[85] His *apodexis* could be seen, precisely, as a report back: does this make him a *theōros*, at least a *theōros sui generis*? Distinctive discourses of **philosophy** and **history** (among others) are certainly emerging during the fifth and fourth centuries, together, crucially, with their distinctive expository strategies. Are these genres, these styles of thinking, ever totally distinct, *per se*? From the point of view of historical ontology, the operative question is rather: how are they *made* distinctive, *sui generis*?

---

[80] The ontological investment in this term is unusually strong, and the ontological ripples it has retrojectively spread from respective 'presents' into the past are evident from antiquity's 'present' (cf. Laks 2018, 76–77 on the attribution to Pythagoras of the neologism 'philosophy') through to the 'present' of the twenty-first century: cf. e.g. Van De Mieroop 2015 on Babylonian 'philosophy'.

[81] For a detailed historical account of the cultural practices associated with *theōria* cf. Rutherford 2013.

[82] When Nightingale describes certain figures as 'sophists', we should recall Cassin 1995, 9, who speaks of the notion of 'the sophists' as a coherent intellectual movement as 'l'artefact platonicien, le produit des dialogues. L'essence de l'artefact est tout simplement de faire du sophiste l'*alter ego* négatif du philosophe: son mauvais autre.' One aim of this essay is to encourage an enhanced awareness of when we translate the fifth-century past into philosophically inflected language, as those who are invested in **philosophy** (most of us, at least some of the time) are prone to do, caught up in the slipstream of Plato's artefact.

[83] Nightingale 2004, 63–68 surveys a number of fifth-century figures. Cf. also Thomas 2006, 61.

[84] Nightingale 2004, 67.

[85] On this phrase cf. Bakker 2002.

2.3 Re-viewing *theōria*. Part 1: *deixis*

Platonic 'philosophy' co-opts and appropriates *theōria* for its particular purposes – with spectacular success: **theory** has come to connote overwhelmingly a process of the mind or soul, but in such a way as to marginalize physical experience. For the moment, let us resist this platonizing strategy by specifically not bracketing off the physical, or accepting a categorical distinction between body and mind. Raymond Tallis, a recalcitrant reader of the Western philosophical tradition and the directions it has (but need not have) taken,[86] has challenged this distinction in his intriguing exploration of the peculiarly human phenomenon of pointing – a gesture we saw was important to Latour in his studies of the production of presence and knowledge. Tallis draws attention to the role of pointing in recognizing that other humans are embodied minds that do not share one's particular point of view and that one may be in a position to rectify a deficit of knowledge on their behalf. Pointing is emphatically not a solipsistic exercise, but involves a pooling of awareness and consciousness. The knowledge it shares is corrigible from a different point of view.[87] We can re-visit and re-view *theōria* with the help of Tallis; and, with the help of Herodotus, recover a viewpoint before Plato wrote so as to appreciate just how daring was Plato's *coup de théâtre*.[88]

Tallis sees consciousness as embodied and explores how vision opens out a vista in which the viewer is surrounded by things to which s/he stands in a relationship, near or far, left or right, in front of or behind; a vista can become a 'field' of vision, 'bounded' by its horizons. That relationship changes as the point and angle of vision change: what was far becomes near, what was left becomes right, what was in front becomes behind, what was over there is now over here. The world at which one looks becomes the world as spectacle, accessible through different points of view, from over here or, at another moment, from over there. This argument emphasizes the importance of first-person awareness of one's embodied self.[89] A sense of *being* that arises out of the first-person awareness *that I am (here)* – Tallis calls this the Existential Intuition – has been overwhelmed by the notion of third-person being: the accumulated prestige of Parmenidean *esti*-thinking, if you will, has long occluded *eimi*-thinking, though there is much to be

---

[86] Explored in a trilogy on human being and knowledge: Tallis 2003, 2004 and 2005.
[87] Cf. Tallis 2010, which builds on his study of the existential significance of the human hand, Tallis 2003.
[88] For some brief and pertinent remarks on pointing and deixis in Herodotus cf. Bakker 2006, 98–101.
[89] Tallis 2004.

gained by seeing them not as wholly discrete phenomena but as complementary.⁹⁰ A change of position can uncover what was previously unseen, and this can be conveyed to others in language: 'over *there* behind the bush is a tiger.' The language is deictic, as is the statement as a whole, pointing to and reporting what one can, and others cannot, see. Tallis calls this 'indexical knowledge'.⁹¹ But the (first-person) knowledge in the form of a statement or report *that* behind the bush there is a tiger can become, as Tallis puts it, deindexicalized,⁹² as its reception shifts it towards a (third-person) mode that elides the mediation to stake a claim for it as a feature of a common world, a pooling or collectivization of consciousness: 'there is a tiger behind the bush'. The deictic aspect of statements can be temporal as well as spatial ('there was a tiger behind the bush'), interrogative rather than indicative ('is there a tiger behind the bush?'), or potential ('there may be a tiger behind the bush'), tense and mood inviting or expressing other aspects or points of view on what 'is the case'.

Back now to Herodotus and Solon's *theōriē*. Solon in the treasury of Croesus both 'looks' and 'considers'; the physical and mental actions are conjoined. Croesus for his part (albeit slyly) seeks to rectify a 'deficit' in his knowledge with the help of Solon. If *theōria* involves a view, then a change of location may enhance it, by offering a different and arguably 'better' point of view, embracing things that were hitherto unobserved: travel does indeed broadens one's horizons. This might, as in the cases of Solon or Herodotus, involve a journey across the earth to places hitherto unvisited. Croesus explicitly says to Solon: 'much talk has reached us about you, on account of your wisdom and your wanderings, of how in seeking wisdom (*philosopheōn*) you have travelled far and wide (*gēn pollēn*) for the sake of *theōriē*' (1.30.2). Solon's own, very brief, response to the question if he, the much-travelled Solon with his immense first-person experience, has ever seen the happiest of all men is an indexical one which points to someone far away who no longer exists: 'Tellus the Athenian' (1.30.3). Solon's first-person *theōriē*

---

90 For Tallis *sum* is altogether more primal than Descartes' *cogito, ergo sum* (2004, 22–89), for it is from the Existential Intuition that all else flows. Tallis 2004, 138–151 appeals to Heidegger above all as the philosopher of embodied 'am'-thinking, and relates his own sense of the significance of 'here' and 'there' to Heideggerian thought. However, he distances himself from Heidegger's (third-person) characterization of human *being* as *Da*-sein (being *there*), suggesting that it needs to be complemented by (first-person) *Fort*-sein (being *here*): Tallis 2004, 141–145. The inertia of the philosophical tradition, manifested in the historical prestige of *esti*-thinking, exerts a drag even on those, like Heidegger, who would seek to think beyond it.
91 Cf. Tallis 2005, 110–117.
92 Cf. Tallis 2005, 117–127.

prompts an answer, Tellus, that is distilled or abstracted from his varied experiences; but the narration of Herodotus that frames and mediates his response takes a further step in the process of deindexicalization by characterizing it in third-person terms, *that* 'this is the case' (*to eon*), which serves further to delocalize and de-temporalize Solon's response. The brevity, and surprise, of Solon's answer prompts Croesus to ask (1.30.4, in a phrasing that keeps the interaction of first-person and third-person modes of being in play): 'How do *you judge* (*krineis*) Tellus *to be* (*einai*) the most blest?' Croesus casts Solon as a *histōr*, one who has witnessed but who must also justify *why* 'this is the case', and Solon goes on to do so: Tellus' city was prosperous, he was the father of outstanding sons and so on.[93]

Solon here, as many have indeed 'pointed' out, is an exemplar for Herodotus and the *historiē* he is doing. To return to Nightingale's formulation which I distanced myself from earlier, Herodotus offers not *historiē per se*, rather, in his scrupulous formulation in the preface, an *apodexis* of his enquiries (a particular act of *deixis* and reportage, an act of mediation). It is not enough to witness X: one must *bear* witness *that* X *is* the case – as Solon does for Croesus when, according to the narration, he 'uses' the *to eon* argument, and as Herodotus himself does when he reports 'the *reason* why (*di'hēn aitiēn*) the Greeks and barbarians fought against each other' – and then generates an enormous text to explain why he judges this to be the case. The *apodexis* of his enquiries has a temporal as well as spatial dimension, and this is crucial to the discourse that is emerging thanks to Herodotus, in two important ways. His address to his audience or readers invites them to be *spectators* of events and figures in the past ('back then') they otherwise could not 'see' (Solon at the palace of Croesus; or Xerxes and his generals discussing in council whether to invade Greece in the opening chapters of Book 7). What is no longer there or exists far away can nonetheless be made *present*, endowed with being through the capacity (which develops as we go along, willy-nilly as well as by design, and in ways we cannot fully anticipate) of language, as well as visual spectacle, for representation. But even more crucially, the emergence of a causal sense involves the indication and association of events and entities (e.g. *phoros*/'tribute') that can be widely separated in time and space, as

---

[93] Cf. Fowler 2006, 29: '[*Historiē*] does not mean "history" until well into the fourth century. Until then the noun and its associated verb *historein* have a more general meaning of "inquiry", "question", "investigate"; related is the noun *histōr* meaning "judge", "expert", or "witness" (i.e., "one who investigates/knows/sees"). Cf. also Asheri/Lloyd/Corcella 2007, 8 n. 23: 'The Homeric predecessor [to *historiē*], ἵστωρ, never appears in Herodotus. It implies the notion of arbitration or judgement between contrasting evidences or opinions.'

they are, to a quite unprecedented extent, in Herodotus as he generates his narrative to apportion *responsibility* for the war between Greeks and barbarians. A cause can be progressively deindexicalized by the elision of the first-person indexical, perspectival aspect which is the *reference*, the *apodexis*, that X is the case.

Re-presentations can come to take on many forms (they are *sui generis*), conjuring up 'spectacles' or 'fields of sense'[94] populated by what Latour called, in his explication of the mode **Reference**, 'remote entities' – things far away or people who have ceased to exist, such as Solon, Croesus or Xerxes, in the case of Herodotus' *apodexis*.[95] This needs to be probed further, to bring out what is distinctive about different fields of sense. Take the case of theatre, which very visibly creates a special and defined space for its representations, and a very distinctive *way of seeing*. In the *Persians* of Aeschylus (472 BC), Xerxes, and the ghost of Darius, are brought to appearance before the spectators, who are aware that they are present *there* on stage, though not *here* off it. This partial existence, there but not here, 'induces a self-consciousness of fictionality', as Simon Critchley puts it.[96] A sense of temporality is also skewed: the *now* on stage (dramatically the aftermath of the defeat of Xerxes in 480 BC) both is and is not the *now* of the spectators. Compare the council of Xerxes in Herodotus: the *now* of the debate (before the invasion of Greece) both is and is not the *now* of his readers. But the representation of direct speech serves to align the temporal experience of readers with characters. In fashioning his field of sense and populating it as he does, Herodotus was undoubtedly interacting with tragedy and its modes of representation (amongst many others), but is also generating something new and distinctive which does not require a physical stage, actors, props and speeches so as to produce presence, and gives an increasingly important role to emergent non-human entities, such as causality, that are *there* (he points explicitly to them in his *apodexis*) in the field of sense and way of seeing he is (to an extent willy-nilly, perhaps) creating.[97]

Rather than pursue this in the detail it craves, let us take the argument in a fresh direction by considering some of the issues it raises in relation to Plato, for

---

[94] I take this phrase from Gabriel 2015b.
[95] Recall that the word *reference* suggests the act of bringing some thing back. For population of fields of sense with entities cf. Kennedy 2020a, especially 243–245.
[96] Critchley 2019, 45.
[97] A capacity to 'see' or sense the presence and agency of the entities that are condensed out of the narratives and descriptions of Herodotus might be facilitated by the representation on stage, by actors, of abstractions such as Power (*Kratos*) and Violence (*Bia*) in the *Prometheus Bound*, or Madness in the *Herakles* of Euripides, or The Better Argument and The Worse Argument in the *Clouds* of Aristophanes.

whom the way of seeing that tragedy generated and the self-consciousness of fictionality associated with it were the source of acute anxiety. His response, as we will see shortly, was to create a fresh way of seeing and a new space, a new field of sense populated with its own entities. But first consider his dialogue *Parmenides*. In it, Parmenides of Elea is said to have come to the Great Panathenaea (a neatly recursive instance of Nightingale's take on *theōria*) in Athens when he was about sixty-five (*Parmenides* 127b), when Socrates was 'very young' (127c). This suggests a so-called dramatic date for the dialogue of 450BC or thereabouts, two or three generations before its composition.[98] Yet, *there* Parmenides *is*, as large as life – and still is, whenever the dialogue is read: the production of presence to which Gumbrecht has drawn our attention. When Parmenides engages in a dialectical conversation, the characteristically Platonic discursive mode, he subjects the youthful Socrates' concept of transcendental Forms (which reflects the arguments put forward in the *Republic*) to a withering critique.[99] The dialogue re-configures, with bare-faced cheek, the past to reflect present interests. To recall Latour's guidance, Parmenides existed when there was no Plato, when Plato's thinking and interest in the dialogue form[100] and the dialectical 'method' had not yet come into being; but Plato's dialogues (in a characteristic move) send ontological ripples into the past, and give us the Parmenides we encounter in the *Parmenides*. The past is being *made* 'present' here, but not in quite the same way as in the discourse of Herodotus, and, for all the affinities the dialogues have with drama,[101] this is not theatre. The issue at stake here is how Plato engineers a fresh kind of 'seeing'.

Rodolphe Gasché, in a stimulating essay entitled *Theatrum Theoreticum*, has sought to forge anew the links of the chain linking theatre and theory which he suggests were broken by Plato.[102] To do so involves wading upstream against the torrent of platonizing discourse:

---

[98] Its composition comes after the *Republic* to which it refers (see below); cf. Rowe 1993, 12: 'a strong body of opinion regards [the *Parmenides*] as the turning-point between the middle and late dialogues.'
[99] Cf. the summary in Clay 2000, 223–224.
[100] On the evidence for dialogue form before Plato, cf. Charalabopoulos 2012, 32–43.
[101] For an exploration of the ways in which the dialogues of Plato both are and are not like theatre, cf. Blondell 2002, 1–52. It is possible that performances of the dialogues were used as a teaching tool in the Academy (cf. Blondell 2002, 25–26) and they were even, perhaps, actually performed on stage, for which cf. Blondell 2002, 23–28 and Charalabopoulos 2012, 104–255.
[102] Gasché 2007, 188–208.

> Does theory, and the seeing that it implies, have a natural affinity, as it were, with the theatrical stage? The Platonic reservations concerning the theater in the *Republic*, and elsewhere, have shaped philosophy's judgment of the theater up to J.L. Austin's description of stage recitation as a parasitic or nonserious use of language. Accordingly, the theater appear to be one of philosophical theory's others. It must seek to radically distinguish itself from, and must have no traffic with, the theater.[103]

Plato's dialogues are, as Latour's modes of existence would have it, acts of **Organization**, structured around a **Fiction** of reportage, which sets the scene for the exchanges. So Socrates begins the *Republic* by telling how he went down *yesterday* to the Peiraeus with Glaucon, son of Ariston (327a), and other dialogues construct even more elaborate contextual frames within which the dialogue is, we are asked to believe, reported *verbatim*.[104] The dialogue is thus organized as an *apodeixis*, but the term is being rendered invisible by the absence of Plato himself and his authorial voice.[105] Of course Plato is not alone in this elision of *apodeixis*. Consider how the *historiēs apodexis* of Herodotus is starting to morph into a new entity *historiē*, as **history** is being (third-person) ontologized in Thucydides' suggestion (1.22.4) that his work is a *ktēma...es aiei*, a possession for all time, with transcendent qualities, rather than *agōnisma es to parakhrēma akouein*, a performance for immediate hearing. The value of the work is presented as transcending any moment of performance – composition, delivery and reception. Thucydides the (artful) reporter fades from view, and rather than 'seeing' *with* the text, we seem to 'see' *through* it. The first instance of the use of the plain term *historiē* to mean **history** seems to be in Aristotle's *Poetics* (1451b2).[106] **History** and **philosophy** in their coming-into-being and distinction from each other overlap and even interact in their suppression of the awareness of the act of mediation, in favour of a way of seeing that looks through acts of mediation to things, people, facts, arguments as though existing *in themselves*. *apode(i)xis* fades from view as these things become progressively deindexicalized into a third-person ontology.

It would be idle to deny that that way of seeing and that kind of ontologizing can have important uses, as a shorthand or black box that lets you just get on with the business at hand. But it needs to be treated with extreme caution. Above

---

103 Gasché 2007, 189.
104 Cf. the analysis of Clay 2000, 15–31 of what he calls the 'dramatic settings' of *Phaedo, Theaetetus, Parmenides* and *Symposium*.
105 On the impact and significance of this cf. Blondell 2002, 39–47; cf. also Clay 2000 for Plato as 'the silent philosopher'.
106 Cf. Fowler 2006, 33 and 42 n. 18 for discussion.

all, there can be dangers in elevating (or reducing) it to a single, unifying, metaphysical 'vision' of *how things are*, of how the 'world' *really is*.[107] Latour is hostile to the notion that any 'in*form*ation' is unmediated, devoid of the attachments and types of organization that make it take on the particular *form* that it has, hostile to the notion that any 'data' is simply 'given'.[108] One of his modes of existence is **Double Click**, named for the 'point and click' facility of graphical user interfaces, which he presents as the 'Evil Genius of the Moderns'.[109] **Double Click**, in its suggestion that we can have instantaneous access to the 'facts' (facts that, as the etymology can remind us, can be viewed as the outcomes of processes of *making*), and that access to truths can be direct and unmediated, looks rather like a bastardized version of the Platonic-Aristotelian tradition of *theōria*, the desire to see things *per se*. Plato, as we shall see shortly, should not be accused of mixing up that desire with its achievement, but it is to Latour that we can look for the bloody-mindedness not to elide the processes, the sheer hard work, that is involved in getting us to where and what we *are* at any point in time. We are in a Faustian pact with **Double Click**, but we rely on it (and another mode, **Habit**) for much of our lives to flow smoothly: we can't be forever unpacking our every thought and action, tracing back in exhaustive detail the chains of reference that make our facts, unless *there is something* that comes to our attention that makes us re-visit a particular chain. Thus, '[t]he error is not that we trust **Double Click** – it's our whole life – but that we slip unwittingly *from omission to forgetting*.'[110] Latour's work might be seen as a life-long devotion to a mission of unforgetting. Not being modern, he operates under a very old sign, *a-lētheia*.

Alētheia is often rendered by the philosopheme 'truth'. But the history of such philosophemes should not be forgotten. Though third-person ontologizing discourses work to suppress *apode(i)xis* in the mediating sense of 'exposition', they re-tool the word to mean 'proof', focussing on the outcome not the process by which that outcome is reached. Geometrical *apodeixis*, which so fascinated Plato,

---

107 It has become traditional to refer to this sense of a single vision of how things really are as 'the God's-eye view' (as e.g. Daston 2000, 1, quoted above), or, in Thomas Nagel's phrase 'The View from Nowhere' (Nagel 1986). Gabriel 2015a sets out to argue that the 'world' in this totalizing sense *does not exist*, except in a meta-metaphysical field of sense as a hypothetical argument.
108 Chains of references that go to fashion 'equipped and rectified knowledge' *matter*: mentioning one's sources may have been another Herodotean innovation (though such references are fairly infrequent); cf. Fowler 1996, 86: '[Herodotus] invented the *problem* of sources.'
109 Latour 2013, 274.
110 Latour 2013, 275; my emphasis.

played a crucial role in this shift of meaning.[111] However, formal geometrical proof achieves its transcendence not by inhabiting some superlunary sphere, but by the *moves* that generate the outcome, the result that was to be demonstrated, being exactly repeatable, any time, any place.[112] 'Proof' is a fine concept, and allows what came in the Platonic-Aristotelian tradition to be known as geometrical 'theorems' to be carried over to new demonstrations – but not if this results in a *failure to notice* or *forgetfulness* of how that point was reached: *alētheia* can express those senses, but itself is re-tooled in third-person ontologically inflected discourses – historical no less than philosophical – to suggest *truth*, simple, *per se*, just *there*. But...just *where*?

2.4 Reviewing theōria: Part 2. New Views from 'here' and 'there'

If speech, language and writing (in Latour's more dynamic modal terms, **Fiction** intersecting with **Organization**) can configure their listeners or audience as viewers of a spectacle, inviting their attention to what they otherwise could not see, it does so by fashioning different, novel, and often unexpected points of view, ways of seeing and fields of sense. The focus will now be on how Plato engineered this. In *Republic* 475c–e, Glaucon and Socrates pursue a line of argument that seeks to distinguish between *philotheamones*, people who love looking at things, and *philosophoi*, lovers of wisdom. Glaucon suggests that the former couldn't be bothered to spend time listening to arguments, but 'run round the city and country Dionysia, never missing a festival, as if they were under contract to listen to every performance.'[113] Glaucon asks: shall we call them *philosophoi*? No, replies Socrates, though they resemble *philosophoi* in a way, because *philosophoi* are those who love to be spectators of the truth (*tous tēs alētheias...philotheamonas*). But how does one become a spectator of the truth? As Gasché would put it, theatre and theory are here being distinguished, and Plato is fashioning a fresh way of seeing. A view from ground level may be inferior ('lower') to the 'superior' vista furnished from higher up; but Plato administers a characteristic twist to this notion by playing about with the relationship between different vertical levels whilst pressing the limits of the physical capacity to achieve

---

111 Cf. Netz 1999, 254–263. Netz 1999, 292–311 baulks at Plato's appropriation of it for his theory of Forms.
112 For much more on these issues see Kennedy 2020c.
113 The translation quoted here comes from Lee 1974, 269.

such a 'superior' point of view. Let us concentrate on three passages which play with points of view to achieve a special perspective and space ('over there') that comes to be identified as 'theoretical' in a 'philosophical' sense that is differentiated not simply from the avid spectatorship dismissed in the *Republic* but, more importantly, from what we might call the horizontal *theōria* practised by Herodotus.

First of all, in *Phaedo* 109b–e, Socrates says he believes the earth to be very large, and that those who live between the pillars of Hercules and the river Phasis (i.e. the world as 'known' to the Greeks through the mediation of figures like Herodotus) live in only a small part of it. He then makes the (frankly) bizarre suggestion that we do not live, as we think we do, on the surface of the earth, but in hollows. However, rather than suggesting we climb to the highest vantage-point, he then compares us to somebody who lives in the depths of the ocean but thinks that he lives on its surface, and observing the sun and the stars through the water, imagines that the sea was the sky. If sluggish or weak, he may never have made it to the surface, and would never, by lifting his head above the water have seen 'our' world (*ton enthade topon*, deictically 'the place here'), and should never have heard from anyone who had seen it how much purer and more beautiful it is. So it is for us, who are unable to reach the upper surface of the air, but if anyone could get wings and fly up and poke his head through, as fish lift their heads (*anakuptontes*) out of the water and see 'the things here' (*ta enthade*), if his nature was capable of holding up as he looked (*theōrousa*), then he would see that it is 'unmistakably the heaven' (*ho alēthōs ouranos*) and 'unmistakably the light' (*ho alēthōs phōs*) and 'unmistakably the earth' (*hē alēthōs gē*).

In much the same way and much the same language, the charioteer in the *Phaedrus* (248a–249c) raises his head into 'the outer place' (*ton exō topon*), the realm of God and the Forms, and, like the fish in the *Phaedo*, 'pops up his head into that which is, being-wise' (*anakupsasa eis to on ontōs*). But like the fish out of water, this is not a place ordinary mortals can inhabit. A separation is enacted between a realm of human experience and a realm of 'things unmistakably' and 'that which is, being-wise'. We cannot normally have access to, visit or see the latter: the 'physical' is gradually becoming distinguished from what will eventually be called the 'meta-physical'. Not even Socrates himself claims knowledge of the Forms, which lie beyond *immediate* human experience, and are elusive: in

Cratylus 439c, Socrates remarks: 'Consider the thing I often *dream* about, my worthy Cratylus: should we say, or shouldn't we, that there is a beautiful in itself or a good in itself, and in this manner each one of the things that are?'[114]

The third passage is, in its own way, no less bizarre. In *Theaetetus* 171, Socrates and Theodorus are discussing the Socrates's characterization of Protagoras's dictum that 'man is the measure of all things' (170e); it is self-refuting, Socrates suggests (171c). Theodorus interjects that 'we are running *down* (*katatheomen*) my friend too hard'.[115] Socrates responds by picking up the verb Theodorus has used, but amending it to say that it isn't clear that we are running *past* (*paratheomen*) what is correct (*to orthon*), thus countering an accusation of personal disparagement with an appeal to the correct meaning of the saying. But what is the 'correct' meaning? Is there a 'correct' meaning? The failure of texts to pin down meaning precisely, once and for all, is a recurrent Platonic neurosis (familiar from the *Phaedrus* above all), the remedy for which is the open-ended conversational arguments that constitute 'the dialectical method'. Protagoras is not there to defend himself, Socrates takes Theodorus to imply. But would even his physical presence to put his side of the argument be a sufficient guarantee of the 'correct' meaning of his dictum, outside of any context in which it is invoked? Socrates replies with a flight of fancy (172d): 'it is likely', he says, 'that Protagoras, being older, is wiser than we are; and if he suddenly popped up (*anakupseie*) from the ground here, from the neck up, he would, in all probability, convict me of talking a lot of nonsense, and you of agreeing with me, and then he would duck down and get away at a run (*katadus an oikhoito apotrekhōn*)'. We can but admire the fast footwork of Socrates himself, as he concedes that 'we must make do with ourselves such as we are, I suppose, and we must always say what seems to us to be the case.' Even a pop-up Protagoras couldn't, even if he wanted to, settle the issue.[116] Protagoras could not be present because, at the dramatic date of this dialogue shortly before the death of Socrates in 399 BC (cf. *Tht.* 142c), he had been dead for about twenty years. Socrates's image, like the fish poking its head out of water in the *Phaedo*, conjures up an intervention from a realm removed from our everyday physical experience – only for Socrates to say 'scrub that'. But the notion, that *somewhere* there *is* the 'correct' meaning, like the seed in *Phaedrus*

---

114 On the language of dreaming as one of the ways Plato bootstraps this separation of realms cf. Kennedy, 2020a, 228–235.
115 For the loyalty of Theodorus here to his old 'teacher' cf. Blondell 2002, 282, 286–287.
116 The contexts in which this dictum has been discussed are myriad, but one conversation should be reported here which I had with Pantelis Michelakis in the Mocha Mocha café in Bristol one day in December 2018 (to give it its contextual frame): does the dictum acknowledge and assert the role of *eimi*-being in putting forward *esti*-being?

(276b–e), has been planted in our minds.[117] Socrates's visualization (*paradeigma*),[118] his deictic sketch or model of that realm, has got us dreaming. Meaning effects and presence effects collude.

At this point, let us return to Nightingale's exploration of the imagery of *theōria*. She has argued that a visit to another realm that we cannot ourselves make needs an intrepid reporter who makes the journey on our behalf and comes back to tell us about it. Two stories in the *Republic*, the Cave and Er, are of crucial importance according to Nightingale,[119] so let us conclude by re-visiting them in the light of what Latour said of the mode of existence (**Reference**) by which 'remote entities' are reached. We do not have direct access to the Forms. The story of the prisoners in the Cave is a narrative modelling (**Fiction** intersecting with **Organization**) of how Socrates envisages the soul as, ideally, 'seeing' the Forms directly. The narrative deploys the imagery of discrete levels of verticality we have been examining. The freed prisoner, compelled to stand up (*anistasthai*, 515c), to look upwards towards the light (*pros to phōs anablepein*, 515c), and make his ascent (*anabaseōs*, 515e) out of the cave, directs his vision upwards towards the sun, which acts as an image of the Form of the Good, and then returns below (*katabas*, 516e) to tell those who remain there what he saw on his journey up there (cf. *anabas* 517a). Glaucon early on interjects (515a) that the image is bizarre (*atopon*) and the prisoners it depicts are *atopous*, bizarre. The adjective *atopos* suggests, 'out of place', and this acts as a subtle trigger for what follows. At the conclusion of the narrative, Socrates remarks to Glaucon of the image (517b): 'you won't disappoint my hopes if you connect the ascent upwards (*tēn..anō anabasin*) and the looking at the things above (*thean tōn anō*) with the soul's way up (*tēs psukhēs anodon*) into the place of reasoning (*ton noēton topon*).' A 'place' has been fashioned that is the object of philosophical *theōria*, a field of sense populated by the entities of third-person *esti* being that is stripped of the embodiment of first-person *eimi* being. The soul can go to a 'place' that the body cannot. At the very end of the *Republic*, Socrates tells how Er was presumed killed in battle, but after his body was taken home and placed on the funeral pyre, he woke up on the twelfth day and recounted how his soul departed (*ekbēnai tēn psukhēn*, 614b) and travelled far to 'some sort of divine place' (*eis topon tina daimonion*, 614c). The judges of the dead tell him that he must become a messenger to men and listen

---

[117] I have explored the metaphysical implications of 'planting the seed' of an idea (with help from Christopher Nolan's 2010 movie *Inception*) in Kennedy 2020a.
[118] On the philosopher as 'model-maker' and Socratic *paradeigmata*, which do not *represent* what exists but allow one to *visualize* something cf. Allen 2010, 38–54.
[119] Nightingale 2004, 76–77 and 99–107.

to and observe everything in the place (*akouein te kai theasthai panta ta en tōi topōi*, 614d; Er is later described as 'the messenger from over there' (*ho ekeithen aggelos*, 619b), and he duly reports back when he wakes on the pyre.

That 'place', 'over there', though inaccessible, is not entirely unfamiliar. Props from current belief systems are redeployed to create a scene of which we are invited to become the new-fangled 'spectators', though we are no more able to enter that scene than the audience of a tragedy, however *philotheamenoi* they may be, can cross the orchestra and become part of the action. For us, now discursively visualized as stuck 'over here', body and soul are conjoined, and we ourselves cannot undertake that sort of *theoretical* journey and view directly 'the things that are, being-wise'. In practical terms (i.e. 'over here'), where *eimi* cannot be definitively separated from *esti*, what attempts to *mediate* 'the things that are' – 'over there' – is the dialectical 'method' (i.e the meta-journey [*hodos*]).[120] Socratic dialogues invite us to become spectators of the give-and-take of conversational argument, a multi-vocal discourse, presented, as it were, in 'real' time that seeks to establish a common world of corrigible knowledge, but one in which nothing is settled once and for all.[121] This is a scene we cannot pop up into (no more than Protagoras could in the *Theaetetus*), but with which we can engage whenever we 'point' to or 'reference' details in the text and weave them into our own *apodeixis*.

Bibliography

Allen, Danielle. 2010. *Why Plato Wrote*, Chichester: Wiley-Blackwell.
Anderson, Greg. 2018. *The Realness of Things Past: Ancient Greece and Ontological History*, New York: Oxford University Press.
Arendt, Hannah. 1994. *Essays in Understanding*, New York: Schocken.
Asheri, David/Alan Lloyd/Aldo Corcella. 2007. *A Commentary on Herodotus Books I-IV*, Oxford: Oxford University Press.
Bakker, E.J. 2002. 'The Making of History: Herodotus' *Historiēs Apodexis*', in E.J. Bakker/I.J.F. de Jong/H. van Wees (eds.), *Brill's Companion to Herodotus*, 3–32. Leiden/Boston/Cologne.

---

[120] 'Path' (*hodos*) was a term Herodotus had used of his narrative: cf. 1.95.1 with Fowler 2006, 42 n. 13. For a major re-examination of this image and its development before Herodotus cf. Folit-Weinberg 2017.

[121] Attempts can, of course, be made (and have repeatedly been made) to reduce that multi-vocal discourse to a univocal one that gets called 'Platonism'; for this cf. Kennedy 2020b, especially 274 n. 57.

Bakker, E.J. 2006. 'The Syntax of *historiē*: How Herodotus Writes', in Dewald, Carolyn/ John Marincola (eds.), *The Cambridge Companion to Herodotus*, 92–102, Cambridge: Cambridge University Press.
Blondell, Ruby. 2002. *The Play of Character in Plato's Dialogues*, Cambridge: Cambridge University Press.
Cassin, Barbara. 1995. *L'Effet sophistique*, Paris: Gallimard.
Cassin, Barbara. 2014. *Sophistical Practice: Toward a Consistent Relativism*, New York: Fordham University Press.
Charalabopoulos, Nikos G. 2012. *Platonic Drama and its Ancient Reception*, Cambridge: Cambridge University Press.
Clay, Diskin. 2000. *Platonic Questions: Dialogues with the Silent Philosopher*, University Park, Pennsylvania: The Pennsylvania State University Press.
Critchley, Simon. 2019. *Tragedy, the Greeks and Us*, London: Profile Books.
Daston, Lorraine (ed.) 2000. *Biographies of Scientific Objects*, Chicago: Chicago University Press.
De Vries, Gerard. 2016. *Bruno Latour*, Cambridge: Polity Press.
Derrida, Jacques. 1995. *Points...Interviews 1974-94*. Translated by Peggy Kamuf, Stanford, CA: Stanford University Press.
Derrida, Jacques/Maurizio Ferraris. 2001. *A Taste for the Secret*. Translated by Giacomo Donis, Cambridge: Polity Press.
Descola, P. 2013 [2003]. *Beyond Nature and Culture*. Translated by J. Lloyd, Chicago: Chicago University Press.
Folit-Weinberg, Benjamin. 2017. *The Figure of the Hodos from Homer to Parmenides*. Diss., Cambridge.
Fowler, R.L. 1996. 'Herodotus and his Contemporaries', *JHS* 116, 62–87.
Fowler, R.L. 2006. 'Herodotus and his Prose Predecessors', in Dewald, Carolyn/John Marincola (eds), *The Cambridge Companion to Herodotus*, 29–45, Cambridge: Cambridge University Press.
Furet, François. 1981. *Interpreting the French Revolution*, Cambridge: Cambridge University Press.
Gabriel, Markus. 2015a. *Why the World Does Not Exist*, Cambridge: Polity Press.
Gabriel, Markus. 2015b. *Fields of Sense: A New Realist Ontology*, Edinburgh: Edinburgh University Press.
Gabriel, Markus. 2018. *Neo-Existentialism*, Cambridge: Polity Press.
Gasché, Rodolphe. 2007. *The Honor of Thinking: Critique, Theory, Philosophy*, Stanford, CA: Stanford University Press.
Gumbrecht, Hans Ulrich. 2004. *Production of Presence: What Meaning Cannot Convey*, Stanford, CA: Stanford University Press.
Hacking, Ian. 1994. 'The Looping Effects of Human Kinds', in D. Sperber/D. Premack/A.J. Premack (eds.), *Causal Cognition: A Multidisciplinary Approach*, 351–94, Oxford: Clarendon Press.
Hacking, Ian. 1995. *Rewriting the Soul: Multiple Personality and the Sciences of Memory*, Princeton: Princeton University Press.
Hacking, Ian. 2002. *Historical Ontology*, Cambridge MA: Harvard University Press.
Hadot, Pierre. 2006. *The Veil of Isis: An Essay on the History of the Idea of Nature*, Cambridge MA: The Belknap Press of Harvard University Press.

Heidegger, Martin. 1962 [1927]. *Being and Time*. Translated by John Macquarrie and Edward Robinson, Oxford: Blackwell Publishing.

Hernández Garcés, Carlos. 2018. *Καιρός, αἰτία and the Experience of Time in Herodotus' Histories: Narrative and the Emergence of Historical Discourse*. Diss., Oslo.

Irwin, Elizabeth. 2018. 'The End of the *Histories* and the End of the Atheno-Peloponnesian Wars', in Thomas Harrison/Elizabeth Irwin (eds.), *Interpreting Herodotus*, 279–334, Oxford: Oxford University Press.

Kahn, Charles H. 2009. *Essays on Being*, New York: Oxford University Press.

Kendon, Adam. 2004. *Gesture: Visible Action as Utterance*, Cambridge: Cambridge University Press.

Kennedy, Duncan F. 2002. *Rethinking Reality: Lucretius and the Textualization of Nature*, Ann Arbor: University of Michigan Press.

Kennedy, Duncan F. 2013. *Antiquity and the Meanings of Time: A Philosophy of Ancient and Modern Literature*, London: IB Tauris.

Kennedy, Duncan F. 2020a. 'Metalepsis and Metaphysics', in Sebastian Matzner/Gail Trimble (eds.), *Metalepsis: Ancient Texts, New Perspectives*, 223–45, Oxford: Oxford University Press.

Kennedy, Duncan F. 2020b. 'Plato and Lucretius on the Theoretical Subject: A Metaphysical Enquiry', in Donncha O'Rourke (ed.), *Approaches to Lucretius*, 259–81, Cambridge: Cambridge University Press.

Kennedy, Duncan F. 2020c. 'Metaphysics and the Mathematical Diagram', in P. Michelakis (ed.), *Media and Classics*, 77–113, Oxford: Oxford University Press.

Kern, Stephen. 2004. *A Cultural History of Causality: Science, Murder Novels, and Systems of Thought*, Princeton: Princeton University Press.

Kirk, G.S./J.E. Raven/M. Schofield. 1984. *The Presocratic Philosophers: A Critical History with a Selection of Texts*. Second Edition, Cambridge: Cambridge University Press.

Kosselleck, Reinhart. 2002. *The Practice of Conceptual History: Timing History, Spacing Concepts*, Stanford, CA: Stanford University Press.

Ladyman, James. 2017. 'An Apology for Naturalised Metaphysics', in M.H. Slater/Z. Yudell (eds), *Metaphysics and the Philosophy of Science: New Essays*, 141–62, Oxford: Oxford University Press.

Ladyman, James/Dan Ross. 2007. *Every Thing Must Go: Metaphysics Naturalized*, Oxford: Oxford University Press.

Laks, André. 2018 [2006]. *The Concept of Presocratic Philosophy: Its Origin, Development, and Significance*. Translated by Glenn W. Most, Princeton and Oxford: Princeton University Press.

Latour, Bruno. 1987. *Science in Action: How to Follow Scientists and Engineers through Society*, Cambridge MA: Harvard University Press.

Latour, Bruno. 1988 [1984]. *The Pasteurization of France*. Translated by Alan Sheridan and John Law, Cambridge MA: Harvard University Press.

Latour, Bruno. 1993 [1991]. *We Have Never Been Modern*. Translated by Catherine Porter, Cambridge MA: Harvard University Press.

Latour, Bruno. 1999. *Pandora's Hope: Essays on the Reality of Science Studies*, Cambridge MA: Harvard University Press.

Latour, Bruno. 2000. 'On the Partial Existence of Existing *and* Nonexisting Objects', in Daston (ed.) 2000, 247–69.

Latour, Bruno. 2004. *Politics of Nature: How to Bring the Sciences into Democracy*. Translated by Catherine Porter, Cambridge MA: Harvard University Press.
Latour, Bruno. 2008. 'Review Essay: The Netz-Works of Greek Deductions', *Social Studies of Science* 38, 441–59.
Latour, Bruno. 2010. 'Coming out as a Philosopher', *Social Studies of Science* 40, 599–608.
Latour, Bruno. 2013a [2012] *An Inquiry into Modes of Existence: An Anthropology of the Moderns*. Translated by Catherine Porter, Cambridge MA: Harvard University Press.
Latour, Bruno. 2013b [2002]. *Rejoicing: On the Torments of Religious Speech*. Translated by Julie Rose, Cambridge: Polity Press.
Latour, Bruno. 2016. *Reset Modernity!* Cambridge MA: MIT Press.
Latour, Bruno. 2018 [2017]. *Down to Earth: Politics in the New Climatic Regime*. Translated by Catherine Porter, Cambridge: Polity Press.
Latour, Bruno/Steve Woolgar. 1986. *Laboratory Life: The Construction of Scientific Facts*. Second Edition, Princeton: Princeton University Press.
Lear, Jonathan. 1988. *Aristotle: The Desire to Understand*, Cambridge: Cambridge University Press.
Lee, Desmond (trans.). 1974. *Plato: The Republic*. Second Edition, Harmondsworth: Penguin Books.
Lloyd, G.E.R. 2015. *Analogical Investigations: Historical and Cross-cultural Perspectives on Human Reasoning*, Cambridge: Cambridge University Press.
Maniglier, Patrice. 2014. 'A Metaphysical Turn? Bruno Latour's *An Inquiry into Modes of Existence*', *Radical Philosophy* 187, 37–44.
Nagel, Thomas. 1986. *The View from Nowhere*, New York/Oxford: Oxford University Press.
Nail, Thomas. 2019. *Being and Motion*, New York: Oxford University Press.
Nightingale, Andrea Wilson. 2004. *Spectacles of Truth in Classical Greek Philosophy: Theoria in its Cultural Context*, Cambridge: Cambridge University Press.
Peters, John Durham. 2015. *The Marvelous Clouds: Toward a Philosophy of Elemental Media*, Chicago: Chicago University Press.
Rowe, C.J. (ed.). 1993. *Plato: Phaedo*, Cambridge: Cambridge University Press.
Ruffing, Kai. 2018. 'Gifts for Cyrus, Tribute for Darius', in Thomas Harrison/Elizabeth Irwin (eds.), *Interpreting Herodotus*, 149–61, Oxford: Oxford University Press.
Rutherford, Ian. 2013. *State Pilgrims and Sacred Observers in Ancient Greece: A Study of Theōria and Theōroi*, Cambridge: Cambridge University Press.
Schmidgen, Henning. 2015. *Bruno Latour in Pieces: An Intellectual Biography*, New York: Fordham University Press.
Shapin, Steven. 1996. *The Scientific Revolution*, Chicago: Chicago University Press.
Tallis, Raymond. 2003. *The Hand: A Philosophical Inquiry into Human Being*, Edinburgh: Edinburgh University Press.
Tallis, Raymond. 2004. *I Am: A Philosophical Inquiry into First-Person Being*, Edinburgh: Edinburgh University Press.
Tallis, Raymond. 2005. *The Knowing Animal: A Philosophical Inquiry into Knowledge and Truth*. Edinburgh: Edinburgh University Press.
Tallis, Raymond. 2010. *Michelangelo's Finger: An Exploration of the Everyday Transcendent*, London: Atlantic Books.
Van De Mieroop. 2015. *Philosophy Before the Greeks: The Pursuit of Truth in Ancient Babylonia*, Princeton: Princeton University Press.

Viveiros de Castro, Eduardo. 2014 [2009]. *Cannibal Metaphysics*. Edited and translated by Peter Skafish, Minneapolis: Univocal Publishing.
Woodruff, Paul (ed.) 2018. *The Oedipus Plays of Sophocles: Philosophical Perspectives*, New York: Oxford University Press.
Zuboff, Shosana. 2019. *The Age of Surveillance Capitalism: The Fight for a Human Future at the New Frontier of Power*, London: Profile Books.

Alexander Meeus
Truth, Method and the Historian's Character: The Epistemic Virtues of Greek and Roman Historians

For good reasons the question of truth is one of the central problems in the theory and philosophy of history,[1] and it was an equally central question already in ancient historiography.[2] In recent decades, however, several scholars have argued for a substantial difference between in ancient and modern understandings of historical truth, the former for instance being limited to impartiality and plausibility, or generally allowing for a much greater degree of – in our terms – subjectivity than would be acceptable nowadays.[3] The undeniable merit of these studies is that they have substantially enhanced our understanding of the often neglected differences between ancient and modern historiography. Yet it seems to me that some in turn understand the rhetorical and literary nature of ancient historiography in equally anachronistic and one-sided terms,[4] and often only in superficial engagement with recent insights developed in the theory and philosophy of history.

Two central points in recent debates about history have been admirably summarised by Fasolt, namely that "our knowledge is linguistically constructed. But, far from making it unreal, that is what makes it knowledge",[5] and that:

I would like to thank Aaron Turner having included me in his excellent conference, and the audience at the conference, especially Katherine Clarke, Jonas Grethlein, Lisa Irene Hau and Jouni-Matti Kuukkanen for their valuable comments; translations of Greek and Latin texts are from the Loeb Classical Library, unless stated otherwise.

---

1 See e.g. Lorenz 1998; Tucker 2004, 255–258 and *passim*; Murphey 2009; Pataut 2009; Kuukkanen 2015, esp. 113–192; Paul 2015, 111–122.
2 See among many others e.g. Marincola's entry ἀλήθεια in the *LHGL* (Marincola 2007a), Gehrke 2014, 86–119 and *passim*, and two recent collective volumes: Ruffell/Hau 2017; Blank/Maier 2018.
3 E.g. Wiseman 1979; Loraux 1980; Woodman 1988; Nicolai 1992 and 2007; Heldmann 2011.
4 See e.g. the counter-arguments in Pelling 1990; Moles 1993; Rhodes 1994; Bosworth 2003; Schepens 2007; Lendon 2009; Schorn 2019.
5 Fasolt 2005, 10. As Lorenz 1997, 40, aptly put it in his argument against idealistic philosophies of history: 'was erdacht wurde, ist ja nicht zwangsläufig fiktional oder imaginär'; cf. even Wiseman 1988, 263 about Thucydides: 'Because he couldn't be sure he got it right, it doesn't mean he made it up.'

> By now the hunt for absolute objectivity seems to have lost most of its old appeal. What has unhappily not yet lost its appeal is absolute subjectivity. Absolute objectivity is gone from the minds of most respectable historians. Absolute subjectivity is very much alive and well. It has not yet sunk in that absolute subjectivity is merely the mirror image of absolute objectivity, and quite as meaningless. It cannot very well sink in unless we take responsibility for knowledge and stop imagining that knowledge can be had without anachronistic self-assertion.[6]

Indeed, the very fact that historical knowledge can only originate through the intellectual activity of a thinking subject makes it inevitably subjective, but that does not automatically imply that it cannot be true. Fasolt's formulation does, however, raise the question of the conditions that allow the historian to achieve valid knowledge and take responsibility for it. In light of this the following statement by an expert on ancient historiography is puzzling in several ways:

> If modern historiography tends to be more or less aware of an absolute truth (which can be the foundation of philosophical thought) or a scientific truth (which is independent of any subjectivity), the truth of ancient historians generally rested upon the impartiality and honesty of the historian, viz. on subjective and relative values.[7]

While much more should also be said about the philosophical problems of the first half of this sentence, that would take us too far. It is the latter part that is relevant here, namely the observation on ancient historiography that stands in marked contrast to a central development of the last decades within the field of epistemology: the important role played by such values as impartiality and honesty in the creation of knowledge has been studied intensively by so-called virtue epistemologists. Whether or not Momigliano was right to claim that 'epistemological questions about the nature, validity, and limits of our objective knowledge of reality have only an oblique importance for historical analysis',[8] it is fundamental that the student of the history of historiography at the very least engages with the questions as to how knowledge comes about and which epistemic standards constitute fair criteria with which to judge past historians.

After a very brief presentation of virtue epistemology follows a short discussion of ancient source theory and the way it makes virtue epistemology a highly relevant tool of analysis. Then follows an overview of some of the epistemic vir-

---

[6] Fasolt 2014, 56. On postmodern approaches to history as mere inversions of positivism, see also Lorenz 1998.
[7] Nicolai 2007, 19.
[8] Momigliano 2016, 40; similarly Tucker (2004, 25) in his investigation on historical knowledge.

tues regularly expressed by Greek and Roman historians. No definitive and complete catalogue of intellectual virtues can be compiled, since there will always be disagreement both large (as between reliabilists and responsibilists, cf. infra, n. 10) and small (i.e. on specific virtues) about what to include or exclude. Even bearing in mind this restriction, the present discussion must remain merely a preliminary survey limited to some of the most common virtues. Neither is there space to elaborate the nuances that distinguish individual authors, to analyse chronological developments or to study the differences between Greek and Roman historians.[9]

1 Epistemic Virtues

The nature of knowledge remains a hotly debated conundrum among philosophers. Many of them hold that true belief is an important dimension of knowledge, but also that true belief alone is not enough. Virtue epistemology is a branch of epistemology which argues that, under certain conditions, true beliefs can be obtained thanks to a particular set of cognitive capacities or ethical qualities, so-called epistemic virtues, or even that the involvement of such capacities or qualities is what turns true belief into knowledge. Examples of such virtues are a good memory, open-mindedness, perservance, accuracy and honesty.[10] Since every field seems to need its set of turns, virtue epistemology is a central

---

9 Much of this ground has of course been covered in much more detail by Marincola 1997 from the perspective of the historians' construction of authority. Heldmann (2011, 16) in my view overstates the difference between Greek and Roman historiography or indeed between Thucydides and Hellenistic historiography as a whole.

10 For recent introductions to virtue epistemology, see Turri et al. 2017 and Battaly 2019. The attentive reader will have noticed that not all of these are what one would traditionally classify as virtues (e.g. having a good memory). This is a philosophically relevant problem to those interested primarily in the definition of virtue, and thus a hotly debated topic dividing the field in so-called responsibilists, whose main concern is with character traits like honesty and open-mindedness, and reliabilists, who focus on faculties like vision or memory. This debate need not detain us here, however, as it is not fundamental to virtue epistemology's practical application to historiography: in this context I would thus agree with the claim of Turri et al. 2017, §3, p. 6, that 'arguments over which are the "real" virtues can seem pointless and counterproductive, since many are the ways of excelling and flourishing intellectually'.

aspect of the so-called value turn in epistemology.[11] The origins of virtue epistemology as a specific school within the field of epistemology lie in the 1980's, but the approach has been anticipated and inspired by many earlier philosophers, including Plato and Aristotle:[12] there is thus no need to consider it an approach alien to or incompatible with the ancient world, although it does not seem applicable to ancient philosophical analyses of knowledge.[13]

In recent years the approach of virtue epistemology has also entered the debates on the theory and philosophy of history.[14] Although different terminology has been used, such as 'cognitive values' or 'epistemic values', I follow Herman Paul's use of the label "epistemic virtues", because it best fits the focus on character and the subjective role of the historian in ancient historiographical theory (cf. infra, section 2).[15] In summarizing his approach, Paul writes that:

> Philosophers of history in the past few decades (…) have focused consistently and almost exclusively on the historian's (published) output, thereby ignoring that historical scholarship is a practice of reading, thinking, discussing, and writing, in which successful performance requires active cultivation of certain skills, attitudes, and virtues. (…) Inspired by a "performative turn" in the history and philosophy of science, [this paper] focuses on the historian's "doings" and proposes to analyze these performances in terms of epistemic virtue. It argues that historical scholarship is embedded in "practices" or "epistemic cultures," in which knowledge is created and warranted by means of such virtues as honesty, carefulness, accuracy, and balance. (…) The better historians perform these virtues, the better they apply the prevalent standards of scholarship, and the better their work will be conceived to be.[16]

The beginning of this statement equally applies to many recent studies of ancient historiography, which have often focussed largely or exclusively on its narrative form. While this was a necessary and undeniably very fruitful change of perspective after the long neglect of the literary aspects, it does entail the risk of neglecting the essential cogntive features of historiography as a written account of actual

---

[11] Turri *et al.* 2017, §1, p. 3. Recently the 'factive turn' in epistemology has been proclaimed, but whether it is in fact a turn my be doubted: see Whiting 2018.
[12] Turri *et al.* 2017, §2, p. 4. Of course, virtue epistemology does deny Aristotle's distinction between moral and intellectual virtues: Zagzebski 1996, 139–158.
[13] Cf. Gerson 2009, 1–13 on differences between ancient an modern epistemology.
[14] See e.g. Tucker 2004, 36–39 and *passim*; Paul 2008 and 2011; Kuukkanen 2015, esp. 121–130; Spiegel 2019.
[15] Turri *et al.* 2017 use 'cognitive', 'epistemic' and 'intellectual' synonymously, as they note in their preliminary remarks (p. 1).
[16] Paul 2011, 1.

past events.[17] Like Paul, I am convinced 'that character traits play important, constitutive roles in the acquisition of scholarly knowledge' but do not intend to answer the central epistemological question whether 'epistemic virtues *best* explain how scholars arrive at justified true beliefs' (emphasis mine). Indeed, it is clear that virtues such as honesty, perseverance, open-mindednes and impartiality are truth-conducive whereas their opposites or not. Thus, it seems to me that an investigation into the epistemic virtues expressed in ancient historiographical and related texts will yield a more nuanced understanding both of the conception of truth held by the ancients and of their thinking on the best way to achieve truth.

2 Source Theory and the Historian's Character in Ancient Historiography

The theory of epistemic virtues appears particularly appropriate for the analysis of ancient historiography because such virtues are mentioned by the historians themselves. Indeed, according to Lucian (*Hist. conscr.* 42), Thucydides distinguished historiographical virtue and vice (διέκρινεν ἀρετὴν καὶ κακίαν συγγραφικήν), and the historian's character figured prominently in ancient historiographical theory. Plutarch wrote an entire essay not on the mistakes in Herodotos' history, but on his κακοήθεια, the character defects that caused these mistakes.[18] What remains of Polybius' extensive polemics against in book 12 is peppered with references to Timaios' character flaws.[19] Arrian, on the other hand, considered Ptolemaios a particularly trustworthy (πιστότερος) authority on Alexander because for a king it was even more shameful (αἰσχρότερον) to lie.[20] These are just some of the most elaborate or famous examples – many more could be added.[21] The connection between the reliability of a witness and his character was by no means specific to historiography: it seems to have been shared by society at large,

---

[17] Let me stress again that this is not to deny the enormous contribution to our understanding of ancient historiography of such pioneering and provocative works as Wiseman 1979 and Woodman 1988. I also discuss this problem from different perspectives in Meeus 2017a and 2018b, 4–14.
[18] Marincola 2015.
[19] Baron 2013, 65–66.
[20] Arr. *Anab.* pr. 2.
[21] See Marincola 1997, 128–174, 285–286, and more recently e.g. also Porod 2013, 239–255, Chrysanthou 2015, Free 2015, 53–59, Marincola 2015, Wiater 2017.

as is clear both from the theory in rhetorical handbooks and from the practice in the law courts and elsewhere.²² An ancient catalogue of the historian's epistemic virtues is to be found in Lucian's treatise:

> τοιοῦτος οὖν μοι ὁ συγγραφεὺς ἔστω, ἄφοβος, ἀδέκαστος, ἐλεύθερος, παρρησίας καὶ ἀληθείας φίλος, ὡς ὁ κωμικός φησι, τὰ σῦκα σῦκα, τὴν σκάφην δὲ σκάφην ὀνομάσων, οὐ μίσει οὐδὲ φιλίᾳ τι νέμων οὐδὲ φειδόμενος ἢ ἐλεῶν ἢ αἰσχυνόμενος ἢ δυσωπούμενος, ἴσος δικαστής, εὔνους ἅπασιν ἄχρι τοῦ μὴ θατέρῳ ἀπονεῖμαι πλεῖον τοῦ δέοντος, ξένος ἐν τοῖς βιβλίοις καὶ ἄπολις, αὐτόνομος, ἀβασίλευτος, οὐ τί τῷδε ἢ τῷδε δόξει λογιζόμενος, ἀλλὰ τί πέπρακται λέγων (*Hist. conscr.* 41).

> That, then, is the sort of man the historian should be: fearless, incorruptible, free, and a friend of free expression and the truth, intent, as the comic poet says, on calling a fig a fig and a trough a trough, giving nothing to hatred or to friendship, sparing no one, showing neither pity nor shame nor obsequiousness, an impartial judge, well disposed to all men up to the point of not giving one side more than its due, in his books a stranger and a man without country, independent, subject to no sovereign, not reckoning what this or that man will think, but stating the facts.

Epistemic virtues also seem to have particular relevance because of the ancient source theory which, unlike our approach to sources, focuses on the historian's doings rather than on the material evidence he is confronted with, as Schepens has demonstrated.²³ Whereas our theory of information starts from the objective materials that contain historical information – such as literary texts, inscriptions or coins – and assumes that the sources speak to us, the ancients saw the subjective means through which the historian gathers his information as his sources. This is clearly exemplified for instance in Herodotos 2.99, claiming that *opsis*, *gnome* and *historie* are his sources: μέχρι μὲν τούτου ὄψις τε ἐμὴ καὶ γνώμη καὶ ἱστορίη ταῦτα λέγουσα ἐστί ('Thus far it is my own sight and judgement and inquiry that say this', trans. Schepens).²⁴ This theory of information is also expressed very tellingly by Athenian ambassadors at the meeting of the Peloponnesians in Thucydides, identifying hearing (ἀκοαί) rather than seeing (ὄψις) as sources (μάρτυρες) for the remote past:

---

22 Marincola 1997, 104 and 128–131.
23 Schepens 2011, esp. 108: "Focusing not on the material medium between the historian and past reality but on the subjective means – capabilities and activities of the researcher – the discussion of sources in Greek historiography is led to incorporate a number of considerations on the personality of the historian, his living conditions, his intellectual or moral qualities". What follows in this section is strongly based on Schepens' article.
24 Schepens 2011, 103–105. On the practical application of the principle expressed here in the rest of book II, see Lloyd 2007, 228–232.

καὶ τὰ μὲν πάνυ παλαιὰ τί δεῖ λέγειν, ὧν ἀκοαὶ μᾶλλον λόγων μάρτυρες ἢ ὄψις τῶν ἀκουσομένων· τὰ δὲ Μηδικὰ καὶ ὅσα αὐτοὶ ξύνιστε, εἰ καὶ δι' ὄχλου μᾶλλον ἔσται αἰεὶ προβαλλομένοις, ἀνάγκη λέγειν (*Thuc.* 1.73.2).

We need not refer to remote antiquity: there the witnesses are the hearings of stories rather than the eyes of those who will hear them told. But to the Median War and contemporary history we must refer, although we are rather tired of continually bringing this subject forward.

The phrasing seems utterly strange to us, in suggesting that the faculties with which the audience receives them rather than the stories themselves are the source, but this appears to be how the ancients thought about the problem.[25] For this reason the role of the historian in 'questioning those who have witnessed the several events' (πυνθάνεσθαι παρὰ τῶν εἰδότων ἕκαστα τῶν πραγμάτων) is so central, as Polybius (12.28a.8–9) points out:[26]

καίτοι γε περὶ τοῦτο τὸ μέρος ἀνάγκη μεγάλα διαψεύδεσθαι τοὺς ἀπείρους· πῶς γὰρ οἷόν τε καλῶς ἀνακρῖναι περὶ παρατάξεως ἢ πολιορκίας ἢ ναυμαχίας; πῶς δὲ συνεῖναι τῶν ἐξηγουμένων τὰ κατὰ μέρος ἀνεννόητον ὄντα τῶν προειρημένων; οὐ γὰρ ἔλαττον ὁ πυνθανόμενος τῶν ἀπαγγελλόντων συμβάλλεται πρὸς τὴν ἐξήγησιν· ἡ γὰρ τῶν παρεπομένων τοῖς πράγμασιν ὑπόμνησις αὕτη χειραγωγεῖ τὸν ἐξηγούμενον ἐφ' ἕκαστα τῶν συμβεβηκότων.

And even in this task men of no experience are sure to be frequently deceived. For how is it possible to examine a person properly about a battle, a siege, or a sea-fight, or to understand the details of his narrative, if one has no clear ideas about these matters? For the inquirer contributes to the narrative no less than his informant, since the very mention of the typical aspects of such events [by the inquirer] guides the narrator to the several things that happened (trans. adapted).[27]

The historian can even consider his own enthusiasm for the historical enterprise as a source, as Diodoros does in his main proem:[28]

ἀφορμῇ δὲ πρὸς τὴν ἐπιβολὴν ταύτην ἐχρησάμεθα μάλιστα μὲν τῇ πρὸς τὴν πραγματείαν ἐπιθυμίᾳ, δι' ἣν πᾶσιν ἀνθρώποις τὸ δοκοῦν ἄπορον εἶναι τυγχάνει συντελείας, ἔπειτα καὶ τῇ ἐν Ῥώμῃ χορηγίᾳ τῶν πρὸς τὴν ὑποκειμένην ὑπόθεσιν ἀνηκόντων.

---

25 Schepens 2011, 105–106.
26 Schepens 2011, 115–117; cf. Marincola 1997, 73–74.
27 This is quite a complicated passage, as is clear from the sometimes rather divergent translations that have been produced of it: Pédech (1961, 150–151) offers a detailed analysis of the vocabulary of the passage and of the structure of the argument, which seems to have inspired Marincola's translation (1997, 73); see also Walbank 1967, 412.
28 Schepens 2011, 109–110.

> As for the resources which have availed us in this undertaking, they have been, first and foremost, that enthusiasm for the work which enables every man to bring to completion the task which seems impossible, and, in the second place, the abundant supply which Rome affords of the materials pertaining to the proposed study.

Such an approach to the question of sources may be puzzling at first sight, but makes sense in a society that did not fundamentally distinguish between oral testimony – regardless of its partiality – and legal documents,[29] and is less surprising when one considers that the concept of objectivity had not yet been invented.[30] Given this focus on the subjective capacities of the historian obtaining the information, rather than on the objective materials containing the information, epistemic virtues affect not only the historian's interpretation of the evidence, as they do in our view, but his very sources.

3 The Epistemic Virtues of Ancient Historiography

The following catalogue presents some of the main epistemic virtues encountered in the ancient historians. Selected passages are quoted under the virtue that is most central to them, but several of these quotations are also relevant to other virtues. Marincola has offered an excellent and detailed discussion of most of these topics with respect to the claims historians made to boost their authority.[31] Although much of what follows is thus not new in itself, in light of the many recent studies treating ancient historiography merely as a branch of rhetoric it seems worth stressing that these claims boost a historian's authority because of their epistemological relevance: while the ancients obviously did not have an explicitly developed virtue epistemology, they were well aware of the evident contribution of such virtues to the creation of reliable knowledge.

3.1 Impartiality

Impartiality is ubiquitous in ancient considerations on historiography and it is the epistemic virtue that has received most attention in recent scholarship on an-

---

[29] Marincola 1997, 104–105.
[30] On the emergence of the concept of objectivity in the nineteenth century, see Daston/Gallison 2007.
[31] Marincola 1997.

cient historiography; many have even argued that to the ancients truth and impartiality can virtually be equated.³² The most famous statement of impartiality is Tacitus' profession in the preface of the *Annals* (I 1.3) that he will write the history of the early principate 'sine ira et studio', without anger or partiality, in contrast to the contemporary authors who had been inspired by fear or hatred.³³ Both sides of the coin are discussed by Diodoros in a polemical fragment from book 21 (17), reproaching Timaios for the misrepresentation that followed from his hatred of the Syracusan tyrant Agathokles and Kallias for distorting the facts in Agathokles' favour:

> Ὅτι οὗτος ὁ ἱστορικὸς τὰς ἁμαρτίας τῶν πρὸ ἑαυτοῦ συγγραφέων πικρότατα ἐλέγξας κατὰ μὲν τἄλλα μέρη τῆς γραφῆς πλείστην πρόνοιαν εἶχε τῆς ἀληθείας, ἐν δὲ ταῖς Ἀγαθοκλέους πράξεσι τὰ πολλὰ κατέψευσται τοῦ δυνάστου διὰ τὴν πρὸς αὐτὸν ἔχθραν. φυγαδευθεὶς γὰρ ὑπ᾿ Ἀγαθοκλέους ἐκ τῆς Σικελίας, ζῶντα μὲν ἀμύνασθαι τὸν δυνάστην οὐκ ἴσχυσε, τελευτήσαντα δὲ διὰ τῆς ἱστορίας ἐβλασφήμησεν εἰς τὸν αἰῶνα. καθόλου γὰρ ταῖς προϋπαρχούσαις τῷ βασιλεῖ τούτῳ κακίαις ἄλλα πολλὰ παρ᾿ ἑαυτοῦ προσθεὶς ὁ συγγραφεύς, τὰς μὲν εὐημερίας ἀφαιρούμενος αὐτοῦ, τὰς δὲ ἀποτεύξεις, οὐ τὰς δι᾿ αὐτὸν μόνον γενομένας, ἀλλὰ καὶ τὰς διὰ τύχην μεταφέρων εἰς τὸν μηδὲν ἐξαμαρτόντα. γενομένου δὲ ὁμολογουμένως αὐτοῦ στρατηγικοῦ μὲν κατὰ τὴν ἐπίνοιαν, δραστικοῦ δὲ καὶ τεθαρρηκότος κατὰ τὴν ἐν τοῖς κινδύνοις εὐτολμίαν, οὐ διαλείπει παρ᾿ ὅλην τὴν ἱστορίαν ἀποκαλῶν αὐτὸν ἄνανδρον καὶ δειλόν. καίτοι γε τίς οὐκ οἶδεν ὅτι τῶν πώποτε δυναστευσάντων οὐδεὶς ἐλάττοσιν ἀφορμαῖς χρησάμενος μείζω βασιλείαν περιεποιήσατο; χειροτέχνης γὰρ ἐκ παίδων γενόμενος δι᾿ ἀπορίαν βίου καὶ πατέρων ἀδοξίαν, ἐξ ὑστέρου διὰ τὴν ἰδίαν ἀρετὴν οὐ μόνον Σικελίας σχεδὸν ὅλης ἐκυρίευσεν, ἀλλὰ πολλὴν τῆς Ἰταλίας τε καὶ Λιβύης τοῖς ὅπλοις κατεστρέψατο. θαυμάσαι δ᾿ ἄν τις τοῦ συγγραφέως τὴν εὐχέρειαν· παρ᾿ ὅλην γὰρ τὴν γραφὴν ἐγκωμιάζων τὴν τῶν Συρακουσίων ἀνδρείαν, τὸν τούτων κρατήσαντα δειλίᾳ φησὶ διενηνοχέναι τοὺς ἅπαντας ἀνθρώπους. διὰ γὰρ τῶν ἐν ταῖς ἐναντιώσεσιν ἐλέγχων φανερός ἐστι τὸ φιλάληθες τῆς ἱστορικῆς παρρησίας προδεδωκὼς ἰδίας ἕνεκεν ἔχθρας καὶ φιλονικίας. διόπερ τὰς ἐσχάτας τῆς συντάξεως πέντε βίβλους τοῦ συγγραφέως τούτου, καθ᾿ ἃς περιείληφε τὰς Ἀγαθοκλέους πράξεις, οὐκ ἄν τις δικαίως ἀποδέξαιτο.

---

32 Woodman 1988, esp. 73–74; Luce 1989; Marincola 1997, 159–161, and 2007a. Such a view seems to a large extent based on a category mistake: Woodman 1988, 73, for instance, writes in his discussion of the letter to Lucceius (*Ad fam.* 5.12) that 'it will be seen from section 3 of the letter that Cicero contrasts truth (*ueritas*) with prejudice (*gratia, amor*), from which it appears to follow that Cicero saw the truth in terms of impartiality'. The contrast, however, is not between two opposite sides of the same spectrum, but between the end of the true-false spectrum the historian should strive for, i.e. truth, and the *obstacle to achieving the truth* that is relevant *in this specific context* of Cicero's request to Lucceius, namely the partiality of a friend (cf. infra, n. 38). Marincola 1997, 160 does also speak of 'the great obstacle to truth'.

33 Heldmann 2011, 11–12, rightly notes that this must not be translated as objectivity, but I do not agree that Tacitus' profession implies that to give one's anger and sympathy free reign was normal in ancient historiography: Tacitus is merely pointing out that because of the temporal distance he is unburdened by these common obstacles to the truth in imperial historiography.

Ὅτι καὶ Καλλίας ὁ Συρακούσιος δικαίως ἂν καὶ προσηκόντως κατηγορίας ἀξιωθείη. ἀναληφθεὶς γὰρ ὑπ' Ἀγαθοκλέους καὶ δώρων μεγάλων ἀποδόμενος τὴν προφῆτιν τῆς ἀληθείας ἱστορίαν, οὐ διαλέλοιπεν ἀδίκως ἐγκωμιάζων τὸν μισθοδότην.

This historian (sc. Timaeus) who had so sharply rebuked earlier historians for their errors, showed very high regard for the truth in the rest of his writings, but the greater part of his history of Agathocles consists of lying propaganda against the ruler because of personal enmity. For since he was banished from Sicily by Agathocles and could not strike back while the monarch lived, after his death he defamed him in his history for all time. For, in general, to the bad qualities that this king did in fact possess the historian adds others of his own invention. He strips him of his successes, leaving him his failures – not only those for which the king was himself responsible, but even those due to ill luck, which he transfers to the score of one who was not at all at fault. And though it is generally agreed that the king was a shrewd strategist, and that he was energetic and confident where courage in battle was called for, yet Timaeus throughout his history incessantly calls him a poltroon and coward. Yet who does not know that of all men who ever came to power, none acquired a greater kingdom with fewer resources? Reared from childhood as an artisan because of scant means and humble parentage, he later, thanks to his own ability, not only became master of nearly all Sicily, but even reduced by arms much of Italy and Libya. One may well marvel at the nonchalance of the historian, who throughout his work praises the people of Syracuse for their courage, but says that he who mastered them surpasses all men in cowardice. The evidence of these contradictions shows clearly that he deserted the honest standard of historical candour to gratify his personal animosity and contentiousness. Consequently we cannot fairly accept the last five books of this writer's history, in which he covers the deeds of Agathocles.
Likewise Callias of Syracuse might justly and fittingly be held liable to censure. For ever since he was taken up by Agathocles and for a great price in gifts sold into bondage Madam History, the mouthpiece of truth, he has never ceased singing dishonest praises of his paymaster.

Although the context is unknown, it seems that by means of these polemics Diodoros is claiming that he himself will give an impartial account.[34] Particularly relevant is the claim that Timaios disregards the truthful frank speech of historiography and abandons all standards of logic because of his partiality, so that his account contradicts the facts.

Lest we understand the virtue of impartiality in fully modern terms, it is important to bear in mind that in antiquity for some the virtue of patriotism could legitimately trump the demand for an impartial report and interpretation of the

---

34 Cf. Marincola 1997, 233–234 on polemics in Diodoros.

facts in historiography.³⁵ Such, however, was surely not the opinion of the best historians, as is made explicitly clear by Polybius (16.14.6–8):³⁶

> ἐγὼ δὲ διότι μὲν δεῖ ῥοπὰς διδόναι ταῖς αὑτῶν πατρίσι τοὺς συγγραφέας, συγχωρήσαιμ' ἄν, οὐ μὴν τὰς ἐναντίας τοῖς συμβεβηκόσιν ἀποφάσεις ποιεῖσθαι περὶ αὐτῶν. ἱκανὰ γὰρ τὰ κατ' ἄγνοιαν γινόμενα τοῖς γράφουσιν, ἃ διαφυγεῖν ἄνθρωπον δυσχερές· ἐὰν δὲ κατὰ προαίρεσιν ψευδογραφῶμεν ἢ πατρίδος ἕνεκεν ἢ φίλων χάριτος, τί διοίσομεν τῶν ἀπὸ τούτου τὸν βίον ποριζομένων;

> Now I would admit that authors should have a partiality for their own country but they should not make statements about it that are contrary to facts. Surely the mistakes of which we writers are guilty and which it is difficult for us, being but human, to avoid are quite sufficient; but if we make deliberate misstatements in the interest of our country or of friends or for favour, what difference is there between us and those who gain their living by their pens?

Thucydides upheld Polybius' principle better than Dionysios of Halikarnassos (*Pomp*. 3) deemed acceptable, so he blamed him for not being sufficiently pro-Athenian; that Herodotos was willing to defend certain foreigners while he accused some Greeks of terrible deeds earned him Plutarch's (*De malign. Her.* 12) condemnation for being *philobarbaros*. The same principle also held in the case of friends, as is attested by Cicero's request (*Ad fam.* 5.12.3) to Lucceius to to have the truth yield precedence to his affection for him: Cicero is very well aware that this is to disregard the laws of history.³⁷ These examples reveal very clearly why the ancients were so concerned about bias: authors were often directly or indirectly involved in the events and even when they were not, patriotic pressure could be strong.

3.2 Truthfulness

The passages in the previous category make a clear distinction between truth and impartiality, especially Polybius 16.14.6–8, and this distinction becomes all the more clear in the following examples concerning the virtue of truthfulness. At the same time, the very attempt to divide intellectual virtues into categories reveals

---

35 Luce 1989, 20–21.
36 That Polybius did not manage to live up to his ideal (cf. Haegemans/Kosmetatou 2005; Rood 2007), is of course a different matter.
37 Cicero does not put forward a different historiographical programme in the letter (*pace* Li Causi *et al.* 2015, 472–473): the rules are the very same, but he asks Lucceius to disregard them: 'et in eo leges historiae neglegas' (V 12.3). Cf. *supra*, n. 32 and *infra*, n. 40–41.

how closely related truth and impartiality are: indeed it raises the question whether honesty is a part of truthfulness or rather a separate virtue that can in this case perhaps be taken to be a synonym of impartiality.[38] In a performative approach to knowledge such as virtue epistemology it becomes eminently clear how sensible it is for the ancients to have placed so much emphasis on the relationship between impartiality and truth.

Of particular importance to the question of truthfulness in ancient historiography is the well-known claim of the orator Marcus Antonius in Cicero's dialogue *De Oratore* II 62–63 that not lying and not omitting anything that is true are universally accepted as the fundamental laws of history:

> *Sed illuc redeo: videtisne, quantum munus sit oratoris historia? Haud scio an flumine orationis et varietate maximum; neque eam reperio usquam separatim instructam rhetorum praeceptis; sita sunt enim ante oculos. Nam quis nescit primam esse historiae legem, ne quid falsi dicere audeat? Deinde ne quid veri non audeat? Ne quae suspicio gratiae sit in scribendo? Ne quae simultatis? Haec scilicet fundamenta nota sunt omnibus, ipsa autem exaedificatio posita est in rebus et verbis.*

> Don't you see how great a task history is for an orator? In terms of fluency of discourse and variety it is probably his greatest task, yet I can't find a separate treatment of the subject anywhere in the rules of rhetoric (and they're easily available for inspection). Everyone of course knows that the first law of historiography is not daring to say anything false, and the second is not refraining from saying anything true: there should be no suggestion of prejudice for, or bias against, when you write. These foundations are of course recognised by everyone, but the actual superstructure consists of content and style. (trans. Woodman)

Though not written by a historian, this passage is nevertheless of great importance because Cicero claims that truthfulness is a universally acknowledged *law* of historiography.[39] Although it has been argued that Cicero develops a rhetorical theory of historiography in which truth actually does not occupy a central place,[40] this interpretation has been convincingly rejected by Leeman, who

---

[38] Cf. Williams 2002, 94: '"Truthfulness", in fact, like the German *Wahrhaftigkeit*, can refer to both Sincerity and Accuracy, and this is entirely natural'.

[39] Brunt 2011, 210: 'It was natural for Cicero to emphasise that the historian must be truthful'. Compare Luc. *Hist. conscr.* 42 for Thucydides laying down the law (ἐνομοθέτησε) about reporting things as they had happened, and 63 for truth and impartiality as the κανὼν καὶ στάθμη ἱστορίας δικαίας, the rule and law for just history.

[40] Woodman 1988, esp. 81–83; 2011, 288–290 with further references. I agree with Woodman that the *fundementa* in this passage are to be understood in relation to the *exaedificatio*, but I do not see why that should make the law of truthfulness any less fundamental to historiography. That the laws do not further concern Cicero does not alter this because, as Woodman himself notes, they are said to be well-known and, more importantly, Cicero is writing a treatise about

demonstrates that the statement about the truth of historiography is an integral part of the argument, not just an interpolation, as Woodman would have it.⁴¹

In his treatise on writing history, Lucian (*Hist. Conscr.* 39) likewise considers truthfulness a central concern of the historian: τοῦ δὴ συγγραφέως ἔργον ἕν–ὡς ἐπράχθη εἰπεῖν ('the historian's one task is to tell the thing as it happened'). While bias is again the only obstacle to achieving the truth that Lucian goes on to mention explicitly, he makes his understanding of truth clear with the phrase ὡς ἐπράχθη, 'as it was done', i.e. as it actually happened.⁴² This reflects his correspondence theory of truth, which we shall also encounter in the next section. Throughout his treatise Lucian places much emphasis on the need for truthfulness, on being an ἀληθείας φίλος and on saying what actually happened (e.g. also 41 τί πέπρακται and 51 πέπρακται γὰρ ἤδη).

Other obstacles apart from bias were known to the ancients, however. Thucydides (1.22.3) already considered faulty memory just as problematic as partiality,⁴³ as did Asinius Pollio (*FRHist* 53 F 8). Plutarch (*Per.* 13.12) in turn points out that while bias is a problem for those writing contemporary history, other problems affect those who wish to find out the truth about events of the past:

οὕτως ἔοικε πάντη χαλεπὸν εἶναι καὶ δυσθήρατον ἱστορίᾳ τἀληθές, ὅταν οἱ μὲν ὕστερον γεγονότες τὸν χρόνον ἔχωσιν ἐπιπροσθοῦντα τῇ γνώσει τῶν πραγμάτων, ἡ δὲ τῶν πράξεων

---

oratory not about history. Furthermore, one must not underestimate the meaning of the word *lex* in this context. As to what truth means to Cicero here, Woodman repeats the category mistake from his interpretation of the letter to Lucceius: see Leeman 1989, 238, Bosworth 2003, 169, and above, n. 32. Li Causi *et al.* 2015, 472, also state that truth is central to the understanding of historiography expressed in our passage, but despite Leeman 1985 they still connect it to a specific Hellenistic theory of history.

41 Leeman 1989. Unfortunately this imporant article has largely gone unnoticed, perhaps because it has been published in Dutch and in a journal that was not easily accessible before it was posted online. Its main argument, however, had already been published in two studies not included in Woodman's bibliography, namely Leeman 1985 and Leeman/Pinkster 1985. Woodman 2011, 288 mentions Leeman's 1989 article, but does not engage with its argument, preferring to limit himself to a refutation of the bad arguments that have been developed against his argument: in so doing he does not even do justice to the contribution of Lendon 2009, that for all its polemics and some flaws does add substance the debate.

42 It is also interesting to note that Lucian puts the historian in the role of a judge rather than an orator, which is the very same point that Cicero also makes: Leeman 1985, 285 ("Or, l'attitude impartiale de l'historien ressemble à celle du juge – le grand absent dans la rhétorique antique – et non pas à celle du plaideur.") and 287. It is also worth noting in the context of epistemic virtue that Lucian in the conclusion to his treatise repeats the idea of an ἴσος δικαστής in speaking of ἱστορίας δικαίας (*Hist. conscr.* 63); earlier he dubs Xenophon a δίκαιος συγγραφεύς (ibid. 39).

43 Cf. also Thuc. 7.8.2 with Williams 2002, 166 and n. 37.

καὶ τῶν βίων ἡλικιῶτις ἱστορία τὰ μὲν φθόνοις καὶ δυσμενείαις, τὰ δὲ χαριζομένη καὶ κολακεύουσα λυμαίνηται καὶ διαστρέφῃ τὴν ἀλήθειαν.

To such degree, it seems, is truth hedged about with difficulty and hard to capture by research, since those who come after the events in question find that lapse of time is an obstacle to their proper perception of them; while the research of their contemporaries into men's deeds and lives, partly through envious hatred and partly through fawning flattery, defiles and distorts the truth.

In his preface to the *Histories*, Tacitus (1.1.1) similarly lists several obstacles to achieving truthfulness, when he writes 'simul veritas *pluribus modis infracta*, primum *inscitia rei publicae* ut alienae, mox libidine adsentandi aut rursus odio adversus dominantis'.[44] While the classical causes of bias are there, *inscitia* is also a possible cause of errors, and it is all the greater among tryannical regimes because it was often impossible for the public to learn about affairs of state taking place in the seclusion of the imperial court.[45] Diodoros (1.5.2) realizes that there may be ignorant mistakes in his work (τὰ δὲ ἀγνοηθέντα), but hopes that these will be corrected by others. Indeed Polybius (12.7) and Diodoros (13.90.6–7) agree that mistakes out of ignorance deserve forgiveness and kind correction, as opposed to deliberate falsehood inspired by bias which should be censured.

Yet the ancients were also aware about other threats to the truth posed for instance by a desire to invent to fill the gaps in one's account or simply to entertain or impress the reader. The *locus classicus* is of course Thucydides' contrast between his own history and those who aim at entertainment, perhaps thinking also of Herodotos (1.22.4). Ktesias (*FGrHist* 688 F 1.15.2 and F 16.62) accused Herodotos and Hellanikos of lying and inventing things, just as Ktesias was often accused of the same practice (FGrHist 688 T 11a–i), at times even along with Herodotos and Hellanikos (Str. 1.2.35).[46] In his criticism of Phylarchos' desire to

---

[44] 'Then too the truthfulness of history was impaired in many ways; at first, through men's ignorance of public affairs, which were now wholly strange to them, then, through their passion for flattery, or, on the other hand, their hatred of their masters'.

[45] Cf. Tac. *Ann*. 3.19 for the observation that even in the case of major events often nothing more than rumours was available; very similar observations in D.C. 53.19–15. Seneca (*Nat*. 7.16.1–2) likewise considers it possible for historians to offer faslehood either deliberately or accidentally through their credulity. Although this is a polemical exaggeration about the unreliability of historians, the intellectual vices Seneca mentions are clearly relevant to the Roman understanding of historiography: the point at hand is a factual mistake about an astronomical phenomenon in Ephoros which has nothing to do with bias. For similar critiques of Herodotos and Ephoros, see Diod. 1.38–39.

[46] Cf. e.g. Diod. 1.69.7 for Herodotos' inventions for the sake of entertaining and impressing the reader.

shock the reader, Polybius (2.56.10) notes that the historian's duty is to report what was actually said and done, however unimpressive it may be.[47] Dionysios of Halikarnassos (*A.R.* 1.7.1, quoted below, section 3.5), on the other hand, asserts in his preface that he has not invented those events described by him that are not found in the accounts of his well-known predecessors like Hieronymos, Timaios or Polybius.

The same standard is also found in the case of speeches: Polybius repeatedly stressed that the historian needs to find out what was actually said and not just make up whatever is plausible (2.56.10, 12.25a.3–25b, 36.1.7). Thucydides (1.22.1), on the other hand admitted that, despite his painstaking research, this has not always been possible and some amount of reconstruction has been necessary, yet without deviating too much from the actual words.[48] Truthfulness, then, was clearly understood in terms of sticking to the facts, and its opposite, falsehood, could occur through all sorts causes, such as bias, ignorace, faulty memory, a desire to entertain or shock the reader, etc.[49]

3.3 Mimesis / Mirroring Reality

Closely related to truthfulness is the particular virtue that concerns the formal, narrative side of the attempt to stick to the facts. This is probably the closest

---

47 τῶν δὲ πραχθέντων καὶ ῥηθέντων κατ' ἀλήθειαν αὐτῶν μνημονεύειν πάμπαν, κἂν πάνυ μέτρια τυγχάνωσιν ὄντα. Eckstein 2013 and Marincola 2013 rightly argue that Polybius is concerned with serious historiographical principles in his criticism of Phylarchos, including the truth, but that does not necessarily exclude that this is one of the instances in which Polybius was less successful in applying his own principles: see Schepens 2005.
48 Whether or not he has sufficiently lived up to that promise is not the question here (cf. e.g. Tompkins 2013). Nevertheless, the harshness of the modern criticism of Thucydides' admission that he has had to reconstruct that which he could not establish with complete certainty can only surprise in the light of the scope and underdetermination of many of the hypotheses that are deemed perfectly acceptable in modern scholarship and that are often not identified as such any more clearly than Thucydides' speeches. Of course, the difference is that Thucydides is not only a historian, but also our only hope of having a reliable picture of many aspects of fith century Greek history; yet from the point of view of the history of historiography that is no reason to judge him by standards more exacting than those with which we measure the historiographical products of our own time. Whether he succeeded or not, his methodological principle of trying to recover the speeches as much as possible with the technology of his time and his honesty in warning the reader of the impossibility of attaining the same standard as with events are an admirable step forward – regardless of the question how well he succeeded.
49 The wide variety of obstacles to the truth is also recognized e.g. by Pelling 1990, 42–43 with n. 65, and Raaflaub 2010, 190.

equivalent the ancients had to what we would call objectivity, but it differs from that concept in important ways: the historian is not supposed to efface the self or avoid personal engagement, and indeed his perspective and his role as author are explicitly acknowledged.[50] Because of the analogy of the historian's account with nature in some of the following passages, one might perhaps label this virtue 'truth-to-nature', a predecessor of objectivity found in eighteenth and nineteenth century science: it rather refered to an ideal-type that represented the essence of an object better than any particular instance actually found in nature.[51] Diodoros and Douris (quoted below) used the concept of mimesis in this context, which has the advantage that it is at least an ancient term, but its meaning in historiographical texts is strongly debated. Another label, perhaps less controversial, would be 'mirroring reality'. This is how Lucian describes it in his treatise on writing history (50), which again lays down the general rule:

> μάλιστα δὲ κατόπτρῳ ἐοικυῖαν παρασχέσθω τὴν γνώμην ἀθόλῳ καὶ στιλπνῷ καὶ ἀκριβεῖ τὸ κέντρον, καὶ ὁποίας ἂν δέξηται τὰς μορφὰς τῶν ἔργων, τοιαῦτα καὶ δεικνύτω αὐτά, διάστροφον δὲ ἢ παράχρουν ἢ ἑτερόσχημον μηδέν· οὐ γὰρ ὥσπερ τοῖς ῥήτορσι γράφουσιν,[52] ἀλλὰ τὰ μὲν λεχθησόμενα ἔστι καὶ εἰρήσεται· πέπρακται γὰρ ἤδη· δεῖ δὲ τάξαι καὶ εἰπεῖν αὐτά. ὥστε οὐ τί εἴπωσι ζητητέον αὐτοῖς, ἀλλ' ὅπως εἴπωσιν.

> He has to make of his brain a mirror, unclouded, bright, and true of surface; then he will reflect events as they presented themselves to him, neither distorted, discoloured, nor variable. Historians are not writing fancy school essays; what they have to say is before them, and will get itself said somehow, being solid fact; their task is to arrange and put it into words; they have not to consider what to say, but how to say it. (trans. Fowler and Fowler)

The historian has to show (δεικνύτω) the events exactly as they appear (ὁποίας ἂν δέξηται) and therefore need not ask himself what to say, but merely how to describe the events that are already there exactly as they are, without twisting

---

[50] Raaflaub 2010, esp. 193 rightly argues that 'to the ancients (...) objectivity was not a goal in itself'.
[51] Daston/Gallison 2007, 55–113 for 'truth-to-nature' as a predecessor to objectivity. For the truth of history in the sense of an ideal-type or general truths see e.g. Moles 1993, 107–110; Hau 2016, 275–277 and 2017, esp. 243–245. This also seems to be the way Dionysios of Halikarnassos understands the concept of *mimesis* in his analysis of Thucydides' speeches in *De Thuc.* 45: Gray 1987, 468–469; Halliwell 2002, 292–293.
[52] Something seems wrong with the Greek text here (see Porod 2013, 569), but the general sense is clear although there is no way to reconstruct the exact wording.

them or changing their colour or shape.⁵³ Such a correspondence theory of truth is obviously naïve, but it was held by most historians in Antiquity and is clearly a much stronger definition of truth than the mere absence of bias.⁵⁴

In his introduction Polybius (1.4.7–11) presents a rather comparable sort of truth-to-nature understanding:

> καθόλου μὲν γὰρ ἔμοιγε δοκοῦσιν οἱ πεπεισμένοι διὰ τῆς κατὰ μέρος ἱστορίας μετρίως συνόψεσθαι τὰ ὅλα παραπλήσιόν τι πάσχειν, ὡς ἂν εἴ τινες ἐμψύχου καὶ καλοῦ σώματος γεγονότος διερριμμένα τὰ μέρη θεώμενοι νομίζοιεν ἱκανῶς αὐτόπται γίνεσθαι τῆς ἐνεργείας αὐτοῦ τοῦ ζῴου καὶ καλλονῆς. εἰ γάρ τις αὐτίκα μάλα συνθεὶς καὶ τέλειον αὖθις ἀπεργασάμενος τὸ ζῷον τῷ τ' εἴδει καὶ τῇ τῆς ψυχῆς εὐπρεπείᾳ κἄπειτα πάλιν ἐπιδεικνύοι τοῖς αὐτοῖς ἐκείνοις, ταχέως ἂν οἶμαι πάντας αὐτοὺς ὁμολογήσειν διότι καὶ λίαν πολύ τι τῆς ἀληθείας ἀπελείποντο πρόσθεν καὶ παραπλήσιοι τοῖς ὀνειρώττουσιν ἦσαν. ἔννοιαν μὲν γὰρ λαβεῖν ἀπὸ μέρους τῶν ὅλων δυνατόν, ἐπιστήμην δὲ καὶ γνώμην ἀτρεκῆ σχεῖν ἀδύνατον. διὸ παντελῶς βραχύ τι νομιστέον συμβάλλεσθαι τὴν κατὰ μέρος ἱστορίαν πρὸς τὴν τῶν ὅλων ἐμπειρίαν καὶ πίστιν. ἐκ μέντοι γε τῆς ἁπάντων πρὸς ἄλληλα συμπλοκῆς καὶ παραθέσεως, ἔτι δ' ὁμοιότητος καὶ διαφορᾶς, μόνως ἄν τις ἐφίκοιτο καὶ δυνηθείη κατοπτεύσας ἅμα καὶ τὸ χρήσιμον καὶ τὸ τερπνὸν ἐκ τῆς ἱστορίας ἀναλαβεῖν.

He indeed who believes that by studying isolated histories he can acquire a fairly just view of history as a whole, is, as it seems to me, much in the case of one, who, after having looked at the dissevered limbs of an animal once alive and beautiful, fancies he has been as good as an eyewitness of the creature itself in all its action and grace. For could anyone put the creature together on the spot, restoring its form and the comeliness of life, and then show it to the same man, I think he would quickly avow that he was formerly very far away from the truth and more like one in a dream. For we can get some idea of a whole from a part, but never knowledge or exact opinion. Special histories therefore contribute very little to the knowledge of the whole and conviction of its truth. It is only indeed by study of the interconnexion of all the particulars, their resemblances and differences, that we are enabled at least to make a general survey, and thus derive both benefit and pleasure from history.

---

53 Cf. Porod 2013, 177: 'so habe auch der Historiker lediglich den schon vorgegebenen Stoff zu bearbeiten, ohne selbst etwas erfinden zu müssen'. Moles 1993, 89 and 110 applies the label *mimesis* also to Lucian's description.

54 Many historians, however, understood that human beings rarely achieved the ideal: e.g. Thuc. 1.22.2 (ὅσον δυνατόν); Ephoros (*FGrHist* 70) F 110 (εἰ δυνατὸν ἦν...); Sall. *Cat.* 4.3 ('*quam uerissume potero*'); Diod. 1.5.2 (διορθόσεως ὑπὸ τῶν δυνατωτέρων) and 13.90.7 (ὡς ἂν ἀνθρώπους ὄντας...); Liv. *praef.* 3 ('pro virili parte'); Amm. Marc. 15.1.1 ('*utcumque potui veritatem scrutari*'), 31.5.10 and 31.16.9; Oros. 1 pr.1 ('*utinam tam efficaciter quam libenter*'). Cf. also Plb. 3.59.1 on practical obstacles.

In not producing an exact image of nature,[55] the historian strays very far from the truth (λίαν πολύ τι τῆς ἀληθείας ἀπελείποντο), and knowledge (ἐπιστήμη) or exact opinion (γνώμη ἀτρεκής) become impossible. By means of the optative ἄν τις ἐφίκοιτο καὶ δυνηθείη in the final sentence Polybius does, however, seem to suggest that in practice one cannot live up to this theoretical ideal completely.

Similarly, Diodoros notes in his preface that in historiography the words, i.e. the description, should agree with the events, i.e. exactly correspond with it,[56] and in a passage in book 20 (43.7), he sets forth the ideal of an exact correspondence with nature:

> ταύτῃ δ' ἄν τις καὶ τὴν ἱστορίαν καταμέμψαιτο, θεωρῶν ἐπὶ μὲν τοῦ βίου πολλὰς καὶ διαφόρους πράξεις συντελουμένας κατὰ τὸν αὐτὸν καιρόν, τοῖς δ' ἀναγράφουσιν ἀναγκαῖον ὑπάρχον τὸ μεσολαβεῖν τὴν διήγησιν καὶ τοῖς ἅμα συντελουμένοις μερίζειν τοὺς χρόνους παρὰ φύσιν, ὥστε τὴν μὲν ἀλήθειαν τῶν πεπραγμένων τὸ πάθος ἔχειν, τὴν δ' ἀναγραφὴν ἐστερημένην τῆς ὁμοίας ἐξουσίας μιμεῖσθαι μὲν τὰ γεγενημένα, πολὺ δὲ λείπεσθαι τῆς ἀληθοῦς διαθέσεως.

> At this point one might censure the art of history, when he observes that in life many different actions are consummated at the same time, but that it is necessary for those who record them to interrupt the narrative and to parcel out different times to simultaneous events contrary to nature, with the result that, although the actual experience of the events contains the truth, yet the written record, deprived of such power, while presenting copies of the events, falls far short of arranging them as they really were.

Since the historian cannot possibly recount two events at once although in reality they took place at the same time, he has to divide them up unnaturally (παρὰ φύσιν) and his account cannot exactly reflect the events (μιμεῖσθαι μὲν τὰ γεγενημένα) but misses much of their actual shape (πολὺ δὲ λείπεσθαι τῆς ἀληθοῦς διαθέσεως).[57] In part also because of the use of the verb μιμεῖσθαι, this passage

---

[55] Cf. Arist. *Poet.* 23 (1459a20–24) with Marincola 2017, *ad loc.*

[56] Diod. 1.2.7: in comparing the benefits of history with those of other types of literature, such as poetry or law codes, he argues that 'while some of them actually pervert the truth, history alone, since in it word and fact are in perfect agreement, embraces in its narration all the other qualities as well as that are useful' (ἔνια δὲ κατεψεῦσθαι τῆς ἀληθείας, μόνην δὲ τὴν ἱστορίαν, συμφωνούντων ἐν αὐτῇ τῶν λόγων τοῖς ἔργοις, ἅπαντα τἆλλα χρήσιμα τῇ γραφῇ περιειληφέναι). It is clear from this context that the meaning is not stylistic propriety but correspondence with reality: after all stylistic propriety can be obtained in any genre, but Diodoros' point is that only his genre actually offers the truth and is thus the most useful kind of literature. See also Schorn 2018, 370.

[57] The passage is often understood as a mere observation about the problem of organizing an account that comprises different parts of the world, but Diodoros' point is far more philosophical

has often been taken to derive from Douris of Samos,[58] who reproached Ephoros and Theopompos for neglecting this dimension of history (*FGrHist* 76 F 1):

> Δοῦρις μὲν οὖν ὁ Σάμιος ἐν τῆι πρώτηι τῶν αὐτοῦ Ἱστοριῶν οὕτω φησίν· «Ἔφορος δὲ καὶ Θεόπομπος τῶν γενομένων πλεῖστον ἀπελείφθησαν· οὔτε γὰρ μιμήσεως μετέλαβον οὐδεμιᾶς οὔτε ἡδονῆς ἐν τῶι φράσαι, αὐτοῦ δὲ τοῦ γράφειν μόνον ἐπεμελήθησαν.»
>
> In the first book of his Histories, Duris of Samos says the following: 'Ephoros and Theopompos are very inferior to the events of their narratives. For they adopted neither any exactness of representation nor any charm in their narrative, but they applied themselves only to the act of writing itself'. (trans. Pownall, BNJ)

Douris seems to have been referring to the two fundamental aims of history, truth and entertainment. It has been rightly observed that in the context in which Photios' transmits this fragment the words τῶν γενομένων may refer to previous historians rather than to the events of history,[59] but it is equally clear from the context that such a comparison with predecessors still concerns the question of representing reality.[60] If Diodoros 20.43.7 does indeed go back to Douris, the verbal echoes rather suggest that the events are meant. Furthermore, in F 32 Douris reports that Eupompos claimed that the sculptor should imitate not his predecessors but nature, and it is likely enough that he had the same approach to historiographical mimesis.[61] However this may be, the conclusion that mimesis is indeed to be understood as 'exact represenation' is confirmed by another fragment of Douris, which perhaps comes from his *Homeric Problems* but contains the same view of mimesis. It concerns his criticism of the Homeric simile in which the Skamandros chasing Achilleus in *Iliad* 21 (257–264) is compared to a man watering his garden (*FGrHist* 76 F 89):[62]

---

than that: cf. Meeus 2018a, 160–161 with further references. Also compare Diod. 16.1.2 on reflecting nature in not breaking up the account of a continuous series of events. Diodoros' language seems to imply a general desire for history to reflect reality exactly as it is: this specific problem of chronology just happens to be an area in which such exact reflection is impossible, and to limit Diodoros' mimesis to this aspect alone is to interpret the text in too narrow a sense, as is clear from 1.2.7 (*contra* Halliwell 2002, 292).
58 Though it need not be a direct quotation: see now Parmeggiani 2016 with further references.
59 Ottone 2015, 215–218.
60 Parmeggiani 2016, 116.
61 Cf. Parmeggiani 2016, 111, although in my view Pseudo-Longinus' criticism of Theopompos (43.2–5) is not relevant here, as it clearly is a stylistic and not a historiographical criticism that is concerned with creating sublime literature at the cost of historical detail.
62 For the relevance of F 89 to the interpretation of F 1 see also Gray 1987, 475–478 (though her interpretation in terms of stylistic propriety seems too narrow to me) and Parmeggiani 2016.

Δοῦρις δ' αἰτιᾶται τὴν εἰκόνα ὡς τοῦ ὀρυμαγδοῦ καὶ τῆς ἀπειλῆς ἐνδεεστέραν καί φησι ταῦτα· "διὰ τὴν ἐν τοῖς κήποις ὑδραγωγίαν <τὸ> ἐκμιμεῖσθαι λανθάνει πως τοὺς ἀναγιγνώσκοντας, ὥστε μηδεμίαν ἔννοιαν λαμβάνειν πρὸς ὃ πεποίηκε".[63]

Douris criticizes the simile as inadequate to the noise and the threat. He also says the following: 'through the irrigation in gardens the imitation escapes the readers in some way, so that they cannot form an idea of what he [scil. Skamandros] did'. (trans. by the present author)

Douris' statement that the gardening parallel does not convey the noise and the threat, thus failing to offer an idea of what Skamandros did (ὃ πεποίηκε), i.e. how violently and dreadfully he chased Achilleus, shows that he was concerned with the exact representation of events. In as far as the brief fragment represents his entire interpretation of the passage, Douris may not have done full justice to Homer's simile in ignoring that Homer was concerned with the parallel of the acceleration of the water. This is perhaps because in this fragment the historian Douris was speaking rather than the literary critic. What he wanted was as exact as possible a representation of reality: whatever its other qualities the peaceful gardening scene gives no idea of the terror of the situation.[64] Whether this Hellenistic understanding of historiographical mimesis was a fundamental innovation or simply a more theoretically developed description of ideas already held before is hard to tell. At least in Lucian's phrasing, however, it seems to represent mainstream historiographical thinking.

3.4 Accuracy

Truthfulness and mimesis of course require the closely related virtue accuracy,[65] which was for instance to be practiced in matters of chronology, as Thucydides

---

[63] If anything is wrong with the Greek text at all, I would suggest inserting τὸ before ἐκμιμεῖσθαι, as I have done here, rather than before τὴν ἐν τοῖς κήποις ὑδραγωγίαν as most editors do: Parmeggiani 2016, 109–111 discusses the various possibilities and concludes that no substantial differences of meaning exist between them.

[64] Halliwell 2002, 289–291, places much stress on the concept of visualisation, but this need not be implied here; it certainly is not relevant to Diod. 20.43.7. See Strasburger 1966, 78–85; Schepens 1998, 104; Parmeggiani 2016.

[65] On accuracy as an epistemic virtue, see Williams 2002, 123–148, and specifically 124 for the reason to consider accuracy a virtue.

states in his criticism of Hellanikos,[66] or Polybius in his long denunciation of Timaios (12.10.4):

> καίτοι διότι τοῦτ' ἴδιόν ἐστι Τιμαίου καὶ ταύτῃ παρημίλληται τοὺς ἄλλους συγγραφέας καὶ καθόλου τῇδέ πῃ τῆς ἀποδοχῆς —λέγω δὲ κατὰ τὴν ἐν τοῖς χρόνοις καὶ ταῖς ἀναγραφαῖς ἐπίφασιν τῆς ἀκριβείας καὶ τὴν περὶ τοῦτο τὸ μέρος ἐπιμέλειαν—δοκῶ, πάντες γινώσκομεν.

> And yet Timaeus's special boast, the thing in which he outvies other authors and which is the main cause of the reputation he enjoys, is, as I suppose we all know, his display of accuracy in the matter of dates and public records, and the care he devotes to such matters.

The fact that accuracy in matters of dates and public records was the basis for Timaios' reputation reveals that this was widely considered an important feature of a work of history.[67] Interestingly, though, at least in the case of chronology Eunapios deemed this pedantic rather than virtuous, but in its extreme form his view seems to be rather exceptional.[68] Timaios seems to have criticised his predecessors for all sorts of errors, which clearly shows that accuracy of fact was valued. Polybius (12.4a.2–6) reports that:

> ἐν αἷς Θεοπόμπου μὲν κατηγορεῖ διότι Διονυσίου ποιησαμένου τὴν ἀνακομιδὴν ἐκ Σικελίας εἰς Κόρινθον ἐν μακρᾷ νηΐ, Θεόπομπός φησιν ἐν στρογγύλῃ παραγενέσθαι τὸν Διονύσιον, [3] Ἐφόρου δὲ πάλιν ἄγνοιαν καταψεύδεται, φάσκων λέγειν αὐτὸν ὅτι Διονύσιος ὁ πρεσβύτερος παρελάμβανε τὴν ἀρχὴν ἐτῶν εἴκοσι τριῶν ὑπάρχων, δυναστεῦσαι δὲ τετταράκοντα καὶ δύο, μεταλλάξαι δὲ τὸν βίον προσλαβὼν τοῖς ἑξήκοντα τρία· [4] τοῦτο γὰρ οὐδεὶς ἂν εἴπειε δήπου τοῦ συγγραφέως εἶναι τὸ διάπτωμα, τοῦ δὲ γραφέως ὁμολογουμένως· [5] ἢ γὰρ δεῖ τὸν Ἔφορον ὑπερβεβηκέναι τῇ μωρίᾳ καὶ τὸν Κόροιβον καὶ τὸν Μαργίτην, εἰ μὴ δυνατὸς ἦν συλλογίζεσθαι διότι τὰ τετταράκοντα καὶ δύο προστεθέντα τοῖς εἴκοσι καὶ τρισὶν ἑξήκοντα γίνεται καὶ πέντε· [6] ἢ τούτου μηδαμῶς ἂν πιστευθέντος ὑπὲρ Ἐφόρου φανερὸν ὅτι τὸ μὲν ἁμάρτημά ἐστι τοῦ γραφέως

> For instance, he accuses Theopompus of stating that Dionysius was conveyed from Sicily to Corinth in a merchant ship, whereas he really travelled in a warship, [3] and again he falsely

---

66 Thuc. 1.97.2: τούτων δὲ ὅσπερ καὶ ἥψατο ἐν τῇ Ἀττικῇ ξυγγραφῇ Ἑλλάνικος, βραχέως τε καὶ τοῖς χρόνοις οὐκ ἀκριβῶς ἐπεμνήσθη ('Hellanicus, it is true, did touch on these events in his Athenian history; but he is somewhat concise and not accurate in his dates', trans. Crawley). Cf. also Diod. 1.3.2 and 1.3.8.
67 Polybius, out to destroy Timaios' reputation, surely would not have written this, had it not been so. On Timaios' reputation for chronological accuracy, see also Diod. 5.1.3.
68 Eunapios *Hist.* F 1; though also compare Dionysios' criticism of Thucydides' arrangent of his narrative according to winters and summers (D.H. *Thuc.* 9.4–10). For Velleius Paterculus (2.48.5–6) chronology is important in detailed accounts, but less so in briefer summaries. Against the older view that Herodotos took no interest in chronology, see Gehrke 2014, 78 with further references.

accuses Ephorus of making a blunder because he tells us that the elder Dionysius began to reign at the age of twenty-three, reigned for forty-two years, and died at the age of sixty-three. [4] For surely no one could say that the mistake here was the author's, but it is obviously the scribe's. [5] Either Ephorus must have surpassed Coroebus and Margites in stupidity if he could not reckon that forty-two added to twenty-three make sixty-five, [6] or as nobody would believe this of Ephorus, the mistake is evidently due to the scribe.

Caesar is generally criticised by Asinius Pollio (*FRHist* 53 F 8) for not having been sufficiently accurate in writing up his *commentarii*:[69]

> *Pollio Asinius parum diligenter parumque integra ueritate compositos putat, cum Caesar pleraque et quae per alios erant gesta temere crediderit et quae per se, uel consulto uel etiam memoria lapsus perperam ediderit;*

> Pollio Asinius thinks that they were not drawn up with much care, or with a due regard to truth; for he insinuates that Caesar was too hasty of belief in regard to what was performed by others under his orders; and that he has not given a very faithful account of his own acts, either by design, or through defect of memory.

When Ammianus (22.8.10) reports the length of the circumference of the Black Sea, he emphasises that he took his information from the most accurate investigators: 'ut Eratosthenes affirmat et Hecataeus et Ptolomaeus aliique huius modi cognitionum minutissimi scitatores'.

3.5 Inquisitiveness

From Ammianus' reference to the most accurate investigators we can conclude the close connection between accuracy and the virtue of inquisitiveness,[70] a virtue that perhaps more than any other was considered characteristic of ancient historiography and even gave the genre its name: the extent of his research seems to have been Herodotos' main innovation and the one that earned him the title of *pater historiae*.[71] In Thucydides' *Methodenkapitel* (1.22.2–3) there is an even stronger emphasis on the necessity of research:

---

69 Interestingly enough, Hirtius *BG* 8 *praef.* 5–6 praises the ease and speed with which Caesar composed the works. Both Pollio's statement and that of Hirtius are cited by Suetonius (*Iul.* 56) who does not explicitly say whom he agrees with, but since he also cites the positive judgment of Cicero's *Brutus* 262, he seems to be inclined rather towards the opinion of Hirtius.
70 Den Boeft *et al.* 1995, 102: 'the scientists in question revelled in detailed research'.
71 On the originality of Herodotos' explicit engagement with sources and their merits, see Fowler 1996, 77–80.

τὰ δ' ἔργα τῶν πραχθέντων ἐν τῷ πολέμῳ οὐκ ἐκ τοῦ παρατυχόντος πυνθανόμενος ἠξίωσα γράφειν, οὐδ' ὡς ἐμοὶ ἐδόκει, ἀλλ' οἷς τε αὐτὸς παρῆν καὶ παρὰ τῶν ἄλλων ὅσον δυνατὸν ἀκριβείᾳ περὶ ἑκάστου ἐπεξελθών. [3] ἐπιπόνως δὲ ηὑρίσκετο, διότι οἱ παρόντες τοῖς ἔργοις ἑκάστοις οὐ ταὐτὰ περὶ τῶν αὐτῶν ἔλεγον, ἀλλ' ὡς ἑκατέρων τις εὐνοίας ἢ μνήμης ἔχοι.

But as to the facts of the occurrences of the war, I have thought it my duty to give them, not as ascertained from any chance informant nor as seemed to me probable, but only after investigating with the greatest possible accuracy each detail, in the case both of the events in which I myself participated and of those regarding which I got my information from others. And the endeavour to ascertain these facts was a laborious task, because those who were eye-witnesses of the several events did not give the same reports about the same things, but reports varying according to their championship of one side or the other, or according to their recollection.

In Lucian's treatise (*Hist. conscr.* 47) research is the historian's first duty:

τὰ δὲ πράγματα αὐτὰ οὐχ ὡς ἔτυχε συνακτέον, ἀλλὰ φιλοπόνως καὶ ταλαιπώρως πολλάκις περὶ τῶν αὐτῶν ἀνακρίναντα, καὶ μάλιστα μὲν παρόντα καὶ ἐφορῶντα, εἰ δὲ μή, τοῖς ἀδεκαστότερον ἐξηγουμένοις προσέχοντα καὶ οὓς εἰκάσειεν ἄν τις ἥκιστα πρὸς χάριν ἢ ἀπέχθειαν ἀφαιρήσειν ἢ προσθήσειν τοῖς γεγονόσι. κἀνταῦθα ἤδη καὶ στοχαστικός τις καὶ συνθετικὸς τοῦ πιθανωτέρου ἔστω.

As to the facts themselves, he should not assemble them at random, but only after much laborious and painstaking investigation. He should for preference be an eye-witness, but, if not, listen to those who tell the more impartial story, those whom one would suppose least likely to subtract from the facts or add to them out of favour or malice. When this happens let him show shrewdness and skill in putting together the more credible story.

Very explicit comments about the necessity of inquisitiveness are also found in Polybius. Particularly telling is the reproach against Timaios that he has not done any research at all concerning the animals and the geography of Africa but seems to relate, as if on purpose, the opposite of the truth: περὶ ὧν οὐδὲν ἱστορήσας Τίμαιος ὥσπερ ἐπίτηδες τἀναντία τοῖς κατ' ἀλήθειαν ὑπάρχουσιν ἐξηγεῖται (12.3.6). Dionysios of Halikarnassos, in turn, wishes to remove any suspicion by those who have read other Greek accounts of Roman history that he has invented everything not found there, and therefore feels the need to stress his extensive research and list his sources (*A.R.* 1.7.1):

βούλομαι καὶ περὶ τῶν ἀφορμῶν εἰπεῖν, αἷς ἐχρησάμην ὅτ' ἔμελλον ἐπιχειρεῖν τῇ γραφῇ· ἴσως γὰρ οἱ προανεγνωκότες Ἱερώνυμον ἢ Τίμαιον ἢ Πολύβιον ἢ τῶν ἄλλων τινὰ συγγραφέων, ὑπὲρ ὧν ἐποιησάμην λόγον ὀλίγῳ πρότερον ὡς ἐπισεσυρκότων τὴν γραφήν, πολλὰ τῶν ὑπ' ἐμοῦ γραφομένων οὐχ εὑρηκότες παρ' ἐκείνοις κείμενα σχεδιάζειν ὑπολήψονταί με καὶ πόθεν ἡ τούτων γνῶσις εἰς ἐμὲ παραγέγονεν ἀξιώσουσι μαθεῖν. ἵνα δὴ μὴ τοιαύτη δόξα παραστῇ τισι περὶ ἐμοῦ, βέλτιον ἀφ' ὧν ὡρμήθην λόγων τε καὶ ὑπομνηματισμῶν προειπεῖν.

> I wish now to say something concerning the sources I used while preparing for my task. For it is possible that those who have already read Hieronymus, Timaeus, Polybius, or any of the other historians whom I just now mentioned as having slurred over their work, since they will not have found in those authors many things mentioned by me, will suspect me of inventing them and will demand to know how I came by the knowledge of these particulars. Lest anyone, therefore, should entertain such an opinion of me, it is best that I should state in advance what narratives and records I have used as sources.

Cicero's admiration of Varro's historical works is inspired among others things by the enormous amount of previously almost inaccessible knowledge about Rome's past researched by the author (*Acad. Post.* 1.3.9):

> *nam nos in nostra urbe peregrinantis errantisque tamquam hospites tui libri quasi domum deduxerunt, ut possemus aliquando qui et ubi essemus agnoscere. tu aetatem patriae tu descriptiones temporum, tu sacrorum iura tu sacerdotum, tu domesticam tu bellicam disciplinam, tu sedum regionum locorum tu omnium divinarum humanarumque rerum nomina genera officia causas aperuisti.*

> We were wandering and straying about like visitors in our own city, and your books led us, so to speak, right home and enabled us at last to realize who and where we were. You have revealed the age of our native city, the chronology of its history, the laws of its religion and priesthood, its civil and its military institutions, the topography of its districts and sights, the terminology, classification and moral and rational basis of all our religious and secular institutions.

Orosius, although his practice of using sources seems to suggest otherwise, was not afraid to imply that he has perused all works of history available at the time in his description of the task Augustine had given him to write of the vices, crimes and disasters of the past: 'you ordered that I collect [these] on the basis of all the records of histories and annals that are to be found at present'.[72] It is only thanks to this research, Orosius submits, that he came to realize that the past was indeed worse than the present, thus emphasising the necessity of the labour.[73]

3.6 Thoroughness

As is already clear from some of the quotations in the preceding section, inquisitiveness in itself is not sufficient if the research is not done thoroughly. Even at those points, for instance, where Polybius ackowledges that Timaios has done

---

[72] Oros. 1pr.10: '*praeceperas ergo, ut ex omnibus qui haberi ad praesens possunt historiarum atque annalium fastis*' (trans. Van Nuffelen).
[73] Oros. 1pr.13; Van Nuffelen 2012, 40.

some research, he still disparages him, alleging that it was poorly and cursorily executed: thus for instance on the animals in Corsica, ὑπὲρ ὧν Τίμαιος κακῶς καὶ παρέργως ἱστορήσας ἐσχεδίασε.[74] Although Polybius often appears to be unfair to Timaios,[75] he also accuses Timaios of having been unfair to his predecessors in pretending he is the only one who has done thorough research (12.26d.3):

> ἐν γὰρ τούτοις τηλικαύτην ἐπίφασιν ποιεῖ διὰ τῆς ἀκριβολογίας καὶ τῆς πικρίας τῆς ἐπὶ τῶν ἐλέγχων, οἷς χρῆται κατὰ τῶν πέλας, ὥστε δοκεῖν τοὺς ἄλλους συγγραφέας ἅπαντας συγκεκοιμῆσθαι τοῖς πράγμασι καὶ κατεσχεδιακέναι τῆς οἰκουμένης, αὐτὸν δὲ μόνον ἐξητακέναι τὴν ἀκρίβειαν καὶ διευκρινηκέναι τὰς ἐν ἑκάστοις ἱστορίας, ἐν οἷς πολλὰ μὲν ὑγιῶς λέγεται, πολλὰ δὲ καὶ ψευδῶς.

> For here he makes such a fine show owing to his accuracy of statement and the bitter tone in which he confutes others that one would think all writers except himself had dozed over events and made mere random shots at what was befalling the world, while he alone had tested the accuracy of everything and submitted to careful scrutiny the various stories in which there is much that is genuine and much that is false.

Yet one of those predecessors, Theopompos of Chios, was praised enthusiastically by Dionysios of Halikarnassos (*Pomp.* 6.2–4) for the way in which he dedicated himself to his research, not simply considering it some pastime:

> μάλιστα δὲ τῆς ἐπιμελείας τε καὶ φιλοπονίας τῆς κατὰ τὴν συγγραφήν· δῆλος γάρ ἐστιν, εἰ καὶ μηδὲν ἔγραψε, πλείστην μὲν παρασκευὴν εἰς ταῦτα παρεσκευασμένος, μεγίστας δὲ δαπάνας εἰς τὴν συναγωγὴν αὐτῶν τετελεκώς, καὶ πρὸς τούτοις πολλῶν μὲν αὐτόπτης γεγενημένος, πολλοῖς δ' εἰς ὁμιλίαν ἐλθὼν ἀνδράσι τοῖς τότε πρωτεύουσι καὶ στρατηγοῖς δημαγωγοῖς τε καὶ φιλοσόφοις διὰ τὴν συγγραφήν· οὐ γὰρ ὥσπέρ τινες πάρεργον τοῦ βίου τὴν ἀναγραφὴν τῆς ἱστορίας ἐποιήσατο, ἔργον δὲ τὸ πάντων ἀναγκαιότατον. γνοίη δ' ἄν τις αὐτοῦ τὸν πόνον ἐνθυμηθεὶς τὸ πολύμορφον τῆς γραφῆς· καὶ γὰρ ἐθνῶν εἴρηκεν οἰκισμοὺς καὶ πόλεων κτίσεις ἐπελήλυθε, βασιλέων τε βίους καὶ τρόπων ἰδιώματα δεδήλωκε, καὶ εἴ τι θαυμαστὸν ἢ παράδοξον ἑκάστη γῆ καὶ θάλασσα φέρει, συμπεριείληφεν τῇ πραγματείᾳ. καὶ μηδεὶς ὑπολάβῃ ψυχαγωγίαν ταῦτ' εἶναι μόνον· οὐ γὰρ οὕτως ἔχει, ἀλλὰ πᾶσαν ὡς ἔπος εἰπεῖν ὠφέλειαν περιέχει.

> Especially admirable are the care and industry which mark his historical writing, for it is clear, even if he had said nothing to that effect, that he prepared himself most fully for his task and incurred heavy expense in the collection of his material. Moreover, he was an eye-witness of many events, and came in contact with many leading men and generals of his day, whether popular leaders or more cultivated persons. All this he did in order to improve

---

[74] Plb. 12.4.4: 'about wich Timaios made a random statement after having researched inadequately and casually' (translation by the present author).
[75] Baron 2013, 72–87.

his History. For he did not (as some do) consider the recording of his researches as a pastime, but as the one thing needful in life. The trouble he took may be inferred from the comprehensiveness of his work. He has related the foundation of nations, described the establishment of cities, portrayed royal lives and peculiar customs, and incorporated in his work everything wonderful or strange found on any land or sea. Nor must it be supposed that this is merely a form of entertainment. It is not so. Such particulars are, it may in general be said, of the greatest utility. (trans. Rhys Roberts)

That a thorough treatment of the affairs of the past is necessary for history to be useful is an idea also expressed by Sempronius Asellio (*FRHist* 20 F 2):

Scribere autem bellum initum quo consule et quo confectum sit et quis triumphans introierit ex eo, et eo libro quae in bello gesta sint non praedicare aut interea quid senatus decreverit aut quae lex rogatiove lata sit neque quibus consiliis ea gesta sint iterare: id fabulas pueris est narrare, non historias scribere.

To write over and over again in whose consulship a war was begun and ended, and who in consequence entered the city in a triumph, and in that book not to state what happened in the course of the war, what decrees the senate made during that time, or what law or bill was passed, and with what motives these things were done—that is to tell stories to children, not to write history.

As Ammianus (23.6.1) argues at the beginning of his geographical digression about Persia, thoroughness also concerns the need to discover and explain unknown details to the reader at some length because an account that is too brief not only reveals a lack of research but is unclear too:[76]

Res adigit huc prolapsa ut in excessu celeri situm monstrare Persidis, descriptionibus gentium curiose digestis, in quibus aegre vera dixere paucissimi. Quod autem erit paulo prolixior textus, ad scientiam proficiet plenam. Quisquis enim affectat nimiam brevitatem ubi narrantur incognita non quid signatius explicet, sed quid debeat praeteriri, scrutatur.

Affairs have reached a point where I am led in a rapid digression to explain the topography of the Persian kingdom, carefully compiled from the descriptions of the nations, in only a few of which the truth has been told, and that barely. My account, however, will be a little fuller, which will be to the advantage of complete knowledge. For anyone who aims at extreme brevity in telling of the unknown tries to discover what he ought to leave out rather than what he may explain more clearly.

---

76 Cf. Sundwall 1996, 625.

3.7 Industriousness

Historians since Thucydides consistently stress that virtues like truthfulness, accuracy, thoroughness and inquisitiveness can only be put to effective use when combined with industriousness, as is clear from many of the above passages, including – yet again – the prescription by Lucian.[77] Having accused most other people of being 'averse to taking pains (ἀταλαίπωρος) ... in the search for the truth' (1.20.3), Thucydides points out that he conducted his research ἐπιπόνως (1.22.3). Later historians would claim not only effort, but even great expenses or dangers.[78] Sallust (*Jug.* 4.3), while forgoing the praise of history itself does not think that his efforts in producing his work can go unmentioned. Justin's preface (2–3) contains extensive praise of the immense labour undertaken by Pompeius Trogus, perhaps echoing the latter's own preface:[79]

> Trogus Pompeius, Graecas et totius orbis historias Latino sermone conposuit, ut, cum nostra Graece, Graeca quoque nostra lingua legi possent: prorsus rem magni et animi et corporis adgressus! Nam cum plerisque auctoribus singulorum regum uel populorum res gestas scribentibus opus suum ardui laboris uideatur, nonne nobis Pompeius herculea audacia orbem terrarum adgressus uideri debet, cuius libris omnium saeculorum, regum, nationum populorumque res gestae continentur?

> Trogus Pompeius composed the history of Greece, and of the whole world, in the Latin tongue, in order that, as our actions might he read in Greek, so those of the Greeks might be read in our language; attempting a work that demanded extraordinary resolution and labour. For when, to most authors who write the history only of particular princes or nations, their task appears an affair of arduous effort, must not Trogus Pompeius, in attempting the whole world, seem to have acted with a boldness like that of Hercules, since in his books are contained the actions of all ages, monarchs, nations, and people? (trans. Watson)

If Trogus perhaps tried to emulate Herakles, Nikolaos of Damaskos took it one step further and in his autobiography claimed to have surpassed him:

> ὁ δὲ μειζόνως ἔτι ὥρμησεν ἐπὶ τὸ πρᾶγμα, πᾶσαν ἀθροίσας τὴν ἱστορίαν μέγαν τε πόνον ὑποστὰς καὶ οἷον οὐκ ἄλλος· ἐν πολλῶι δὲ χρόνωι φιλοπονήσας ἐξετέλεσεν αὐτήν, ἔλεγέ τε ὡς τοῦτον τὸν ἆθλον Εὐρυσθεὺς εἰ προύτεινεν Ἡρακλεῖ, σφόδρα ἂν αὐτὸν ἀπέτρυσεν.

> He embarked upon the enterprise in grand style, gathering all historical events and making a great effort without equal; and having dedicated to it a lot of time and labor, he brought

---

[77] Luc. *Hist. conscr.* 47; Thuc. 1.22.2–3; Marincola 1997, 148–158.
[78] Expenses: Theopompos FGrHist 115 T 20a = F 26, T 28a; Jos. *BJ* 1.16. Dangers: e.g. Plb. 3.59.7, 12.27.4, 12.28a.5; Diod. 1.4.1.
[79] Meeus 2018a, 152 n. 15 with further references.

it to an end. He said that if Eurystheus had imposed on Herakles such a labor, it would have worn him out. (trans. Favuzzi, *BNJ*)

It seems that to Nikolaos, then, industriousness was a fundamental epistemic virtue to the historian – to such an extent that even the greatest hero of the past would have been seriously challenged by the task.[80]

3.8 Careful and Logical Reasoning

Conducive as it was to accuracy and thoroughness, laborious research alone was not enough: the historian also needed to be careful in his interpretations and logical in his arguments, or as Lucian (*Hist. conscr.* 43) put it: 'his thought should be coherent and intelligent' (ὁ μὲν νοῦς σύστοιχος ἔστω καὶ πυκνός).[81] Herodotos understood this very well and regularly developed detailed and explicitly logical arguments to disprove mistaken views, such as that of the Ionians about the meaning of the name Egypt which also impacted the question about the oldest people on earth: with a combination of evidence and logic Herodotos (2.15–18) constructs a meticulous argument in order to arrive at the truth of the matter – in the process he seems to show a lack of sympathy with those unable to think correctly.[82] Thucydides likewise stresses the need for clear and logical thinking, for instance in his argument about the value of ruins as an indication of past greatness.[83]

Poor reasoning and contradictions also constitute an aspect of Diodoros' criticism (21.17) of Timaios cited above (section 3.1). Polybius had similar criticism of Timaios (12.4b–4c.1, 12.15, though cf. 8.10.11) and especially of Theopompos, whom he accused of treating Philip II in a way that contradicted his initial assessment of him (8.10.1, μαχόμενα λέγει πρὸς τὴν αὐτοῦ πρόθεσιν). He concluded from this that Theopompos must either be a liar and flatterer (ψεύστην καὶ κόλακα) in his initial statement or entirely foolish and childish (ἀνόητον καὶ μειρακιώδη) in his more detailed assessment of the king (8.11.2).[84] Polybius did not

---

80 For the connection between Herakles, toil and virtue, see e.g. Ring 2010, 37–39.
81 The translation 'intelligent' or 'wise' is preferable to Kilburn's well-knit: see LSJ s.v. πυκνός and the detailed discussion by Porod 2013, 531–532.
82 See Thomas 2000, 168–212 for a detailed discussion of this and other examples.
83 Thuc. 1.10; cf. Reynolds 2009. Also compare the very similar argument in Diod. 2.5.5–7.
84 At 16.28.4 Polybius in a similar instance pre-emptively explains that he is not contradicting himself: ποιοῦμαι δὲ τὴν τοιαύτην διαστολήν, ἵνα μή τις ἡμᾶς ὑπολάβῃ μαχόμενα λέγειν ἑαυτοῖς, ἄρτι μὲν ἐπαινοῦντας Ἀτταλον καὶ Ῥοδίους, Φίλιππον δὲ καταμεμφομένους, νῦν δὲ τοὐναντίον

mean that a historian's interpretation must not be nuanced, but rather that he must offer a coherent and non-contradictory overall judgment. For the same reason Sallustius at the end of the introduction to the *Bellum Jugurthinum* (5.3) stated that he needed to go back in time a little, so as to place the events in context and justify his view of them. In discussing the question of the priority of the Spartan or Kretan constitutions Ephoros (*FGrHist* 70 F 149) argued against those who deemed it simple-minded (εὔηθες) to assume that a colony in imitating the constitution of its mother-city could improve upon its model: he posited the principle that one must not take it as a given that the present situation situation is always an indication of past conditions, as these can change quite drastically. He thus illustrated the need for the historian to keep an open mind and avoid dogmatic fallacies.

3.9 Experience

The previous examples all concern features of the historian's practice that are virtues in an obvious sense. According to reliabilist virtue epistemologists (cf. supra, n. 10), however, the more relevant qualities are those that allow someone to be secure in their judgment, such as good vision or a good memory. We have already encountered some references to faulty memory (Thuc. 1.22.3, Pollio *FRHist* 53 F 8; supra 3.2 and 3.5). The most common such quality found in ancient historiographical thinking, though, is undoubtedly political insight and experience: Lucian (*Hist. conscr.* 34) claimed that the historian must possess σύνεσίν τε πολιτικὴν καὶ δύναμιν ἑρμηνευτικήν, 'political understanding and power of expression'. He qualified the former as something that cannot be learned (ἀδίδακτόν τι τῆς φύσεως δῶρον), though at *Hist. conscr.* 37 we find the more common view that the historian needs personal experience in managing public affairs:

> καὶ τοίνυν καὶ ἡμῖν τοιοῦτός τις ὁ μαθητὴς νῦν παραδεδόσθω, συνεῖναί τε καὶ εἰπεῖν οὐκ ἀγεννής, ἀλλ' ὀξὺ δεδορκώς, οἷος καὶ πράγμασι χρήσασθαι ἄν, εἰ ἐπιτραπείη, καὶ γνώμην στρατιωτικήν, ἀλλὰ μετὰ τῆς πολιτικῆς καὶ ἐμπειρίαν στρατηγικὴν ἔχειν, καὶ νὴ Δία καὶ ἐν στρατοπέδῳ γεγονὼς ποτε καὶ γυμναζομένους ἢ ταττομένους στρατιώτας ἑωρακὼς καὶ ὅπλα εἰδὼς καὶ μηχανήματα, ἔτι δὲ καὶ τί ἐπὶ κέρως καὶ τί ἐπὶ μετώπου, πῶς οἱ λόχοι, πῶς οἱ ἱππεῖς καὶ πόθεν καὶ τί ἐξελαύνειν ἢ περιελαύνειν, καὶ ὅλως, οὐ τῶν κατοικιδίων τις οὐδ' οἷος πιστεύειν μόνον τοῖς ἀπαγγέλλουσι.
>
> So give us now a student of this kind – not without ability to understand and express himself, keensighted, one who could handle affairs if they were turned over to him, a man with

('I make this express statement lest anyone should think I contradict myself, as but lately I praised Attalus and the Rhodians and blamed Philip, and now I do the reverse').

the mind of a soldier combined with that of a good citizen, and a knowledge of generalship; yes, and one who has at some time been in a camp and has seen soldiers exercising or drilling and knows of arms and engines; again, let him know what 'in column', what 'in line' mean, how the companies of infantry, how the cavalry, are manoeuvred, the origin and meaning of 'lead out' and 'lead round', in short not a stay-at-home or one who must rely on what people tell him.

The same idea occurs in Polybius' 12th book (12.17–22, 12.25f) which accused Kallisthenes, Ephoros, Theopompos and Timaios of lacking the necessary understanding to give adequate accounts of battles. Such experience was necessary not simply to be able to write about such events with vividness (12.25h.5), but as we have seen above (section 2), in order to be able to question eye-witnesses in a suitable manner (12.28a.8–9).

While Roman historians were primarily displaying their social status in listing the offices they had held,[85] they did thus also underline their experience and expertise to write about public affairs. This is surely the case in Ammianus' casual mention that he had been a soldier in his concluding statement (31.16.9):

Haec ut miles quondam et Graecus, a principatu Caesaris Nervae exorsus, ad usque Valentis interitum, pro virium explicavi mensura: opus veritatem professum numquam (ut arbitror) sciens silentio ausus corrumpere, vel mendacio. Scribant reliqua potiores, aetate et doctrinis florentes. Quos id (si libuerit) aggressuros, procudere linguas ad maiores moneo stilos.

These events, from the principate of the emperor Nerva to the death of Valens, I, a former soldier and a Greek, have set forth to the measure of my ability, without ever (I believe) consciously venturing to debase through silence or through falsehood a work whose aim was the truth. The rest may be written by abler men, who are in the prime of life and learning. But if they chose to undertake such a task, I advise them to forge their tongues to the loftier style.

3.10 Traditionalism

The last example is an ancient epistemic virtue that most scholars in the post-enlightenment world would – at least in principle – not deem conducive to knowledge, namely traditionalism.[86] Although the traditionalism of historians

---

85 Marincola 1997, 141.
86 For traditionalism as an epistemic virtue, or in his terminology a cognitive value, see e.g. Tucker 2004, 38–39 and 79; Paul 2011, 15 n. 48: 'Although "traditionalist" is a derogatory, pejorative label (…) those identified with this label (Biblical scholars before Jean Astruc, J.G. Eichhorn, and W.M.L. de Wette) made knowledge-claims just as did "critical" students of Scripture. Obviously, the types of knowledge these groups of scholars produced were markedly different,

does not seem to have been as extreme as that of the philosophers who had a stake in the authority of the founder of their school,[87] they did have a similar respect for the authority of some of their early predecessors or for local oral traditions. This also explains why they so often relied on a single source, often cited authorities rather than sources and felt obliged to report even traditions they did not believe.[88] Even Thucydides sometimes reports such traditions, despite his polemics against traditionalism in book 1.[89] In a historiographical context the most explicit statement of the principle that tradition guarantees truth is to be found in Josephus (c. *Ap.* 1.26–27):[90]

> τῆς μὲν γὰρ ἀληθοῦς ἐστι τεκμήριον ἱστορίας, εἰ περὶ τῶν αὐτῶν ἅπαντες ταὐτὰ καὶ λέγοιεν καὶ γράφοιεν. οἱ δ' εἰ ταὐτὰ γράψειαν ἑτέρως, οὕτως ἐνόμιζον αὐτοὶ φανεῖσθαι πάντων ἀληθέστατοι. λόγων μὲν οὖν ἕνεκα καὶ τῆς ἐν τούτοις δεινότητος δεῖ παραχωρεῖν ἡμᾶς τοῖς συγγραφεῦσι τοῖς Ἑλληνικοῖς, οὐ μὴν καὶ τῆς περὶ τῶν ἀρχαίων ἀληθοῦς ἱστορίας καὶ μάλιστά γε τῆς περὶ τῶν ἑκάστοις ἐπιχωρίων.

> For the proof of historical veracity is universal agreement in the description, oral or written, of the same events. On the contrary, each of these writers, in giving his divergent account of the same incidents, hoped thereby to be thought the most veracious of all. While, then, for eloquence and literary ability we must yield the palm to the Greek historians, we have no reason to do so for veracity in the history of antiquity, least of all where the particular history of each separate foreign nation is concerned.

While not in itself related to historiography, it is interesting to compare Diodoros' discussion of Chaldaian wisdom: he admired that they all share the same opinions because knowledge is passed down from father to son, as opposed to the Greek philosophers who in the hope of financial gain constantly desired to come up with new ideas rather than 'following in the path of their predecessors', so that in the end they are 'unable to believe at all with firm conviction' and 'simply

---

but that is precisely what their different sets of epistemic virtues explain'. I wish to stress that I understand traditionalism as a label of an epistemic virtue of the past in a neutral, descriptive sense.

87 See for instance the special justification apparently required for criticizing Plato at D.H. *Pomp.* 1.15 or especially at Aristid. *Or.* 2.1–12, where the length and nature of the argument that the truth of a particular view cannot be determined by the authority of those who hold it, shows how widespread the opposite idea was. See also Isoc. *Panath.* 149–150 with Marincola 2014.
88 See Marincola 1997, 95–117 and 281–185; Meeus 2017b.
89 See e.g. Thuc. 1.9.2, 4.120.1, 6.2; Marincola 1997, 283–284.
90 Cohen 1988, 3 rightly notes that the *Against Apion* 'is basically an extended essay on historiography'. Josephus clearly expected it to make sense to a Graeco-Roman audience.

wander in confusion'.[91] Polybius (3.9.1–5), however, indirectly confirms that respect for authoritative predecessors was a common attitude concerning historiography too, when in discussing an implausible statement in Fabius Pictor he offers a plea for the epistemic virtue of testimonial justice:[92]

> τίνος δὴ χάριν ἐμνήσθην Φαβίου καὶ τῶν ὑπ' ἐκείνου γεγραμμένων; οὐχ ἕνεκα τῆς πιθανότητος τῶν εἰρημένων, ἀγωνιῶν μὴ πιστευθῇ παρά τισιν — ἡ μὲν γὰρ [παρὰ] τούτων ἀλογία καὶ χωρὶς τῆς ἐμῆς ἐξηγήσεως αὐτὴ δι' αὑτῆς δύναται θεωρεῖσθαι παρὰ τοῖς ἐντυγχάνουσιν — ἀλλὰ τῆς τῶν ἀναλαμβανόντων τὰς ἐκείνου βύβλους ὑπομνήσεως, ἵνα μὴ πρὸς τὴν ἐπιγραφὴν ἀλλὰ πρὸς τὰ πράγματα βλέπωσιν. ἔνιοι γὰρ οὐκ ἐπὶ τὰ λεγόμενα συνεπιστήσαντες ἀλλ' ἐπ' αὐτὸν τὸν λέγοντα καὶ λαβόντες ἐν νῷ διότι κατὰ τοὺς καιροὺς ὁ γράφων γέγονε καὶ τοῦ συνεδρίου μετεῖχε τῶν Ῥωμαίων, πᾶν εὐθέως ἡγοῦνται τὸ λεγόμενον ὑπὸ τούτου πιστόν. ἐγὼ δὲ φημὶ μὲν δεῖν οὐκ ἐν μικρῷ προσλαμβάνεσθαι τὴν τοῦ συγγραφέως πίστιν, οὐκ αὐτοτελῆ δὲ κρίνειν, τὸ δὲ πλεῖον ἐξ αὐτῶν τῶν πραγμάτων ποιεῖσθαι τοὺς ἀναγινώσκοντας τὰς δοκιμασίας.

> One may ask why I make any mention of Fabius and his statement. It is not from apprehension lest it may find acceptance from some owing to its plausibility; for its inherent unreasonableness, even without my comment, is self-evident to anyone who reads it. But what I wish is to warn those who consult his books not to pay attention to the title, but to facts. For there are some people who pay regard not to what he writes but to the writer himself and, taking into consideration that he was a contemporary and a Roman senator, at once accept all he says as worthy of credit. But my own opinion is that while not treating his authority as negligible we should not regard it as final, but that readers should in most cases test his statements by reference to the actual facts.

General opinion about foreign lands can be trumped by local traditions, although the reporting author may refuse to vouch for the truth of it, as Sallust (*Jug.* 17.7) does in his description of Africa:

> *Sed qui mortales initio Africam habuerint quique postea accesserint aut quo modo inter se permixti sint, quamquam ab ea fama, quae plerosque obtinet, diuersum est, tamen, uti ex libris Punicis, qui regis Hiempsalis dicebantur, interpretatum nobis est utique rem sese habere cultores eius terrae putant, quam paucissimis dicam. Ceterum fides eius rei penes auctores erit.*

---

91 Diod. 2.29.3–6; cf. Cic. *De orat.* 1.47 for the idea that the Greek philosophers are more fond of argument than of truth. Compare, however, the rather different perspective at 3.6.2–4, where Diodoros contrasts 'arguments such as are accepted by a simple-minded nature, which has been bred in a custom that is both ancient and difficult to eradicate' with a Greek education and the study of philosophy: it seems that Diodoros found conflicting ideas on the matter equally convincing and was unable – or felt no need – to make up his mind.
92 Turri *et al.* 2017, §10.2, p. 29: testimonial *injustice* 'occurs when someone's assertions are accorded less (or more) credence than they deserve because of prejudice of some kind, such as bias regarding identities like gender, race, ethnicity, or age'.

> I shall offer the following brief account, which, though it differs from the general opinion, is that which was interpreted to me from the Punic volumes said to have belonged to King Hiempsal, and which the inhabitants of that country believe to be consistent with fact. For the truth of the statement, however, the writers themselves must be responsible.

Not only for the history of distant lands, unless one had personally visited them,[93] but also for older times the historian often had little choice but to follow an ancient authority (Plb. 4.2, 9.2.1–2); unless no reliable one was available at all (Liv. 8.40.3–5), however, they often did not seem to consider this a fundamental problem. This also explains why myth features so prominently in many historiographical texts, even when the historian realises that he cannot establish the truth of these ancient traditions (cf. e.g. Diod. 4.1 and 4.8, Liv. *praef.* 6–9).

4 Concluding Remarks

The sweeping discussion offered here obviously cannot do full justice to all aspects of the texts analyzed or cover all the ways in which they affect our understanding of ancient historiography. Further questions need to be asked and studied in a more systematic way, for instance what the ancient historians meant with the concepts interpreted here in such terms as truth, accuracy and thoroughness, how this varied among individual authors, or how it developed chronologically.[94] Besides knowing how strong the theoretical definition of these virtues was, one also needs to ask how close to the ideal a historian needed to come in order to appear to have fulfilled it. Nevertheless, some conclusions emerge quite clearly.

First of all, the idea that 'knowledge is created and warranted by means of such virtues as honesty, carefulness, accuracy, and balance', and that 'the better historians perform these virtues, the better they apply the prevalent standards of scholarship, and the better their work will be conceived to be',[95] seems to have been held in Antiquity too. The wide range of epistemic virtues covered in this preliminary survey thus contradicts the popular view that to the ancient historians truth meant nothing – or not much – more than plausibility and the absence

---

[93] E.g. Amm. 23.6.30: '*ut scriptores antiqui docent, nosque vidimus*' ('as the writers of old say, and as I myself have seen').
[94] Of course, much important work – too much to mention it all – has already been done in this respect, especially for the most famous authors: extremely helpful are the volumes of the *Lexicon historiographicum Graecum et Latinum*.
[95] Paul 2011, 1, cf. *supra*, section 1.

of bias: with virtues like truthfulness, accuracy, thoroughness, a mimetic representation of reality, clear and logical reasoning, industriousness, inquisitiveness and experience their theoretical understanding of truth clearly implied a commitment to a representation of past events exactly as they had happened – although most realized that such an ideal could not be realized completely.

In line with their source theory and the importance they attached to the historian's character, the ancients had a clear understanding of the inevitable subjectivity involved in creating and transmitting historical knowledge and of the responsibilities and skills required to achieve the truth in such a subjective endeavour – although they had no concepts equivalent to subjective and objective. Given that historians had to live up to other virtues such as patriotism or often even wrote in the service of a particular state or ruler, the risk of bias was much higher than it is in a modern academic context that generally does not consider patriotism a virtue to be displayed in scholarship. Furthermore, both authors and audience belonged to a culture that deemed practical usefulness central to the study of the past and historians were often actively involved in politics.[96] Moreover, the historians were in competition with other reporters of past events such as orators and poets who could legitimately prefer the moral virtues over the epistemic ones.[97]

Perhaps it is not surprising, then, that the most commonly mentioned virtue is impartiality, not only because the likelihood of a historian being biased was much higher, but also because bias is an epistemic vice that can easily annihilate the positive effects of all other virtues, even if a historian is committed to practicing those. This is one area in which there was a fundamental difference between history and rhetoric since for the orator partiality often was required. The virtue of mimesis as it is understood in the quotations from Douris, Diodoros and Lucian places further limits on the rhetoric of historiography in the sense that it merely serves to represent historical reality and must not in any way distort the events. Moreover, many of the other virtues, such as accuracy and inquisitiveness, indirectly constrain the author's rhetorical freedom: however baffling the contents of ancient works of ancient historiography may sometimes appear, one cannot

---

[96] See Marincola 2017, xlii–xlvi.
[97] Grethlein 2010; Gehrke 2014; Schorn 2018, 365–391.

claim that in theory "the first plausible story was good enough", for such a narrative would not reflect the industry, inquistiveness and accuracy required of the historian.[98]

The passages discussed above also served to establish authority, especially those taken from prefaces or polemics with predecessors, and in fashioning an authoritative persona the historians referred to the highest ideals of ancient historiography, as Marincola has demonstrated.[99] Whether or not the historians always lived up to those ideals or whether they may have had ulterior motives in expressing them are different questions, which do not, however, impact the relevance of these texts for the identification of the epistemic virtues of ancient historiography. I hope to have shown that an analysis of these passages in terms of virtue epistemology adds a further perspective to our understanding of ancient historiography and reveals the necessity of bringing together ancient and modern philosophies of history: knowing both their epistemic culture and our own is essential if we want to grasp both the differences and the similarities between ancient and modern historiography.

Although the ancient writers of history upheld strict standards of truth, they did not always live up to these in a way that would satisfy us because their list of epistemic virtues and ours do not completely overlap, because the standards for practicing particular virtues may have been lower, and because the hierarchy between the virtues seems to have been somewhat different too. The ancients could for instance often rank inquisitiveness lower than traditionalism, for cultural as well as practical reasons.[100] Since the end of the *Querelle des anciens et des modernes* and especially since the enlightenment, however, most would no longer consider traditionalism an epistemic virtue at all,[101] whereas it has been argued in recent times that inquisitiveness is at the heart of a virtue-based approach to truth.[102] Bridging the chasm between the epistemic cultures of earlier historians and our own is a challenge that has been described as 'the historian's equivalent to life in zero gravity, a state impossible to achieve on earth'.[103] Thus it is both remarkable and potentially misleading how many epistemic virtues we seem to

---

98 *Contra* Wiseman 1979, 48. It is interesting to compare Wiseman's statement to an observation by Finley (1983, 23 n. 61) on modern scholarship and 'the common practice of pretending (or hoping) that the best we have is good enough'.
99 Marincola 1997.
100 Cf. Meeus 2017b.
101 Cf. Paul's view quoted above (n. 86) that traditionalist is a 'derogatory, pejorative label'.
102 Miscevic 2007 and 2016; Watson 2015.
103 Phillips 2013, 5.

share with the ancients;[104] those that we do not share are the hardest to undertsand for us, and they may in that sense reveal the most about the differences between ancient and modern historiography – along with those modern academic virtues that seem to fail completely in the works of ancient writers of history such as objectivity.[105] Virtue epistemology can thus add analytical clarity to such fundamental questions as whether the ancients possessed a methodology for choosing between different accounts of the past.[106] As long as they explicitly concerned themselves with the question how to acquire reliable knowledge in a particular field and did so in a way that satified the requirements of their own epistemic culture, one can in my view speak of a methodology. It is self-evident that this methodological thinking had to be very different from our own, given the in some ways very different epistemic cultures. Entertaining the theoretical possibility that one day our own methods will appear equally antiquated is not simply modest, it is a plausible expectation – and is to be hoped for if humanity is to make further progress.

Bibliography

Battaly, Heather (ed.) (2019), *The Routledge handbook of virtue epistemology*, New York.

Blank, Thomas/Maier, Felix K (eds.) (2018), *Die symphonischen Schwestern: Narrative Konstruktion von Wahrheiten' in der nachklassischen Geschichtsschreibung*, Stuttgart.

Brunt, Peter A. (2011), "Cicero and Historiography", in John Marincola (ed.), *Oxford Readings in Greek and Roman Historiography*, Oxford, 207–240 (originally published in *ΦΙΛΙΑΣ ΧΑΡΙΝ: Miscellanea di studi classici in onore di Eugenio Manni*, Rome 1980, I, 311–340).

Bosworth, A. Brian (2003), "*Plus ça change*… Ancient Historians and their Sources", in *Classical Antiquity* 22, 167–197.

Cohen, Shaye J.D. (1988), "History and Historiography in the *Against Apion* of Josephus", *History & Theory Beiheft* 27, 1–11.

---

104 It is in this respect that the critical questions of Wiseman 1979, Woodman 1988 and others have been most beneficial.

105 I have already refered to the emergence of objectivity in the nineteenth century, see above, n. 30 and 50–51. One may therefore wonder whether it makes sense to ask whether the ancients strove for objectivity, as is often done: e.g. Moles 1993, 114; Reynolds 2009, 364.

106 This is denied by Marincola 1997, 286: 'the various methods by which ancient historians choose different versions cannot be said to establish an historical methodology. Rather, sources are chosen (when they are chosen) because of rhetorical criteria – reliability, numbers, "persuasiveness", the character of the writer'. Apart from the rhetorical status of such qualities, however, their epistemic virtuousness should also be taken into account.

Chrysanthou, Chrysanthos S. (2015), "P. Oxy. LXXI 4808: *Bios*, Character, and Literary Criticism", *Zeitschrift für Papyrologie und Epigraphik* 193, 25–38.

Daston, Lorraine/Gallison, Peter (2007), *Objectivity*, New York.

Den Boeft, Jan, et al. (1995), *Philological and Historical Commentary on Ammianus Marcellinus XXII*, Groningen.

Eckstein, Arthur M. (2013), "Polybius, Phylarchus, and Historiographical Criticism", in *Classical Philology* 108, 314–338.

Fasolt, Constantin (2005), "The Limits of History in Brief", *Historically Speaking* 6.5, 5–10.

Fasolt, Constantin (2014), *Past Sense: Studies in Medieval and Early Modern European History*, Leiden.

Finley, Moses I. (1983), *Politics in the Ancient World*, Cambridge.

Fowler, Robert L. (1996), "Herodotos and His Contemporaries", *Journal of Hellenic Studies* 116, 62–87.

Free, Alexander (2015), *Geschichtsschreibung als Paideia. Lukians Schrift 'Wie man Geschichte schreiben soll' in der Bildungskultur des 2. Jahrhunderts n. Chr.*, (Vestigia 69), München.

Gehrke, Hans-Joachim (2014), *Geschichte als Element antiker Kultur: Die Griechen und ihre Geschichte(n)* (Münchener Vorlesungen zu antiken Welten 2), Berlin.

Gerson, Lloyd P. (2009), *Ancient Epistemology*, Cambridge.

Gray, Vivienne J. (1987), "Mimesis in Greek Historical Theory", *The American Journal of Philology* 108, 467–486.

Grethlein, Jonas (2010), *The Greeks and Their Past: Poetry, Oratory and History in the Fifth Century BCE*, Cambridge.

Gross, Alan G. (2006), *Starring The Text: The Place of Rhetoric in Science Studies*, Carbondale.

Haegemans, Karen/Kosmetatou, Elizabeth (2005), "Aratus and the Achaean Background of Polybius", in Guido Schepens and Jan Bollansée (eds), *The Shadow of Polybius. Intertextuality as a Research Tool in Greek Historiography* (Studia hellenistica 42), Leuven, 123–139.

Halliwell, Stephen (2002), *The aesthetics of mimesis: ancient texts and modern problems*, Princeton, NJ.

Hau, Lisa I. (2016), *Moral History from Herodotus to Diodorus Siculus*, Edinburgh.

Hau, Lisa I. (2017), 'Truth and Moralising: The Twin Aims of the Hellenistic Historiographers', in Ian Ruffell and Lisa I. Hau (eds), *Truth and History in the Ancient World: Pluralising the Past*, New York, 226–249.

Heldmann, Konrad (2011), *sine ira et studio. Das Subjektivitätsprinzip der römischen Geschichtsschreibung und das Selbstverständnis antiker Historiker* (Zetemata 139), München.

Kuukkanen, Jouni-Matti (2015), *Postnarrativist Philosophy of Historiography*, Basingstoke.

Leeman, Anton D. (1985), "L'historiographie dans le De oratore de Cicéron", *Bulletin de l'Association Guillaume Budé* 3, 280–288.

Leeman, Anton D. (1989), "Antieke en moderne geschiedschrijving. Een misleidende Cicero-interpretatie", *Hermeneus* 61, 235–241.

Leeman, Anton D./Pinkster, Harm (1985), *M. Tullius Cicero, De Oratore libri III*, Vol. 2, *Buch I, 166–265; Buch II, 1–98*, Heidelberg.

Lendon, J. E. (2009), "Historians Without History: Against Roman Historiography", in Andrew Feldherr (ed.), *The Cambridge Companion to the Roman Historians*, Cambridge, 41–61.

Li Causi, Pietro, et al. (2015), *Marco Tullio Cicerone, De oratore: traduzione e commento*, Alessandria.

Lloyd, Alan B. (2007), "Book II", in David Asheri et al., *A Commentary on Herodotus Books I–IV*, Oxford, 219–378.

Loraux, Nicole (1980), "Thucydide n'est pas un collègue", in *Quaderni di Storia* 12, 55–81 (now in John Marincola (ed.), *Oxford Readings in Greek and Roman Historiography*, Oxford, 19–39 as "Thucydides Is Not a Colleague").

Lorenz, Chris (1997), *Konstruktion der Vergangenheit: Eine Einführung in die Geschichtstheorie*, Köln.

Lorenz, Chris (1998), "Can Histories be True? Narrativism, Positivism, and the 'Metaphorical Turn'", *History & Theory* 37, 309–329.

Marincola, John (1997), *Authority and Tradition in Ancient Historiography*, Cambridge.

Marincola, John (2007a), "ἀλήθεια", in: *Lexicon historiographicum Graecum et Latinum* 2, Pisa, 7–29.

Marincola, John (ed.) (2007b), *A Companion to Greek and Roman Historiography*, 2 vols., Malden, MA.

Marincola, John (ed.) (2011), *Oxford Readings in Greek and Roman Historiography*, Oxford.

Marincola, John (2013), "Polybius, Phylarchus, and "Tragic History": A Reconsideration", in Bruce Gibson/Thomas Harrison (eds), *Polybius and His World. Essays in Memory of F.W. Walbank*, Oxford, 73–90.

Marincola, John (2014), "Rethinking Isocrates and Historiography", in Giovanni Parmeggiani (ed.), *Between Thucydides and Polybius: The Golden Age of Greek Historiography*, Washington D.C., 39–61.

Marincola, John (2015), "Plutarch, Herodotus, and the Historian's Character", in Rhiannon Ash et al. (eds), *Fame and Infamy: Essays on Characterization in Greek and Roman Biography and Historiography*, Oxford, 83–95.

Marincola, John (2017), *On Writing History from Herodotus to Herodian*, London.

Megill, Allan and McCloskey, Deirdre (1987), "The Rhetoric of History", in John S. Nelson et al. (eds), *The Rhetoric of the Human Sciences: Language and Argument in Scholarship and Public Affairs*, Madison, 221–238.

Meeus, Alexander (2017a), "Ctesias of Cnidus: Poet, Novelist or Historian?", in Ian Ruffell and Lisa I. Hau (eds), *Truth and History in the Ancient World: Pluralising the Past*, New York, 172–201.

Meeus, Alexander (2017b), "Compilation or Tradition? Some Thoughts on the Methods of Historians and Other Scholars in Antiquity", *Sacris Erudiri* 56, 395–413.

Meeus, Alexander (2018a), "History's Aims and Audience in the Proem to Diodoros' *Bibliotheke*", in Lisa I. Hau et al. (eds.), *Diodoros of Sicily: Historiographical Theory and Practice in the* Bibliotheke (Studia Hellenistica 58), Leuven, 149–174.

Meeus, Alexander (2018b), "Introduction: Narrative and Interpretation in the Hellenistic Historians", in *idem* (ed.), *Narrative in Hellenistic Historiography* (Histos Suppl. 8), Newcastle upon Tyne, 1–22.

Miscevic, Nenad (2007), "Virtue-Based Epistemology and the Centrality of Truth (Towards a Strong Virtue-Epistemology)", *Acta Analytica* 22, 239–266.

Miscevic, Nenad (2016), "Curiosity – The Basic Epistemic Virtue", in Chienkuo Mi et al. (eds), *Moral and Intellectual Virtues in Western and Chinese Philosophy: The Turn toward Virtue*, New York, NY, 145–163.

Moles, John L. (1993), "Truth and Untruth in Herodotus and Thucydides", in: Christopher Gill and T.P. Wiseman (eds), *Lies and Fiction in the Ancient World*, Exeter, 88–121.

Momigliano, Arnaldo D. (2016) [1974], "The Rules of the Game in the Study of Ancient History", *History & Theory* 55, 39–45.

Murphey, Murray (2009), "Realism about the Past", in Aviezer Tucker (ed.) *A Companion to the Philosophy of History and Historiography*, Malden, MA, 181–189.

Nicolai, Roberto (1992), *La storiografia nell'educazione antica* (Biblioteca di MD 10), Pisa.

Nicolai, Roberto (2007), "The Place of History in the Ancient World", in John Marincola, *A Companion to Greek and Roman Historiography*, 2 vols., Malden, MA., 13–26.

Ottone, Gabriella (2015), "La critica a Eforo e Teopompo: nuove prospettive ermeneutiche a proposito del F 1 di Duride di Samo", in Valérie Naas and Mathilde Simon (eds), *De Samos à Rome: personnalité et influence de Douris (Modernité classique 5)*, Paris, 209–242.

Parmeggiani, Giovanni (2016), "Sulle critiche di Duride di Samo ad Omero (FGrHist 76 F 89) e a Eforo e Teopompo (FGrHist 76 F 1)", *Eikasmos* 27, 105–119.

Pataut, Fabrice (2009), "Anti-Realism about the Past", in Aviezer Tucker, (ed.) *A Companion to the Philosophy of History and Historiography*, Malden, MA, 190–198.

Paul, Herman (2008), "The Epistemic Virtues of Historical Scholarship; or, the Moral Dimensions of a Scholarly Character", *Soundings: An Interdisciplinary Journal* 91, 371–387.

Paul, Herman (2011), "Performing History: How Historical Scholarship Is Shaped by Epistemic Virtues", *History & Theory* 50, 1–19.

Paul, Herman (2015), *Key Issues in Historical Theory*, Abingdon.

Pédech, Paul (1961), *Polybe, Histoires, Livre XII* (Collection des Universités de France), Paris.

Pelling, Christopher (1990), "Truth and Fiction in Plutarch's Lives", in D.A. Russell (ed.), *Antonine Literature*, Oxford, 19–52.

Phillips, Mark (2013), *On Historical Distance*, New Haven, CT.

Porod, Robert (2013), *Lukians Schrift 'Wie man Geschichte schreiben soll'. Kommentar und Interpretation*, Wien.

Raaflaub, Kurt A. (2010), "Ulterior Motives in Ancient Historiography: What Exactly, and Why?", in Lin Foxhall et al. (eds), *Intentional History: Spinning Time in Ancient Greece*, Stuttgart, 189–210.

Reynolds, Joshua J. (2009), 'Proving Power: Signs and Sign-inference in Thucydides' *Archaeology*", *Transactions of the American Philological Association* 139, 325–368.

Rhodes, P.J. (1994), "In Defence of the Greek Historians", *Greece & Rome* 41, 156–171.

Ring, Abram (2010), "Heraclean Historians", *Syllecta Classica* 21, 35–64.

Rood, Tim (2007), "Polybius", in Irene J.F. de Jong/René Nünlist (eds), *Time in Ancient Greek Narrative* (Studies in Ancient Greek Narrative 2; Mnemosyne Suppl. 291), Leiden, 165–81.

Ruffell, Ian/Hau, Lisa I. (2017), *Truth and History in the Ancient World: Pluralising the Past*, New York.

Schepens, Guido (1998), "Geschiedschrijving als Pyrrhusoverwinning: enkele reflecties vanuit de antieke historiografie", in Johan Tollebeek et al. (eds), *De lectuur van het verleden: opstellen over de geschiedenis van de geschiedschrijving aangeboden aan Reginald de Schryver*, Leuven, 89–107.

Schepens, Guido (2005), "Polybius' Criticism of Phylarchus", in Guido Schepens and Jan Bollansée, (eds), *The Shadow of Polybius. Intertextuality as a Research Tool in Greek Historiography* (Studia hellenistica 42), Leuven, 141–164.

Schepens, Guido (2007), "History and *Historia*: Inquiry in the Greek Historians", in John Marincola, *A Companion to Greek and Roman Historiography*, 2 vols., Malden, MA, 39–55.

Schepens, Guido (2011), "Some Aspects of Source Theory in Greek Historiography", in John Marincola, *Oxford Readings in Greek and Roman Historiography*, Oxford, 100–118 (originally published in *Ancient Society* 6 [1975], 257–274).

Schepens, Guido/Bollansée, Jan (2005) (eds), *The Shadow of Polybius. Intertextuality as a Research Tool in Greek Historiography* (Studia hellenistica 42), Leuven.

Schorn, Stefan (2018), *Studien zur hellenistischen Biographie und Historiographie* (Beiträge zur Altertumskunde 345), Berlin.

Schorn, Stefan (2019), "Rhetorik und Historiographie", in Michael Erler and Christian Tornau (eds), *Handbuch Antike Rhetorik* (Handbücher Rhetorik 1), Berlin, 627–654.

Spiegel, Gabrielle M. (2019), "The Limits of Empiricism: The Utility of Theory in Historical Thought and Writing", *Medieval History Journal* 22, 1–22.

Strasburger, Hermann (1966), *Die Wesensbestimmung der Geschichte durch die antike Geschichtsschreibung* (Sitzungsberichte der wissenschaftl. Gesellschaft an der J.W. Goethe-Universität Frankfurt am Main 5, 1966, 3), Wiesbaden.

Sundwall, Gavin A. (1996), "Ammianus Geographicus", *The American Journal of Philology* 117, 619–643.

Tompkins, Daniel P. (2013), "The Language of Pericles", in Antonis Tsakmakis/Melina Tamiolaki (eds.), *Thucydides between history and literature* (Trends in Classics Suppl. 17), Berlin, 447–464.

Tucker, Aviezer (2004), *Our Knowledge of the Past: A Philosophy of Historiography*, Cambridge.

Tucker, Aviezer (2009) (ed.), *A Companion to the Philosophy of History and Historiography*, Chichester.

Turri, John et al. (2017)[2], "Virtue Epistemology", in Edward N. Zalta (ed.), *The Stanford Encyclopedia of Philosophy* (Summer 2018 Edition), URL = <https://plato.stanford.edu/archives/sum2018/entries/epistemology-virtue/>.

Van Nuffelen, Peter (2012), *Orosius and the Rhetoric of History*, Oxford.

Walbank, Frank W. (1967), *A Historical Commentary on Polybius*, vol. II, *Commentary on Books VII–XVIII*, Oxford.

Watson, Lani (2015), "What Is Inquisitiveness", *American Philosophical Quarterly* 52, 273–287.

Whiting, Daniel (2018), review of Veli Mitova (ed.), *The Factive Turn in Epistemology*, Cambridge 2018, in *Notre Dame Philosophical Reviews* 2018.08.29 (https://ndpr.nd.edu/news/the-factive-turn-in-epistemology/).

Wiater, Nicolas (2017), "Expertise, 'character' and the 'authority effect' in the early Roman history of Dionysius of Halicarnassus", in Jason König and Greg Woolf (eds), *Authority and expertise in ancient scientific culture*, Cambridge, 231–259.

Williams, Bernard (2002), *Truth and Truthfulness: An Essay in Genealogy*, Princeton, NJ.

Wiseman, T.P. (1979), *Clio's Cosmetics: Three Studies in Greco-Roman Literature*, Leicester.

Wiseman, T.P. (1988), review of Woodman, Anthony J (1988), *Rhetoric in Classical Historiography. Four Studies*, in *Classical Review* 38, 262–264.

Woodman, Anthony J. (1988), *Rhetoric in Classical Historiography. Four Studies*, London.

Woodman, Anthony J. (2011), "Cicero and the Writing of History", in John Marincola, *Oxford Readings in Greek and Roman Historiography*, Oxford, 241–290.

Zagzebski, Linda Trinkaus (1996), *Virtues of the Mind: An Inquiry into the Nature of Virtue and the Ethical Foundations of Knowledge*, Cambridge.

Jonas Grethlein
The Universal in the Particular: A Core Dilemma of Historicism in Antiquity

Historicism continues to be a fuzzy concept. Generally associated with the modern idea of history which emerged around 1800, Historicism has been seen as a major rupture with Enlightenment thought. Some scholars, however, have challenged this view, emphasizing that Enlightenment historians such as Schlözer and Gatterer in fact laid the groundwork for Ranke, Droysen and Meinecke.[1] Another open question concerns the scope of Historicism: is it mainly a school of thought within the field of history or is it more broadly a change of attitude that affected the humanities in general with strong repercussions outside academia?[2] And finally a question as to its contemporary legacy: is the reign of Historicism over, as for example Fukuyama, Hartog and Gumbrecht seem to think, or do we still find ourselves, in one or another metamorphosed form, under its sway?[3]

No matter what answers we are inclined to give to these questions, we are likely to agree that Historicism is predicated on the conviction that human life and culture can only be understood as historical. This implies a special view of historical processes. Historicists take it for granted that events, forming parts of developments, are in themselves unique and individual. As Ranke famously put it, historical epochs are "immediate to God". This observation is more explosive than it may appear at first sight. It not only leads to a considerable degree of relativism, but also challenges an approach to the past that has been and continues to be powerful, namely historical comparison. By no means does Historicism rule out historical comparison – it is of course possible to juxtapose all sorts of things, and the use of the same terms for different events makes implicit comparison inevitable. But from a Historicist perspective, the value of comparisons is strictly limited. Comparing is of little help when it comes to elucidating what is most important: the unique nature of historical processes.[4]

In the first part of this paper, I will use Droysen's *Historik* to illustrate the Historicist emphasis on individuality and juxtapose it with another modern

---

1 Whereas, for example, Muhlack (1991) elaborates on the break between Enlightenment and Historicism, the contributors to Bödeker (1986), emphasize the continuity.
2 See Oexle (1996, 139–200), who makes a case against limiting Historicism to history as a discipline.
3 Fukuyama 1992; Hartog 2003; Gumbrecht 2010.
4 On the concept of comparison (not only historical) and its intricacies, see, e.g., Felski/Friedman 2013, and Epple and Erhart 2015.

school of thought, namely Anglophone positivism. Unlike their Historicist colleagues, positivists are highly invested in the idea of historical laws and put a premium on what is general in history. The dichotomy of the particular and the universal is a core issue of modern ideas of history, and yet it has, as I wish to show, a prehistory in antiquity. In order to outline the ancient engagement with this supposedly modern issue, I shall interrogate Aristotle's *Poetics* and Thucydides' *History* in the second part of this paper. Finally, having set our ancient testimonies under the lens of a modern debate, I will conversely reassess this modern discussion in light of the ancient backdrop. The tension between the particular and the universal will play out not least in how ancient thinking bears on the modern question. Aristotle and Thucydides cannot help us to settle the issue definitely, but they allow us to see it from a range of new perspectives. In particular, the *Poetics* and the *History of the Peloponnesian War* will alert us to the role that narrative can play for what Giorgio Agamben has described as the paradigmatic mode of thinking.

1 Historical Uniqueness and Comparison: Historicism versus Positivism

Rooted in Romanticism and indebted to hermeneutics, Historicism emphasizes the individual nature of historical events. Take for example Droysen, whose *Historik*, first published in 1868, is arguably the most important Historicist reflection on history and a work that continues to be of paramount value in the eyes of some theoreticians.[5] Droysen does not deny the general a place in history; however, he allocates it not in laws, but in "the continuum of the ongoing historical work", which "connects the single facts of history and assigns value to each of them in its individual way. In fact, it assigns only value to those that are individual".[6] As a consequence of the individual nature of historical events, historians do not explain, but interpret: "We do not explain. Interpretation is not an explanation of what is later by means of what is earlier, but it is, as it were, a construction of what we have, a slackening and unraveling of this inconspicuous material in the wealth of its moments, the countless threads, that have been gathered up in one

---

[5] E.g. Rüsen 1983–1989.
[6] Droysen 1974, 29: "Kontinuität der fortschreitenden geschichtlichen Arbeit… die einzelnen Tatsachen der Geschichte verbindet und jeder in ihrer individuellen Art ihren Wert gibt, nur denen, die individueller Art sind, einen Wert gibt".

knot, which become vivid again through the art of interpretation and start to speak".[7]

This emphasis on the individuality of events does not leave much space for the idea of comparison in the *Historik*. When Droysen elaborates on heuristics, he discusses analogy as a means of closing gaps in our sources.[8] Beyond this, however, comparison plays no role in *Historik*. Comparativism has no power to illuminate historical developments which are shaped by the will of individuals and are therefore unique in their dynamics. This position can also be found in philosophical hermeneutics, for example when Gadamer objects to Dilthey's predilection for comparativism. Comparison, Gadamer argues, "presupposes the independent nature of the recognizing subjectivity that already has one and the other at its disposal... It is therefore doubtful that the method of comparison is really adequate for the idea of historical comprehension. Is it not rather the case that a technique, which is at home in certain areas of natural science and prevalent in some areas of the humanities, e.g. inquiries into language, law and culture, is elevated from an inferior to a prominent status of importance for our historical understanding, which provides fake legitimization to superficial and disconnected reflection?"[9]

When understood as the attempt to capture the particular, historiography requires a special form of its own. Droysen distinguishes four modes in which historians can present their work: the inquiring, the narrative, the didactic and the discursive modes. His polemical argument against the widely spread assumption that history is part of *les belles lettres* reveals that narrative is Historicism's mode of choice. This affinity to narrative chimes well with the emphasis on the particular; narratives are well suited to do justice to the singularity of historical events

---

7 Ibid. 163: "Wir erklären nicht. Interpretation ist nicht Erklärung des Späteren aus dem Früheren, des Gewordenen als ein notwendiges Resultat der historischen Bedingungen, sondern ist die Deutung dessen, was vorliegt, gleichsam ein Lockermachen und Auseinanderlegen dieses unscheinbaren Materials nach der Fülle seiner Momente, der zahllosen Fäden, die sich zu einem Knoten verschürzt haben, das durch die Kunst der Interpretation gleichsam wieder rege wird und Sprache gewinnt".
8 Ibid. 335. Cf. Bichler 1978, 5–8.
9 Gadamer 1972, 220: "die Unabhängigkeit der erkennenden Subjektivität, die über das eine wie das andere verfügt, bereits voraus.... Man muß deshalb bezweifeln, ob die Methode des Vergleichens der Idee der historischen Erkenntnis wirklich genügt. Wird hier nicht ein Verfahren, das in bestimmten Bereichen der Naturwissenschaft zu Hause ist und auf manchen Gebieten der Geisteswissenschaften, z.B. der Sprachforschung, der Rechtswissenschaft, der Kunstwissenschaft usw., Triumphe feiert, aus einem untergeordneten Hilfsmittel zu zentraler Bedeutung für das Wesen historischer Erkenntnis emporgesteigert, die oft nur oberflächlicher und unverbindlicher Reflexion eine falsche Legitimierung verschafft?"

and developments.¹⁰ It is not incidental that Kracauer, when he argues that history is a non-science and, at least primarily, unconcerned with laws, mentions the telling of stories as its core business.¹¹

Now we should insist at this venture that the idea of the general is not alien to Historicism. Its proponents heavily critique Hegel and his idea of world history constituted by the concept of Spirit, and yet they themselves take for granted the notion of universal history.¹² Besides Romanticist hermeneutics, the tradition of Idealism has left its imprint on Historicism. Droysen unabashedly speaks of the idea and Ranke finds a force ("Kraft") at work in world history. Still, the universal of which they speak operates only through the particular and cannot be fully comprehended since history is still in a state of flux. The historian is therefore confined to the particular. It is in this sense that Meinecke defines Historicism as "the attempt to replace a generalizing view of forces in human history with an individualizing view".¹³

The individualizing view is part and parcel of the notion of history on which Historicism is premised. As Reinhart Koselleck demonstrated, the turn of the nineteenth century saw the disintegration of what he called the "horizon of expectations" and the "space of experiences".¹⁴ New experiences, most notably the experience of the French Revolution, transcended the "horizon of expectations" and made it difficult to extrapolate future events. At the same time, the past was reconceptualized as a dynamic development, a shift that is tangible in the German term "Geschichte". The plural "Geschichten" metamorphosed into the singular "Geschichte", which signifies both the events of history themselves as well as historical accounts of them. The singular "Geschichte" expresses an understanding of historical processes as unique in their dynamic and beyond the grasp of universal categories. As this shows, the infatuation of Historicism with the particular is bound with its notion of temporality. It is the temporal dynamics of history that renders things particular; the general would have to be exempt from the flux of time.

The interest in the general, however, was to resurface again in a new form in the twentieth century. Positivist theoreticians tried to close the gap between history and science, endowing the former with the putative objectivity of the latter.

---

10 Droysen 1974, 273; 282.
11 Kracauer 1969, 32.
12 Cf. Gadamer 1972, 185–191.
13 Meinecke, 1959, 2: "Ersetzung einer generalisierenden Betrachtung geschichtlich-menschlicher Kräfte durch eine individualisierende Betrachtung". For a critique of Meinecke's approach to Historicism as too narrow, see Oexle 1996.
14 Koselleck 2004, 3–69.

For them, history is not so much an idiographic as a nomological discipline. Whereas Historicists consider their main task to be interpretation, scholars such as Carl Hempel and Ernest Nagel declare that the core business of the historian is explanation.[15] Whether explicitly or implicitly, historians deduce nomological conclusions in order to find the causalities at work in history. Laws permit them to explain how one state emerges from another. The covering law model or, more moderately, probabilistic models thus stand at the core of history.

On the positivist account, historians aim less at finding universal laws than at using them to explain specific events. Nonetheless, the universal assumes a central place that it does not have in Historicism. It is only with the help of general laws that the historian can explain the course of history. Now that statistics and probabilities have been placed center stage, comparison is also endowed with a central role. The laws on which historical analysis is based derive essentially from comparison. The evaluation of causal factors and their effects also depends on comparison. Even theories that abandon Hume's legacy and discard the idea of laws rely on comparison to find causes.[16]

If history is based on laws and probabilities, it also employs different modes of expression from the kind of history which is predicted on the unique character of events. Coherent narration is replaced by texts featuring arguments, theoretical reflections and charts as well as calculations. While Theodor Mommsen received the Nobel Prize in Literature for recognition of his *Roman History*, many works associated with the Annales school, for example, are barely different from sociological and economic analysis. Besides putting a premium on comparison, the focus on the universal seems to undercut the primacy of narrative in history.

The preference for a narrative presentation which aims at the individual, on the one hand, or an analysis that privileges structures, on the other, is often ideologically charged.[17] A case in point is the so-called Lamprecht Dispute, a major and highly emblematic controversy among German historians at the end of the nineteenth century and the beginning of the twentieth century.[18] As the author of four volumes on German economy in the Middle Ages ("*Deutsches Wirtschaftsleben im Mittelalter*") Karl Lamprecht had gained some recognition.[19] The German history that he began to publish in several volumes in the 1890s,

---

15 See, e.g., Hempel 1967; 1978; Nagel 1968; Murphey 1973; Stegmüller 1969.
16 Lorenz 1997, 231–284.
17 Cf. Bichler 1990.
18 E.g. Oestreich 1969, 320–363; Schorn-Schütte 1984; Geier/Homann 1993.
19 Lamprecht 1885–1886.

however, attracted fierce criticism.[20] Such prominent colleagues as von Below, Rachfahl und Meinecke wrote devastating reviews of it. The rejection of Lamprecht in Germany went so far that academic journals started to ignore his work altogether. What had Lamprecht done? He had dared to substitute the kind of political historiography cultivated by the Rankeans with a morphological account in which social and economic factors are key. Lamprecht focused not on the State, but on what he designated the "conditions" ("Zustände"). Instead of confining himself to the particular and elucidating the unique course of events, he engaged in comparative analysis and concentrated on the typical. In stigmatizing Lamprecht, Germany's conservative historians successfully defended their conception of history which foregrounds the particular as well as the role of the State. Their success, however, was only temporary: in the 1960s their legacy lost its credit more and more and Social History, developing approaches not dissimilar to Lamprecht's own, began to dominate the field for several decades.[21]

Ironically, the tables were turned in what was arguably the most prominent public debate in which German historians engaged in the twentieth century.[22] The so-called *Historikerstreit*, which was centered on the contested uniqueness of the Holocaust as an event, came to a head in 1986. In this case, it was conservative historians that capitalized on the business of comparison. Ernst Nolte, for example, called Auschwitz a "copy" of Archipel Gulag and "the frightened response to the destructive activities of the Russian revolution".[23] He was heavily attacked by Habermas and liberal historians, who vehemently opposed this comparison, which in their eyes relativized the crime of Nazi Germany.[24] The striking reversal of roles – now Social Historians refute a comparison which is championed by their conservative colleagues – is due principally to the object of controversy and should not detract from the high esteem in which Social Historians generally hold comparisons. It underlines, however, that the issue of the universal and the particular in history is more than a methodological point, that it is also imbued with ideological assumptions.

---

[20] Lamprecht 1891–1909.
[21] Marc Bloch, one of the founding fathers of the Annales school attended Lamprecht's lectures at Leipzig, but it seems that Lamprecht's influence on the Annales school was minor. This being said, critics of the Annales school aligned it with Lamprecht. Cf. Schöttler 2015.
[22] Cf. Bichler 1990, 170–171. The most important contributions to the Historikerstreit in 1986 are assembled in Augstein *et al.* 1987.
[23] Nolte 1987, 32: "die aus Angst geborene Reaktion auf die Vernichtungsvorgänge der Russischen Revolution".
[24] In addition to Augstein *et al.*, see also Wehler 1988.

The particular versus the universal, uniqueness versus recurrence – this is a core dilemma of history in the modern era, as Siegfrid Kracauer, to whom we will return at the end of this paper, in particular noticed. Here we have seen some of the far-reaching ramifications of this dilemma: on the one hand, the Historicist focus on the particular puts little stock in comparison while privileging interpretation and relying on narrative. On the other hand, the positivist belief in laws and structural forces espouses comparison and replaces interpretation with explanation, narrative with analysis. But indissoluble as it may seem, the tension between the individual and the general can be mitigated. Koselleck, best known for his argument supporting the notion of development behind modern conceptualizations of history, speculated in an essay what history would be like if there were either only repetition or only innovation. Neither seems possible, he argues: "The historical nature of man, or, theoretically phrased, historical anthropology, is couched between the two poles of this hypothetical thought-experiment (*Gedankenexperiment*), that is ongoing repetitiveness or permanent innovation".[25] Even a historian who privileges individuality in the Historicist tradition will have to rely on the same terms when speaking about different events.[26] Instead of pitting the particular against the universal, it seems more fruitful to envisage them as two complementary perspectives on history, as Reinhold Bichler notes: "All historical events can be examined from the viewpoint of their singleness or that of their general and comparable nature".[27] The move from the level of history to that of historiography relaxes the tension between the universal and the particular, but it cannot ultimately resolve it; the question still remains as to where historians should place their emphasis.

The salience of the dichotomy of the particular versus the universal for the modern idea of history makes it easy to overlook the traces of this distinction in classical antiquity. In the second part of this paper, I will consider two examples which illustrate the premodern engagement with the relationship between the universal and the particular. At first sight, Aristotle and Thucydides put forward diametrically opposed views, but their positions are more nuanced than it may seem from preliminary inspection. Instead of making singleness and recurrence

---

25 Koselleck 2010, 98: "Die geschichtliche Natur des Menschen, oder wissenschaftstheoretisch formuliert, die historische Anthropologie ist angesiedelt zwischen diesen beiden Polen unseres Gedankenexperiments stetiger Wiederholbarkeit oder ständiger Innovation".
26 Ibid., 110. See also Lorenz 1997, 269.
27 Bichler 1990, 191: "Es lassen sich alle historischen Begebenheiten unter dem Aspekt ihrer Besonderheit und unter dem ihrer Allgemeinheit und Vergleichbarkeit untersuchen".

opposite poles of a dichotomy, both authors seek to mediate between the two. They will also alert us to a function of narrative that deserves our attention.

2 The Universal and the Particular in Aristotle's *Poetics* and Thucydides' *History of the Peloponnesian War*

In *Poetics* 9, Aristotle famously juxtaposes poetry and historiography. Whereas history is concerned with events "that actually occurred", poetry is free to deal with "what could have happened". This makes the works of poets "more philosophical and more serious" than those of historians, for "poetry speaks more of universals, history of particulars" (1451b5–7). Scholars have not failed to note that Aristotle here seems to anticipate the Historicist focus on the particular.[28] The opposite view, which places its trust in the universal, is not difficult to find in antiquity. An exemplary use of the past was very popular: poets and orators frequently drew lessons from the past, and ancient historians were inclined to engage in historical comparison. Even Thucydides, who was held in high esteem by many Historicists of the nineteenth century, above all for his espousal of historiographical accuracy, evokes the universal in a central reflection on the purposes of his historiography: the results of his efforts may be less delightful for listening:

> Yet if they are judged useful by any who wish to look at the plain truth about past events and those that at some future time, in accordance with human nature, will recur in similar or comparable ways, that will suffice. It is a possession for all time, not a competition piece to be heard for the moment that has been composed (1.22.4).

Human nature, being constant across all time, permits the historian to compare different historical events directly, as well as to conjecture what may happen in the future. The claim of offering the readers a possession for all time radically opposes the program of Historicism, as John Moles observes: "There would be no more radical challenge to historicism in any of its forms".[29]

As we see, both positions – on the one hand, the emphasis given to the unique nature of historical events, and on the other, the assertion of a universal dimension – can be found in classical antiquity. There is obviously irony in that

---

28 Cf., e.g., Iggers 1971, 43 n. 1; Bichler 1990, 171.
29 Moles 2001, 199.

Thucydides aims at a truth that goes beyond the reconstruction of particular events and therefore seems to aim at what for Aristotle distinguishes poetry from historiography. But are the views of the philosopher and the historian really irreconcilable, the former being an advocate of historical individuality, the latter championing the worth of historical comparison? This may be our first impression; a closer look however will reveal that despite the different thrusts of their arguments Aristotle and Thucydides take both perspectives into account.

Let us begin with Aristotle. After discussing the form, length and unity of the poetic plot in chapters 7 and 8 of the *Poetics*, he tackles poetic mimesis through a comparison with historiography in chapter 9. It is not form that distinguishes poetry from historiography. One could versify Herodotus' work, for example, and it would still remain historiography:

> The difference lies in the fact that one speaks of events which have occurred, the other of the sort of events which could occur. It is for this reason that poetry is both more philosophical and more serious than history, since poetry speaks more of universals, history of particulars. The universal comprises the kind of speech or action which belongs by probability or necessity to a certain kind of character – something which poetry aims at despite its addition of particular names. The particular, by contrast, is (for example) what Alcibiades did or experienced (1451b4–11).

There has been much discussion about Aristotle's concept of the universal (*ta katholou*) which renders poetry distinct from historiography and more similar to philosophy.[30] He does not seem to be thinking of abstract entities, Platonic ideas or moral principles. This would not tie in with the significance that he ascribes to the vividness of poetic representation (1455a22–26). The course of the argument indicates that plot is pivotal to Aristotle's understanding of the universal: Chapters 7 and 8 are fully devoted to plot, and the comparison of poetry with historiography in chapter 9 forms part of the discussion of how the unity of plot can be achieved. When Aristotle returns to the notion of the universal in chapter 17, it is again discussed in the context of plot.[31] Most importantly, probability and necessity, which define the universal in chapter 9, do not signify the relation between representation and reality in the sense of naturalism. What they refer to is immanent plausibility, a key criterion of plot. I therefore follow Stephen Halliwell when he argues: "This means that universals are related to causes, reasons, motives,

---

30 E.g. Halliwell 2002, 193–206; Aristoteles, *Poetik*, transl. and comm. A. Schmitt (Darmstadt: Wissenschaftliche Buchgesellschaft, 2008), 372–426 with further literature.
31 Cf. Halliwell 2002, 194–195.

and intelligible patterns of human life in the structure of a dramatic poem as a whole".[32]

Whereas poetry aims at a closed plot that reveals universals about characters and actions, historiography concentrates on the particular – to keep with Aristotle's example, on what Alcibiades did and suffered, no matter whether it adds up to a plot or not. A later passage makes clear that historiography does not require action which conforms with the laws of probability. In chapter 23, Aristotle argues that poetic composition ought to be different from the historian's work, for in historiography "one need not find the exposition of a unitary action but all the contingently connected events which happened to one or more persons in a particular period of time" (1459a22–4).

Now poets, unlike philosophers, do not engage in abstract meditations, but narrate stories from which the universal can be gleaned. The tragedians in particular employ historical names in such a way that guarantees the possibility of the action, which, besides plausibility, marks another criterion of good poetry (1451b15–19). Indeed, poets can take not only names, but entire subjects from history:

> And he is just as much a poet even if the material of his poetry comprises actual events, since there is no reason why some historical events should not be in conformity with probability, and it is with respect to probability that the poet can make his poetry from them (1451b27–32).

This implies that historiography can also reveal the universal. History *can* but need not, feature the kind of probability which is indispensable to poetry. If there is this kind of probability in a course of events, then the particular on which the historian focuses encapsulates the universal. This means: the particular that defines historiography is not opposed to the universal – history can be the realm of the universal as understood by Aristotle.

Aristotle's *Rhetoric* corroborates the argument that he acknowledges a universal dimension which renders history open to comparison. In a discussion of exempla together with fables as an important means of rhetoric, Aristotle points out that exempla lend themselves in particular to deliberative oratory, "for future events are, by and large, similar to past events" (*Rhet.* 2.20, 394a7–8). Before this, in a discussion of the skills of the deliberative orator, Aristotle has emphasized

---

[32] Halliwell (2002, 195; 1987, 109) rightly stresses that Aristotle here engages with Plato's criticism of poetic mimesis. In particular the thesis that poetry is "more philosophical and more serious" responds to Plato's assertion that poetry is "play and not serious (*spoude*)" (*resp.* X 602b).

that military counseling can benefit from the works of historians just as legal advisers may draw on ethnographic reports (*rhet.* 1.4, 1360a30–7).[33] The assertion that history has lessons to offer is based on the assumption that particular events harbor universal aspects that can be transferred to other events. In order to stress the salience of the universal in poetry, Aristotle juxtaposes it with historiography and its focus on the particular. And yet, as my reading of the *Poetics* and the brief glance at the *Rhetoric* demonstrate, the universal may also be found in the particulars of history.

What about Thucydides, whose promise to provide the reader with a possession for all times seems to pose a radical challenge to the singleness of historical events? The very passage in which Thucydides makes his claim qualifies the assumption of transhistorical constants. Thucydides asserts that his work will allow readers "to look clearly" at future events. The visual imagery underlines the credit that Thucydides gives to an investigation which elucidates human nature. His work will make visible not only the Peloponnesian War, but also what is still to come in the future. At the same time, Thucydides sounds a note of caution when he adds that these things "will recur in similar or comparable ways". The constant element of human nature need not articulate itself in simple repetitions.

Thucydides' sensitivity to the uniqueness of historical events is even more pronounced when he comments on the stasis that ruined Corcyra in 427. He describes this civil war in great detail, for "later the rest of Hellas was also in turmoil, with rival efforts everywhere by the popular leaders to bring in the Athenians and the oligarchs, the Lacedaemonians" (3.82.1). The analysis of the disintegration is valid beyond the Peloponnesian War:

> And during the civil wars the cities suffered many cruelties that occur and will always occur as long as men have the same nature, sometimes more terribly and sometimes less, varying in their forms as each change of fortune dictates (3.82.2).

Human nature is constant, but manifests itself in varying forms. While giving the universal a central place in his work, Thucydides remains aware of the individuality of historical events.

In fact, right after promising his readers insights into human nature in Book 1, Thucydides stresses the unique character of his war. The Peloponnesian War outshone other wars, not least the Persian Wars, through its length and fierceness:

---

[33] See also Halliwell 2017, 200.

> For never had there been so many cities captured or left desolate, some by barbarians and others by the Hellenes as they fought each other (and some cities even changed population after they were taken), nor were there so many men exiled or slaughtered, both in the war itself and because of faction (1.23.2).

Even natural catastrophes were more frequent than ever before.[34] That being said, the uniqueness that Thucydides claims for the Peloponnesian War does not rule out its comparison with other wars. On the contrary, being not so much qualitatively as quantitatively different from other wars, the Peloponnesian War, through its unprecedented dimension, is particularly apt to highlight what is transtemporal.[35] Thucydides has chosen an event that makes the universal visible.

Thucydides' self-fashioning will strike modern historians as odd. Can an analysis that presents itself as a rigid reconstruction of what happened at one point simultaneously aim at shedding light on the universal? How does the proclaimed usefulness of Thucydides' account square with its accuracy? Is objectivity not at loggerheads with attempts to instrumentalize history? For Thucydides there is no contradiction. Only a critical reconstruction of particular events has the capacity to illuminate the workings of human nature. To "see clearly" the past is the prerequisite for the ability to envisage the future. The universal from which the reader will benefit is encapsulated in the particular and can only be revealed through its meticulous reconstruction.

One of the few ancient treatises on the theory of history, Lucian's *On how to write history* illustrates that ancient writers in general were inclined to see no tension between the accuracy and practical use of historiography. Adherence to facts is crucial to Lucian's idea of historiography: "The historian's sole task is to tell the tale as it happened" (39). Lucian then mentions Thucydides and links the truth of history to its use (42):

> For Thucydides says that he is writing a possession forever rather than a prize-essay for the occasion, that he does not welcome fiction but is leaving to posterity the true account of what happened. He brings in, too, the question of usefulness and what is, surely, the purpose of sound history: that if ever again men find themselves in a like situation they may be able, he says, from a consideration of the records of the past to handle rightly what now confronts them (42).

---

[34] Here Thucydides implicitly compares the Peloponnesian War with the Persian Wars through an allusion to Herodotus' statement that Greece suffered more during the reigns of Dareius, Xerxes, and Artaxerxes than in the twenty generations before (Hdt. 6.98.2).
[35] Cf. Moles 1993, 109.

Far from mutually exclusive, factual accuracy and the usefulness of history in comparison are closely entwined with each other in Lucian's argument. For Lucian, as for most ancient writers, the main danger to truth is that the historian looks to his contemporary audience. Then fear and flattery are likely to corrupt the account:

> This, as I have said, is the one thing peculiar to history, and only to truth must sacrifice be made. When a man is going to write history, he must ignore everything else. In short, the one yardstick to keep in view is not your present audience but those who will meet your work thereafter (39).

If bias generated by present concerns is the primary enemy of truth, history forges an alliance with the future that will reveal its usefulness. The permanent benefit one receives from historiography signals that its account was not engineered to pursue personal interests. The universal, which makes historical comparison possible, is not opposed to the particular, but rather proves the accuracy of an account.

It is not least the way in which Thucydides expresses the universal that helps dissolve its tension with the particular. There are only few passages in which Thucydides explicitly points out that he is now touching on something general that will help the reader to understand his own time better. Besides the Corcyrean *stasis*, the detailed description of the plague contains one of these assertions. Rejecting speculations about the causes of the epidemic, Thucydides notes (2.48.3):

> I will say what it was like in its course and describe here, as one who had the plague myself and saw others suffering from it myself, the symptoms by which anyone who studies it cannot possibly fail to recognize it with this foreknowledge, if it ever strikes again (2.48.3).[36]

Note, however, the object of Thucydides' comments: only the symptoms of a disease, not human nature, for instance the human desire for power that shapes history. The *History of the Peloponnesian War* sketches an anthropology, but presents it less in explicit reflections than through narrative.

Let me single out three means by which Thucydides embeds the universal in his account of the particular. The first element is the speeches, which fulfil various functions in the *History of the Peloponnesian War*.[37] On the one hand, speeches let the reader envisage the past as a form of the present. Thucydides certainly does not render what was actually said and artfully interweaves the

---

[36] Against the thesis that Ranke's famous dictum of "wie es eigentlich gewesen" is a translation of this passage in Thucydides, see Stroud 1987.
[37] On the speeches in Thucydides, see Stadter 1973; Scardino 2007.

speeches with his own narrative. Nonetheless the speeches render the point of view held by a historical agent and provide an assessment of the situation without the benefit of hindsight that is enjoyed by the historian and his readers. On the other hand, Thucydides has the speakers comment not only on the situation at hand, but also on factors that go beyond it and allow the reader to see the universals at work.

The two extended pairs of speeches from book 3, the Mytilenean Debate (3.36–49) and the Plataian Dialogue (3.52–68), may illustrate this general dimension evoked by the speeches.[38] The Athenian assembly first decides to execute the male population of Mytilene, which has defected from the Attic-Delian League. Then, however, this vote becomes the object of another meeting. Whereas Cleon defends the initial decision and points out the constraints to which an Empire such as the Athenian is subjected, Diodotus argues that an act of mercy would greatly benefit Athens. Diodotus' opinion carries the day; the Athenians spare the Mytileneans. After the Mytilenean Debate has put the spotlight on Athenian politics, the Plataian Dialogue illustrates the foreign policy of Sparta. The Plataians, former allies of Sparta and now brought to their knees after a two-year siege, conjure up their glorious past, especially their merits in the Persian Wars. The Thebans, who lost an army in Plataia, present a rather different history in which the Plataians appear as hopeless traitors. Furthermore, they address Sparta's current interests. Following this argument, the Spartan judges have all male Plataians killed.

These two sets of speeches are not only about the fate of the Mytileneans and Plataians. They are also about more than Athens' and Sparta's treatment of their allies in general. Thucydides has the speakers comment on nothing less than the relation between power and law and the tension between the exigencies of the present and the legacy of the past. The reasoning of the speakers brings universal categories into play; it invites the readers to view the particular event as a model for the larger forces operating in history. It is therefore not surprising that Koselleck, when he discusses the possibility of lessons to be learnt from the past, adduces pair of speeches from Thucydides: "Thucydides' Melian Dialogue about

---

38 From the rich scholarship see, for example, Winnington-Ingram 1965; MacLeod 1983, 92–102; and the literature in Hornblower 1991 on 3.37–50, on the Mytilenean Debate *ibid*. 421 and MacLeod 1983, 103–22; Debnar 1996; Grethlein 2012, 57–75 on the Plataian Dialogue.

power and law is *mutatis mutandis* a key also for the situations of Hácha facing Hitler in 1939 and Dubček facing Breschnew in 1968".[39]

No less surprisingly, if more disconcertingly for the liberal historian, the meditation on power that can be found in these and other speeches is a major reason for why Thucydides is so popular with Political Realists.[40] Besides Hobbes and Machiavelli, Thucydides is a central source for attempts to capture the laws of power politics in such theoreticians as Hans Morgenthau and Edward Hallett Carr. Their interpretations of Thucydides concentrate especially on the Melian Dialogue. The Athenian's assertion that "justice is what is decided when equal forces are opposed, while those superior do what they can and the weaker ones have to suffer" has come to be used as an essential creed of Political Realism, and the destruction of the Melians by the Athenians is adduced as evidence that on the great cold stage of world politics there is only one thing that really counts: self-interest.

The political influence of this reading of the *History of the Peloponnesian War*, and in particular of its speeches, ought not to be underrated. The architects of the Iraq Wars frequently invoked Thucydides – or Fake-Thucydides, as when Colin Powell presented as Thucydidean the claim that "of all manifestations of power, restraint impresses men most," a quotation which actually stems from Frank Byron Jevons' *A History of Greek Literature*.[41] The current President of the US has not outed himself as an avid reader yet, but the spell of Thucydides on the White House seems to be unbroken.[42] Steve Bannon and Herbert Raymond McMaster advertised their esteem for Thucydides, when just before a visit of a Chinese delegation Graham T. Allison, the author of *Destined for War: Can America and China Escape Thucydides' Trap?*, was sighted in the White House.

The reception of Thucydides in Political Realism illustrates the appeal of the universals in the speeches. The obvious shortcomings of most of these interpretations simultaneously throw into relief the special dynamic that Thucydides bestows upon his reflections on human nature by using speeches. Even if speeches evoke universal categories, they remain utterances of characters which by no means need to reflect Thucydides' position. Most speeches are opposed by counter-speeches which Thucydides tends to endow with similarly strong arguments.

---

39 Koselleck 2003, 263: "Der Melier-Dialog des Thukydides über Macht und Recht bleibt *mutatis mutandis* ein Schlüssel auch für die Situation, in der sich Hácha gegenüber Hitler 1939, Dubček gegenüber Breschnew 1968 befunden haben".
40 Harloe 2012. Cf. Morley 2014, 167.
41 Sharlin 2004, 12–28.
42 Crowley 2017.

The claims of speeches also need to be weighed in the narrative context. The claims made by the speakers sometimes illuminate the course of events; at other times they sit uncomfortably with it or are even in outright contradiction. How, for example, can Political Realists deduce from the Mytilenean Debate the doctrine of "might is right" if the politics of radical self-interest defended by the Athenians ultimately leads to Athens' downfall? Far from conveying clear-cut messages, Thucydides uses the speeches to introduce general categories as prisms that refract the action.

The second means that Thucydides deploys to flag the universal in his account of the particular can be found in the combination of speeches and narrative. Ancient readers did not fail to notice Thucydides' peculiar style.[43] He has a preference for abstract nouns and indulges in transforming adjectives, infinitives and participles into nouns. As students of Greek have to learn painfully, the ensuing words and constructions are often highly idiosyncratic. Frequently, Thucydides personifies the newly created nouns and makes them into the subject of actions. He is also fond of the passive voice and likes to substitute prepositional expressions for contact clauses. Condemned as heavy and opaque by ancient critics, this style nonetheless helps to convey a specific idea of history. Not men but abstract forces seem to make history. Most importantly for my argument, Thucydides' style emphasizes the general behind the individual.

Particularly striking examples of these stylistic idiosyncrasies can be found in the Corcyrean *stasis*. After a detailed description of the changes in society, Thucydides notes for example (3.82.8): "The cause of this was power through greed and ambition" (πάντων δ' αὐτῶν αἴτιον ἀρχὴ ἡ διὰ πλεονεξίαν καὶ φιλοτιμίαν). The English translation is barely comprehensible, but the same has to be said about the Greek original. Instead of writing, say, "The Corcyreans did all of this, because they were greedy and ambitious and wanted power," Thucydides lays down a heavy collocation of nouns, in which power, greed and ambition seem to have lives of their own. The expression silently substantiates the claim, quoted above, that the events of Corcyra illustrate the course of any civil war. Agency has passed from men in a specific situation to abstract entities operating throughout history.

In addition to speeches and this stylistic preference for nouns, analogies are a third means through which Thucydides draws his reader's attention to the universal dimension of history. His account features large- as well as small-scale patterns. It has been shown, for example, that the account of the Deceleian War

---

43 E.g. Dionysius of Halicarnassus, *Pomp.* 3.17.2–5; *Thuc.* 24.51–6.

(415–404) echoes the description of the Archidamian War (431–421).⁴⁴ The second half of the Peloponnesian War proved far more detrimental to Athens than the first, but the same mechanisms can be detected in both. Greed and fear drive cities into conflicts which they are ultimately unable to win. The irrational forces of politics are particularly tangible in the Sicilian Expedition, which not only paves the way for Athens' downfall, but also mirrors the Peloponnesian War as a whole.⁴⁵

Thucydides also seems to rely on patterns in his reconstruction of the ancient past. He does not cast doubt on the historicity of the Trojan War, but feels compelled to rectify the Homeric version of it.⁴⁶ His comment on the Greeks' motivation in particular bears out the assumption that the recent and remote pasts both work along similar lines. Thucydides argues that, instead of following the Tyndarid oath, the Greek allies obeyed the power of Mycenae, especially at sea. Fear, adduced by Thucydides as a major reason here, also looms large in the Peloponnesian War. As Thucydides describes it, many cities joined the Attic-Delian league out of the fear of Athens' naval power. Other corrections of Homer's view also seem to be premised on analogical reasoning. The length of the Trojan War, Thucydides argues, did not reflect the fierceness of the conflict, but was due to issues of supply, just as a lack of supply sealed the fate of the Sicilian expedition. Likewise, the thesis that the Greek army in the Trojan War was relatively small corresponds with the critique of the Athenians for not sending enough troops to Sicily.

Only rarely does Thucydides make the parallels between events explicit.⁴⁷ Essential aspects of the past are not highlighted through comments, but emerge implicitly from allusions and correspondences within a carefully crafted narrative.⁴⁸ Not unlike Greek tragedy, which shuns clear answers and raises complex questions, the *History of the Peloponnesian War* requires an active reader. When we read Thucydides, we ourselves have to spot the links and parallels woven into the narrative and assess them in light of the concepts laid out in the speeches.

As Thucydides' meditation on his historiographical purposes demonstrates, his deeper interest lies with what is transhistorical, and most notably human na-

---

44 Rawlings 1981.
45 E.g. Stahl 1973, 76–77.
46 Cf. Hunter 1982, 197–198; Kallet 2001, 97–112.
47 A prominent exception is the comparison of the battle in the Syracusan harbor with the siege of Pylos (Thuc. 7.71.7).
48 E.g. Strasburger 1982, 538; Hornblower 1987, 41–42.

ture. This being said, Thucydides does not approach the general through propositional claims, but in the form of narrative. The lack of abstraction is made up for by narrative vividness. Most importantly, Thucydides' narrative balances the universal with the particular. It aims at the universal without extracting it from the particular. Thucydides considers the universal in the particular, he views human nature in the mirror of history. Patterns, speeches and a stylistic preference for nouns allow him to make the general visible behind the individual.

Nonetheless, the tension between the particular and the universal has survived at least in Thucydides' reception history. As Neville Morley has demonstrated, many modern historians, not exclusively, but especially in the nineteenth century praised Thucydides as a timeless model of what a historian should be like.[49] Other scholars, however, keenly observed the gap that separates Thucydides' work from the modern historian's practice. George Grote, for example, contended that Thucydides gave too much credit to myth and Francis M. Cornford even declared him "mythhistoricus". The very tension that the *History of the Peloponnesian War* attempts to dissolve, returns and continues in its modern reception.

On first impressions it had seemed that Aristotle and Thucydides pursued opposite agendas about singleness and repetition in history. We have seen, however, that their positions are not all that different from each other. Aristotle defines historiography through the particular, but does not exclude the possibility that it reflects the universal. Thucydides, one could say, makes this possibility the model of his work, which aims at seeing the transtemporal in the past. We are inclined to consider the tension between the universal and the particular a key question of our modern idea of history, and yet the example of Aristotle and Thucydides illustrates that this same tension was already the object of piercing reflections in antiquity. The philosopher and the historian concentrate on opposite aspects – the former on the singleness of historical events, the latter on recurrences – but both integrate the opposite aspects into their picture: while the particular does not rule out the universal, the desire for insights into human nature can only be fulfilled through an investigation of specific events.

---

49 Morley 2014.

3 Narrative as a Representation of the Universal in the Particular

A modern thinker, who reflected piercingly on the relation between the universal and the particular as well as the transtemporal and the temporal, is Siegfrid Kracauer. In *History. The Last Things before the Last*, he tries to do for history what he does for photographic media in *Theory of Film*; in fact, he bases his meditation on history on its analogy with photographic representation. Like photography, historiography requires 'the "right" balance between the realistic and formative tendencies': 'In exact analogy to the photographic approach, the "historical approach" comes true only if the historian's spontaneous intuition does not interfere with his loyalty to the evidence but, conversely, benefits his empathetic absorption in it.'[50] One of the characteristics that history shares with photography is the focus on the specific. Kracauer is therefore critical of positivist attempts to study history as a realm regulated by laws. History, he contends, takes place in the 'anteroom'[51] and is concerned with 'the last things before the last'.

At the same time, Kracauer does not fully subscribe to the approaches of Historicists, who gave preference to the individual and had difficulties to conceptualize the universal. He rejects the 'transcendental' solution of Ranke, Droysen and others, who took for granted a transtemporal truth but place it outside historical time, as well as the immanence of Dilthey, for whom man's historicity excluded an eternal truth.[52] Instead, Kracauer believes that history, through its cataract-like temporality, embraces the general as well as the particular. Both levels, though, are hard to reconcile; they do not map onto each other and coexist 'side by side'.[53] The 'structure of the historical universe' is, as Kracauer puts it, 'nonhomogeneous'.[54] It may be possible to derive general conclusions from an analysis of the particular, and yet the general will fail to capture fully the particular.

My analysis of ancient reflections on the tension between the universal and the individual offers a fresh perspective which yields an alternative view. Thucydides in particular draws our attention to narrative as a medium that not only lends itself to capturing the uniqueness of historical processes, but simultaneously has the capacity to express the general. In Thucydides' hands narrative has

---

50 Kracauer 1969, 56.
51 Ibid. 191.
52 Ibid. 195–200.
53 Ibid. 200.
54 Ibid. 136.

turned out to be a form that can mediate between the particular and the universal, enshrining the transtemporal in the report of specific events. Narrative makes it possible to account for the general in its individual articulation; it has the capacity to present recurrences as the single acts they simultaneously are.

Narrative thus allows us to transform the dichotomy or 'side by side' as which Kracauer defines the relation between the universal and the particular. Giorgio Agamben's notion of the paradigmatic, I suggest, furnishes a conceptual framework for this reassessment of the two putative poles in narrative. In a discussion of Foucault and Kuhn and in defense of his own mode of inquiry, Agamben describes the paradigm as a form of thinking that is neither inductive nor deductive.[55] As he has it, the paradigm "moves from one singularity to another and, without betraying itself, transforms each case into the exemplar of a general rule that is impossible to establish a priori". The universal has no independent existence; it is constituted only through the presentation of the particular in the paradigm. Agamben traces the paradigmatic in various places, in grammatical examples, in Warburg's *Pathosformel*, in Kant's definition of aesthetic judgment as something that exists without rule but is nonetheless more than subjective, to name just a few; he even suggests envisaging the hermeneutic circle as paradigmatic: there is no *aporia* if we replace the duality of part and whole or, in Heidegger's temporal version, of before and after with the notion of an intelligibility that is constituted through the phenomenon.

One of the reasons Agamben elaborates on the method of paradigmatic thinking is the critique that he in his previous works reveled in archetypes. Against this objection, Agamben insists that such concepts as *Muselmann* or the 'state of exception' do not try "to explain Modern Age by going back to a ground or historical origin... but they are paradigms serving to make intelligible a series of phenomena...".[56] That being said, the discomfort with the status of Agamben's central concepts is not entirely incomprehensible; the highly abstract nature of his meditations invites the critique of archetypal thinking. Narrative, on the other hand, lends itself to paradigmatic reasoning, and it is as odd as it is revealing that it is not mentioned by Agamben. As the example of the *History of the Peloponnesian War* illustrates, narrative has the capacity to linger on the particular and simultaneously to make visible the universal that would not exist without the particular.

The ancient reminder of what narrative can do is, I think, particularly helpful in the current climate of theory. For decades scholars followed Hayden White's

---

55 Agamben 2009.
56 Ibid. 37.

lead and put a premium on emplotment as narrative's essential contribution to history. In the last fifteen years, however, a growing disenchantment with the linguistic turn has also reached the theory of history. Intellectual energies that had been fully devoted to linguistic representation now fuel the desire for presence. Ankersmit, once a champion of tropology, now chews over the kind of immediacy with which we experience history, not unlike the sublime. Runia, arguably the most prominent proponent of the "New Romantics," deems a metonymic bond with the past more essential than its metaphorical emplotment. Given these thinkers' shared opposition to the linguistic turn, it is not surprising that theoreticians of presence tend to bypass narrative or even reject it as a form of mere representation.[57]

Ancient writers, however, invite us to reconsider the verdict of the New Romantics and to reassess the role of narrative in history beyond Hayden White's tropology. Elsewhere I have used ancient historiography to make a case that narrative is more than representation.[58] Narrative can, with due qualification, restore presentness to the past. Temporal orchestration, direct speech and focalization are means by which a historian can forego hindsight and present the past as it was experienced. Not least through its sequential form, narrative triggers experiences in readers, a point emphasized by cognitive and phenomenological approaches, and thus has the capacity to make them re-experience the past in the frame of "as-if". The argument of this paper gestures towards another capacity of narrative. Historians concerned with structures and comparison put little stock in narrative; some even consider it unscientific. Thucydides' *History of the Peloponnesian War*, however, thought-provokingly suggests that narrative can establish a link between the particular and the universal in history. Narrative permits us to satisfy the longing for the universal in history without neglecting our obligations towards the individual. In stories the particular can become general and simultaneously remain unique.

Bibliography

Agamben, Giorgio (2009), *The Signature of All Things. On Method* (trans. L. D'Isanto and K. Attell), New York.

---

57 Ankersmit 2005; Runia 2006, 1–29. Gumbrecht, one of the most prominent theoreticians of presence, shares the dislike of narrative, cf. Gumbrecht 1997; 2006, 299–318. See also the essays in Ghosh/Kleinberg 2012, and for further literature Grethlein 2014, 327 n. 56.
58 Grethlein 2010, 315–335; 2013; 2014.

Ankersmit, Frank R. (2005), *Sublime Historical Experience*, Stanford, CA.
Augstein, Rudolf, *et al.* (1987), "Historikerstreit": Die Dokumentation der Kontroverse um die Einzigartigkeit der nationalsozialistischen Judenvernichtung, München.
Bichler, Reinhold (1978), "Die theoretische Einschätzung des Vergleichens in der Geschichtswissenschaft," in Franz Hampl/Ingomar Weiler (eds), *Vergleichende Geschichtswissenschaft: Methode, Ertrag und ihr Beitrag zur Universalgeschichte*, Darmstadt, 1–58.
Bichler, Reinhold (1990), "Das Diktum von der historischen Singularität und der Anspruch des historischen Vergleichs: Bemerkungen zum Thema Individuelles versus Allgemeines und zur langen Geschichte deutschen Historikerstreits", in Acham, K. (ed.), *Teil und Ganzes: Zum Verhältnis von Einzel- und Gesamtanalyse in Geschichts- und Sozialwissenschaften*, München.
Bödeker, Hans E. (ed.) (1986), *Aufklärung und Geschichte: Studien zur dt. Geschichtswissenschaft im 18. Jh.* [Internationales Kolloquium im Aug. 1981 im Max-Planck-Institut für Geschichte in Göttingen], Göttingen.
Crowley, Michael (2017), "Why the White House Is Reading Greek History," *Politico*.
Debnar, Paula (1996), "The Unpersuasive Thebans (Thucydides 3.61–67)", *Phoenix* 50, 95–110.
Droysen, Johann G. (1974), *Historik: Vorlesungen über Enzyklopädie und Methodologie der Geschichte*, ed. R. Hübner, 7th ed., Darmstadt.
Epple, Angelika/Erhart, Walter (eds) (2015), *Die Welt beobachten: Praktiken des Vergleichens*, Frankfurt.
Felski, Rita/Friedman, Susan S. (eds) (2013), *Comparison: Theories, Approaches, Uses*, Baltimore, MD.
Fukuyama, Francis (1992), *The End of History and the Last Man*, New York, NY.
Gadamer, Hans-Georg (1972), *Wahrheit und Methode: Grundzüge einer philosophischen Hermeneutik*, 3rd ed., Tübingen.
Geier, Wolfgang/Homann, Harald (eds) (1993), *Karl Lamprecht im Kontext: Ein Kolloquium*, Leipzig: Institut für Kulturwissenschaften i. Gr. der Universität Leipzig.
Ghosh, Ranjan/Kleinberg, Ethan (eds) (2012), *Presence: Philosophy, History, and Cultural Theory for the Twenty-First Century*, Ithaca, NY.
Grethlein, Jonas (2010), "Experientiality and Narrative Reference: With Thanks to Thucydides", *History and Theory* 49, no. 3, 315–335.
Grethlein, Jonas (2012), "The Use and Abuse of History in the Plataian Debate", in Jonas Grethlein/Christopher B. Krebs (eds), *Time and Narrative in Ancient Historiography. The "Plupast" from Herodotus to Appian*, Cambridge, 57–75.
Grethlein, Jonas (2013), *Experience and Teleology in Ancient Historiography: Futures Past from Herodotus to Augustine*, Cambridge.
Grethlein, Jonas (2014) "Time, Tense and Temporality in Ancient Greek Historiography", in *Oxford Handbooks Online*.
Grethlein, Jonas (2014), "Future Past: Time and Teleology in (Ancient) Historiography", *History and Theory* 53, 309–330.
Gumbrecht, Hans Ulrich (1997), *In 1926. Living at the Edge of Time*, Cambridge, MA.
Gumbrecht, Hans Ulrich (2006), "Aesthetic Experience in Everyday Worlds. Reclaiming an Unredeemed Utopian Motif", *New Literary History* 37, 299–318.
Gumbrecht, Hans Ulrich (2010), *Unsere breite Gegenwart*, Berlin.
Halliwell, Stephen (1987), *The Poetics of Aristotle. Translation and* Commentary, London.
Halliwell, Stephen (2002), *The Aesthetics of Mimesis: Ancient Texts and Modern Problems*, Princeton.

Halliwell, Stephen (2017), "Was Aristotle a Literary Historian?", in Jonas Grethlein/Antonios Rangakos (eds), *Griechische Literaturgeschichtsschreibung: Traditionen, Probleme und Konzepte*, Berlin, 189–211.
Harloe, Katherine (ed.) (2012), *Thucydides and the Modern World: Reception, Reinterpretation and Influence from the Renaissance to the Present*, Cambridge.
Hartog, François (2003), *Régimes d'historicité: présentisme et expériences du temps*, Paris.
Hempel, Carl G. (1967) "The Function of General Laws in History", in Patrick Gardner (ed.), *Theories of History*, 8th ed., New York.
Hempel, Carl G. (1978), "Explanation in Science and History", in William Herbert Dray (ed.), *Philosophical Analysis and History*, Westport, CT.
Hornblower, Simon (1987), *Thucydides*, London.
Hornblower, Simon (1991), *A Commentary on Thucydides*, vol. I, Oxford.
Hunter, Virginia J. (1982), *Past and Process in Herodotus and Thucydides*, Princeton, NJ.
Iggers, Georg G. (1971), *Deutsche Geschichtswissenschaft: Eine Kritik der traditionellen Geschichtsauffassung von Herder bis zur Gegenwart*, München.
Kallet, Lisa (2001), *Money and the Corrosion of Power in Thucydides: The Sicilian Expedition and its Aftermath*, Berkeley, CA.
Koselleck, Reinhart (2003), "Stetigkeit und Wandel aller Zeitgeschichten. Begriffsgeschichtliche Anmerkungen," in Reinhart Koselleck (ed.), *Zeitschichten. Studien zur Historik*, Frankfurt, 246–245.
Koselleck, Reinhart (2004), *Futures Past: On the Semantics of Historical Time*, transl. Keith Tribe, New York.
Koselleck, Reinhart (2010), "Wiederholungsstrukturen in Sprache und Geschichte", in Dutt, Carsten (ed.), *Vom Sinn und Unsinn der Geschichte: Aufsätze und Vorträge aus vier Jahrzehnten*, Berlin, 96–114.
Kracauer, S. (1969), *History. The Last Things before the Last*, New York, NY.
Lamprecht, Karl (1885–1886), *Deutsches Wirtschaftsleben im Mittelalter: Untersuchungen über die Entwicklung der materiellen Kultur des Platten Landes auf Grund der Quellen zunächst des Mosellandes*, 3 vols., Leipzig.
Lamprecht, Karl (1891–1909), *Deutsche Geschichte*, 12 vols., Berlin.
Lorenz, Chris (1997), *Konstruktion der Vergangenheit: Eine Einführung in die Geschichtstheorie*, Köln.
MacLeod, Colin W. (1983), *Collected Essays*, Oxford.
Meinecke, Friedrich (1959), *Die Entstehung des Historismus*, Hans Herzfeld/Carl Hinrichs (eds.), München.
Moles, John (1993), "Truth and Untruth in Herodotus and Thucydides," in Christopher Gill (ed.), *Lies and Fiction in the Ancient World*, Exeter, 88–121.
Moles, John (2001), "A False Dilemma. Thucydides' History and Historicism", in Stephen J. Harrison (ed.), *Texts, Ideas, and the Classics: Scholarship, Theory, and Classical Literature*, Oxford, 195–219.
Morley, Neville (2014), *Thucydides and the Idea of History*, London.
Muhlack, Ulrich (1991), *Geschichtswissenschaft im Humanismus und in der Aufklärung: Die Vorgeschichte des Historismus*, München.
Murphey, Murray G. (1973), *Our Knowledge of the Historical Past*, Indianapolis.
Nagel, Ernest (1968), *The Structure of Science: Problems in the Logic of Scientific Explanation*, 2nd ed., London.

Nolte, Ernst (1987), "Zwischen Geschichtslegende und Revisionismus?", in Augstein, Rudolf, *et al.* (eds), "Historikerstreit": Die Dokumentation der Kontroverse um die Einzigartigkeit der nationalsozialistischen Judenvernichtung, München, 13–35.

Oestreich, Gerhard (1969), "Die Fachhistorie und die Anfänge der sozialgeschichtlichen Forschung in Deutschland," *Historische Zeitschrift* 208, 320–363.

Oexle, Otto G. (1996) "Meineckes Historismus. Über Kontext und Folgen einer Definition", in Otto G. Oexle/Jörn Rüsen (eds), *Historismus in den Kulturwissenschaften: Geschichtskonzepte, historische Einschätzungen, Grundlagenprobleme*, Köln, 139–200.

Rawlings, Hunter R. III (1981), *The Structure of Thucydides' History*, Princeton, NJ.

Runia, Eelco (2006), "Presence," *History and Theory* 45, 1–29.

Rüsen, Jörn (1983–1989) *Grundzüge einer Historik*, 3 vols., Göttingen.

Scardino, Carlo (2007), *Gestaltung und Funktion der Reden bei Herodot und Thukydides*, Berlin.

Schorn-Schütte, Luise (1984), *Karl Lamprecht: Kulturgeschichtsschreibung zwischen Wissenschaft und Politik*, Göttingen.

Schöttler, Peter (2015), Die *"Annales"–Historiker und die deutsche Geschichtswissenschaft*, Tübingen.

Sharlin, Shifra (2004), "Thucydides and the Powell doctrine," *Raritan: A Quarterly Review* 24, 12–28.

Stadter, Philip (ed.) (1973), *The Speeches in Thucydides: A Collection of Original Studies with a Bibliography*, Chapel Hill.

Stahl, Hans-Peter (1973), "Speeches and Course of Events in Books Six and Seven of Thucydides", in Philip A. Stadter (ed.), *The Speeches in Thucydides: A Collection of Original Studies with a Bibliography*, Chapel Hill, 60–77.

Stegmüller, Wolfgang (1969), *Probleme und Resultate der Wissenschaftstheorie und Analytischen Philosophie*, Band I: Wissenschaftliche Erklärung und Begründung, Berlin.

Strasburger, Hermann (1982), "Die Entdeckung der politischen Geschichte durch Thukydides," in Walter Schmitthenner/Renate Zoepffel (eds), *Studien zur alten Geschichte*, vol. II, Hildesheim, 527–591.

Stroud, Ronald S. (1987), "'Wie es eigentlich gewesen' and Thucydides 2.48.3", *Hermes* 115, 379–382.

Wehler, Hans-Ulrich (1988), *Entsorgung der deutschen Vergangenheit? Ein polemischer Essay zum "Historikerstreit"*, München.

Winnington-Ingram, Reginald P. (1965), "ΤΑ ΔΕΟΝΤΑ ΕΙΠΕΙΝ: Cleon and Diodotus," *Bulletin of the Institute of Classical Studies* 12, 70–82.

Part II: **Transcending Representation and Reality**

Aske Damtoft Poulsen
Teleology with a Human Face: 'Sideshadowing' and its Effects in Tacitus' Treatment of Germanicus (*Annals* 1–2)

Introduction

An historiographer's philosophy of history, what (s)he means by 'doing history', may – broadly speaking – be approached from two perspectives: the scholar investigates either theoretical remarks or historiographical praxis. This paper on Tacitus' *Annals*, an annalistic account of Roman history from the death of Augustus to the death of Nero (AD 14–68) written at the beginning of the second century AD, opts for the latter.[1] Rather than attempting to provide a comprehensive description of Tacitus' conception of his historical endeavour through analysis of his theoretical remarks (which are both few and often notoriously unreliable as paradigmatic statements), we will investigate an example of his historiographical praxis, more specifically the tension between teleology and experientiality in his treatment of Germanicus, the adopted son and presumed successor of Tiberius (emperor AD 14–37) until his suspicious death in AD 19. By analysing the negotiation of this specific tension (of particular importance in historical narrative) in the treatment of this specific character, we will not only explore Tacitus' historiographical praxis but also shed light on the philosophy of history wherein this praxis is embedded.[2]

I wish to express my gratitude to Ellen O'Gorman, Arne Jönsson, Monika Asztalos, and Christina S. Kraus for their comments on various earlier versions of this paper. Thanks are due also to Richard Alston, at whose "Tacitus for the 21st Century"-workshop (Royal Holloway, 1 April 2019) I received valuable feedback on its main ideas.

---

1 In its original state the *Annals* presumably consisted of eighteen books, of which, sadly, seven have been lost (5, 7–10, 17–18). The preserved narrative covers the years AD 14–29, 31–37, and 47–66, meaning that we lack a one-and-a-half-year period in the latter half of Tiberius' reign (29–31), the entire account of Caligula's reign (37–41), the first six years of Claudius' reign (41–47), and the last two years of Nero's reign (66–68).
2 For a nuanced attempt to grapple with (the problems of uncovering) the overarching philosophy of history in Tacitus' works, see Griffin 2009. Griffin notes that (p. 168) "no one who has considered these questions has emerged with a plausible picture of Tacitus as a thinker. On the contrary, opinions are divided between those who blame him for muddle-headedness and those who justify the muddle." See also footnote 14 below on the tension between *fatum* ('fate') and *fortuna* ('fortune') in Tacitus.

More specifically, we will attempt to pinpoint the cause of a widely shared readerly experience of the *Annals*, for while undoubtedly an impressive literary achievement, it can be a miserable experience to make one's way through the text: year after year, emperor after emperor, Rome seems to sink ever deeper into a quagmire of moral decay, political incompetence, and overt authoritarianism. In the words of Sir Ronald Syme, "the *Annales* convey the traveller through a bleak land without light or hope."[3] If the endeavour of the philologist is to explain why she feels the way she does about a text, then the specific aim of this paper is to make sense of this readerly experience of the *Annals*. We will do so through analysis of (i) its negotiation of the tension between teleology and experientiality and (ii) the emotional responses elicited from the reader by this negotiation in the treatment of Germanicus in *Annals* 1–2. Starting from the premise that a narrative of decline is not in itself enough to elicit the emotions experienced by Syme and others, we will – by investigating episodes in which alternative futures are imagined, so-called 'side-shadowing' – demonstrate the potential of the *Annals* to induce in the reader a sensation not only of hopelessness, but also helplessness and regret.[4]

The paper is divided in three parts. Part one presents the terms teleology, experientiality, and side-shadowing and considers their applicability to ancient historiography in general and the *Annals* in particular. Part two investigates side-shadowing effects in the treatment of the unrealised civil war between Tiberius and Germanicus in *Annals* 1–2. It argues that the hopelessness, helplessness, and regret experienced by readers may be explained by the discrepan-

---

[3] Syme 1958, 545; cf. Trilling 1976/2012, 435: "we are aware of him [Tacitus] as one of the few great writers who are utterly without hope". See also Ash 2006, 89: "entering Tacitus' world is not straightforwardly pleasurable, but it does have a certain compulsion and fascination to it, as the audience becomes steeped in the guilty pleasures of watching a disaster narrative unfold." Griffin (2009, 168–72), arguing that Tacitus appears to wield (and shift between) four main modes of interpretation – divine intervention, fate (i.e. an unalterable chain of natural causes), destiny, and fortune/chance –, notes that (p. 171) "on each occasion, Tacitus invokes the explanation that produces the effects he wants, and what he usually wants is a gloomy effect."

[4] On the arousal of emotions in ancient historiography, see Levene 1997/2012 and Marincola 2003. As noted by Marincola, the portrayal and arousal of emotions constituted a key part of the ancient historiographical endeavour, serving not only a didactic-persuasive but also an experiential function, that is, (p. 315) "to give the reader the vicarious experience of what it was like to be there and thus to encourage understanding of the events in the narrative." On the role of emotions in ancient strategies of persuasion, see Kaster 2006 – who notes that the arousal of emotions is discussed primarily in rhetorical treatises – and the articles collected in Sanders & Johncock (eds.) 2016. On the arousal of emotions in ancient rhetoric, see esp. Quintilian on *enargeia* (*Inst.* 6.2, 8.3.61–71, 9.2.40–3); cf. Webb 2009, 87–106.

cy between the futures they are being encouraged to imagine and the future they know will come to pass and in which they find themselves as both readers of the narrative and descendants of its characters. Part three situates the analysis within a broader discussion of the relationship between teleology and experientiality, inevitability and openness in the *Annals*.

1 Teleology, Experientiality, and Side-shadowing

As noted by Jonas Grethlein, all narratives oscillate between teleology and experientiality, between explaining events from a position of hindsight and representing the experiences of the people who live through them. This tension, however, gains special significance in historiography, since historians (ancient as well as modern) are expected to construct an explanatory narrative while simultaneously remaining faithful to actual experiences and actual historical causes, that is, to let events guide narrative and not vice-versa.[5] The negotiation of the tension between teleology and experientiality in an historical narrative thus reveals authorial notions of what history is, or is supposed to be. In the words of Grethlein, "the historian can capitalize on the advantage of hindsight or try to render the past as it was experienced by the historical agents."[6] Historical narratives that (for good reasons) capitalise on hindsight in order to explain the past often struggle to accommodate the lived experiences of the historical agents, including the futures they imagined, feared, or strove to realise.[7] Histor-

---

[5] Grethlein 2013, 22. On the question of truth (and its relation to partiality) in ancient historiography, see Woodman (1988, 70–95) on Cic. *Fam.* 5.12 and *De or.* 2.51–64, with references also to Sall. *Cat.* 4.2–3 and *Hist.* 1.6, and Tac. *Hist.* 1.1.3 and *Ann.* 1.1.3; cf. Marincola 1997, 158–174. See also footnote 10 below on the rhetorical turn in ancient historiography.
[6] Grethlein 2013, 6.
[7] Cf. Trilling 1976/2012, 438: "to minds of a certain sensitivity, 'the long view' is the falsest historical view of all, and indeed the insistence on the length of perspective is intended precisely to overcome sensitivity – seen from sufficient distance, it says, the corpse and the hacked limbs are not so very terrible, and eventually they begin to compose themselves into a 'meaningful pattern'." On the potential of experiential (i.e. anti-deterministic/fatalistic) historiography to 'resurrect' the past, see Ricoeur 2004, 381–382: "The historian has the opportunity to carry herself in imagination back to a given moment of the past as having been present, and so as having been lived by people of the past as the present of their past and as the present of their future ... People of the past once were, like us, subjects of initiative, of retrospection, and of prospection. The epistemological consequences of this consideration are substantial. Knowing that people of the past formulated expectations, predictions, desires, fears, and projects is to fracture historical determinism by retrospectively reintroducing contingency into history."

ical narratives that focus on the experiences of historical agents, on the other hand, tend to suspend hindsight and thus present the past as more open-ended. To describe the underlying temporal dynamics at play in historiographical texts, Grethlein adopts and adapts Reinhart Koselleck's term 'futures past':

> Besides entwining retrospect with prospect, the term captures the asymmetry between characters and historians – what is still future for the former, is already past for the latter – and signifies the point that regulates the balance between experience and teleology: the stronger the future in a given narrative's 'futures past', the stronger its focus on experience; the more the 'futures past' is treated as past, on the other hand, the more prominent becomes its teleology.[8]

---

[8] Grethlein 2013, 12; cf. Grethlein 2010, 323. See also Aron 1938, 181: "La retrospection crée une illusion de fatalité qui, après coup, confèrent une apparante nécessité à l'issue effective." On the influence of hindsight on ancient and modern claims about the inevitability of the Principate, see Low 2013b and Grethlein 2013, 325–326. Noting the debate on whether historians should exercise or eschew hindsight when attempting to explain the fall of the Republic, Grethlein (reassuringly and somewhat predictably) takes up a position between the trenches (p. 354): "The combination of both [experience and teleology] is crucial to historical explanation: we need to know where history is heading, but also how it got there." On the inevitability (or not) of the fall of the Roman Republic, see Meier 1966, Brunt 1971 and 1988 (esp. pp. 68–92, 240–280), Gruen 1974, Deininger 1980, Bleicken 1995, Welwei 1996, Eder 1996, von Ungern-Sternberg 1998, Morstein-Marx & Rosenstein 2006, Girardet 2007 (cf. Hurlet 2008) and 2017, Jehne 2009, and Hölkeskamp (ed.) 2009, esp. the paper by Walter. As noted by Gildenhard, Gotter, Havener & Hodgson 2019, the conception of history promoted by the imperial regime maintained the impossibility of alternatives and thus entailed a "Destruction of History", that is, (p. 3) "the apparent elimination of contingency from the historical process in the service of power – the transformation of historical time, in other words, from a realm of kaleidoscopic unpredictability with ever-shifting re-configurations, in which, in principle, almost anything is possible and nothing is (entirely) certain, into a realm of necessity that manifests the unfolding of an at least partially predetermined script, which includes the imaginary possibility of history coming to an end altogether." While modern scholars – by ending chronological accounts of Roman history at the Battle of Actium and uncritically adopting the self-descriptions promoted by Augustan culture (e.g. the 'Augustan Age') – long abetted this destruction of history (p. 4–6), more recent scholarly treatments have challenged the claim that the imperial regime was the preordained endpoint of the Roman Republic, not least the articles gathered in Gildenhard et al. (p. 25): "the papers in this volume wrestle with ... the ways in which the *princeps* has managed to smooth over – and smother – the complexities of the historical record"; see esp. Hodgson 2019, 39: "One of the common themes of this book is to take issue with the presumption that the Augustan principate was a solution without an alternative to an inevitable crisis. Whether or not the crisis was inevitable, I aim to show that people did put forward alternatives, if without a great deal of success." For an attempt to write a chronological history of the period 44 BC – AD 14, see Richardson 2012.

The focus of the present investigation is not on the actual experiences of those who lived through the first five years of Tiberius' reign and his (supposed) conflict with Germanicus, but on the ways in which such experiences are portrayed by Tacitus and their effects on the reader of the *Annals*. As noted by Grethlein, the experientiality of historical agents and consequent openness of the past may be recreated through various literary devices, so-called 'side-shadowing' devices. Coined by literary critic Gary Saul Morson for his work on modern fiction, side-shadowing describes the ways in which novelists restore the possibility of possibility in their narratives. In Morson's words, the fundamental lesson of side-shadowing is that

> to understand a moment is to grasp not only what did happen but also what else might have happened. Hypothetical histories shadow actual ones. Some nonactual events enjoy their own kind of reality: the temporal world consists not just of actualities and impossibilities but also of a third, in-between category: real, though unactualized, possibilities.[9]

While the potentially far-reaching interpretive implications of side-shadowing in historiography are immediately apparent, its applicability for historiographical texts is only affirmed when their literariness is accepted.[10] When the historian is recognised as a manufacturer of narrative, her texts are simultaneously burdened with a teleological drive and empowered to creatively challenge it.

In his analysis of Thucydides' *Peloponnesian War*, Grethlein demonstrates that, despite their strong tendency for closure, hindsight, and teleology, ancient historiographical texts do accommodate devices that may restore openness to the past and let the reader – through a momentary suspension of her superior knowledge – re-experience the experiences of historical agents: debates highlight the alternative decisions and futures with which historical agents grappled, introspection reveals expectations, narratorial uncertainty may be used to

---

9 Morson 1998, 602; cf. Morson 1994.
10 Grethlein 2013, 18. On the literariness of ancient historiography, see esp. Wiseman 1979 and 1998 and Woodman 1988; cf. Feldherr 2009, 6–8; Ash 2012, 8–11. The theoretical roots of the so-called 'rhetorical turn' in ancient historiography were formed in the wake of Hayden White's work on the rhetorical elements of historiography. As noted by White 1973, the transformation of past events into narrative entails the construction of a plot. The historian not only chooses which events to include but must also put them together into a coherent whole. This construction of plot is the most obvious act of fictionalisation carried out by the historian, since by it she decides what the events mean: to the events she adds the story (White 1973, esp. 1–42). For an all-out attack on Wiseman, Woodman, and their successors, see Lendon 2009. For more nuanced discussions of the debate between 'traditionalists' and 'rhetorical historians', see Laird 2009 and Marincola 2009, 15.

mimic that of historical agents, the relation of rumours implies other possibilities, 'Beinahe-episodes' (i.e. things that almost happened) suggest that other outcomes were possible, and explicit counterfactuals develop such outcomes. As noted by Grethlein, side-shadowing devices, although fictive, restore an important aspect of the past, namely its experientiality: "The sacrifice of literal truth in a positive sense permits a reference to and 're-presentation' of the openness of the past."[11] The reader both learns about the experience of historical agents and re-experiences them. In this way, side-shadowing devices enable readers to experience the past as the open-ended present that it once was, including its various latent futures.

Roman readers would have been accustomed to think in terms of counterfactuals due to their rhetoricised education, especially their training in the composition of *suasoriae*, *controuersiae*, and *ethopoeia*. They would therefore instinctively have related to the deliberative situations that pervade historiographical texts, had little difficulty 'retrospecting' the inherent openness of such situations, and quickly recognised the possibility that different decisions could have led to different outcomes.[12] It should be stressed, however, that although the reader of an historiographical text faces an openness similar to that of its characters and is, like them, forced to conjecture about the future, she may, unlike them, shift to the teleological perspective at any time. In other words, a complete convergence between reader and character experiences is (normally) precluded by the former's superior knowledge of the past, the implications of which will be discussed in the subsequent analysis.

As demonstrated by Grethlein, the *Annals* as a whole inclines towards experientiality rather than teleology:[13] mimetic devices such as vividness and the

---

[11] Grethlein 2010, 328; cf. Grethlein 2013, 45–8. On the potential of rumours to activate alternative realities, see also Morson 1998, 604. On the rhetorical force of counterfactuals in historiography, see Kożuchowski 2015, esp. p. 339: "Cognitive curiosity is not a standard stimulus for which we employ counterfactuals in everyday life. We do so for emotional reasons (Olson, Roese, and Deibert 1996), such as the need to reconsider the causes of our failures and achievements, or to reassure ourselves that the choices we made were right. ... Counterfactuals are rhetorical formulas that allow us to emphasize the importance of certain decisions, developments, and events from the past by stressing their consequences which never materialized, but nevertheless seem evident to us."

[12] On Roman education and rhetoric, see Clark 1957, Kennedy 1972, Bonner 1977, and Bloomer 1997; cf. Grethlein (2013, 22) on *futurum fuisse*. See also Morson 1998, 603: "In its inclusion of contrary-to-fact expressions and tenses, our language displays an appreciation of potentialities in excess of actualities – of the surplus of temporalities."

[13] Grethlein 2013, 168–171. Grethlein analyses Germanicus' visit to the Teutoburg Forest (pp. 133–140), Germanicus' death (pp. 140–154), and the Pisonian conspiracy (pp. 156–167).

frequent overlap between narratorial and character uncertainty allow for a convergence of reader and character experiences, the annalistic framework precludes the use of narrative units which stretch over several years (although, as noted by Grethlein, the annalistic format is never rigidly imposed and becomes increasingly flexible in the Claudian and Neronian books) and lets the reader experiences events 'with' the characters, prolepses tend to be vague about what exactly will happen in the future (and thus might even facilitate a convergence of reader and character experiences), and authorial interventions stress both the qualitative similarity between past and present (cf. 3.55.5 on the discussion of the development of luxury) and the role of coincidence as an historical force (cf. 3.18.4 on the future succession of Claudius).[14] An exhaustive identification of all possible side-shadowing devices in the *Annals* would be a momentous undertaking, as even a quick glance at books 1–2 reveals a multitude of passages where openness is restored to the past. While fully-fledged counterfactuals are absent, 'Beinahe-episodes', rumours, narratorial uncertainty, debates, and moments of introspection feature prominently.[15]

A final point calls for attention before we proceed to the analysis proper. While the textual presence of side-shadowing devices may be demonstrated and a consequent awakening of readerly curiosity presumed, their precise effects on the narrative and the reader's experience thereof are difficult to determine. Morson appears to assume that the alternative realities summoned by side-shadowing automatically reveal inevitability to be an illusion and thus subvert

---

14 Grethlein 2013, 167–177; cf. Griffin 2009, 182–183. For an example of how the annalistic format might leave things 'hanging', see the division of the war against Tacfarinas into three different books (2.52, 3.20–1, 73–74, 4.23–26); cf. Devillers 1991. On the tension between *fatum* (fate) and *fortuna* (fortune) in Tacitus, see Kroymann 1952; Walker 1952, 244–254; Syme 1958, 521–527; Luce 1986/2012; Davies 2004, 166, 171–176; Griffin 2009, 168–172; Shannon 2014, 276–277; Woodman 2016, 181–183; Shannon-Henderson 2019, 20–22.

15 For 'Beinahe-episodes', see e.g. Fabius Maximus telling his wife about Augustus' visit to Agrippa Postumus (1.5.1–2), the Roman army under Caecina almost re-enacting the Varian disaster (1.61–68), Germanicus being recalled by Tiberius when at the point of defeating the Germani (2.26.2–5), Maroboduus retreating after having fought Arminius to a draw (2.46.4–5), and Germanicus saving Piso's life at sea (2.55.3). On how the report of rumours about Germanicus' death and narratorial uncertainty regarding their validity allow for multiple pasts to coexist, see Grethlein 2013, 154. For debates, see e.g. 1.4.2–5 on Augustus' possible successors, 1.17–9 between Junius Blaesus and his mutinous soldiers, 1.29.3 on how to suppress the mutiny in Pannonia, and 1.36 on how to suppress the mutiny in Germania. For moments of introspection, see e.g. Tiberius' reasons for pretending reluctance in assuming power at 1.7.6–7, Augustus' thoughts on his possible successors at 1.13.2, and reactions to the mutinies in Pannonia and Germania among the Roman people and Tiberius at 1.46–7.

the teleology of the narrative.¹⁶ This, however, appears not to be the case. Firstly, the most famous example of a counterfactual thought experiment in Roman historiography, Livy's Alexander-digression, explicitly and elaborately denies that Rome's rise could have been prevented even if the Macedonian king had brought his army to Italy (Livy 9.17–19). With the alternative historical development summoned only to be rejected, teleology is confirmed rather than challenged. Secondly, since alternative futures are usually only implicitly and cursorily acknowledged in the *Annals*, it is difficult to see if any of them are (consistently) supported by whatever hints may be uncovered from the text.

Grethlein's discussion of side-shadowing in the account of the Pisonian conspiracy in *Annals* 15 illustrates the combined force of these two points. Alternative futures are repeatedly imagined by Tacitus and the conspirators: Subrius Flavus conceives of an impulse to kill Nero on stage or in the city (15.50.4), Epicharis fails to draw the marines into the conspiracy (15.51.1–3), the conspirators consider killing Nero in Piso's villa (15.52.1), Piso – allegedly – fears that the people might bestow power on L. Silanus or Atticus Vestinus (15.52.2–3), the conspirators envisage the murder in detail (15.53.1–3), Flavius Scaevinus almost manages to conceal the conspiracy when defending himself (15.55.2–4), and Piso refuses to test the loyalty of the soldiers or speak to the people in a final attempt to salvage the situation (15.59). In Grethlein's analysis, the presence of these alternative paths not only adds suspense to the narrative and restores presentness to the past, but also illustrates the conspiracy's political insignificance:

> the dense web of alternative scenarios throws into relief the fact that the Pisonian Conspiracy did not offer a true alternative. The multiple possible developments entertained by Tacitus contrast with the absence of a real political alternative and thereby intimate that, questionable as it is, the principate may have become the only viable political system.¹⁷

Grethlein thus concludes that Tacitus' detailed narration of the conspirators' various (unrealised) plans – rather than implying that things could have gone differently – highlights the political insignificance and inevitable failure of the conspiracy to offer a true alternative to Nero's rule.¹⁸ In the following analysis,

---

16 Morson 1998, 601.
17 Grethlein 2013, 159. On the (possible) significance(s) of the Pisonian conspiracy, see also Ash 2018, 21–22.
18 Cf. O'Gorman 2006a on the virtual (i.e. side-shadowed) history of the Pisonian dynasty. In O'Gorman's analysis, the recurring references to possible Pisonian pretenders in the *Annals* suggest that, while the imperial name and family might have differed, the Principate as a

then, I shall not assume that side-shadowing automatically subverts teleology, but rather explore the various ways in which it plays with readerly expectations of teleology and its concomitant potential to elicit specific emotional responses. More specifically, I shall demonstrate how the restoration of openness to the past in the treatment of Germanicus in *Annals* 1–2 induces in the reader – especially a contemporary Roman reader – a mixture of hopelessness, helplessness, and regret.[19]

2 Germanicus and the Civil War that Never Was

In this part I will investigate how side-shadowing effects are created in the treatment of the conflict between Tiberius and Germanicus in *Annals* 1–2. I will (a) demonstrate how the conflict is construed as an extension of the civil wars of the late Republic, (b) highlight the opposition between other peoples' hopes that Germanicus will challenge Tiberius and his own (increasingly remarkable) refusal to do so, and (c) discuss reader and character experiences of these hopes. But first some words on Tacitus' Germanicus.

As noted by Kraus, "the Tacitean portrait of Germanicus is famously ambivalent."[20] He is not only courageous and eminently likeable but also, at times, hopelessly and ridiculously incompetent. In Pelling's analysis, Germanicus functions (for better and worse) as a contrast to Tiberius: young, affable, accessible, and popular among all classes of society, but also impetuous, theatrical, careless, and quick to despair. While I do not intend to challenge Pelling's well-argued claim that Germanicus' failure arises from his being out of place – "brilliantly anachronistic" – in the world of the Principate,[21] I wish to turn attention

---

system of government was inevitable. For the claim that Tacitus was unable to imagine an alternative to the Principate, see Giua 2014, 53.

[19] On the capacity of side-shadowing to induce regret, see Morson 1998, 600.

[20] Kraus 2009, 110; cf. Shotter 1968; Ross 1973; Williams 1989, 141–146; Pelling 1993; Pigoń 2008; Williams 2009; Manolaraki/Augoustakis 2012. On Germanicus as both a reader of traces of the past and an image of the past read by others, see O'Gorman 2000, 46–69.

[21] Pelling 1993, 78; cf. O'Gorman 2000, 46–47. As noted by Baxter 1972 and Bews 1972–3, there is a multitude of Vergilian intertexts in Tacitus' treatment of Germanicus. In Baxter's (admittedly incomplete; cf. Woodman 2009 on Verg. *G.* 3.544–5, Vell. Pat. 129.3, and Tac. *Ann.* 2.45.3) analysis, 47 of the 61 Vergilian intertexts in *Annals* 1–2 occur when Germanicus is involved. However, a closer look at these occurrences reveals that 32 of them are gathered in treatments of Germanicus' Germanic campaigns, with 4 during the mutiny, 3 during his eastern travels,

to a more tangible cause of his failure, the appreciation of which will allow for a more nuanced discussion of his role in, and readerly responses to, *Annals* 1–2: his consistent refusal to challenge Tiberius. In contrast to his energetic leadership while on campaign in Germania, Germanicus is remarkably and frustratingly passive both when assigned the task of suppressing a mutiny in the empire's most powerful army and when faced with the increasingly aggressive insubordination of a dangerous political rival appointed by the emperor.[22] In the end, I believe, the appeal to anachronism as an explanation of Germanicus' failure to (at least try to) change the course of history risks obscuring the hope that he personified and becoming an apology for his passivity. By suggesting that he was somehow innately unable to act differently, it divests him of his responsibility and lets him off the hook too easily, too comfortably.

2.1 The (civil) conflict between Germanicus and Tiberius

The conflict between Tiberius and Germanicus, which takes the form of an ever-threatening but never-realised civil war, is a recurrent theme in *Annals* 1–2. It attaches itself seamlessly onto the civil war that ended the Republic and established Augustus' one-man rule, which is summarily narrated a staggering four times in the first ten chapters of Book 1: twice by Tacitus' authorial persona (1.1.1, 1.2.1), once by those who praise Augustus (1.9.3–5), and once by his critics (1.10.1–4). The latter's designation of his celebrated imperial peace as 'bloody' (*pacem ... cruentam*, 1.10.4) is largely corroborated by the subsequent narrative, in which the Principate increasingly resembles an institutionalised form of civil conflict.[23] Not only does Tiberius' rule claim Roman blood from the very outset (cf. the murder of Agrippa Postumus at 1.6.1), it is characterised by a latent conflict between the emperor and Germanicus, his nephew and adopted son.[24]

---

and 3 in his death scene. In other words, the epic (and potentially archaising) language used by Tacitus to portray Germanicus is significantly less dominant when he interacts with Romans.

22 Cf. Pigoń 2008, who notes the contrast between Germanicus' vigorous activity during the Germanic campaign and his passivity and dependence on others during the mutiny.

23 Sailor 2008, 190; cf. Christ 1978, 482; Woodman 1988, 186–190; 1992/1998; Martin/ Woodman 1989, 226–227; Sage 1991, 3397–8; Ash 1999, 2009; 2018, 10–11, 27; O'Gorman 2000, 20–45; Kraus 2009, 105; Damon 2010; Low 2013a, 11–12, 28–31, 55, 132–133, 233–275; Strunk 2017, 62–67. On how Tacitus implies that the civil war of the late Republic continues into Augustus' Principate, see Keitel 1984, 312–317, 325; cf. Low 2013a, 92–93.

24 Cf. Kraus 2009, 105; see also Low 2013a, 11–12, 132–133.

The civil nature of the conflict is strengthened by several factors. Firstly, Germanicus not only has Augustus and Mark Antony as great-uncle and grandfather respectively (2.53.2), the two major players in the final stage of the civil war that ended the Republic, he is also the son of the allegedly republican sympathiser Drusus the Elder (see below on 1.33.1–2). Secondly, the family ties between Tiberius and Germanicus are consistently stressed, intra-familial conflict being a common metaphor of civil war in Roman literature: Germanicus is hated by his uncle Tiberius (*patruus*, 1.33.1) and grandmother Livia (*auia*, 1.33.1), yet remains on affectionate terms with his paternal cousin and brother-through-adoption Drusus the Younger (*frater*, 2.42.6; cf. 1.76.3, 2.26.4, 2.42.6), despite the family intrigues surrounding them and the popular fear that these two young men might tear the state apart (1.4.5).[25] Thirdly, like the civil war that brought an end to the Republic, the conflict between Tiberius and Germanicus is widely seen as a struggle between freedom and servitude: while Tiberius' succession is greeted with a rush into servitude by all classes of Roman society (1.7.1), to the fate of Germanicus is tied a hope of a restoration of freedom (see below). Moreover, although the conflict is fought mostly in the shadows (and mostly by Tiberius), the possibility of a fully-fledged civil war is noted already at 1.3.5, when the aging Augustus puts Germanicus in charge of eight legions in Germania and orders Tiberius to adopt him. Upon Augustus' death at 1.7.6, Tiberius' feigned reluctance to assume power in the senate is caused by his fear that Germanicus might use his formidable army and popular support to mount a challenge against him. The potentially cataclysmic consequences of this latent civil conflict are felt most strongly in the account of the mutiny among the legions stationed in Germania, which is dominated by civil war terminology and imagery throughout.[26] It is to this account that I now turn.

---

25 For *frater* in the sense paternal cousin, see Cic. *Fin.* 5.1, *Att.* 12.7.1, Suet. *Calig.* 15.2, Ov. *Her.* 8.28. Alternatively, Germanicus and Drusus might be designated *fratres* because Germanicus was adopted by Drusus' father, Tiberius. War between brothers is one of the most frequently recurring civil war motifs in Roman literature: see e.g. Verg. *G.* 2.495–510, *Aen.* 2.291–295, Prop. 1.7.1–2, Hor. *Epod.* 7, Livy 1.7, Luc. 1.95, Tac. *Hist.* 3.51; cf. Wiseman 1995, 143–144; Bannon 1997, 149–188.
26 Cf. *ciuilium armorum* at 1.49.1, *furor* (cf. Jal 1963, 422: "un véritable synonyme de *bellum ciuile*") at 1.49.3, *furens* at 1.35.5, 1.40.2, 1.42.1, *uaecors/uaecordia* at 1.32.1, 1.39.2 (cf. Sallust's portrait of Catiline at *Cat.* 15.5), and *rabies* at 1.31.3, 1.39.6; cf. Woodman 2006 and Ash 2009, 90. Low (2013a, 36–75) reveals intertexts with the civil wars of the late Republic and AD 68/69. On the potential of the mutiny to unleash another destructive civil war, see O'Gorman 2000, 48.

2.2 The undefined and unrealised *spes Germanici*

The accounts of the 14 AD mutinies among the legions in Pannonia (1.16–30) and Germania (1.31–52) constitute the first major blocks of narrative in the *Annals*. The mutinies break out when news of Augustus' death and Tiberius' succession reach the soldiers. While order is re-established fairly quickly in Pannonia by Drusus the Younger, Germanicus struggles to suppress the mutiny among the legions in Germania. Matters are complicated not only by the greater strength of the Germanic legions, but also by their hope that Germanicus will lead them in a bid for the purple (1.31.1): "The German legions were disrupted – all the more violently [than the Pannonian legions], given their greater numbers, and with high hopes (*magna spe*) that Germanicus Caesar would be unable to suffer the command of another and would entrust himself to the legions, who would handle everything by their own force."[27] When Germanicus appears on the scene to restore order, the soldiers vocally express their readiness to follow him against Tiberius (see below on 1.35.3). Between these two expressions of military support, the reader is presented with the following description of Germanicus' popularity among the people and their hopes in him (1.33.1–2):

> being himself [Germanicus] the offspring of Drusus (Tiberius's brother) and the grandson of Augusta, but tense from his uncle's and grandmother's concealed hatred of him, their reasons for which were all the more bitter because unjust. (The memory of Drusus among the Roman people was considerable, and it was believed that, if he had been in charge of affairs, he would have given them back their freedom. Hence goodwill towards Germanicus, and the same hope. For the young man had the instinct of an ordinary citizen and a remarkable affability quite different from Tiberius' conversation and look, arrogant and dark as they were).
>
> ipse Druso fratre Tiberii genitus, Augustae nepos, sed anxius occultis in se patrui auiaeque odiis, quorum causae acriores quia iniquae. quippe Drusi magna apud populum Romanum memoria, credebaturque, si rerum poti<t>us foret, libertatem redditurus; unde in Germanicum fauor et spes eadem. nam iuueni ciuile ingenium, mira comitas et diuersa a Tiberii sermone uultu, adrogantibus et obscuris.

Rather than an objective description of Germanicus' character and aims, the passage offers a glimpse of how he was perceived by others: hated by his uncle Tiberius and grandmother Livia, and ascribed republican sympathies by the Roman people. In fact, what starts out as a seemingly objective character sketch

---

[27] All translations of the *Annals* are from Woodman 2004; text from Heubner 1994. On the soldiers' desire to rally behind Germanicus and carry him to power, see Pelling 1993, 68–69.

(with mention of ancestors and family relationships) quickly becomes focalised through the people, whose hope that he will restore freedom appears to colour their interpretation of his behaviour and the significance they attach to his ancestry. The memory of his father Drusus as a potential liberator is explicitly noted as the source wherefrom (*unde*) the same goodwill and hope (*fauor et spes eadem*) arose towards Germanicus.[28] The mention of his citizenlike instincts and remarkable affability is then attached to the line of reasoning, through the explanatory conjunction 'for' (*nam*), almost as a wishful confirmation of its validity: (i) Germanicus is Drusus' son, (ii) Drusus would have restored freedom, (iii) doesn't Germanicus exhibit some traits that might suggest that he too would restore freedom? With this popular focalisation established, we can recognise that, while the attribution of citizenlike instincts and remarkable affability to Germanicus is not necessarily mistaken, the significance attached to them (i.e. proof of republican sympathies and a desire to restore freedom) is clearly blown out of proportion: while undoubtedly positive attributes, they hardly suggest a desire on the part of Germanicus to uproot the Principate and jeopardise his own expected succession.[29] The popular focalisation is further underlined by the contrast with Tiberius' unpleasant disposition at the end of the passage. The focus on the emperor's arrogant and dark demeanour (conversation and look) situates the reader as a contemporary listener-observer, whose limited auditory and visual access to the imperial family constrains her ability to form reliable hypotheses about what is really going on at court. As will be discussed in more detail in the next section, however, a complete convergence between reader and character experiences is precluded by the reader's superior knowledge of the past.

In order to divulge insights into Germanicus' own ideas about himself, his role, and his future, the passage must be contextualised within the surrounding narrative, that is, the soldiers' explicit readiness to follow him against Tiberius and his own refusal to lead them. In fact, contrary to the narratologically prepared next step, that Germanicus – notified that Rome's strongest army wishes to put him on the throne and aware that he is hated by Tiberius and Livia –

---

[28] Drusus is said to have proposed to Tiberius that they should compel Augustus to reinstate the Republic (Suet. *Tib.* 50.1; cf. Levick 1999, 19). Rumours claimed that he was poisoned by Augustus because of his republican sympathies (Suet. *Claud.* 1.4–5). His death, which occasioned a *Consolatio ad Liuiam*, was chosen by Livy as the endpoint of his 137-book history of Rome. On Roman beliefs in the inheritance of family traits, see Roller 2018, 54–55 (with further bibliography) and 125–132.

[29] For the argument that the people's enthusiasm for Germanicus is misguided, see Edelmaier 1964, 148–173; Ross 1973; cf. Pelling 1993, 64–67.

might at least assess the pros and cons of revolt, he reacts to the chaotic (and potentially dramatically career-enhancing) situation by redoubling his loyalty to the emperor (1.34.1): "Yet, the closer Germanicus now was to that highest of all hopes (*summae spei*), the more emphatically did he strive on Tiberius' behalf." He sets off hurriedly to the camp and delivers a speech in praise of Tiberius. Undismayed, the soldiers again express their willingness to follow him in a bid for the purple, adding to their complaints about the harshness of military discipline and their demand to be paid the money promised by Augustus (1.35.3) "words of auspicious omen for Germanicus; and, if he wanted the command, they demonstrated their readiness." Germanicus, however, replies that he would rather take his own life than commit such an outrage (1.35.4–5). The real indication of Germanicus' nature, then, is his decision *not* to challenge Tiberius, which is all the more extraordinary when seen in the light of his popularity among the soldiers and his awareness of the hatred with which he is viewed by the emperor. Even though he has both a reasonable cause to rebel and Rome' most powerful army within his grasp, he opts out. Germanicus' loyalty to Tiberius despite his awareness of the emperor's animosity towards him is stressed again when he omits mention of himself on his Germanic victory monument in order not to arouse resentment (2.22.1) and when he complies with a request to return from Germania, (2.26.5) "although his understanding was that those [Tiberius' reasons] were fabrications and that through resentment he was being dragged away from the honor already won." In spite of his consistent and extraordinary loyalty, however, the emperor continues to distrust his adopted son.[30]

When Germanicus is despatched to settle matters in the east, Tiberius simultaneously appoints Cn. Piso as governor of Syria. Although Tacitus refrains from stating as a certainty that Tiberius told Piso to oppose his adopted son, he does note that Piso himself did not (2.43.4) "have any doubt that he had been

---

30 Tiberius' distrust is well-illustrated by his mixed reaction when news of Germanicus' suppression of the mutiny in Germania reaches Rome: delight that military discipline has been restored but concern about his adopted son's increased goodwill among the soldiers. In the subsequent senate meeting, Tiberius attempts to diminish Germanicus' accomplishments by highlighting instead those of his own son, Drusus (1.52); cf. Pelling 1993, 71. See also his disapproval of Germanicus' visit to the battlefield where Varus was defeated by the Germani (1.62.2), his distrust of the motives of Germanicus' wife Agrippina the Elder as she prevents the dismantling of a bridge across the Rhine and welcomes the Roman soldiers back into Gaul (1.69), his use of disturbances in the east as a pretext to remove Germanicus from his legions in Germania (2.5.1; finally achieved at 2.26.2–5), and his rumoured instructions to Cn. Piso to oppose Germanicus in Syria (2.43.4).

selected for installation in Syria to curb Germanicus' hopes (*ad spes Germanici coercendas*)". The phrase illustrates not only the lack of knowledge about what Tiberius might or might not have said to Piso, but also succinctly restates both the immensity and the vagueness of the hopes attached to Germanicus.[31] While the despatch of an important nobleman such as Piso and the seriousness with which he embraces his task suggest a belief that Germanicus' hopes are of a substantial (and dangerous) nature, they are left wholly unspecified. Not only Piso and the Roman people but also the reader is left to conjecture what or indeed whose these hopes are: the *spes Germanici* appear to have taken on a life of their own to the point that Piso can hardly know if he is supposed to oppose Germanicus' own hopes (subjective genitive) or the hopes others had in him (objective genitive). While the circumstances of Piso's mission are left ambiguous, the absurdity of ascribing rebellious designs to Germanicus is immediately made clear. Although the imperial court divides itself into factions supporting Germanicus and Drusus, Tiberius' son, respectively, (2.43.6) "the brothers were exceptionally affectionate, and unshaken by the conflicts of their kin." The stress on Germanicus' innocence at the very moment when his end draws near not only intensifies the perception of Tiberius as paranoid and arouses pity for Germanicus' impending death, but also underlines yet again the implausibility that he would ever try to live up to the hopes attached to him by the soldiers and people.

Germanicus' actions in the east reaffirm both his potential danger and his unswerving loyalty to Tiberius, his opportunities to change the course of his story as well as his consistent refusal to do so. His symbolic visit to the civil war battlefield of Actium and his trip to the key imperial province of Egypt evoke his origins in and capability to carry out civil war respectively. When he decides to visit Actium and pay his respects to his ancestors while his fleet is being repaired, the narrator intervenes to remind the reader that Augustus had been his great-uncle and Mark Antony his grandfather (2.53.2).[32] When Tiberius rebukes him for entering Egypt, the narrator again intervenes to point out that Augustus had expressly forbidden senators and illustrious equestrians to enter the province without permission in order to prevent a potential challenger from taking control of Rome's food supply.[33] As noted from the outset, however, Germani-

---

[31] Cf. Grethlein 2013, 143.
[32] On Germanicus' visit to Actium, see O'Gorman 2000, 62–69.
[33] The historical authenticity of the hopes placed in Germanicus is hinted at in one of the 'Oxyrhyncus papyri' (*P. Oxy* 2435), whose recording of a speech that he delivered in Alexandria notes also the crowd's emotional interruptions. Their cries of "Good luck!" and "Live on, a

cus' interest in Egypt arises not from its strategic importance but from its history and culture. While Tiberius looks on anxiously as a potential challenger enters Egypt and tampers with the prices of crops, to Germanicus these public matters are merely pretexts for sightseeing on the Nile (2.59–61). In addition to stressing the unlikelihood of Germanicus planning a revolt, then, these passages betray either remarkable carelessness or an inability to fully grasp the danger of being considered the emperor's rival.[34]

Germanicus' business in the east presents him with several opportunities to confront Cn. Piso, at whose hands he will later allegedly be murdered (2.71–2).[35] Not only does he save Piso from shipwreck (2.55.3), he thrice declines to take action against him despite his blatantly threatening transgressions: stirring up soldiers and provincials (2.55.4–6), refusing to obey orders (2.57.1–3), and throwing insults during a dinner party (2.57.4). While the opportunities for alternative action and concomitantly alternative futures are constantly stressed, Germanicus' refusal to act is underlined most clearly when Piso and his wife Plancina successfully stir up the soldiers stationed in Syria, (2.55.6) "because there had spread a concealed rumour that such developments were not contrary to the commander's will. All this was known to Germanicus, but turning his attention to the Armenians was a more immediate concern."[36] The reader is reminded both of Germanicus' knowledge that Piso is causing trouble and of his awareness that Tiberius ('the commander') might be supporting him. While the relation of the rumour does not explicitly incriminate the emperor, it rekindles in the reader's mind the earlier mention – made in the authorial voice – of Germanicus' anxiety about "his uncle's and grandmother's concealed hatred of him" (see above on 1.33.1). This awareness of the emperor's hatred and his consequent anxiety haunt (our reading of) Germanicus until his death, adding further poignancy to his refusal to act.

---

longer life!" sound somewhat ominous from a position of hindsight. On the papyrus, see Sherk 1988, 60. On the genuineness of the threat posed by Germanicus (e.g. the parallels between his actions and those of Piso and Sejanus), see Pelling 1993, 71–72.
34 Cf. Pelling 1993, 72; Kraus 2009, 111–112; Low 2013a, 43–45.
35 Cf. Sailor 2019, 104. On how narratorial uncertainty (including the transmission of rumours and suspicions) about how Germanicus died and who might have caused his death mimics that of and aligns the reader with the historical agents, see Grethlein 2013, 140–156; cf. Griffin 2009, 176: "[rumours] are facts, if not about the state of affairs, then about the state of mind of those affected by them." On the ambiguity of Piso's character as both enemy of Germanicus and champion of freedom, see Williams 1989, 146; Pelling 1993, 83–84; Low 2013a, 97.
36 Cf. Grethlein 2013, 143–144.

Germanicus' own aspirations remain an enigma even after his death.[37] When he finally addresses "my hopes" in his deathbed speech to his friends, he leaves their substance unspecified and the identity of those who entertain them ambiguous (2.71.2): "Anyone who was moved by my hopes (*spes meae*),[38] by kindred blood, even by resentments toward me in my lifetime – they will shed tears that a once flourishing survivor of so many wars has fallen to womanly foul play." In this way, Germanicus allows his listeners (and Tacitus' readers) to draw their own conclusions. Neither those who imagined him a champion of freedom nor those who wished for him to become emperor need restrain their pity or renounce their anger at his alleged murder. Clarification would only risk alienating possible avengers. It is, yet again, the potential effect of the hopes rather than their exact nature which takes centre stage.

After Germanicus' death, the reader is presented with the reactions (i) at the funeral ceremony in Syria, (ii) when news of his faltering health and (soon after) death reach Rome, and (iii) at the funeral ceremony in Rome.[39] At the funeral ceremony in Syria, the talk among the attendees includes a favourable comparison with Alexander the Great, which leads to an explicit counterfactual (2.73.3): "If he had been the sole arbiter of affairs, they said, with royal prerogative and name (*quod si solus arbiter rerum, si iure et nomine regio fuisset*), he would have achieved military glory more readily, just as he excelled in clemency, restraint, and the other good qualities." Germanicus is seen as a would-be king rather than a would-be liberator, as underlined by the comparison with Alexander the Great and the mention of "royal prerogative and name". After Piso's unsuccessful attempt to take control of Syria (2.74–81), the scene switches to Rome, where news of Germanicus' faltering health cause pain and anger (*dolor ira*, 2.82.1) among the people. Claiming that this had been reason for Germanicus' despatch to the east, they recall that his father Drusus (another potential liberator) had also died under mysterious circumstances (2.82.2): "Their elders had spoken altogether truly about Drusus: rulers were prone to be displeased with citizen-

---

37 Although Germanicus remains curiously and pointedly vague about the nature of his own hopes throughout the text, he does seem to cultivate his relationship with this particular 'divine quality' (cf. Clark 2007), as witnessed in his consecration of a shrine to Hope at 2.49.2; cf. O'Gorman 2000, 48.
38 The possessive pronoun *meae* may be understood both/either subjectively (as in Woodman's translation: "my hopes") and/or objectively, in the sense "hopes in me (entertained by others)"; for the latter use of the possessive pronoun, see Kühner/Stegmann 1976, 599 (§ 116.2.5); cf. Menge 1960, 54; Georges & Georges 1976, *s. v. 'meus'* and *'tuus'*.
39 Cf. Pelling 1993, 78. On Tiberius' (lacklustre) mourning behaviour, see Vekselius Forthcoming.

like instincts in their sons, and they had been cut off only because they had aspired to incorporate the Roman people under equal rights, with freedom restored." The people in Rome thus reaffirm their belief that Germanicus, like Drusus, had intended to supervise a restoration of the Republic. Upon news of his death, they react with groans and sorrow (*gemitus ... maerebant*, 2.82.3), and, after a rumour about his recovery has been quashed and his death is finally confirmed, their pain returns sharper than before (*acrius doluit*, 2.82.5). At the beginning of *Annals* 3, Germanicus' widow Agrippina the Elder returns to Rome with his ashes, which are laid to rest in the mausoleum of the Julio-Claudian family (3.4.1): "The day ... was sometimes desolate in its silence, sometimes restless with sobbing (*ploratibus*). The streets of the City were full, torches shining out across the Plain of Mars. There soldiers with arms, magistrates without insignia, and the people in their tribes kept shouting that the state had collapsed and no vestige of hope remained (*nihil spei reliquum clamitabant*)." Seemingly oblivious to the fact that the hopes they had pinned on him were not the same, soldiers, magistrates, and people unanimously lament their lost saviour and share a sensation of hopelessness.[40]

2.3 Reader and character experience of the *spes Germanici*

At the end of his analysis of experientiality and teleology in the *Annals*, Grethlein explores how the gap between Tacitus and his characters is reduced by the introduction of a future historiographical text as a telos in the narrative.[41] Through an analysis of the trial of the historian Cremutius Cordus (4.32–3), he demonstrates that the characters are aware of their future inclusion in historiographical works and adjust their actions correspondingly. In this way, future historians – or, at least, their spectres – become historical agents in the narrative of the past: "The embedding of future historiographic records as telos in the world of the action establishes a bridge between the historian and the historical agents."[42] At the end of the current section, I will suggest that the readers too ought to be welcomed into the story-world as future historical characters, char-

---

[40] On the *spes Germanici*, including their vagueness, see also O'Gorman 2000, 47–49. As noted by O'Gorman, the various hopes attached to Germanicus, like his family – his grandfather Mark Antony (at least according to Augustan propaganda) a would-be king in the eastern mould, his great-uncle Augustus a civil warlord turned princeps, his father Drusus a republican, his son Caligula and grandson Nero autocratic emperors –, span the political spectrum.
[41] Grethlein 2013, 172–179.
[42] Grethlein 2013, 177.

acters who – unlike those of the past – still have the opportunity to act and who will be judged by subsequent generations if they do not.

On a fundamental level, the mention of the *spes Germanici*, the hopes placed in Germanicus by others, allows the reader to access the minds and desired futures of the various characters: the soldiers wish for a warlord who can give them swifter discharge, higher pay, lighter burdens, more protection from their superiors, and the opportunity to win rewards (1.31.4, 1.35.1–3; cf. 1.16.1); the people hope for a republican liberator who will restore their freedom (1.33.2, 2.82.1); the emperor fears the revolt of a rival (1.7.6, 1.52.1); and Germanicus himself appears to await – with a hopefulness tinted by trepidation (cf. especially his awareness of Tiberius' and Livia's hatred of him at 1.33.1) – the emperor's death and his own succession. While none of these futures come to pass, the descriptions of their existence and influence on events provide the reader with insights into the experiences of a wide range of historical agents.

The reader's superior knowledge of the past means that reader and character experiences remain – at least until Germanicus' death – unaligned. The reader cannot share the hopefulness of the Roman soldiers (1.31.1) or the Roman people (1.33.2) when they imagine Germanicus as either a civil warlord who will increase military pay or a liberator who will restore civic freedom. What for the characters are still actual hopes (in an open future) are for the reader already unrealised hopes (in a closed past): she knows that they will not be fulfilled. The characters' experiences are witnessed but not re-experienced by the reader, whose concomitant emotional response is coloured by her knowledge of Germanicus' subsequent death and the suspicious circumstances surrounding it. She is not only prevented from sharing their emotions of hope, but effectively positioned as a helpless spectator to the imminent destruction of these hopes. Where the characters feel a mixture of hope and dread, the reader thus experiences hopelessness and helplessness, as well as pity for the nescient characters and – with the Roman state plunging deeper into servitude after Germanicus' death – mounting regret that no action was taken to save the young prince.[43]

---

[43] On the meaning of regret (*paenitentia*) and a taxonomy of its uses in ancient Rome, see Kaster 2005, 66–83. As noted by Kaster, the Romans – or, at least, Aulus Gellius (17.1.9) – connected *paenitentia* with *paene* ('almost') and *paenuria* ('shortfall'). Kaster's definition of the emotion is worth quoting in full (p. 68): "If I say *me paenitet*, I mean that I feel not only a *displeasure* but also a *desire*, a more or less marked contrafactual urge: the thought is not simply 'I am dissatisfied that X' but rather 'I am dissatisfied that X rather than Y – and I would undo the state of affairs if only I could'. Just because the emotion proceeds from a relative assessment, it always carries with it the awareness of – and the desire for – some preferred alternative: that is how *paenitet* differs from the simple displeasure of *non placet*. The desire is integral

The relationship between nescient characters and an omniscient audience (and the particular experiential dissonance produced by this relationship) in historiography mirrors that of other kinds of ancient literature in which the finale is known in advance by the audience, most notably epic and tragic poetry.[44] Since Tacitus' treatment of Germanicus has more in common with the latter – especially due to the lack of a clearly designated and readerly approved telos by which otherwise meaningless events can be justified (but note also the intra-familial nature of the conflict with Tiberius) –, I will here focus on tragedy.[45] My observations should not be seen as an untimely resurrection of 'tragic history' as a term used to distinguish between emotional-rhetorical and rational-scientific historiography,[46] but rather as an acknowledgment of the similarity between the audience-character relationship in *Annals* 1–2 and tragic plays and

---

to the structure of the thought; to put it another way, if there were no desire, no wish to undo the gap between the 'is' and the 'should be', there would simply *be* no distress."

44 On the common roots of epic poetry and historiography in tragedy, see Walbank 1960. On the capability of both tragic and narrative texts to facilitate a convergence between audience and character experiences through *energeia*, i.e. vivid description, see Levene 1997/2012, 212–213.

45 Epic poems usually have a more clearly designated and divinely sanctioned telos. In Vergil's *Aeneid* the suicide of Dido and the murder of Pallas, while heart-breaking, derive meaning from their positions within a narrative that points towards the Augustan present. The audience, while encouraged to contemplate the cost of empire, can at least take solace in this overarching telos. The death of Germanicus, on the other hand, is meaningless. It plays no role in the creation of something greater. On the specifically tragic connotations of intra-familial conflict, see Hall 2010, 3. For an illustration of the difficulty (if not impossibility) of upholding a strict distinction between tragic and epic characteristics, see Manolaraki/Augoustakis 2012 on Germanicus as a tragic hero in the mould of Silius Italicus' (epic) Hannibal. The tragic potential of Germanicus' life was exploited by the French writer Antoine-Vincent Arnault in his 1816 tragedy 'Germanicus'.

46 For a rejection of the usefulness of the term 'tragic history', see Marincola 2003, 298–299. Marincola (pp. 285–288) demonstrates that the study of emotions in ancient historiography was long warped by (i) simplistic readings of Aristotle's identification of pity and fear as the primary tragic emotions at *Poet.* 6.1449b.27–8 and Polybius' attack on his historiographical colleague Phylarchus for arousing inappropriate emotions in his readers at 2.56.3–13 and (ii) the concomitant postulation of a 'tragic school' of ancient historiography; cf. Walbank (1972, 34–40) and Fornara (1983, 120–34). On the arousal of pity and fear in ancient historiography in general and the specific arousal of pity in Tacitus' account of the fall of Vitellius (*Hist.* 3.36–86), see Levene 1997/2012. As noted by Marincola (pp. 301–302, 314), ancient historiography *qua* rhetoric is intimately connected with the arousal of appropriate emotions – and not only pity and fear – for the purpose of education and persuasion. His wilfully unsystematic survey (pp. 302–314) touches on emulation, friendliness, enmity, hatred, anger, disgust, weariness, grief, impatience, satiety, joy, and sadness.

as a way to shed light on the readerly experience of Tacitus' treatment of Germanicus. Given that tragic plots were drawn primarily from a stock of well-known mythical and historical stories, the tragic spectator (like the historiographical reader) would normally possess a knowledge of the outcome denied to the characters of the play. In the words of Hall, "the tragic spectator knows much more than the characters – is almost as omniscient as the gods – yet has absolutely no power to intervene. Watching a tragedy is like sitting in the seat of a god, but bound in shackles."[47] The audience-character relationship in tragedy, then, is characterised not only by an inequality in knowledge and the invariable distance between scene and semi-circular seating area, but also by an inherently frustrated desire on the part of the audience to erase the inequality, overcome the distance, and intervene in the plot.

Tacitus' treatment of Germanicus is constructed similarly, that is, it manipulates the audience-character relationship in a similar way and with/for similar emotional effect. The readerly experience of the narrative may thus fruitfully be seen through the lens of the tragic arousal and release of emotions.[48] By envisaging Germanicus' death as a lost opportunity to break the downwards trajectory of Roman history (rather than a meaningful part of a progression towards something better) and forcing the reader to witness the alternative futures imagined by his contemporaries – futures that she knows will not come to pass –, the narrative harnesses the emotional potential inherent in the knowledge inequality between them to devastating effect.[49] In short, Tacitus' reader is subjected to the emotion identified by Hall as distinctive of the tragic spectator: a frustrated desire to intervene in the plot, or, in other words, a mixture of helplessness and hopelessness.

When news of Germanicus' death is brought to Rome (2.82), however, and when the Roman people at his funeral in Rome sob and shout that no vestige of hope remains (3.4.1), the readerly experience is gradually aligned with that of the characters of the text. While the reader could neither share the characters' pre-mortem feeling of hopefulness (instead feeling a mixture of hopelessness and helplessness) nor identify completely with their first bout of pain and anger occasioned by the news of his faltering health (2.82.1–2), she can at least partly

---

[47] Hall 2010, 8. My (admittedly somewhat simplistic) transgression into the realm of tragedy is indebted also to Segal 1996 and Rabinowitz 2008. On the potential of tragedy to embrace alternative futures, see Hall 2010, 7; cf. Eagleton 2003.
[48] Cf. Hall 2010, 6.
[49] On Germanicus' ignorance and lack of self-awareness as reminiscent of tragic heroes, see Santoro L'Hoir 2006, 92–97; cf. Manolaraki/Augoustakis 2012.

embrace their sorrow and pain when his death is finally confirmed (2.82.3–5) and, by the time of the funeral in Rome, may effortlessly share their post-mortem feelings of sadness and hopelessness (3.4.1). At this point the characters' knowledge has, so to speak, caught up with that of the reader: they both know that Germanicus is dead and they both suspect Tiberius' involvement.

With this gradual convergence of reader and character experiences, we have moved, in the terminology of Levene, from 'analytic' to 'audience-based' emotion.[50] While 'analytic' emotion entails letting the reader react with an emotion potentially different from the one felt by a character (e.g. the portrayal of a character's fear *in such a way* that the reader feels pity for the character), 'audience-based' emotion entails persuading the reader to feel the same emotion as a character (e.g. the portrayal of a character's pity *in such a way* that the reader also feels pity for whomever the character pities). The difference, as noted by Levene, is between witnessing ('analytic') and re-experiencing ('audience-based') a character's emotion. When brought to bear on the readerly experience of Tacitus' treatment of Germanicus, we may put it like this: While the reader's awareness of the inevitable disappointment of the characters' hopes serves to transform them into hopelessness and helplessness at the point of reception and precludes a strong re-experience of their anger and pain upon the first news of his faltering health, the only constraining factor in her appropriation of their pain at the news of his death and their sadness and hopelessness at his funeral in Rome is her temporal distance from the events.

The comparison with the tragic audience-character relationship is illuminating also by way of their differences. In tragedy the release of emotions is achieved at the moment when spectator and character knowledge are synchronised, that is, at the very end.[51] Although the convergence of reader and character experiences during the public lament at Germanicus' funeral in Rome resembles that which occurs at the end of a tragic play, the emotional release experienced by the reader of Germanicus' death diverges from that experienced by the tragic spectator for two reasons. Firstly, while the funeral facilitates a release of emotion by bringing the characters up to date and putting an end to the story of the conflict between Germanicus and Tiberius, it also functions as a new beginning by re-establishing a disparity of knowledge between reader and characters. The convergence of experiences, in other words, does not last long.

---

50 Levene 1997/2012, 213–214: cf. Marincola 2003, 294.
51 On the importance of uniting characters and spectators in 'common grief', see esp. Segal 1996. The general purpose of tragedy and the specific meaning of 'katharsis' are still intensely debated: cf. Halliwell 2011, 208–265.

In fact, a new popular hope is introduced even before the funeral is over (3.4.2): "turning to heaven and the gods, they prayed (*precarentur*) that [Agrippina's] progeny would be untouched and would outlive those prejudiced against her." While this prayer/hope will admittedly be partially granted (though not for the greater good of Rome), the reader's superior knowledge of the future immediately serves to re-establish the experiential dissonance between reader and characters. Where the characters hope for a better future, the reader is already dreading the pitiful end of Agrippina (exiled to the island of Pandataria, where she will either starve herself or be starved to death on Tiberius' orders; cf. *Ann*. 6.25, Suet. *Tib*. 53) and the brutal reigns of her son Caligula and grandson Nero.[52] Secondly, Tacitus' contemporary roman readers do not possess the comfort of distance enjoyed by the tragic spectator, that is, the knowledge that the events portrayed happened a long time ago, almost in a different world.[53] There is no such emotional distancing at work in the treatment of Germanicus, for unlike most Greco-Roman tragedies (the exception being the *fabulae praetextae*, of which the pseudo-Senecan *Octavia* is our only extant example) the *Annals* is set in a past in whose shadow Tacitus' contemporaries still live. The Roman readers inhabit the same story-world as the characters, whose descendants they are and for whose choices they suffer the consequences.

This position of the Roman readers within the story-world and as inheritors of the narrative's outcome enables the arousal of 'analytic' regret. Unlike hope, which requires an open future, regret necessitates a closed past, a past, moreover, by which the reader's present has been shaped. Since the characters of the text can always imagine sudden changes, they cannot judge the significance of the events that take place around them. Their ability to feel regret, that is, is severely limited by their lack of hindsight. They do not know that only one of Germanicus' and Agrippina's six children will die of natural causes (cf. footnote 52 above). Tacitus' contemporary readers, on the other hand, who are both sufficiently distant from the events and have an obvious stake in their outcome, are eminently well-positioned to feel regret.

---

52 Among the six children of Agrippina and Germanicus, five died in their twenties: Nero Julius Caesar and Drusus Caesar were murdered on the orders of Tiberius and/or his praetorian prefect Sejanus (AD 30/31 and 33, respectively), Julia Drusilla died of an illness in the reign of Caligula (AD 38), Caligula himself was murdered in a palace conspiracy (AD 41), and Julia Livilla was murdered on the orders of her uncle Claudius (AD 41/42). Agrippina the Younger, who was married to and allegedly poisoned Claudius, made it to 43 years, when she was executed by her son Nero (AD 59).
53 Cf. Hall 2010, 8–9; nor are Tacitus' readers provided with a light-hearted satyr-play at the end of the day; cf. Hall 2010, 237.

This regret – enabled by the knowledge of future events and intensified by the stress on Germanicus' many lost opportunities to challenge Tiberius and Piso – is given substance by a persistent intratextual relationship with the narrative of a contemporaneous civil war among the Germani. Starting with the introduction of the chieftain Arminius as "the rabble-rouser of Germania" (*turbator Germaniae*, 1.55.2) in the middle of Book 1, this Germanic civil war continues intermittently until Arminius' death and posthumous designation as "undoubtedly the liberator of Germania" (*liberator haud dubie Germaniae*, 2.88.2) at the end of Book 2. The parallelism with the Roman civil conflict between Tiberius and Germanicus is especially apparent in their shared focus on freedom vs. slavery and family dissension: while Germanicus personifies the popular hope of liberation from the autocracy imposed by his uncle/adoptive father and grandmother (but conspicuously avoids fighting his cousin/brother), Arminius defends Germanic freedom by fighting a father-in-law, a brother, and an uncle, before he is finally killed by unnamed relatives.[54] The importance of Arminius for the appreciation of Germanicus is underlined by Tacitus' deliberate eschewal of chronology when placing Arminius' death and obituary at the end of Book 2 in AD 19 (he did not die until 2 years later). Where the reader expects to find Germanicus, who falls "to the snares of his own people" (*suorum insidiis*, 2.73.2) earlier in the same book, she is instead confronted with Arminius, who falls "to the cunning of his kinsmen" (*dolo propinquorum*, 2.88.2). The parallel is clear and invites reflection, especially in light of Tiberius' immediately preceding pointed and public refusal to poison the Germanic leader, which brings to mind his possible involvement in Germanicus' death.[55]

The many parallels between the civil conflicts in Rome and Germania accentuate the key difference in outcome. Unlike the unrealised civil war between Tiberius and Germanicus, the internal strife among the Germani ends in free-

---

[54] Note also that (i) Tacitus is the first author who portrays Germania as a fatherland (*patria*), (ii) his portrayal of Arminius evokes characters and episodes in Roman civil strife, (iii) Arminius' showdown with the rival Germanic king Maroboduus is intertextually linked to episodes of Roman civil conflict, and (iv) Arminius' four main speeches revolve around the contrast between freedom and slavery, the key terms in all Roman civil wars. For a more detailed discussion of the conflict in Germania as a civil war and its parallels with events in Rome, see Damtoft Poulsen 2018, 81–90. The similarity between "the decision which confronts the German in the face of Roman invasion and the decision which confronts the Roman in the face of the principate" is noted also by Williams 1989, 143. On the parallels between Germanicus and Arminius, see Pelling 1993, 79–81. On Tacitus' verdict on Arminius and his legacy, see Straub 1980.

[55] Cf. Walker 1952, 124; Syme 1958, 266–267; Grethlein 2013, 147; see also Low 2013a, 13, 24–28, 65–75.

dom. In this way, the Germanic civil war 'side-shadows' the events unfolding in Rome. While an impetus for comparison is created by similarities in theme and plot structure, the crucial difference in outcome – which demonstrates that civil war does not always end in one-man rule – stresses the openness of the past when it was still a present and challenges the reader to reflect on the alternative historical paths on which Rome could have embarked. By appreciating the parallels between Roman and Germanic history, in other words, we can deflate the myth of the Principate as the inevitable endpoint of the Republic.[56] Thus, while the hopes attached to Germanicus and his refusal to act upon them raise the possibility of alternative 'futures past' and awaken readerly curiosity about these, the persistent intratextual relationship with the Germanic civil war illustrates how such an alternative might look: war and chaos, to be sure, but also freedom and glory. In this way, openness is restored to the past and the reader is left with a sensation of regret that Germanicus did not challenge the emperor.[57]

It might be worthwhile, before the conclusion, to raise two questions whose attempted answers – due to the ambiguous nature of the text – must remain somewhat fuzzy. Firstly, why does Germanicus remain loyal to Tiberius? Although introduced specifically as a counterweight to the emperor (1.3.5; cf. 1.7.6), the designated successor remains extraordinarily passive in his dealings with both Tiberius and Piso, time and again declining opportunities to challenge them. While revolutionary designs and republican ideals are projected on him by the soldiers and people respectively, he appears to have no interest in embracing either the role of opportunistic warlord or liberator of the state. Since his own motives and aims (on which Tacitus is agonizingly silent) disappear behind the various layers of unrealised expectations, he remains merely a receptacle for other characters' hopes (the soldiers, the people) and fears (Tiberius, Livia). No amount of readerly interrogation can reveal the reasons behind his decisions. Does he simply – as is perhaps suggested by the contrast with his Germanic double, Arminius – lack conviction and determination? For while

---

56 Cf. Haynes 2003, 18–19.
57 On historiographical intertextuality and emotions, see O'Gorman 2006b, esp. 115–116: "The 'peculiarly intangible logic' of repetition in historical discourse, as we have seen, owes part of its intangibility – and much of its power – to its association with affects, to its capacity to evoke not only past events but past modalities and emotions. ... Intertextuality plays a crucial role in the representation of past time as a present from which the historical subject's memories, hopes, fears and experiences can be imagined by the historian as a collection of modalities, within which the historian's own retrospective viewpoint can also be acknowledged without subsuming the past to the present's concerns."

Germanicus remains passive, Arminius demonstrates remarkable decisiveness and tenacity in his struggle for Germanic freedom, a struggle which includes some significant defeats on the battlefield and earns him the laudatory description "equivocal in battles but not defeated in war" (*proeliis ambiguus, bello non uictus*, 2.88.2).

Alternatively, does Arminius merely possess a greater willingness to accept the costs of resistance? It is perhaps a too harsh reading which criticises Germanicus for not accepting the soldiers' offer to start a civil war, especially considering his sense of moral obligation towards fatherland, family and gods (*pietas*). The characteristics which hold him back – his loyalty to his adopted father and outrage at the soldiers' readiness to fight fellow Romans (1.35.4–5), his efforts (more successful than those of Arminius; cf. 1.58.6) to keep his wife and son from harm during the Germanic mutiny (1.42.1), and his ability to remain on affectionate terms with Drusus, his brother-through-adoption, despite the intrigues at court (2.42.6) –, are they not positive traits, after all?[58] Moreover, not only might a civil war bring unimaginable destruction (cf. *Histories* 1–3 on the post-Neronian civil wars), the soldiers have less than idealistic motives. The mutiny among the Pannonian legions, to which the mutiny among the legions in Germania is assimilated (cf. 1.31.1), arises (1.16.1) "not from any novel causes except that it was a change of princeps which offered the license for disruption and, resulting from civil war, the hope of prizes." Rather than a champion of freedom, the soldiers are looking for an intrepid warlord willing to put his own and the state's health into their hands. The conundrum is delicately – if only implicitly – posed: at what point is it legitimate to unleash forces beyond one's control in order to rid the state of an autocrat?

Secondly, what would have happened if Germanicus had marched the Germanic legions against Tiberius and taken power? Would his citizenlike disposition and remarkable affability (1.33.2: *ciuile ingenium, mira comitas*; cf. 1.71.3, 2.13.1, 2.72.2, 2.82.2) have facilitated a restoration of the Republic,[59] or would his impetuosity (cf. his less-than-faultless handling of the mutiny in Germania at 1.31–51), disregard for proper boundaries (cf. his spontaneous trip to Egypt at 2.59), love of the East (cf. his grand tour at 2.53–2.61, including the donning of Greek attire at 2.59.1), and flair for the theatrical (cf. his attempted suicides at 1.35.4 and 2.24.2) have turned him into an emperor in the mould of his grandson Nero? Again, the parallel Germanic civil war might be illuminating. As noted by

---

[58] Baxter (1972, 248–251) notes that Germanicus shares these characteristics with Virgil's Aeneas. On Aeneas as a model for Germanicus, see also Bews 1972–1973, 38–39.

[59] On *ciuilitas* and *comitas* as virtues of pro-senatorial emperors, see Wallace-Hadrill 1982.

Low, the dichotomy between Arminius the liberator and Arminius the would-be king suggests that Germanicus too incorporates both possibilities.[60] While there are admittedly no clear signs in the text that he would have restored the Republic,[61] this is a result of his refusal to commit to any sort of political programme rather than a clear disavowal of republicanism. Given that Germanicus never attained the Principate and that the Principate changed (or uncovered hidden traits of) those who held supreme power (Tiberius at 6.51.3, Nero at 14.52.1, Galba at *Hist.* 1.49.4, Vespasian at *Hist.* 1.50.4), it seems that a final verdict on Germanicus as would-be liberator/emperor must remain elusive. In short, hope is kindled and put out without its actual potential being made clear – and the reader is left to contemplate what might have been and to rue an unrealised opportunity to reassert freedom in Rome.

3 Conclusions

In the analysis above, we demonstrated how side-shadowing effects are created and alternative 'futures past' constructed in *Annals* 1–2 through recurrent mentions of the hopes placed in Germanicus and his refusal to act upon them. This restoration of openness to the past, however, does not necessarily entail that the text is fundamentally anti-teleological. While Grethlein rightly claims that it is "impossible to distil a coherent philosophy of history from the *Annals* that would support a strong teleological view",[62] the general trajectory of Rome under the Julio-Claudians in the *Annals* is clear enough: irreversibly downwards. Firstly, regardless of how the end of Nero's reign was narrated in the final (sadly unpreserved) books, we can – thanks to the survival of *Histories* 1–3 – safely posit the destructive civil wars of 68/69 AD as the vantage point of the *Annals* as a whole.[63] The narrative is headed towards cataclysmic destruction, or at least the promise thereof. Secondly, numerous prolepses insinuate horrors yet to come. Although typically vague about how future events will play out, they leave no doubt about the general trajectory: the murder of Agrippa Postumus is "the first [criminal] act (*primum facinus*) of the new [Tiberian] principate" (1.6.1), Tiberius reacts mildly to popular unrest in the theatre because (1.54.2) "he did not yet (*nondum*) dare to turn them in a harder direction", the murder of

---

[60] Low 2013a, 71.
[61] Cf. Williams 1989, 141–144; Low 2013a, 25–26, 54, 71–72, 92–127.
[62] Grethlein 2013, 171.
[63] On the significance of the historian's selection of vantage point, see Grethlein 2013, 6–8.

Junius Silanus is "the first death (*prima ... mors*) in the new [Neronian] principate" (13.1.1), and the senator Rubellius Plautus avoids Nero's wrath as he "for the present (*ad praesens*) was passed over in silence" (13.22.2).[64] Thirdly, while the text does include passages wherein a downward trajectory is challenged, these are drowned out by the predominating tone of decline. For example, praise for a speech composed by Seneca for Nero (13.3.1) is immediately followed by an analysis of the gradual decline of oratory among the emperors (13.3.2–3).

Appreciation of the narrative's regressive teleological drive is crucial for a nuanced understanding of its side-shadowing effects, for the particular force of historiographical side-shadowing lies in the space between teleology and experientiality. Given that the main plot and endpoint of the narrative are well-known by its readers, the potential for actual suspension of knowledge is obviously limited. Since such a narrative can never create the same sense of openness as a fictional narrative, it follows that the effects of side-shadowing in historiography cannot be analogous to fiction: rather than to create suspense by suspending the reader's knowledge of the outcome, historiographical side-shadowing elicits emotions by feeding on that very knowledge. Moreover, and specifically for those who read historiographical texts about their own past, the particular emotions elicited depend on the teleological drive of the text and the specific shape of its side-shadowing devices. In whig histories of modern European nation states, the combination of a progressive teleological drive with the overcoming of political and biological obstacles is likely to induce in the national reader a sensation of pride in the accomplishments of her ancestors and gratefulness not only for the seemingly perpetual progress of society but also for her own privileged position at its forefront.[65] The side-shadowing effects produced in the *Annals* are of an entirely different hue: the combination of a regressive teleological drive with a series of unrealised opportunities for political change induces in the Roman readers neither pride nor gratefulness, but rather helplessness in watching events unfurl, vexation towards those who failed to resist, regret over lost opportunities to change the course of history, and hopelessness in knowing that they themselves occupy the end-point in a story of

---

64 Cf. Walker 1952, 68; Grethlein 2013, 169–170.
65 Butterfield 1931; cf. Cosgrove 2000 and Burrow 2008, 443–445; see also Grethlein 2013, 3–4. On American whig historiography, see Hijiya 1994, esp. 283–288. On the power of teleological philosophies of history to make sense of the world and our experience in it, see Carr in this volume.

unremitting decline.⁶⁶ This is possible due to the position of the reader at the point towards which the narrative unequivocally leads, inside the (future of the) text, so to speak. This involvement of the reader in the narrative in a way unachievable in fiction creates a tension between text and reader which imbues the side-shadowing with devastating rhetorical potential. The reader is not only encouraged to wonder "what if Germanicus had tried?" but also induced with a sense of regret: "If only Germanicus had at least tried!".⁶⁷

In addition to such unhelpfully unproductive feelings, however, one might perhaps detect also the creation of more constructive and politically significant emotions in the Roman reader: shame over his own political passivity in the face of oppression and guilt for his collaboration with the imperial regime. While not exactly a call to arms, the *Annals* does force Tacitus' contemporary readers to take a long hard look in the mirror. One does not, after all, need to advocate active revolt in order to produce subversive literature. In short, despite its predetermined endpoint (the fall of the Julio-Claudian dynasty and outbreak of civil war), the narrative's suggestion that things could have turned out differently if certain people had acted differently allows the reader to imagine alternatives.⁶⁸ The restoration of the possibility of (other) possibilities, i.e. the acknowledgement that choices or chance were involved in the realisation of the particular future that came to pass, is a challenge to the narrative's teleological drive. In other words, although Tacitus presents the trajectory of the Julio-Claudian dynasty as consistently downwards, he also makes it clear that this is because his characters act immorally, cowardly, or, in the case of Germanicus, not at all. Tacitus' philosophy of history, then, incorporates both helplessness and guilt, and is perhaps best described as teleology with a human face.⁶⁹

---

66 The Roman reader cannot absolve his own ancestors by blaming only Germanicus. The entire Roman people has lost the will to resist (1.7.1): "but at Rome there was a rush into servitude from consuls, fathers, equestrians."
67 On Agricola as another Tacitean character who declines to challenge the emperor, see Haynes 2014, 41.
68 Cf. footnote 8 above on how the conception of history promoted by the imperial regime maintained the impossibility of alternatives to one-man rule.
69 Cf. Griffin 2009, 172; Grethlein 2013, 178–179.

Bibliography

Aron, Raymond (1938), *Introduction à la philosophie de l'histoire: Essai sur les limites de l'objectivité historique*, Paris.
Ash, Rhiannon (1999), *Ordering Anarchy: Armies and Leaders in Tacitus' Histories*, London.
Ash, Rhiannon (2006), *Tacitus*, Bristol.
Ash, Rhiannon (2009), "Fission and fusion: shifting Roman identities in the Histories", in: Anthony J. Woodman (ed.), *The Cambridge Companion to Tacitus*, Cambridge, 85–99.
Ash, Rhiannon (2012), "Introduction", in: Rhiannon Ash (ed.), *Oxford Readings in Classical Studies: Tacitus*, Oxford, 1–35.
Ash, Rhiannon (2018), *Tacitus: Annals book 15*, Cambridge.
Bannon, Cynthia J. (1997), *Brothers of Romulus: Fraternal Pietas in Roman Law, Literature, and Society*, Princeton, NJ.
Baxter, Robert T. S. (1972), "Virgil's influence on Tacitus in Books 1 and 2 of the *Annals*", *Classical Philology* 67, 246–69.
Bews, Janet (1972–3), "Virgil, Tacitus, Tiberius, Germanicus", *Proceedings of the Virgil Society* 12, 35–48.
Bleicken, Jochen (1995), *Gedanken zum Untergang der römischen Republik*, Stuttgart.
Bloomer, W. Martin (1997), *Latinity and Literary Society at Rome*, Philadelphia.
Bonner, Stanley Frederick (1977), *Education in Ancient Rome: From the elder Cato to the younger Pliny*, London.
Brunt, Peter A. (1971), *Social Conflicts in the Roman Republic*, London.
Brunt, Peter A. (1988), *The Fall of the Roman Republic: and Related Essays*, Oxford.
Burrow, John (2008), *A History of Histories: Epics, Chronicles, Romances and Inquiries from Herodotus and Thucydides to the Twentieth Century*, New York.
Butterfield, Herbert (1931), *The Whig Interpretation of History*, London.
Christ, Karl (1978), "Tacitus und der Principat", *Historia* 27, 449–87.
Clark, Donald Lemen (1957), *Rhetoric in Greco-Roman Education*, New York.
Clark, Anna J. (2007), *Divine Qualities: Cult and Community in Republican Rome*, Oxford.
Cosgrove, Richard A. (2000), "Reflections on the Whig Interpretation of History", *Journal of Early Modern History* 4.2, 147–67.
Damon, Cynthia (2010), "Intestinum Scelus: Preemptive Execution in Tacitus' *Annals*", in: Brian Breed/Cynthia Damon/Andreola Rossi (eds.), *Citizens of Discord: Rome and Its Civil Wars*, Oxford, 261–72.
Damtoft Poulsen, Aske (2018), *Accounts of Northern Barbarians in Tacitus' Annales*, Lund.
Davies, Jason P. (2004), *Rome's Religious History: Livy, Tacitus and Ammianus on Their Gods*, Cambridge.
Deininger, Jürgen (1980), "Explaining the Change from Republic to Principate in Rome", *Comparative Civilisations Review* 4.4, 77–101.
Devillers, Olivier (1991), "Le Rôle des passages relatifs à Tacfarinas dans les Annales de Tacite", in: Attilio Mastino (ed.), *L'Africa romana: Atti dell'VIII convegno*, Sassari, 203–11.
Eagleton, Terry (2003), *Sweet Violence: An Essay on the Tragic*, Oxford.
Edelmaier, Wilfried (1964) *Tacitus und die Gegner Roms*, diss. Heidelberg.
Eder, Walter (1996), "Republicans and Sinner: The Decline of the Roman Republic and the End of a Provisional Arrangement", in: Wallace, Robert W./Harris, Edward M. (eds.), *Transi-*

tions to Empire: Essays in Greco-Roman History, 360–146 B.C. in honor of E. Badian, London/Norman, OK.

Feldherr, Andrew (2009), "Introduction", in: Andrew Feldherr (ed.), *The Cambridge Companion to the Roman Historians*, Cambridge, 1–8.

Fornara, Charles W. (1983), *The Nature of History in Ancient Greece and Rome*, Berkeley, CA.

Georges, Karl Ernst/Georges, Heinrich (1976), *Ausführliches lateinisch-deutsches Handwörterbuch*, 2 vols., 14th ed., Hannover.

Gildenhard, Ingo/Gotter, Ulrich/Havener, Wolfgang/Hodgson, Lousie (2019), "Attending to the Past: On the Politics of Time in Ancient Rome", in: Ingo Gildenhard et al. (eds.), *Augustus and the Destruction of History: The Politics of the Past in Early Imperial Rome*, Cambridge, 1–36.

Girardet, Klaus M. (2007), *Rom auf dem Weg von der Republik zum Prinzipat*, Bonn.

Girardet, Klaus M. (2017), *Januar 49 v.Chr.: Caesars Militärputsch: Vorgeschichte, Rechtslage, politische Aspekte*, Bonn.

Giua, Maria Antonietta (2014), "Pace e libertà dall'*Agricola* agli *Annales*: il Tacito incompiuto di Arnaldo Momigliano", in: Olivier Devillers (ed.), *Les opera minora et le développement de l'historiograpie tacitéenne*, Bordeaux, 45–57.

Grethlein, Jonas (2010), "Experientiality and 'Narrative Reference', with thanks to Thucydides", *History and Theory* 49.3, 315–35.

Grethlein, Jonas (2013), *Experience and Teleology in Ancient Historiography: Futures Past from Herodotus to Augustine*, Cambridge.

Griffin, Miriam T. (2009), "Tacitus as a historian", in: Anthony J. Woodman (ed.), *The Cambridge Companion to Tacitus*, Cambridge, 168–83.

Gruen, Erich S. (1974), *The Last Generation of the Roman Republic*, Berkeley, CA.

Hall, Edith (2010), *Greek Tragedy: Suffering under the Sun*, Oxford.

Halliwell, Stephen (2011), *Between Ecstasy and Truth: Interpretations of Greek Poetics form Homer to Longinus*, Oxford.

Häußler, Reinhardt (1965), *Tacitus und das historische Bewußtsein*, Heidelberg.

Haynes, Holly (2003), *The History of Make-Believe: Tacitus on Imperial Rome*, Berkeley, CA.

Haynes, Holly (2014), "The In- and Outside of History: Tacitus with Groucho Marx", in: Olivier Devillers (ed.), *Les opera minora et le développement de l'historiograpie tacitéenne*, Bordeaux, 31–44.

Heubner, Henricus (ed.) (1994), *P. Cornelii Taciti, Libri qui supersunt – Tom. 1: Ab excessu diui Augusti*, Stuttgart/Leipzig.

Hijiya, James A. (1994), "Why the West Is Lost", *The William and Mary Quarterly* 51.2, 276–92.

Hodgson, Lousie (2019), "*Libera Res Publica*: The Road Not Taken", in: Ingo Gildenhard et al. (eds.), *Augustus and the Destruction of History: The Politics of the Past in Early Imperial Rome*, Cambridge, 39–58.

Hurlet, Frédéric (2008), "Le passage de la République à l'Empire: Questions anciennes, nouvelles réponses", *Revue des études anciennes* 110, 215–36.

Hölkeskamp, Karl-Joachim (ed.) (2009), *Eine politische Kultur (in) der Krise? Die "letzte Generation" der römischen Republik*, Munich.

Jehne, Martin (2009), *Der große Trend, der kleine Sachzwang und das handelnde Individuum: Caesars Entscheidungen*, Munich.

Kaster, Robert A. (2005), *Emotion, Restraint, and Community in Ancient Rome*, Oxford.

Kaster, Robert A. (2006), "Rhetoric and Emotion", in: Ian Worthington (ed.), *A Companion to Greek Rhetoric*, Oxford, 411–25.

Keitel, Elizabeth (1984), "Principate and civil war in the Annals of Tacitus", *American Journal of Philology* 105, 306–25.
Kennedy, George A. (1972), *The Art of Rhetoric in the Roman World*, Princeton, NJ.
Kożuchowski, Adam (2015), "More than true: the rhetorical function of counterfactuals in historiography", *Rethinking History: The Journal of Theory and Practice* 19, 337–56.
Kraus, Christina S. (2009), "The Tiberian Hexad", in: Anthony J. Woodman (ed.), *The Cambridge Companion to Tacitus*, Cambridge, 100–15.
Kroymann, Jürgen (1952), "Fatum, Fors, Fortuna und Verwandtes im Geschichtsdenken des Tacitus", in: *Satura: Früchte aus der antiken Welt, O. Weinreich zum 13. März 1951 dargebracht*, Baden-Baden, 130–60.
Kühner, Raphael/Stegmann, Carl (1976), *Ausführliche Grammatik der Lateinischen Sprache: Zweiter Teil (Satzlehre, erster Band)*, 5th ed., Darmstadt.
Laird, Andrew (2009), "The rhetoric of Roman historiography", in: Andrew Feldherr (ed.), *The Cambridge Companion to the Roman Historians*, Cambridge, 197–213.
Lavan, Myles (2013), *Slaves to Rome: Paradigms of Empire in Roman Culture*, Cambridge.
Lendon, Jon E. (2009), "Historians without history: Against Roman historiography", in: Andrew Feldherr (ed.), *The Cambridge Companion to the Roman Historians*, Cambridge, 41–61.
Levene, David S. (1997/2012), "Pity, fear and the historical audience: Tacitus on the fall of Vitellius", in: Rhiannon Ash (ed.), *Oxford Readings in Classical Studies: Tacitus*, Oxford, 209–233. (orig. published in Susanna Morton Braund/Christopher Gill (eds.), *The Passions in Roman Thought and Literature*, Cambridge, 128–49.)
Levick, Barbara (1999), *Tiberius the Politician*, London.
Low, Katherine Anna (2013a), *The Mirror of Tacitus? Selves and Others in the Tiberian Books of the Annals*, diss. Oxford.
Low, Katherine Anna (2013b), "*Memoriae eximere*: AD 41 and the Survival of Republicanism under the Principate", in: Anton Powell (ed.), *Hindsight in Greek and Roman Historiography*, Swansea, 201–21.
Luce, Torrey James (1986/2012), "Tacitus' Conception of Historical Change: The Problem of Discovering the Historian's Opinions", in: Rhiannon Ash (ed.), *Tacitus: Oxford Readings in Classical Studies*, Oxford, 339–56. (orig. published in I.S. Moxon/J.D. Smart/A.J. Woodman (eds.), *Past Perspectives: Studies in Greek and Roman Historical Writing*, Cambridge, 143–57.)
Manolaraki, Eleni/Augoustakis, Antony (2012), "Silius Italicus and Tacitus on the Tragic Hero", in: Victoria Emma Pagán (ed.), *A Companion to Tacitus*, Oxford/Malden, MA, 386–402.
Marincola, John (1997), *Authority and Tradition in Ancient Historiography*, Cambridge.
Marincola, John (2003), "Beyond Pity and Fear: the Emotions of History", *Ancient Society* 33, 285–315.
Marincola, John (2009), "Historiography", in: Andrew Erskine (ed.), *A Companion to Ancient History*, Oxford, 13–22.
Martin, Ronald H./Woodman, Anthony J. (eds.) (1989), *Tacitus: Annals book IV*, Cambridge.
Meier, Christian (1966), *Res Publica Amissa: Eine Studie zu Verfassung und Geschichte der späten römischen Republik*, Wiesbaden.
Menge, Hermann (1960), *Repetitorium der lateinischen Syntax und Stilistik*, 13th ed., Munich.
Morson, Gary Saul (1994), *Narrative and Freedom: The Shadows of Time*, New Haven, CT.
Morson, Gary Saul (1998), "Sideshadowing and Tempics", *New Literary History* 29.4 (*Critics without Schools?*), 599–624.

Morstein-Marx, Robert/Rosenstein, Nathan (2006), "The Transformation of the Republic", in: Rosenstein, Nathan/Morstein-Marx, Robert (eds.), *A Companion to the Roman Republic*, Oxford and Malden, MA.
O'Gorman, Ellen (2000), *Irony and Misreading in the Annals of Tacitus*, Cambridge.
O'Gorman, Ellen (2006a), "Alternate Empires: Tacitus's Virtual History of the Pisonian Principate", *Arethusa* 39, 281–301.
O'Gorman, Ellen (2006b), "Intertextuality, Time and Historical Understanding", in: Alexander Lyon Macfie (ed.), *The Philosophy of History*, Basingstoke, 102–17.
Olson, James M./Roese, Neal J./Deibert, Ronald J. (1996), "Psychological Biases in Counterfactual Thought Experiments", in: Philip E. Tetlock/Aaron Belkin (eds.), *Counterfactual Thought Experiments in World Politics: Logical, Methodological and Psychological Perspectives*, Princeton, NJ, 296–300.
Pelling, Christopher (1993), "Tacitus and Germanicus", in: Torrey James Luce/Anthony J. Woodman (eds.), *Tacitus and the Tacitean Tradition*, Princeton, NJ, 59–85.
Pigoń, Jakub (2008), "The Passive Voice of the Hero: Some Peculiarities of Tacitus' Portrayal of Germanicus in Annals 1.31–49", in: Jakub Pigoń (ed.), *The Children of Herodotus: Greek and Roman Historiography and Related Genres*, Newcastle, 287–303.
Rabinowitz, Nancy Sorkin (2008), *Greek Tragedy*, Malden, MA.
Richardson, John S. (2012), *Augustan Rome 44 BC to AD 14: the Restoration of the Republic and the Establishment of the Empire*, Edinburgh.
Ricoeur, Paul (2000/2004), *Memory, History, Forgetting*, Chicago. Transl. by Kathleen Blamey & David Pellauer. (orig. published as *La mémoire, l'histoire, l'oubli*, Paris.)
Roller, Matthew B. (2018), *Models from the Past in Roman Culture: A World of Exempla*, Cambridge.
Ross, David O. (1973), "The Tacitean Germanicus", *Yale Classical Studies* 23, 209–27.
Sage, Michael M. (1991), "The Treatment in Tacitus of Roman Republican History and Antiquarian Matters", *Aufstieg und Niedergang der römischen Welt* II 33.5, 3385–3419.
Sailor, Dylan (2008), *Writing and Empire in Tacitus*, Cambridge.
Sailor, Dylan (2019), "Arminius and Flavus across the Weser", *Transactions of the American Philological Association* 149.1, 77–126.
Sanders, Ed/Matthew Johncock (eds.) (2016), *Emotion and Persuasion in Classical Antiquity*, Stuttgart.
Segal, Charles (1996), "Catharsis, Audience, and Closure in Greek Tragedy", in: Michael S. Silk (ed.), *Tragedy and the Tragic: Greek Theatre and Beyond*, Oxford, 149–72.
Shannon, Kelly E. (2014), "Aetiology of the Other: Foreign Religions in Tacitus' *Histories*", in: Christiane Reitz/Anke Walter (eds.), *Von Ursachen sprechen: Eine aitiologische Spurensuche/Telling Origins: On the Lookout for Aetiology*, Hildesheim, 271–300.
Shannon-Henderson, Kelly E. 2019. *Religion and Memory in Tacitus' Annals*, Oxford.
Sherk, Robert K. (1988), *Translated Documents of Greece & Rome 6 – The Roman Empire: Augustus to Hadrian*, Cambridge.
Shotter, David Colin Arthur (1968), "Tacitus, Tiberius and Germanicus", *Historia* 18, 194–214.
Strunk, Thomas E. (2017), *History after Liberty: Tacitus on Tyrants, Sycophants, and Republicans*, Ann Arbor, MI.
Straub, Johannes (1980), "*Liberator haud dubie Germaniae*: Zeitkritik im Urteil des Tacitus über Arminius", *Würzburger Jahrbücher für die Altertumswissenschaft* 6, 223–231.
Syme, Sir Ronald (1958) *Tacitus*, Oxford.

Trilling, Lionel (1976/2012), "Tacitus Now", in: Rhiannon Ash (ed.), *Oxford Readings in Classical Studies: Tacitus*, Oxford, 435–40. (orig. published in Lionel Trilling, *The Liberal Imagination: Essays on Literature and Society*, New York, 198–206.)

Vekselius, Johan (Forthcoming), "Tiberius and Tears: Grief and Genre", in: Aske Damtoft Poulsen/Arne Jönsson (eds.), *Usages of the Past in Roman Historiography*, Leiden/Boston.

von Ungern-Sternberg, Jürgen (1998), "Die Legitimitätskrise der römischen Republik", *Historische Zeitschrift* 266.3, 607–24.

Walbank, Frank W. (1960), "History and Tragedy", *Historia* 9, 216–34.

Walbank, Frank W. (1972), *Polybius*, Berkeley, CA.

Walker, Bessie (1952), *The Annals of Tacitus: A Study in the Writing of History*, Manchester.

Wallace-Hadrill, Andrew (1982), "*Civilis Princeps*: Between Citizen and King". *Journal of Roman Studies* 72, 32–48.

Webb, Ruth (2009), *Ekphrasis, Imagination and Persuasion in Ancient Rhetorical Theory and Practice*, Farnham and Burlington, VT).

Welwei, Karl-Wilhelm (1996), "Caesars Diktatur, der Prinzipat des Augustus und die Fiktion der historischen Notwendigkeit", *Gymnasium* 103, 477–97.

White, Hayden (1973), *Metahistory: The Historical Imagination in Nineteenth-Century Europe*, Baltimore, MD.

Williams, Bronwyn (1989), "Reading Tacitus' Tiberian *Annals*", *Ramus* 18, 140–66.

Williams, Kathryn F. (2009), "Tacitus' Germanicus and the Principate", *Latomus* 68, 117–30.

Wiseman, T.P. (1979), *Clio's Cosmetics: Three Studies in Greco-Roman Literature*, Leicester.

Wiseman, T.P. (1995), *Remus: A Roman Myth*, Cambridge.

Wiseman, T.P. (1998), *Roman Drama and Roman History*, Exeter.

Woodman, Anthony J. (1988), *Rhetoric in Classical Historiography: Four Studies*, London/New York.

Woodman, Anthony. J. (1992/1998), "Nero's alien Capital: Tacitus as paradoxographer (*Annals* 15.36–7)", in: Anthony J. Woodman (ed.), *Tacitus Reviewed*, Oxford, 168–189. (orig. published in Anthony J. Woodman/Jonathan Powell (eds.), *Author and Audience in Latin Literature*, Cambridge, 173–188.)

Woodman, Anthony J. (transl.) (2004), *Tacitus: the Annals*, Indianapolis/Cambridge.

Woodman, Anthony J. (2006), "Mutiny and madness: Tacitus' *Annals* 1.16–49", *Arethusa* 39, 303–29.

Woodman, Anthony J. (2009), "Introduction", in: Anthony J. Woodman (ed.), *The Cambridge Companion to Tacitus*, Cambridge, 1–14.

Woodman, Anthony J. 2016. *The Annals of Tacitus: Books 5 and 6*, Cambridge.

Katherine Clarke
Minding the Gap: Mimetic Imperfection and the Historiographical Enterprise

1 Historiography: Looking at and Through the Text

Historiography,[1] 'the writing of history', must be one of the most ill-defined terms in our repertoire and its ambiguity lies productively at the heart of this volume.[2] On the one hand, it refers to the activity of modern scholarship, the attempts of historians in the modern world to write about the past, using a variety of approaches and conceptual frameworks, viewing the evidence through different prisms, often reflecting contemporary preoccupations or historical contexts. On the other, it refers to the study by modern historians of attempts by historians in the ancient world to do the same. Historiography is conducted at various levels and degrees of remove, both a past reality in its own right and a representation of reality at the same time.

The duality inherent in the term is neatly articulated in the course outline for an undergraduate paper in the Modern History degree at the University of Oxford,[3] which claims that 'Historians commonly approach the study of historical writing in two quite distinct ways: either by study of the techniques which we hold to be immediately relevant today, or by looking at the "history of history", as for example by focussing on classic texts in Western historical writing'. The paper's initial focus is on the latter, and it places centre-stage, 'the close reading of texts which really will bear close reading — reading being still the most fundamental of all historical "methods".' The essential meaning of historiography, 'the writing of history', covers a range of possibilities, but as practitioners of ancient historiography, we tend to mean the latter of the two interpretations above, that

---

[1] The sub-heading refers to the work of Ankersmit (1994), much of whose work on the philosophy of history has focused on the layered nature of the historiographical enterprise and on the historical text as a lens through which to view the past as well as an object of study in its own right.
[2] See Becker 1938, 20–28, for an early modern attempt to define the field as 'the study of the history of historical study' (20), which he sees as a piece of intellectual history in its own right.
[3] Historiography: Tacitus to Weber.

is *reading* works of history, pushing the act of *writing* into the hands of our ancient counterparts.⁴

Nevertheless, continuities in the writing of history across time are evident, and I shall argue for a close relationship between our own historical enterprise and that of our ancient predecessors, noting that the observations made by historians in the ancient world concerning the opportunities and constraints might reflect also on our own writing of history. I therefore propose to explore the core question of historiography, 'How do historians make history?',⁵ by reading what some historians in the ancient world have written about that process. As well as illuminating our reading of those historians as sources, by enhancing our understanding of their enterprise, this will also cast light on our own approaches to the writing of history.

Historiography is a self-reflexive enterprise, involving multiple layers of interpretation in which ancient practitioners, whose works we study, are engaged in a similar activity to that of their modern readers. It is an aspect of the ancient world which we study through its reduplication in the medium of its original production, making it unlike any other type of ancient evidence.⁶ Furthermore, the self-consciously analytical nature of ancient historiography aligns it closely with our modern enterprise. Ancient historiography does not simply reflect something of its contemporary society but is already a deliberate attempt to interpret events, situations, individuals, and to shape responses to them, and this tension between historical writing as a window through which to view the past as well as a feature of the past, an object of viewing in its own right, is one to which I shall return.

Since both ancient and modern historiography set out explicitly to offer an intellectually conceived and verbally expressed construction of the past, the notion of 'reconciliation' might appear superfluous. But the relationship between these enterprises is more complex than simple parallelism. The 'ancient' and 'modern' historiographies are distinguished by distance from the object of study, but they are also 'layered' enterprises, with modern historiography characterized as the study of ancient attempts to represent the past, turning ancient historiography into a piece of intellectual history in its own right. These coexistent but

---

4 The 'Historiography' paper based in Oxford's Classics Faculty also defines historiography as a reading exercise, focused on 'the history of history': 'Greek and Roman historical writers offer us a remarkable collection of narratives... This option focuses on particularly rewarding sections from some of the best-known historians.'
5 Faculty of History, University of Oxford, 'Disciplines of History' course description.
6 See Cameron 1989a, 4, for historiography as a 'text upon text', where the historian has to read and interpret materials before creating his own text.

interwoven and enmeshed interpretations of what precisely constitutes the historiographical enterprise are mutually supportive.[7] Thus the gap between ancient and modern historiography may be bridged in many ways.

2 Bridging Ancient and Modern: Parallel Historiographical Enterprises

One apparent discontinuity, however, between ancient and modern historiography is the very purpose of writing history, declared by many ancient historians particularly in the Roman tradition to be primarily didactic and moralizing. Livy's 'lessons of every kind set out as on a conspicuous monument, from which you may choose which to imitate and which to avoid' (1 Preface 9–10) and Diodorus Siculus' proclamation that 'the understanding of the failures and successes of others, which is gained by the study of history, offers an education which is free from actual experience of ills' (1.1.1) both indicate that the historian's task is to teach. The validity of this claim was under critical scrutiny already in the Greek world, implied not least in Thucydides' pessimistic doubting of the capacity of any human truly to learn from the past.[8] As Thucydides notes in relation to both the plague at Athens and *stasis* in Corcyra,[9] the propensity for tragic events to repeat periodically meant that it was useful to record the symptoms so that a named diagnosis might be made more quickly in future, but there could be no expectation that such knowledge would avert the disaster next time.[10] The same pertained to the pathology of the state.[11] Nevertheless, in spite of Thucydides' reservations, didacticism was a strong thread in Roman historiography.

---

[7] Cameron 1989a, 5: 'Thus history-writing is not a simple matter of sorting out 'primary' and 'secondary' sources; it is inextricably embedded in a mesh of text.'
[8] See the classic scholarly treatment of the theme by Rutherford 1994. Pownall 2004 and Hau 2016 both offer illustrations of how the moralizing tendency in ancient historiography is played out.
[9] For the plague, see Thucydides 2.48.3: εἴ ποτε καὶ αὖθις ἐπιπέσοι; for *stasis* in Corcyra, 3.82.2: γιγνόμενα μὲν καὶ αἰεὶ ἐσόμενα, ἕως ἂν ἡ αὐτὴ φύσις ἀνθρώπων ᾖ.
[10] Thucydides 2.48.3: 'But I shall describe how it progressed, and the symptoms by which anyone who knows them beforehand may recognize the illness, if it should ever strike again.'
[11] See Thucydides' account of civil strife or *stasis* at 3.82.2: 'Many difficult things struck the cities on account of civil strife, such as happen and always will happen as long as human nature remains the same.'

This moralizing mission seems hard to relate to modern historiography, not least because of the changed role of the historian in society. The modern disjunction between historiography and statecraft, so tightly linked in the ancient world, entails a change in readership away from those who might need instruction in practical politics through study of the past. The ancient readership comprising the educated élite, including the ruling class of statesmen, is replaced most obviously in the modern world by two distinct groupings – an educated élite, comprising academics rather than statesmen, and a broader audience for so-called 'popular' history, as presented in accessible books, websites, and television programmes. Neither group is inclined to be 'taught' moral lessons by the historian.

However, various challenges can be made to this contrasting model. The involvement of contemporary historians in the development and formulation of public policy suggests that the notion of historical study as influential on the conduct of political life might still persist, although not through lessons learnt from the distant past as recommended by Livy and Diodorus. If there remains some continuity of influence on policy makers, then there are continuities too associated with another modern audience for historiography, the general public, in the form not of moral and political instruction, but of entertainment. As Pliny (*Epistles* 5.8) optimistically notes when contemplating the genre: 'history cannot fail to give pleasure whatever style is adopted' [sc. by contrast with poetry and oratory]. It is perhaps significant that Pliny, in the same letter, also discusses the potential of historiography as a means of winning fame and immortality for the historian.[12] Here, the celebrity of some of the modern historians who bring the past to a wider audience through a range of entertainment media springs to mind,[13] suggesting a point of comparison between ancient and modern historiography as produced for its entertainment-value by those who seek renown.

Indeed, while the grand narratives of ancient historians such as Thucydides and Tacitus may have been aimed at a relatively restricted and highly educated readership of the ruling élite, it is worth remembering that not all ancient historiography fitted this mould. The fragmentary remains of the vast numbers of local historians who flourished particularly in the Hellenistic period, suggest another major function for historiographical versions of the past, namely to instil and foster civic pride in the glorious history of a place, with the story often taken right

---

12 Pliny, *Epistles* 5.8.1: 'It seems to me a particularly fine thing not to let fall into oblivion those who deserve immortality, and to spread the fame of others together with one's own' (*aliorumque famam cum sua extendere*).
13 Mary Beard, David Starkey, and Michael Wood are all figures in the UK with a major public persona linked to their presentation of the Ancient World.

back to the heroic period. The civic context for live performances of these historical works forces us to modify the picture of ancient historiography being produced solely or predominantly for an élite and restricted readership, as well as giving an insight into the extraordinary fame and honours attached to polished practitioners.[14]

Although the didactic purpose of ancient historiography seems misplaced in a modern context, nevertheless the related commemorative function of historiography forms a continuous bridge from the ancient to the modern worlds. Herodotus' declared intent to put on display his enquiry so that 'so that things done by man might not be obliterated by time, nor great and wonderful deeds, some displayed by the Hellenes, some by the non-Greeks, fall into oblivion',[15] set the model for recollection of the past being central to historiography, and not necessarily for moralising reasons. There is, however, an implicit connection between commemorating the past and avoiding the repetition of its failures, and this is true of the modern world too, perhaps most notably in the context of warfare. As seen above, rather counter-intuitively, this continuity between ancient and modern thinking links not the rarefied world of ancient readership with the rarefied world of modern academia, but rather the former with the broader audience of popular history. It is the general public to whom the message of, for example, Remembrance Day, is directed, and they who are urged not to forget past horrors; not the readers of scholarly tomes. Again, perhaps we see here reflected differences in the political and cultural context in which ancient and modern historiography take place, with the lessons of history being now directed more clearly to the people at large than to the ruling oligarchy of statesmen.

The question of why people write history, in either the ancient or the modern worlds, yields a range of responses, some of which indicate continuity and some disjunction between these two worlds. The same is true concerning the issue of constraint over what the historian may write and in what terms. The restrictions on historians at least under the tight reins of the Roman Principate are explicitly set out by Tacitus. At the start of the *Histories* he notes a marked shift in historiographical freedom heralded by the Battle of Actium:

> While they were relating the affairs of the Roman people, they wrote with equal eloquence and freedom. After the battle had been fought at Actium, and it was in the interests of peace that all power should be brought together in one man, those great intellects passed away.

---

14 See Clarke 2008, 304–369, and most recently Thomas 2019, for extensive discussion of *polis*–histories.
15 Herodotus, *Histories*, Preface: ὡς μήτε τὰ γενόμενα ἐξ ἀνθρώπων τῷ χρόνῳ ἐξίτηλα γένηται, μήτε ἔργα μεγάλα τε καὶ θωμαστά, τὰ μὲν Ἕλλησι τὰ δὲ βαρβάροισι ἀποδεχθέντα, ἀκλεᾶ γένηται.

> At the same time, truth was compromised in many ways; at first, through men's ignorance of public affairs, as though these were no longer their business, and soon through their passion for flattery, or, on the other hand, their hatred of domination.[16]

More resonantly, Tacitus' reference to book-burnings in the forum under the reign of Domitian (*Agricola* 2), as censorship hits both authors and their output, brings home the precarious place of the historian and his books under oppressive regimes: 'savagery raged against not only the authors themselves, but also their books' (*neque in ipsos modo auctores, sed in libros quoque eorum saevitum*). The crime in this case is to not to have written history, but to have written it 'wrongly', by praising opponents of the Principate. Thus not only dissidence but also the commemoration of dissidence is liable to penalty, and the writing of history becomes an act of opposition in its own right. More dramatically still, Tacitus' foregrounds at *Ann.* 4.34–5 the figure of the censured historian, Cremutius Cordus, put on trial for treason for writing the wrong kind of history, telling the wrong kinds of lessons, making the wrong people into heroes for emulation.[17]

By contrast, most modern academics would count themselves safely distanced from book-burning and other form of severe censorship, confident of joining Tacitus' Cremutius in the claim that no one cares what they write about the distant past: 'the ancient historian has few critics – nobody minds if he overpraises the Carthaginian (or Roman) army...' (*Ann.* 4.33). But this is to underplay the power of historiography and the investment made in particular versions of the past. One need look no further than controversy over treatments of episodes in twentieth-century history or colonial history across the centuries to realise that telling the 'right' version does matter and that not all versions are equally acceptable. Even if moral didacticism may seem less pressing within modern historiography than among the Roman historians, nevertheless any shaped historical narrative needs to persuade the reader that the 'correct' moral judgements attributing praise and blame have been drawn.

Fundamental questions concerning the scope of historiography – how far back should our study of the past delve, where does history start, and how should the span of time past be divided up – also clearly pertain to both the ancient and

---

16 Tacitus, *Histories* 1.1: Note the variation between this and the start of Tacitus' *Annals*, where he places the decline in historiographic freedom after rather than before the reign of Augustus. The lack of transparency in public affairs and the consequences for historiographical integrity are outlined also by Cassius Dio 53.19.

17 Tacitus, *Annals* 4.34: 'When Cornelius Cossus and Asinius Agrippa were consuls, Cremutius Cordus was tried on the novel charge, heard then for the first time, of publishing a work of history, in which he had praised Brutus and said that Cassius was the last of the Romans.'

the modern worlds. Again, the ancient historians provide a cue, with Tacitus turning the question of where to start from a brain-teaser into an opportunity for political comment. Famously, the opening of the *Annals* makes mileage out of the suggestion that Roman imperial history actually began in the regal period, by opening the account of the period 'after the death of Augustus' (*ab excesso divi Augusti*) with the observation that 'from the beginning, Rome was ruled by kings' (*urbem Romam a principio reges habuere*).[18]

In many cases, setting the limits could be seen as more a problem than an opportunity. The periodization of Ancient History in universities and schools offers some clues as to the complexity of this question for modern syllabus-setters,[19] and the academic debate about the interface between archaeology and history is, indeed, not so far removed from the musings of ancient historians over when their study should begin. For all, the issue is primarily one of evidence. Thucydides (1.21) criticizes the evidence provided by poets and *logographoi*, whose prime purpose was to please the audience and whose subject-matter was mostly swamped by τὸ μυθῶδες owing to the passage of time, a criticism which fits uncomfortably with Thucydides' own archaeology and early history of Sicily. Only two or three generations were seen as representing the limit of historical memory,[20] in order to fulfil the criteria of accuracy and knowledge.

Outside the works of 'great historians', however, there was considerable enthusiasm for the realm of myth. The extant fragments of local Greek historiography positively embrace the opportunity to span the mythical, heroic age and the present day, allowing the latter to benefit from the *kudos* of the former.[21] Universal historians too remained, in practice, unconstrained by the self-imposed discipline of Thucydides. According to Diodorus Siculus (4.1.2), Ephorus avoided the ancient mythological period because of its difficulty (δυσχέρεια), presumably due to lack of evidence,[22] but he still took his narrative back to the return of the Heracleidae (4.1.3).[23] Ancient authors insisted that Ephorus was carefully vetting

---

18 Tacitus, *Annals* 1.1.1. This in spite of the oft-repeated protestation under that Principate that the *principes* were *not reges*; cf. Dio 52.40 and 53.17. See Clarke 2002.
19 *Exempli gratia*, in Oxford, Greek History used to start in 776 BC, the supposed date of the first Olympic Games; it was then moved 650 BC, leaving the world of early Mediterranean history to 'Greek Archaeology'.
20 See, for example, Finley 1975, 27.
21 On this, see Clarke 2008, 195–203.
22 See *FGrH* 70 F9, for this point implied. On Ephorus, see Clarke 2008, 96–98.
23 Note that Diodorus continues with the point that Kallisthenes and Theopompos likewise 'steered clear of ancient myths' (ἀπέστησαν τῶν παλαιῶν μύθων). See Parmeggiani 1999. Marincola 1997, 117–127, offers an excellent discussion of Diodorus 4.1.1–4 on myth in history.

the strength of reliable sources,[24] but the return of the Heracleidai still seems rather remote. Strabo's praise of Ephorus (*Geography* 10.3–4) for his early history of the Aetolians, for example, culminates in the judgement that he 'gave the best account of the foundation of cities, kinships, migrations, and original founders' (10.3.5), which makes attractive Schepens' suggestion that Ephorus was a key player in bridging the gap between the 'pre-history' concerning Panhellenic myths and sagas and the recent history of the Persian and Peloponnesian wars.[25] This sense of bridging allows us to reconcile Ephorus' care for sources and disdain for the most remote past, with his evident inclusion of a past which far predated that of Herodotus. Diodorus himself regularly blurs the boundary between *spatium mythicum* and *spatium historicum*.[26] The parameters of the chronological scope of historiography were clearly a subject for dispute in both the ancient and the modern worlds.[27]

Concern over evidence might seem to be belied by the lack of explicit scholarly apparatus in ancient historical works, which distinguishes ancient from modern attempts to write history.[28] However, the earliest known exponents of the historiographical tradition, such as Herodotus and Hecataeus, illustrate the importance of having strong grounds for the facts and the narratives propounded. Herodotus uses not only autopsy (or professed autopsy), but also oral accounts and some written sources, leading to the notion that his work of history is literally a setting out of the evidence and a display of how to use it in a way which was superior to that of contemporaries and near predecessors, such as Hecataeus.[29] Setting out evidence, weighing it up, acknowledging variant accounts, thinking about value of material evidence – all are methods with which any modern historian would recognize.[30] Furthermore, the methods for using documentary evidence such as inscriptions could become a matter of historiographical controversy in their own right, as when Polybius criticizes Timaeus' false citation of the

---

24 See Schepens 1977, 96, for Ephorus' famed *akribeia* or 'accuracy'.
25 Schepens 1977, 97.
26 See Clarke 1999b, 255–256.
27 See Clarke 2008, 98–106, on the blurring of *spatium mythicum* and *spatium historicum*.
28 See, however, Lenfant who has explored extensively the phenomenon of citation by ancient historians. See, for example, Lenfant 1999, 2005, 2013.
29 See Herodotus, *Histories*, Preface for his work as a ἱστορίης ἀπόδεξις, with Bakker 2002, on the meaning of this phrase.
30 Note how many Herodotean stories hinge on an object, such as 1.66.4 chains at Tegea; 5.77.2 shackles on the Acropolis. See Harris 2018, Dewald 1993, Bassi 2014. See Tacitus *Annals* 3.16, 3.19, 4.53 for different types of documentary evidence.

epigraphy concerning the foundation of Locri (12.9–10).³¹ Competitive interaction with other historians also underpinned Dionysius of Halicarnassus' preoccupation with sources, noting that those who have already read Hieronymous, Timaeus, Polybius and others and see material in his work that is not in theirs might accuse him of invention and 'will demand to know how I came to know those details' (1.7.1). The need to prove his evidential credentials prompts Dionysius to tell the reader what narratives and records he has used (*logoi* and *hypomnematismata*). Furthermore, he claims to have spent twenty-two years in Rome, learning Latin and gathering information both orally and from a long list of Roman annalists.³²

All of this suggests that the use of sources was more critical, knowing, and wide-ranging among ancient historians than is sometimes assumed.³³ They were using a combination of primary, documentary, material, epigraphic evidence *and* the accounts of earlier and other contemporary historians – secondary sources, which put them at two removes from what they were writing about. Here we find a self-consciousness about not only directly handling the past these ancient historians were describing, but also being part of a literary continuum with which they need to be critically engaged.³⁴ In this way some ancient historians strongly foreshadow our own two-fold attempts to write ancient history – a history of the past and a history of historiography itself.

---

31 On this fascinating passage, see Langslow 2013, 167–169.
32 See also Diodorus Siculus 1.4.2–5 for the claim to have learned Latin and used all the *hypomnemata*.
33 See, however, West 1985, for a systematic analysis of Herodotus' citation of both Greek and Oriental inscriptions in his work, in which she detects an occasionally casual approach to epigraphy, which is nevertheless explicable in terms of the predominantly oral culture in which he was operating and in which 'such inanimate, and indeed at times deceptive, testimony' as inscriptions might seem of peripheral value compared to that of oral *logoi* (305).
34 For the notion of continuators and a succession of historiography to stand alongside the continuum of history, see Clarke 1999b, 259–260. See Marincola 1997, 12, for the creative imitation of one's predecessors and the representation of reality as two forms of *mimesis*; also Gray 1987, 467. Schepens 1975, argues that the third-century Duris of Samos' mimetic programme focuses on 'imitation' of reality itself, not of previous artists or writers, thereby acknowledging the latter as a possible interpretation.

3 Bridging Reality and Representation: Translating Reality into Text

The self-consciously dual nature of both ancient and modern historiographical enterprises, concerned with both past realities and with literary attempts at their representation, serves to reinforce the ongoing continuum of historiography. Alongside the methodological similarities of purpose, freedom, scope and evidence, all of which bridge the gap between ancient and modern works of historiography, the duality of historiography as both a feature of the world, a reality worthy of its own study, and a representation of past reality, focuses attention of another form of bridging which lies at the heart of all historiographical enterprises – precisely that between reality and artistic representation. In a much-cited work, Frank Ankersmit argued that the historical text is 'no longer a layer *through* which one looks (either at a past reality or at the historian's authorial intention), but something which the historiographer must look *at*'.[35] This seems to capture perfectly both what connects ancient and modern historiography, with the latter both *looking at* and *looking through* the former, and what characterizes all historiography as a reflection of reality that is of interest in its own right.[36]

The perplexing relationship between reality and its representation, like so many other methodological issues in historiography, is articulated explicitly by ancient authors. The fact that historical works are representative and constructed brings the problem of organization into sharp focus.[37] Polybius notes when embarking on a monumental piece of historiography, one needs to know the beginning, middle and end before it is possible to start writing history (5.32.3–4), articulating a challenge which faces every historian trying to marshal his or her work and ideas into shape. The idea is echoed by Diodorus Siculus, with the comment that 'it should be the special care of historians to give attention to everything that may be of utility, and especially to the arrangement (οἰκονομία) of the varied material they present' (5.1). The challenge of translating a multi-dimensional reality into a literary text is articulated by Diodorus more fully later in his work:

---

[35] Ankersmit 1994, 128.
[36] See Bassi 2014, 174, for acute comments on 'the connection between the historical past and the historical text in the philosophy of history' and an effective use of Ankersmit's 'use of visual metaphors to refer to the epistemological dilemma that lies at the heart of historical narrative since the linguistic turn, namely, the relationship between the reality of the past and the rhetorical structures that shape that reality.'
[37] See Moles 1993, 94, for the idea that 'Herodotus is not just commemorating history: he is creating it'.

One might criticize historical narrative when one sees that in life many different actions happen at same time, but that those who record them must interrupt the narrative and distribute different times to simultaneous events, in an unnatural way. The result is that the actual experience of the events contains the truth, but the written record, deprived of such power, mimics events, but falls far short of the true arrangement (ὥστε τὴν μὲν ἀλήθειαν τῶν πεπραγμένων τὸ πάθος ἔχειν, τὴν δ' ἀναγραφὴν ἐστερημένην τῆς ὁμοίας ἐξουσίας μιμεῖσθαι μὲν τὰ γεγενημένα, πολὺ δὲ λείπεσθαι τῆς ἀληθοῦς διαθέσεως) (20.43).

The identification of historiography as a form of *mimesis* offers many productive and interesting ways to think about the relationship between reality and representation, but let us first scrutinize the organizational challenges.

The axes of time and space within historical narratives form the matrix within which the reality of the world is imperfectly mapped into a literary form. It is clear that all literary attempts to represent reality need to find some way to convey in linear form the simultaneously spatial and temporal location, direction, and progression of the world under discussion, and that the relative dominance given to the different elements of time and space is an authorial choice.[38] Whether time prevails as the overriding organizing principle, with spatial breadth figuratively spinning off to the sides; whether the driving force is a spatial one, with temporal depth drilling down intermittently, as in Strabo's work;[39] whether the two planes of time and space are more evenly handled, resulting in a 'woven' narrative, such as those offered by Polybius and Diodorus himself[40] – it is no surprise that it is the context of such methodological wrangling over how to represent what is effectively a 3–D reality in the 2–D world of the text that Diodorus makes his comments on the mimetic nature of historiography and the inability of the text perfectly to capture reality.

Historians in the ancient world make considerable mileage out of this organizational challenge, playing with the temporal and spatial frameworks which cause such narratalogical difficulties in order to draw out interpretative value. Take, for example, the opening of Tacitus' *Annals*.[41] Here the temporal dimension is inevitably at the fore; the annalistic form which traditionally characterizes Roman historiography raises the expectation that the regular ticking of the magisterial clock will articulate the following narrative, with the only challenge being the one identified by Diodorus, namely that the multiple venues for action will

---

[38] See Clarke 1999b.
[39] Clarke 1999a, 245–293.
[40] On woven narratives, see Clarke 1999b, 274–275.
[41] Tacitus, *Annals* 1.1.1: *urbem Romam a principio reges habuere*. See Clarke 2002 for discussion of this opening.

require the author to mesh together a narrative that has to suspend or even rewind temporal progression in order to encompass multi-locational action. The opening sentence, however, casts doubt on the likelihood that Tacitus' *Annals* will be this kind of conventional annalistic narrative. By starting with the words *urbem Romam*, Tacitus opens up the possibility that the spatial breadth of his work will be the global stage which Polybius (and Diodorus) had found difficult to tame into a linear narrative. Polybius had made the claim that Rome's empire resulted in a global history that moved as one with no multiple venues to worry about once the *symploke* had taken place and history had become 'corporate' or 'like a single body' (*somatoeide*), but later writers like Diodorus suggested otherwise. In the hands of Livy, the *urbs* and the *orbis terrarum* would again blend into an organic whole, one which was overburdened by its own magnitude (Livy 1 Preface 4: *iam magnitudine laboret sua*), but it is by no means clear whether this will be the case for Tacitus. Indeed, his own comments later in the work (4.32) indicate that the days of global excitement and the associated grand narrative died with the Republic. But in the opening two words of the *Annals* it remains an open question as to whether the work is going to be about the *urbs Roma* in its confined or its extended form.

Furthermore, the idea that the ticking of the magisterial clock will be the metronome which anchors the literary representation to the reality of Roman political life is called into question within this first sentence. *urbem Romam a principio reges habuere* – 'the city of Rome was, from the beginning, ruled by kings'. The regular cycle of Republican magistracies may not, after all, provide the heartbeat for Rome's history, but rather the longer and unpredictable articulation by reigns, whether they be of kings, dominant figures of the Republic, or emperors. Thus Tacitus plays with the reader's likely expectations about how the narrative of Roman history may be paced and spaced; about how he will deal with the difficulties of representation. His political comment is enmeshed within this historiographical question.[42] Doubts about the political reality have ramifications for the historiographical representation precisely because historiography makes claims to truth and accuracy which set it apart from fiction, as will be explored below. But, because the act of mimesis is imperfect, the process always poses a challenge and offers a fertile ground for analysis.

---

[42] See Ginsburg 1981, for the argument that Tacitus deliberately makes the Republican annalistic structure, with its chronological sequence and consular punctuation marks, cosmetically central but historically insignificant to his account.

A spatial parallel is offered by Strabo's *Geography*, where the primary organizing principle is unsurprisingly that of space, but where a different mimetic dilemma is in play – how to represent within the spatially organized text change over time, both on the global scale and within communities. Strabo rises to this challenge with a range of tactics, drilling down from the real, conceptual and literary plane of the 'map' into the chronological dimension to offer potted histories of individual places and thereby making his text 3-D in terms of the time-space matrix; and simultaneously but implicitly building up broad geographical layers which offer a synchronic survey of 'how the world is' at particular key phases of the past – the Homeric world, the age of colonization, the growth of Rome's empire, the current peaceful glorious Augustan age. For an author who wins little acclaim, it is a complex, multi-layered and sophisticated piece of literary representation.[43]

Some ancient authors explicitly draw attention to the need for historiography to find ways of mapping narrative time and space to the ever-shifting configurations of political or 'real' time and space, while others illustrate it implicitly by their own literary choices. The mimetic gap acts as a *locus* for creativity at all levels, in terms of both authorial choice and later interpretation, illustrating the duality of historiography as a writing *and* reading activity.

4 The Mimetic Mirror: Exploiting the Gap

Diodorus' comment that historiography is not and cannot be the same thing as history itself, but entails a gap between reality and representation, bridged by some mimetic process, requires further discussion.[44] The inherently representational nature of historiography, reinforced by Hayden White's work on formal-

---

[43] See Clarke 1999a, especially 245–293.
[44] See Gray 1987, 481–482, for the view that Diodorus here stresses second-hand versus true reality, rather than using *mimesis* as a technical term of literary criticism. However, the latter concept of *mimesis* was clearly also relevant to historiographical writings. At 469, she notes that for writers such as Dionysius of Halicarnassus, 'the meaning of *mimesis* in history is the recreation of reality, encompassing recreation of both character and emotion.' Aristotle's *Poetics* are clearly a key text. See 1447a on poetry and other artistic forms as a 'representation of life' (πᾶσαι τυγχάνουσιν οὖσαι μιμήσεις τὸ σύνολον), with representation understood in the sense that life presents to the artist the phenomena of sense, which the artist re-presents in a variety of media, imposing a coherence and pattern in the process.

ism, might appear to disengage the literary representation entirely from the reality it mimics.⁴⁵ As Momigliano importantly noted, however, historiography is characterized by claims to truth which set it apart from fictive literary forms, and this has been reiterated by countless scholars of ancient historiography.⁴⁶ The concern for truth and accuracy, repeated throughout the history of Classical historiography, whether it be manifested in Thucydidean *aletheia* or Tacitean concern over the effects on truthful discourse brought by the exigencies of the Principate, implies a relationship between reality and representation which is close and meaningful. Historiography claims to offer a truthful representation of its subject. It is not fiction,⁴⁷ but rather it claims to be mimetic of reality. But Diodorus reminds us that, in addition to the gap between ancient and modern attempts to write history, there is also a gap that lies at the heart of any historiographical enterprise – the crucial, definitive, and tantalizing disjunction between reality and representation; the failure of the narrative to *be* the reality, however much some ancient historians may attempt to blur the distinction.⁴⁸

For Diodorus the catalyst for these observations is the particular problem of how one can represent in a linear account events which happen simultaneously – just one of the difficulties facing the historian, the creator of the representation. Diodorus is surely right that historiography can only mimic the events it represents, and that it can never replicate reality, although constituting a new reality as a piece of intellectual history in its own right. For Diodorus, this is a 'falling

---

45 See White 1973. See Ankersmit 1994, 194, for a strong expression of this concern: 'we may wonder whether the postmodernist theory of historical writing (...) still leaves room for the authenticity of historical experience. That is, for an authentic experience of the past in which the past can still assert its independence from historical writing.'
46 Momigliano 1981. Note Cicero *De Oratore* 2.35–36 on history as 'the illumination of true reality' (*lux veritatis*). See Rood 1998, 10, for the view that 'What distinguishes historical texts from fiction is the reader's assumption that they relate 'what actually happened' and discussing 'history as a discourse of the real'; also Pitcher 2009, viii, for the idea that treating historical writings as works of literature sometimes 'stands accused of strategically ignoring the fact that works of *history*, unlike most works of art, place themselves in a very particular relation to what some of us still like to think of as reality'; Cameron 1989b, 33: 'Historical narrative is distinguished from fictional narrative by its presumed connection with real events, in fact with truth', while Wheeldon 1989, 44, points out that the reception of historical works as 'truthful' is largely determined by generic expectation, which dictates that history concerns *res gestae* rather than *res fictae* or *res fabulosae*.
47 Except in so far as all narrative is constructed. See Greenwood 2006, 66: 'In this sense fiction is intrinsic to historical narrative *qua* narrative, as long as we are clear that in this context, fiction is used in its primary sense to mean 'the creation of form in language'.
48 See, for example, Livy's claim to have 'written the real events of the Roman people' (*res populi Romani perscripserim*) 1 Preface 1.

short'; the 'written record' is 'deprived of the power' of the reality. In Gorgias' terms, *logos* has the power to depict reality in such a way that 'the soul endures through the words a suffering *of its own*' [my italics] (ἴδιόν τι πάθημα) – importantly close but not identical to the actual event.[49]

But this gap, the imperfect and compromised nature of historiography as a substitute for reality, offers an interpretative opportunity. As has been seen, there are many similarities in methodology between ancient and modern historiographies which allows us to consider them as parallel enterprises, but the observation made by Diodorus brings us back to the idea that the prime interpretation of 'historiography' for us entails 'reading ancient historians', historiography as an academic venture focused on the study of ancient historical texts, which explores and exploits the existence of the 'gap' between reality and representation, and considers various ways in which that gap is bridged, what mimetic devices are used so that the literary construct of the text meaningfully reflects the truth of the reality. This is the enterprise that historiographers are primarily engaged in: analysing the mimetic relationship between history and historiography; thinking about how historians bridge the gap, what devices they use to capture something of the 'essence', the 'truth', Thucydides' *sympase gnome*.[50] The different prisms through which we read ancient historians thus facilitate a dialogue between clues fed to us by the text and our own interrogative frameworks.

Ancient authors use a variety of images to analyse this mimetic process, many of them strongly visual.[51] Capturing a version of the truth is frequently articulated in terms of vividness,[52] with this goal of *enargeia* foremost. Wiseman's work on the possible origins of Roman historiography in the world of the *ludi Romani* serves to highlight how naturally history may be thought of in dramatic

---

49 Gorgias 82 B11.9 DK, with Meier 2018, 303 n. 45.
50 See Thucydides 1.22 on his recording of speeches not verbatim, but: 'keeping as close as possible to the general meaning of what was truly said' (ἐχομένῳ ὅτι ἐγγύτατα τῆς ξυμπάσης γνώμης τῶν ἀληθῶς λεχθέντων). See Greenwood 2006, 64. At 57–59, Greenwood interestingly discusses the idea of truth as the product of literary invention. Moles 1993, 106, observes the complexity of Thucydides' conception of truth at 1.22, noting that 'his speech material is a mixture of factual truth and imaginative truth, specific truth and general truth'.
51 See, for example, Plutarch *Moralia* 347a: 'the most effective historian is he who, by a vivid representation of emotions and characters, makes his narration like a painting'.
52 Walker 1993, 374, notes, 'As fiction, ancient historiography frequently sets as its goal verisimilitude – understood as a likeness to reality, and not as a fidelity to "the facts" – and its success was often measured, by ancient critics and historians alike, by the degree to which the representation is "visually perceived" by the reader.'

terms, and indeed Greek historians also frequently write of history as a spectacle.[53] But perhaps the most analysed account of the process by which historical reality is brought to the mind's eye of a reader is that by Lucian, *How to Write History* 51, in which the historian is exhorted to make his mind like a mirror which will reflect events as they really were. 'Above all, let him bring a mind like a mirror (κατόπτρῳ ἐοικυῖαν), clear, gleaming-bright, accurately centred, displaying the shape of things just as he receives them, free from distortion, false colouring, and misrepresentation.'[54] It is, according to Lucian, not for the historian to invent the facts, which have already taken place, but to arrange them and put them into words. Like a work of sculpture, the historical text is fashioned and displayed 'as vividly as possible' (εἰς δύναμιν ἐναργέστατα). The height of the historiographical craft is achieved 'when a hearer subsequently thinks that he can see what is being told to him' (ὅταν τις ἀκροώμενος οἴηται μετὰ ταῦτα ὁρᾶν τὰ λεγόμενα).

The image of the mirror perfectly encapsulates the tension between the idea that historiography must reflect a pre-existing reality, but that it will inevitably do so imperfectly and with some element of distortion.[55] As Moles helpfully articulates,[56] 'Both the historian ... and his readers ... are engaged in a process of 'looking' (*skopein*). Thus the historian's mimēsis of events, the product of his 'seeing' and 'looking', is like a mirror, at which he invites his readers to 'look'. But for the readers, as for the historian himself, the process of 'looking' is complex: to 'look' is not only to 'see' in a physical sense, but to 'contemplate', to 'attempt to understand', to 'reflect on'.' Moles' formulation issues a timely reminder of the multilayered process of viewing, interpretation, and writing that links our modern historiography with that of the historians whose works we study, both as windows through which to view past reality and as artefacts in their own right. The lens through which each writer 'reads' and 'writes' the reality which he represents, just as his decisions concerning the mapping of the world onto a linear text, are precisely what demand our attention as the focus of our modern reading of ancient texts. Historiography is a mimetic literary enterprise in which historical meaning is embedded in narrative structure and style, as well as in the configuration of time and space.

---

53 Wiseman 1994, 19. See Polybius 1.2.1; 1.64.3; 3.1.4; 9.9.10 for the spectacular nature of history.
54 On this passage, see the excellent discussion of Moles 1993, who observes (89) 'Surely *mimesis* through the medium of a mirror is as close to reality as one can get?'
55 See Moles 1993, 110, for the idea that what readers see in a historian's mirror 'is not a simple reflection of events but a reflection of specifics and general truths, and of the past, the present and the future'.
56 Moles 1993, 110.

5 Herodotus: Master of Mimesis

These complexities are amply illustrated in the *Histories* of Herodotus. In terms of translating a complex reality of vast chronological and spatial scope into a single linear literary representation, it is hard to think of an ancient historian who faced a greater challenge.[57] In addition, however, the text of Herodotus illustrates how historiography may be seen as a mimetic literary enterprise in which historical meaning is embedded in narrative structure and style. In an iconic scene in Book 4 of the *Histories*, where Herodotus has Darius march to where the Bosporus was bridged and sail to the so-called Wandering rocks to sit on a headland and view the Pontus, at the most basic level Herodotus offers himself a perfect opportunity to show off his extraordinary geographical knowledge:

> But Darius... sitting on a headland, viewed the Pontus, a sight worth seeing (ἀξιοθέητον). For it is the most wonderful of all the seas. Its length is 11,100 stades, and its breadth 3,300 stades at the point where it is widest. The channel at the entrance of this sea is 4 stades across; the narrow neck of the channel, called the Bosporus, across which the bridge was thrown, is about 120 stades long. The Bosporus reaches as far as the Propontis; and the Propontis is 500 stades wide and 1,400 long; its outlet is the Hellespont, which is 7 stades in width and 400 in length. The Hellespont empties into a gulf of the sea which is called the Aegean (485).

But the scene is far more complex than this. As is common in the *Histories*, Herodotus' elevated authorial viewpoint from which he looks down from afar on the vast stretches of land that make up the continents, separated by seas, straits, or major rivers, is here complemented by a further viewpoint which is focalized closer to the ground through a player in the narrative. The technique of inserting scenes within scenes and layers of spectating focuses the reader's attention on the process of viewing and representation.[58]

Darius' reaction to the sight that meets his eyes as he sits magisterially above the Black Sea provides the cue for the reader to share his wonder.[59] The Pontic sea is not only 'worth seeing' (ἀξιοθέητον), but exceeds all other seas in the wonder it inspires. Herodotus' authorial viewpoint through which he allows us not only to share Darius' wonderment but also to join with him, Herodotus, in gazing

---

[57] See Gould 1989, 42–62, for Herodotus' weaving together of micro- and macro-*logoi*. Clarke 2018, *passim*, addresses questions of spatial representation.
[58] Walker 1993, 376.
[59] See Grethlein 2015, 312, for the idea that 'narrative is not only a means of representation (as opposed to presence), but that it also has the capacity to trigger experiences in its recipients'.

down upon the scene of that wonderment heightens the sense of marvel and reinforces the self-consciously constructed and representational nature of these layered views. As elsewhere, here Herodotus justifies his own sense of amazement through quantification, giving the dimensions in detail as he presents a miniature geography of the region, which brings home the interconnected sequence of seas, trickling down to the central Mediterranean. The shift in focalization from Darius to Herodotus hinges on the spectacle of the Pontus. In fact, it is left unclear whether the positive assessment of the Pontus belongs to Darius or Herodotus or both.[60] Herodotus thereby offers a double-layering to the focalization, allowing the reader to view the world through Darius' eyes, but additionally sharing his own, more distant, perspective, in which Darius is a feature of the scene and the scope of his gaze is extended imaginatively by Herodotus from the point at which he is sitting right down to the outflow into the Aegean.[61] In these two different but intertwined perspectives Herodotus the author marvels at nature and at man's productive relationship with it, but the Persians view the same world with desirous and destructive eyes.[62] Herodotus' sense of geographical space is entangled with the more resonant and morally charged geographical vision of some of his characters. Here the creation of alternative focalisations or different representational frames opens up key interpretative questions over Herodotus' alignment with or opposition to or view of characters in the work. Of course, *all* perspectives fall within the all-encompassing scope of Herodotus as author of the work, but the consciously constructed nature of the narrative offers scope for the reader's viewpoints and responses to be shaped by the historian.

Furthermore, the literary device by which both the natural wonder of the connected seas and the human figure of Darius as their spectator are brought before the eyes of the reader is reinforced by the way in which the natural marvel is immediately followed in the narrative by the celebration of man's achievements. When Darius sails back to the bridge designed by Mandrocles of Samos, he indulges in yet more spectating – this time of the Bosporus itself. It is another natural feature viewed here, but the choice of viewing point is significantly no longer

---

[60] See Christ 1994, for similar blurring in perspective between Herodotus and Darius at other key geographical features in the narrative – the river Tearus, the river Peneus.
[61] Walker 1993, 373, notes that the figure of the historian as spectator of events illustrates the professed concern for autopsy. Herodotus' distanced perspective calls to mind Polybius' stress on the panoptic viewpoint of the historian, viewing the entirety of world history moving as though it were a single body.
[62] See Clarke 2018, 65–66.

the rocks but a bridge, and one which will span the continents. Here Darius celebrates another human marvel, namely the vast scale of his gathered army, which is inscribed on two pillars in Assyrian and Greek, a landscape of man's making.[63]

The triumph of man in creating everlasting wonders is emphasized by the reciprocal honours paid by Darius and Mandrocles (4.88). In return for Darius' thanks to Mandrocles, the latter has a picture made of the bridging of the Hellespont and of Darius sitting over it watching the army crossing.[64] The wondrous efforts of nature and especially of man are brought together through the medium of artistic representation, commemorating the marvellous sight of Darius marvelling at not nature as we first saw him, but now the achievements of man in conquering the sea he had so admired. This painting adds yet another, third, layer to the focalization of Darius as viewer of the works of nature and of man, as now the viewpoint of the painter is inserted between that of Darius and that of the historian, and the telescopic reach of this narrative stretches out still further.

As Grethlein has noted, the insertion of an actual piece of artwork into the narrative at this point, focused on one of the players as internal viewer, highlights the iconicity of such 'viewing' scenes.[65] Although, as Grethlein argues, various scenes of survey in the narrative, by freezing the moment of the narrative viewer's gaze, offer an experience to the reader similar to that of viewing a painting,[66] the inclusion of actual works of art lifts the mimetic theme to new levels. Here, the painting which Herodotus had probably seen on Samos and from which he may have drawn inspiration for his description of other 'survey' scenes, such as the depiction of Xerxes with his troops at Abydos (7.44) or at Doriscus (7.60–61),[67] interrupts and simultaneously enriches the line of viewing which would naturally have flowed from the reader through Herodotus then Darius and finally to the natural wonder of the Bosporus.

---

[63] 4.87. The pillars were afterwards carried by the Byzantines into their city and used to build the altar of Orthosian Artemis, except one column covered with Assyrian writing that was left beside the temple of Dionysus at Byzantium.
[64] For a fuller discussion of this painting, see West 2013. West interestingly suggests that the iconography of the painting probably resembled that of survey scenes in Persian art, as on the Bisitun relief.
[65] Although see Grethlein 2015, 320, for further nuance on the effect of telescopic viewings: 'When we concentrate on a picture in a picture or a film in a film, the awareness that what we see in the first place is only a picture or film fades without completely vanishing.'
[66] Grethlein 2013, 194.
[67] See Asheri, Lloyd, and Corcella (2007) *ad* 4.88, for Herodotus' use of the painting on Samos.

In fact, Herodotus alludes directly to artistic evidence only rarely in his work. At 2.73, he refers to the phoenix, a bird which he has never seen, except in a picture (2.73.1: ἐγὼ μέν μιν οὐκ εἶδον εἰ μὴ ὅσον γραφῇ). Herodotus' description of the bird is naturally dependent on the accuracy of this representation, a qualification which he makes explicit: 'It is of this size and appearance, if it really resembles the picture' (2.73.2: εἰ τῇ γραφῇ παρόμοιος). The clear understanding that the picture might not 'tell the truth' neatly expresses the imperfect mimesis of representative art, in a way which reminds the reader that this is a feature also of the historiographical account itself.[68]

Elsewhere, the imperfection of mimesis is illustrated through another artistic production, the map shown by Aristagoras to Cleomenes of Sparta when seeking his support for the Ionians against Persian aggression (5.49). The representational nature of the work of art is reinforced by the fact that it evokes a verbal commentary from Aristagoras, interpreting and articulating, this time in the medium of words rather than pictures, the geography of Asia. It is clear that neither the map nor the description can perfectly replicate the reality on the ground, the juxtaposition of two different versions being a stark reminder of this. Both words and images offer a mimesis, here designed to be mutually reinforcing.[69] But the fact that the map and its description act as catalysts for Herodotus' own verbal account of the Persian Royal Road, mapped out in terms of distances, guard-stations, and rivers (5.52–3), brings the author into the self-conscious mimetic frame and adds the likelihood of dissonance.[70] As it turns out, Herodotus' independent account of the geography of Asia acts as guarantor that Aristagoras was indeed broadly speaking the truth about when he claimed that the journey from the sea to Susa was three months, but Herodotus can go further in improving the precision of the distance, adding three days to the journey-length (5.54).[71] The provisional and contestable nature of the representation is thus reinforced.

In this episode, the mimetic nature of the work of art not only produces a certain degree of inaccuracy in the leap between reality and representation, but this gap is creatively exploited by Aristagoras in order to manipulate Cleomenes' view of Asia, enhancing his vision of the lands he might rule. West notes the lack

---

[68] See Tacitus, *Annals* 6.28, for a strikingly similar account of the phoenix and its habits.
[69] Barker, Bouzarovski, and Pelling 2016, note that 'this episode invites us to consider what difference it makes to depict space using words rather than images' (5).
[70] Branscome 2010; Branscome 2013, 105–149, discusses Aristagoras as a foil to Herodotus' superior knowledge.
[71] See also Hornblower 2013, *ad* 5.54, for the ongoing competition for accurate knowledge of the route. Hornblower notes a third-century AD papyrus (*P. Oxy.* LXV 4455) querying Herodotus' results.

of conventions concerning cartographic scaling in this period,[72] which Aristagoras is almost successful in exploiting to lead Cleomenes to underestimate the distance from Sparta to Susa.[73] Only when the savvy Spartan insists on knowing the distances being represented, does the deception fail. But in fact, Aristagoras at no point makes false claims about the size of Asia, simply leaving the truth unsaid. His deception concerns the benefits on offer, not the distances involved. At any rate, the constructed and mimetic nature of works of art within the text and of the text itself is reinforced.

Bringing these thoughts back to Mandrocles and his painting of Darius, if we are thinking about the gap between reality and representation in historiography, Herodotus' literary representation of an artistic representation of a scene in which the Persian king constructs a vision of the reality of which Herodotus himself is also a viewer, illustrates quite how engaged and interested ancient historians were in the whole process of creating narratives which bore a meaningful and 'truthful' relationship to reality while being self-consciously constructed and 'deprived of the power to convey the true experience of events', but nevertheless could 'mimic or imitate or represent' them. Mimetic imperfection perhaps, but one which offers a rich and fertile field of study for modern historiographers. As has been well observed,[74] the phenomenon of *mise en abyme* or embedded tales, the representation of spectators in historical narrative, and the inclusion of visual artistic depictions all serve to indicate a high level of self-consciousness about the processes of reading, viewing and interpretation, as reality is somehow translated onto paper.

Herodotus' inclusion of a painting in this chain of views emphasizes the representational nature of all the layers, including that of his own text. The master of mimesis, the arch-film-director, zooming his lens in and out, drawing the reader's attention to the act of framing and the ways in which viewers, including some of his characters, may *mis*represent reality, falls in turn within the reader's frame of analysis as an object of viewing, interpretation, framing, representation

---

[72] For the notion of cartographic space as elastic, see Aristophanes, *Clouds* 215–216, where Strepsiades proposes increasing the distance between Sparta and Athens on the map:
ὡς ἐγγὺς ἡμῶν. τοῦτο πάνυ φροντίζετε,
ταύτην ἀφ' ἡμῶν ἀπαγαγεῖν πόρρω πάνυ.
'How close it is to us. Take great care to move it far away from us.'
As Dover 1970, *ad loc.* notes, 'Strepsiades thinks of a map as a magical means of bringing places nearer together or further apart'.
[73] West 2012, 165.
[74] See, for example, Grethlein 2013, 2015; Walker 1993.

in his own right and the subject of modern historiography. The coalescence between reader and spectator extends to all levels of the mimetic process. But, interesting though the viewers and viewed, the history and the historical text are, it is the gaps between them which offer depth of meaning and resonance in historical interpretation.

Bibliography

Ankersmit, Frank (1994), *History and Tropology. The Rise and Fall of a Metaphor*, Berkeley.
Asheri, David/Lloyd, Alan/Corcella, Aldo (2007), *A Commentary on Herodotus Books 1–1V*, Oxford.
Bakker, Egbert J. (2002), "The Making of History: Herodotus' *Histories Apodexis*", in Egbert J. Bakker/Irene J.F. de Jong/Hans van Wees (eds), *Brill's Companion to Herodotus*, Leiden, 3–32.
Barker, Elton/Stefan Bouzarovski/Christopher Pelling (2016), "Introduction: Creating New Worlds out of Old Texts", in Elton Barker/Christopher Pelling/Stefan Bouzarovski/Leif Isaksen (eds), *New Worlds from Old Texts. Revisiting Ancient Space and Place* Oxford, 1–21.
Bassi, Karen (2014), "Croesus' Offerings and the Value of the Past in Herodotus' Histories", in Christoph Pieper/James Ker (eds), *Valuing the Past in the Greco-Roman World: Proceedings from the Penn-Leiden Colloquia on Ancient Values VII*. Mnemosyne Supplement 369, Leiden, 173–96.
Becker, Carl (1938), "What is Historiography?", *American Historical Review* 44, 20–8.
Branscome, David (2010), "Herodotus and the Map of Aristagoras", *Classical Antiquity* 29, 1–44.
Branscome, David (2013), *Textual Rivals. Self-Presentation in Herodotus' Histories*, Ann Arbor, MI.
Cameron, Averil (1989a), "Introduction: the writing of history", in Averil Cameron (ed.), *History as Text. The Writing of Ancient History*, London, 1–10.
Cameron, Averil (1989b), "Introduction to M.J. Wheeldon, "True Stories": the reception of historiography in antiquity", in Averil Cameron (ed.), *History as Text. The Writing of Ancient History*, London.
Christ, Matthew R. (1994) "Herodotean Kings and Historical Enquiry", *Classical Antiquity* 13, 167–202.
Clarke, Katherine (1999a), *Between Geography and History. Hellenistic Constructions of the Roman World*, Oxford.
Clarke, Katherine (1999b), "Universal perspectives in historiography", in Christina Kraus (ed.), *The Limits of Historiography: Genre and Narrative in Ancient Historical Texts*, Leiden, 249–80.
Clarke, Katherine (2002) "*In arto et inglorius labor*: Tacitus' anti-history", in Alan K. Bowman/Hannah Cotton/Martin Goodman/Simon R.F. Price (eds), *Representations of Empire. Rome and the Mediterranean World*, Oxford, 83–103.
Clarke, Katherine (2008), *Making Time for the Past: Local History and the Polis*, Oxford.

Clarke, Katherine (2018), *Shaping the Geography of Empire: Man and Nature in Herodotus'* Histories, Oxford.
Dewald, Carolyn (1993), "Reading the World: The Interpretation of Objects in Herodotus' Histories", in Ralph M. Rosen/Joseph Farrell (eds), *Nomodeiktes: Greek Studies in Honor of Martin Ostwald*, Ann Arbor, 55–70.
Dover, Kenneth J. (1970), *Aristophanes'* Clouds, Oxford.
Finley, Moses I. (1975), "Myth, Memory and History", in Moses I. Finley, *The Use and Abuse of History*, London.
Ginsburg, Judith (1981), *Tradition and Theme in the* Annals *of Tacitus*, Salem.
Gould, John (1989), *Herodotus*, London.
Gray, Vivienne (1987), "Mimesis in Greek Historical Theory", *American Journal of Philology* 108, 467–86.
Greenwood, Emily (2006), *Thucydides and the Shaping of History*, London.
Grethlein, Jonas (2013), *Experience and Teleology in Ancient Historiography: 'Future Past' from Herodotus to Augustine*, Cambridge.
Grethlein, Jonas (2015), "Aesthetic Experiences, Ancient and Modern", *New Literary History* 46, 309–33.
Harris, Edward M (2018), "Herodotus and the Social Contexts of Memory in Ancient Greece: the Individual Historian and his Community", in Zosia Archibald (ed.), *The Power of the Individual in Ancient Athens: Essays in Honour of John K. Davies*, London, 79–113.
Hau, Lisa (2016), *Moral History from Herodotus to Diodorus Siculus*, Edinburgh.
Hornblower, Simon (2013), *Herodotus. Histories Book* V, Cambridge.
Langslow, David (2013), "Archaic Latin Inscriptions and Greek and Latin Authors", in Peter Liddell/Polly Low (eds), *Inscriptions and their Uses in Greek and Latin* Literature, Oxford, 167–95.
Lenfant, Dominique (1999), "Peut-on se fier aux « fragments » d'historiens? L'exemple des citations d'Hérodote", *Ktèma* 24, 103–21.
Lenfant, Dominique (2005), "'Polybe et les 'fragments' des historiens de Rhodes Zénon et Antisthène (XVI,14–20)", in Guido Schepens/Jan Bollansée (eds), *The Shadow of Polybius. Intertextuality as a Research Tool in Greek Historiography*. Studia Hellenistica 42, Leuven, 183–204.
Lenfant, Dominique (2013) "The Study of Intermediate Authors and its Role in the Interpretation of Historical Fragments", *Ancient Society* 4, 289–305.
Maier, Felix K. (2018), "Dealing with the Invisible - War in Procopius", in Alexander Kampakoglou/Anna Novokhatko (eds), *Gaze, Vision and Visuality in Ancient Greek Literature*, Berlin/Boston, 289–307.
Marincola, John (1997), *Authority and Tradition in Ancient Historiography*, Cambridge.
Moles, John L. (1993), "Truth and Untruth in Herodotus and Thucydides", in Christopher Gill and T.P. Wiseman (eds), *Lies and Fiction in the Ancient World*, Liverpool, 88–121.
Momigliano, Arnaldo (1981), "The Rhetoric of History and the History of Rhetoric: On Hayden White's Tropes", in Elinor S. Shaffer (ed.), *Comparative Criticism. A Year Book, iii*, Cambridge, 259–68.
Parmeggiani, Giovanni (1999), "Mito e *spatium historicum* nelle *Storie* di Ephoro di Cuma", *Rivista Storica dell'Antichità* 29, 107–25.
Pitcher, Luke (2009), *Writing Ancient History: An Introduction to Ancient Historiography*, New York.

Pownall, Frances (2004), *Lessons from the Past: The Moral Use of History in Fourth-Century Prose*, Ann Arbor.

Rood, Tim (1998), *Thucydides. Narrative and Explanation*, Oxford.

Rutherford, Richard B. (1994), "Learning from history", in Robin Osborne/Simon Hornblower (eds), *Ritual, Finance, Politics*, Oxford, 53–68.

Schepens, Guido (1975), "Ἔμφασις und ἐνάργεια in Polybios' Geschichtstheorie", *Rivista Storica dell'Antichità* 5, 185–200.

Schepens, Guido (1977), "Historiographical Problems in Ephorus", in *Historiographia antiqua. Commentationes lovanienses in honorem W. Peremans septuag. Editae*, Louvain, 95–118.

Thomas, Rosalind (2019), *Polis Histories, Collective Memories and the Greek World*, Cambridge.

Walker, Andrew D. (1993), "*Enargeia* and the Spectator in Greek Historiography", *Transactions of the American Philological Association* 123, 353–77.

West Stephanie (1985), "Herodotus' Epigraphical Interests", *Classical Quarterly* 35, 278–305.

West, Stephanie (2012), "Skylax's problematic voyage: a note on Herodotus IV 44", *Eikasmos* 23, 159–67.

West, Stephanie (2013), "'Every Picture Tells a Story': A Note on Herodotus 4.88", in Boris Dunsch/Kai Ruffing (eds), *Herodots Quellen-Die Quellen Herodots. Classica et Orientalia,* Bd 6, Wiesbaden, 117–128.

Wheeldon, M.J. (1989), ""True Stories": the reception of historiography in antiquity", in Averil Cameron (ed.), *History as Text. The Writing of Ancient History*, London, 36–63.

White, Hayden (1973), *Metahistory: The Historical Imagination in Nineteenth-Century Europe*, Baltimore, MD.

Wiseman, T.P. (1994), *Historiography and Imagination. Eight Essays on Roman Culture*, Exeter, 1–22.

Inger N.I. Kuin
The Life of the Biographer: Plutarch's Presence in *Sulla*, *Antony* and *Otho*

1 Introduction

Plutarch's *Parallel Lives* are a feat. The variety of featured subjects, the liveliness of the narration, the bridging of disparate periods and societies, and their moral-ethical ambition are unparalleled.[1] Most remarkably Plutarch's biographical project makes the lives of historical subjects far removed in time fully present and pertinent to his contemporaries. With apparent ease the author manages to bring Pericles' lifeworld as close to the Roman reader as Otho's. In so far as men and women must always strive to live virtuous lives, for Plutarch it makes no difference if one takes a worthy friend or a man of the (distant) past for an example.

Compared to other ancient authors Plutarch is strikingly present in his corpus. Eunapios in his *Lives of the Philosophers* writes that Plutarch 'sprinkled' (ἐγκατέσπειρεν) his books with information about his own life, so that readers who pay close attention might trace these references, and reconstruct the facts of Plutarch's life from them (*VS* 454). Although Eunapios is too optimistic about the possibility of gathering a coherent biography of the author from his works, he is right about the frequent inclusion of autobiographical material.[2] Plutarch writes at length about his beloved hometown of Chaironeia, family members and friends feature in many dialogues, and his priesthood at Delphi left a clear mark in his works. There is, however, a significant difference between the philosophical essays, *Moralia*, and the *Parallel Lives* in this regard: in the *Moralia* autobiographical tidbits are scattered throughout, while in the *Lives* they are extremely rare.

The rarity of autobiographical content in the *Parallel Lives* must be understood in light of Plutarch's programmatic stance according to which he, and his readers through him, can freely connect with historical figures through representations of character as displayed in deeds small and large. (Conversely, in the *Moralia* the persona of Plutarch as author and thinker centers the philosophical

---

[1] I thank audiences at the Reconciling Ancient & Modern Philosophies of History / Historiography conference (2016), the OIKOS Impact of Empire Work in Progress Day (2017), and the OIKOS Anchoring Innovation Expert Meeting (October 2017) for their helpful questions and comments. Preliminary research for this chapter has been carried out as part of the After the Crisis research project at Groningen University and the OIKOS Anchoring Innovation research agenda.
[2] Cf. Lamberton 2001, 3–4.

reflection.) In the *Parallel Lives* generally speaking Plutarch has no need to allude to his own experiences. The author's connection to the experiences of his subjects is a fundamental given, and is performed in such a way that the reader is expected to enter into a relationship with men of the past just as effortlessly. But, in some of the *Lives* we do suddenly catch a glimpse of Plutarch himself or a family member. In this chapter I will study the rare (quasi) autobiographical moments in Plutarch's *Lives*, pursuing several central questions. First, can we identify any patterns in the author's decision about when to 'intrude' into his subjects' lives? Second, what effect do the moments of authorial presence have on the reader? And, thirdly, what can these autobiographical exceptions tell us about Plutarch's overall methodology in the *Parallel Lives*?

Before investigating the autobiographical moments of the *Lives*, it will be necessary to revisit several well-known programmatic prologues, where Plutarch comments explicitly on his approach and aims with respect to biography. I will focus on how Plutarch reflects on the relationships between the four implicated parties in each set of *Parallel Lives*: author, reader, and two protagonists. Next, I will discuss in chronological order the three *Lives* in which autobiographical elements feature most prominently: *Antony*, *Sulla*, and *Otho*. The protagonists of the first two *vitae* (or their troops) spent time in the biographer's home country of Boeotia during the (civil) wars of the first century BCE. This raises the question of whether in these works the adverse effects that the campaigns of Sulla and Antony had on the lives of Plutarch's forefathers affected his presentation of events. *Otho*, one of only four unpaired *Lives*, is the latest subject on whom Plutarch is known to have written a biography. For Plutarch the circumstances of Otho's reign, which dates to the author's early twenties, were germane to his own experiences in Rome and in Italy.

In the *Parallel Lives* Plutarch creates autobiographical connections in three different ways: through the landscape, through specific objects, and through storytelling. If we consider these three media as distinct modes of remembering, which can of course be combined by the author, it becomes apparent that all three are core concepts in twentieth and twenty-first century philosophy of history. The importance of place and landscape to historical memory was influentially raised by Pierre Nora, precipitating a massive body of research on *lieux de mémoire*, from antiquity to modern history.[3] The power of objects to embody and activate the past has also emerged as a prominent line of inquiry. Both landscape

---

[3] Nora 1984–1992; 1989. On memory and history, with reference to Nora, see Assman 2011 [1992]: 1–59 (on Assman see further below). For a critical appraisal of the mnemonic turn, especially in the field of Ancient History, see Berliner 2005; cf. Grigoropoulos *et al.* 2017.

and objects allow for the perception of continued, immediate experience, which Ankersmit, Runia, and Carr have presented as an antidote to the ever increasing distance between historical events and our understanding of them in the wake of history's linguistic turn.[4] A fascinating fictional example of this material turn in history is a recent Flemish novel, titled *Vloekhout* (*Curse Wood*). The protagonist is a speaking piece of wood that was part of the cross of Jesus, becomes the surface for an icon in czarist Russia, and, after being used in target practice by Bolsheviks, is restored by the avant-garde painter Malevich.[5] An object that mediates the experience of history for modern audiences through its materiality has been given a speaking voice by the literary author. Finally, storytelling, in the form of oral history, became fully entrenched in historiographical methodology in the second half of the twenty-first century.[6] While it does not offer the same hope of 'escape' from Hayden White's emplotment as places and objects do,[7] oral history, just *like* places and objects, draws on experience as the site of memory and therefore of history, focusing on individual, first person accounts of events.

It is worth repeating that in Plutarch's *Parallel Lives* moments of personalized memory through place, object, and oral (family) history are exceptions. In general he understands history as a country that is universally accessible for all those who are willing to pay attention to its lessons, presented and organized by him as biographer. A larger aim of this chapter, therefore, will be to reflect on the differences between what we might call Plutarch's philosophy of history and its modern counterpart(s). If the exceptional subjective moments in Plutarch's emphatically intersubjective project seem like its most modern elements, what does this entail for the intersubjectivity of the modern experience-based approach to history?

---

[4] For Ankersmit (2005, 4–5) the concept of memory, 'an experience or re-experience of the remembered past', takes the place of history, in order to bypass the historiographical tradition. Runia (2006, 2010) has proposed that objects can serve as carriers of memory, and can give us unmediated access to the past. Carr (2014), building on this work, proposes a phenomenological approach to configure history as experience. Grethlein (2013), connecting narratology theory to the experience paradigm, has argued that ancient authors, including Plutarch, through their narrative and style work to let readers experience historical events, see further below.
[5] De Boose 2018.
[6] Started by Allan Nevis at Columbia University in the late 1940s, who founded the Columbia Center for Oral History there in 1948. Paul Thompson (1978) laid out its methodological underpinnings in *The Voice of the Past*, which continues to be of great influence, Thompson and Bornat 2017, vii. On storytelling in ancient historiography see e.g. Kuin 2017a.
[7] White 1980.

2 Plutarch's Philosophy of History

In the *Parallel Lives* programmatic statements are concentrated in the introductions to individual pairs. Their contents are treated in detail by Duff in his monograph *Plutarch's Lives. Exploring Virtue and Vice*,[8] and what follows is indebted to his discussion. Though Duff warns against extrapolating comments from specific *Lives* to apply them to the collection as a whole, when read together these programmatic passages do offer a general outline of Plutarch's intention for the project. As such they provide the methodological context for understanding the role of autobiographical moments in his historical writing.

From a modern perspective Plutarch's *Parallel Lives* are strictly speaking not historiography but biography. For the author, however, there was no clear cut distinction between the two, as seems to have been the case for ancient authors more generally.[9] In the introduction to the *Alexander – Caesar* Plutarch appears to juxtapose *historiai* and *bioi* ('lives'), suggesting that this pair belongs to the latter category.[10] Yet, in many other programmatic passages he refers to the *Lives* as *historia(i)*.[11] Even keeping in mind the differences between ancient and modern understandings of historiography, there should be no hesitation to treat Plutarch's *Lives* as historiography. He himself viewed his project within the tradition of Thucydides' historical writing,[12] and this will be my point of departure as well.

Plutarch's self-fashioning as historiographer is, in contrast to some of his famous predecessors, never predicated on autopsy of the events described, and he only rarely mentions seeing the sites where they took place.[13] Rather, he presents himself as being uniquely dedicated to gathering source materials: he brings together what is already known with what has escaped others. Even well-known sources he is able to present in a new light, paying special attention to their bearing on issues of character and virtue.[14] Plutarch derives his authority as a historiographer from his research and interpretative skills, and this is what he claims to

---

[8] Duff 1999, 13–51.
[9] Cf. Grethlein 2013, 92.
[10] *Alex. – Caes.* 1.2: οὔτε γὰρ ἱστορίας γράφομεν, ἀλλὰ βίους. E.g. De Blois (2014, 267) takes this as programmatic for the corpus as a whole, but Duff (1999, 21) shows that it is a type of *recusatio* — why another work on Alexander? — specifically for *Alex.*
[11] E.g. *Thes. – Rom.* 1.2, 1.4–5; *Per. – Fab.* 1.1. See for further references Duff 1999, 18 n. 14.
[12] E.g. *Nik. – Crass.* 1.5. On Plutarch and Thucydides see Pelling 2002, 117–142.
[13] E.g. Thuc. 1.22.2; Hdt. 1.8.2; cf. Marincola 1997, 63–85.
[14] E.g. *Art.* 8.1; *Nik.* 1.5; *Dem.* 1–2.

offer to readers: thanks to his strengths as a researcher, thinker, and writer, Plutarch and his audiences are in a unique position to understand and learn from noteworthy historical individuals.[15]

In the prologue of the *Lives of Aemilius and Timoleon* Plutarch explicitly places himself alongside the reader, showing that they enter into a relationship of emulation with historical figures together. He confesses that he began to write the *Lives* for the sake of others, his readers, but that he has come to realize that he is 'staying on and enjoying it' for his own sake.[16] In this phrase Plutarch makes striking use of geographical vocabulary. The first verb can mean both 'to stay in the same place' and 'to continue' (to do something); the second verb, however, has the specific meaning of 'loving a place' or 'dwelling gladly' somewhere (*BDAG*). The author conceptualizes the past as seen through the lives of his subjects not merely as a foreign country that can easily be reached through the medium of his writing, but even as an especially desirable destination — all the while, importantly, no physical travel is necessary.

Plutarch goes on to describe, in the same prologue, that he and his readers look to the lives of the biographical subjects as into a mirror, in order to adorn and approximate one's life to *their* virtues. Looking in this mirror ultimately amounts to 'spending time together' (συνδιατήσει) and even 'living together' (συμβιώσει) with the men of the past who 'are received as guests through history each in turn'.[17] Plutarch primarily envisions a get together between himself or the reader with individual men of the past, 'each in turn'. But, if we zoom out and take into account the project of the *Lives* as a whole, we have to imagine a double mirror or even a crowded dinner party. Not only is Plutarch aligning himself with the reader with respect to their shared privilege of relating to virtuous men of the past, but the comparative nature of the *Lives* means that the virtues of one man, a Greek, are always presented to the reader alongside the virtues of a second man, a Roman. Plutarch's readers travel to two different pasts, which are brought together through the intervention of the author. A major assumption, then, underlies this double mirror or crowded dinner party, namely that *through historical writing* time and place can be traversed. Plutarch understands the lives of Greeks and Romans as self-evidently mutually illuminating and accessible for ethical purposes to himself and his readers.[18]

---

15 Compare *Per.* 2.4 with Duff 1999, 37–42.
16 *Aem.* 1.1: ἐπιμένειν δὲ καὶ φιλοχωρεῖν.
17 *Aem.* 1.1–1.2: ἐπιξενούμενον ἕκαστον ἐν μέρει διὰ τῆς ἱστορίας.
18 There is, of course, something jarring about the mirror-metaphor of *Aem.* 1.1: instead of one's own reflection, we see the reflection of two others, whom we try to approximate in virtue by

In the opening of his *Lives of Demosthenes and Cicero* Plutarch discusses the merits of living in a small versus a large city. Taking allegedly insignificant Keos and Aigina as examples, which produced important actors and poets, Plutarch argues that not only artists but especially virtuous men can thrive in small places. Even though to a historian living in a large place offers the advantage of having access to more written sources and lots of people and their memories, Plutarch chooses to live in his native Chaironeia. As has been noted this passage can be read as self-praise: small cities produce virtuous artists, and Plutarch is from a small place.[19] But, I would suggest that in this passage too we can discern a programmatic layer.

Plutarch's discussion of being from a small or a large place has direct bearing on the subjects of the pair: Demosthenes, of course, was from Athens, while Cicero was from the Italian town Arpinum. The two orators are separated by a few centuries, a language, and their very different hometowns, yet they obviously shared attainment in virtue through oratory and their public life. The observation that one can be equally virtuous coming from a small or a large place contributes, then, to the viability of the comparison of the two orators. Likewise, readers coming from a small town are encouraged to view the *Lives* as being relevant to them even if they are about 'big men': after all, Plutarch's own humble surroundings do not prevent him from relating their lives to his own. The discussion of small and large cities, just as the mirror-metaphor, underlines the insistence on translatability and intersubjectivity that is at the root of Plutarch's biographical project: radically different historical subjects can mutually elucidate each other, and, writer and reader can simultaneously interact with historical subjects radically different from each other and from them – just as well, in fact, as when everyone were to be at the same dinner party.

The intricate relationship between author, readers, and subjects that the programmatic statements lay out explicitly, is expressed implicitly in the narrative of the *Lives*. Plutarch often weaves the importance of ethical emulation into the coming of age stories of his subjects: Themistokles was inspired by Miltiades' virtue, and Theseus by Herakles' exploits.[20] These moments confirm the value of studying the virtues of others, and the *Lives* allow readers to follow Themistokles' and Theseus' example in looking to other virtuous men for models of behavior – there is, again, a doubling of exemplarity here. Another element is the blurring

---

studying them. For this issue and further scholarship on the mirror-metaphor see Zadorojnyi 2010.

19 *Dem.* 1–2; cf. Pelling 2002, 271–272.
20 *Thes.* 6.6, 25.4; *Them.* 3.3–4; cf. Duff 1999, 50–51.

between Plutarch's own voice as narrator and the viewpoint of characters within the *Lives* with respect to their ethical stance. Chrysanthou has recently pointed out how the ambiguity as to whether certain evaluative comments should be attributed to the narrator or to a character 'breaks down the barrier between the in-text characters and the external audience', encouraging the readers to be immersed in the action, and evaluate it for themselves.[21] In this case the blended moral evaluation by the in-text characters and narrator serves as an example to the audience to try to do the same. In similar vein, Grethlein has analyzed how Plutarch uses vivid description (*enargeia*) to allow audiences to experience events from the viewpoint of the protagonist, as if they are unfolding, with the ultimate purpose of drawing in readers to evaluate the action morally.[22]

Taken together, the programmatic statements from the *Lives* show that for Plutarch the applicability and ethical utility of the experiences of people far removed in time and place is a given. It is for this reason that Plutarch's connections of history to himself and his family are remarkable: from the perspective of his methodology they are not *needed*. In the quasi autobiographical moments to which we will now turn, Plutarch temporarily bypasses his customary insistence on the *universality* of the ability to interact with the past, presenting instead a *particular* point of contact. Pelling, in a brief survey of some of the passages that I will discuss, notes that such connections add to the narrator's authority and 'convey a world where the past has vitality'.[23] Such an analysis, however, glosses over the fact that for Plutarch the past has vitality no matter what, leaving the question of why the author includes autobiographical elements in the *Lives* when he does unanswered. It is to this question that I will now turn, proceeding chronologically through the *Lives* of Sulla, Antony, and Otho.

3 Plutarch on Sulla in Boeotia

Plutarch's *Life of Sulla* has been studied primarily as a problematic *Life*, because Sulla, of course, is a less than obvious candidate as a historical role model of virtue. At the same time, Plutarch does not use the story of Sulla as simple apotreptic either. Especially in the *synkrisis* his final verdict of Sulla is surprisingly positive, emphasizing his successes in war, and his selflessness in fighting abroad for

---

[21] Chrysanthou 2018, 65.
[22] Grethlein 2013, 92–130.
[23] Pelling 2002, 269.

Rome, while his peers were attacking him back home (*Lys.–Sul. synkr.* 5). For this reason Duff has argued that the *Lives of Lysander and Sulla* seeks to problematize the moral status of both protagonists, and to 'force the reader to assume a more active role in assessing the good and the bad'.[24]

Aside from its moral ambivalence, the *Life of Sulla* is also remarkable for the large role that Greece plays as a stage for the actions of the protagonist. Plutarch includes in great detail Sulla's campaigns in Achaia and Boeotia during the First Mithridatic War, which arose out of ongoing haggling between Rome and Pontos over influence in the Black Sea region. By the time Sulla landed at Epiros in 87 BCE Eupator was in control of most of Greece and Asia Minor. After Sulla's difficult but ultimately successful siege of Athens, fighting moved to Boeotia where he beat Mithridates' general Archelaos in two major battles at Chaironeia, Plutarch's hometown, and Orchomenos respectively.

Plutarch describes Sulla's siege of Athens with an emphasis on the violence and cultural destruction committed by him and his soldiers.[25] In the comparison, though, he contrasts Sulla positively with Lysander with respect to their treatment of Athens: Sulla left the city free and independent (*autonomos*) after taking it, while Lysander appointed savage and lawless (*paranomos*) tyrants.[26] Sulla's relation with Athens in Plutarch bears out Duff's analysis of the parallel pair as challenging readers to consider difficult moral questions, in this case, the contradiction between the bloodshed and destruction caused by Sulla's siege, and its (putatively) positive result of restored 'freedom' for Athens.

The account of the fighting in Boeotia in the *Life of Sulla* contains similar contradictions. On the one hand, Plutarch's hometown of Chaironeia was largely spared thanks to the intercession of Chaironeians fighting in Sulla's army (*Sul.* 15.8), while other Boeotian towns were razed to the ground (*Sul.* 26.4). Throughout his descriptions of the events of the First Mithridatic War in his home country Plutarch subtly reminds the reader of his personal connection to the region, and, therefore, to these events. He does this through references to stories told by the locals, first person plural descriptors applied to (features of) the region, and the inclusion of (implied) autopsy in his account. This material is juxtaposed with his

---

[24] Duff 1997, 182. Compare Stadter (1992) who reads the pair as an ethical message about the dangers of excessive ambition even, or especially, in talented men.
[25] *Sulla* 12–14; cf. Duff 1997, 182; Kuin 2018, 620–622.
[26] *Lys.–Sul. synkr.* 5. Plutarch's inclusion of the notion that Sulla restored Athens to freedom fits with Sulla's self-presentation as protector of the legacy of the city, of which traces can also be found in Appian (*Mith.* 39), and in Athenian coinage from the period, cf. Kuin 2017b, 163–166; Badian 1976, 115–116.

typical reliance on historiographic sources, including, in this case, Sulla's *Memoirs*.

Plutarch transitions from his account of the siege of Athens to the next stage of the war by explaining why Sulla transferred his army into Boeotia, and how he came to be reunited with the forces of his general Hortensius. In bringing this about the help of a certain Kaphis was pivotal: he knew the terrain so well that he was able to slip Hortensius and his men by Mithridates' troops unnoticed, using an alternative route. Plutarch describes this Kaphis as 'being one of ours'.[27] This phrase has bothered scholars because earlier on in the *Life* we have already met at some length a Kaphis working in the service of Sulla, who is there said to be from Phokis, and not from Plutarch's native Boeotia (*Sull.* 12). Some scholars assume that he is the same Kaphis, which is plausible enough, and choose to emend the text in order to fix the 'problem'.[28] This, however, seems unnecessary.

The salient piece of information about Kaphis in the passage is his knowledge of the region. Since he is from neighboring Phokis, he would likely be similarly well-versed in the topography of the area as a Boeotian. This becomes even clearer when we consider the other parties in the passage: Phokians and Boeotians would certainly have a shared advantage over both the Roman generals and the 'barbarians' fighting for Mithridates in terms of understanding the lay of the land. Plutarch can represent Kaphis as 'one of ours' on account of his role as a Greek serving Romans, and trying to promote local interests: earlier on in the *Life* he tried, albeit unsuccessfully, to prevent Sulla from confiscating treasuries from the sanctuary at Delphi (*Sull.* 12). As his narrative continues Plutarch will feature several Boeotians attempting the same balancing act.[29]

As Sulla's army presses on, Mithridates' general Archelaos prepares to set out for Chaironeia. The Chaironeians fighting in Sulla's army beg him not to give up their city. Sulla sends one legion to the city, and lets the Chaironeians join them. Plutarch briefly notes a disagreement in the sources about which tribune led the

---

27 *Sull.* 15.3: ἡμέτερος ὤν.
28 Robert 1960, 82–84; cf. Flacelière and Chambry 1971, 336.
29 It is worth noting that nowhere in the *Lives* does Plutarch use ἡμέτερος specifically to mean, 'ours', i.e. 'belonging to Boeotians/Chaironeians'. There are only six other instances of ἡμέτερος (excluding direct quotations) in the *Lives*, referring to humans in general (*Num.* 12.1), Plutarch as an individual (*Them.* 32.6, *Dem. Cic. synkr.* 1.1), Plutarch's generation (*Them.* 32.6), and those living under Roman law (*Sol.* 21.7, twice). On Greek-speaking authors using first person pronouns and possessives to refer to 'Roman(s)' see Swain 1996, 313–314 (who does not mention Plutarch in this context).

legion to Chaironeia (Gabinius or Ericius), and then concludes: 'Indeed, so narrowly did *my* city escape the danger'.³⁰ In the next section Plutarch describes oracles that were given in Lebadeia in the cave of Trophonios — an oracular site in Boeotia that rose to great prominence in the imperial period — in between the battles of Chaironeia and Orchomenos, predicting a second victory for the Romans in the area within a short time. Plutarch tells us that he gained this information from two different kinds of sources. On the one hand he points to 'the natives', i.e. his fellow Boeotians, who are still talking about these oracles; on the other hand he cites the tenth book of Sulla's own *Memoirs* as a source.³¹ Both passages, in fact, jump ahead to the conclusion of the battles of which Plutarch goes on to give an account (*Sul.* 17.3–20.4).

In the account of the battle Plutarch continues to show his connection to the region. In describing the landscape near Chaironeia, he mentions Thurion, 'a hill *we* call Orthopagos'.³² Two brave Chaironeians, named Homoloïchos and Anaxidamos, offer to cut off Mithridates' soldiers that are stationed at Thurion, using their superior knowledge of the local terrain, just like Kaphis. They are successful, and after the battle they are honored with a trophy at Thurion on which, Plutarch writes, 'it says in Greek letters that Homoloïchos and Anaxidamos were the bravest'.³³ Plutarch also mentions another trophy erected by Sulla with the names of Ares, Nike, and Aphrodite (*Sul.* 19.5), referencing, most likely, Sulla's own explanation for the inclusion of these gods,³⁴ and he adds: 'on his trophies in *my* country his name is written in this way: Lucius Cornelius Sulla Epaphroditos.'³⁵ Plutarch's descriptions of Sulla's trophies have to a remarkable extent been corroborated by archeological finds,³⁶ and in the narrative he gives a strong impression of having studied the trophies himself — it would be hard to imagine why he

---

30 *Sul.* 14.1: ἡ μὲν οὖν πόλις ἡμῶν παρὰ τοσοῦτον ἐξέφυγε τὸν κίνδυνον.
31 *Sul.* 17.1: περὶ ὧν οἱ μὲν ἐπιχώριοι πλείονα λέγουσιν ὡς δὲ Σύλλας αὐτὸς ἐν δεκάτῳ τῶν ὑπομνημάτων γέγραφε…
32 *Sul.* 17.4: ὄρος, ὃ καλοῦμεν Ὀρθόπαγον.
33 *Sul.* 19.5: γράμμασιν Ἑλληνικοῖς ἐπισημαῖνον Ὁμολόϊχον καὶ Ἀναξίδαμον ἀριστεῖς.
34 Eckert 2016, 120.
35 *Sul.* 34.2: καὶ παρ' ἡμῖν ἐν τοῖς τροπαίοις οὕτως ἀναγέγραπται 'Λεύκιος Κορνήλιος Σύλλας Ἐπαφρόδιτος'; cf. *Mor.* 318d: καὶ τὰ παρ' ἡμῖν ἐν Χαιρωνείᾳ τρόπαια καὶ τὰ τῶν Μιθριδατικῶν οὕτως ἐπιγέγραπται.
36 Inscription at Thurion for Homoloïchos and Anaxidamos: *SEG* 41:448, cf. Camp *et al.* 1992. Trophy at Orchomenos with the gods' names: Kountouri *et al.* 2018; cf. Eckert 2016, 121. As far as we can tell Sulla is *not* called Epaphroditos on these inscriptions, but they are highly fragmentary. Pausanias (9.40.7) mentions two trophies erected by Sulla in Chaironeia to mark his victory over Mithridates, but gives no information about the inscriptions.

would not have done so — while also referencing other sources, specifically Sulla's memoirs.

In Plutarch's account of the aftermath of the fighting both physical objects and local storytelling remain important. He concludes his narrative of the battle of Orchomenos, which had Mithridates' soldiers too afraid to offer much resistance, with the following, chilling summation:

> The marshes were filled with the blood of the dead, and the lake with their corpses, so that even to this day many bows, helmets, fragments of steel breastplates, and swords of barbarian make are found buried in the mud, although almost two hundred years have passed since this battle.[37]

Appian's version of the narrative adds to this the unnerving image of Mithridates' soldiers drowning, not knowing how to swim, and begging for mercy in a language not understood by their enemies (*Mith.* 50). But Plutarch's focus on weaponry still being found sets up a tangible connection between the battle and his own time, explicitly drawing attention to the timespan that is traversed by contemplating these gruesome finds. It appears likely that Plutarch saw some of the — reputed — remains from the battle himself, or at the very least he spoke with locals who had.

The final passage from the *Life* that I will discuss concerns events some time after the conclusion of the First Mithridatic War. Plutarch writes that Sulla, who had been spending some time in Athens, travelled to the hot springs of Aidepsos to alleviate pain from his numb and swollen feet. While there some fishermen from Halai come up to him and offer him high quality fish. Sulla is delighted with the fish and says to them: 'What? Is any man from Halai still alive?'[38] Plutarch explains in an aside that after the battle of Orchomenos Sulla and his troops destroyed three Boeotian cities while pursuing the enemy. He continues to describe the terror of the fishermen at Sulla's comment. Sulla, however, smiled, and told them to be on their way in peace. Plutarch concludes: 'The men of Halai say that from this the fishermen drew the courage to return to their city.'[39]

In the passage Plutarch, again, includes a local oral tradition, underlining his connection to the region.[40] More importantly, the inclusion of the story of

---

37 *Sul.* 21.4: καὶ κατέπλησαν ἀποθνήσκοντες αἵματος τὰ ἕλη καὶ νεκρῶν τὴν λίμνην, ὥστε μέχρι νῦν πολλὰ βαρβαρικὰ τόξα καὶ κράνη καὶ θωράκων σπάσματα σιδηρῶν καὶ μαχαίρας ἐμβεβαπτισμένας τοῖς τέλμασιν εὑρίσκεσθαι, σχεδὸν ἐτῶν διακοσίων ἀπὸ τῆς μάχης ἐκείνης διαγεγονότων.
38 *Sul.* 26.3: 'ἔτι γὰρ ζῇ τις Ἁλαίων;'
39 *Sul.* 26.4: Ἁλαῖοι μὲν ἐκ τούτου λέγουσι θαρρήσαντες αὖθις εἰς τὴν πόλιν συνελθεῖν.
40 Cf. Flacelière and Chambry 1971, 340.

Sulla's cruel quip bears testimony to the grave danger that the Chaironeians were in at the time, and how fortunate their narrow escape was. If events had turned out slightly differently, if, for instance, the Chaironeians in Sulla's army had not been able to convince Sulla to protect their city, Plutarch's countrymen could have been the fishermen from this story — refugees whose city has been destroyed by a callously jocular Roman general.

Throughout his narrative of the fighting in and near Boeotia during the First Mithridatic War Plutarch signals his personal connection to the place and to this episode in Sulla's career. Nonetheless, the private element never overshadows Plutarch's customary methodology. He still uses historiographical sources and, even though he narrates these events from a particular rather than a universal point of view, he appeals to the reader to consider Sulla together with him. The story of Boeotia in the First Mithridatic War encapsulates the complexity and volatility of the character of Sulla in the *Life* as a whole. Sulla's virtues are on display in his effective execution of the battles of Chaironeia and Orchomenos, and in his willingness to answer the pleas of the Chaironeians and to honor them for their service. Yet, the dangerous cruelty that is also produced by his ambition is made tangible through the buried mass of armor of the defeated soldiers of Mithridates, and emerges again in his casual joke about the destructions his army wrought elsewhere in Boeotia.

4 Plutarch on Antony in Alexandria and Boeotia

With Plutarch's *Life of Antony* we jump forward in time about fifty years, and this makes a significant difference: it puts the events described within the lifetime of Plutarch's relatives, notably, as we will see, his grandfather and his great-grandfather. Within the *Parallel Lives* the *Lives of Demetrios and Antony* stands out for being explicitly introduced as a pair of 'bad' *Lives*. Plutarch suggests that just as it is beneficial for flute students to hear good and bad playing, reading good and bad *Lives* will make the audience enjoy the good *Lives* more, and encourage them even more strongly to imitate those (*Dem.* 1.6). After introducing Demetrios Poliorketes and Marc Antony as the protagonists, he adds, with reference to Plato, that 'great natures exhibit great faults as well as great virtues'.[41] We would expect,

---

[41] *Dem.* 1.7: καὶ κακίας μεγάλας, ὥσπερ ἀρετάς, αἱ μεγάλαι φύσεις ἐκφέρουσι. Duff (1999, 48–49) convincingly connects the passage to *Resp.* 491d–492a, 495b.

then, in contrast to the *Life of Sulla*, a more straightforwardly apotreptic representation of Marc Antony, but there are moments in the *Life* where the readers are drawn in and implicated in the fate of Antony and Cleopatra to such an extent that they almost *have* to sympathize with the pair's plight. Perhaps sympathy and apotreptic need not be as fully at odds with one another as they would seem to be at first glance: after Plutarch has put the reader in the bad protagonist's shoes, the emotional impact of his demise on the audience will be even greater, and the message of the danger of great faults in great natures even more meaningful.[42]

In the *Life of Antony* there are two passages featuring members of Plutarch's family at some length. In one instance this is because Antony, like Sulla, found himself on campaign in Boeotia at a certain point in his career; the other instance concerns Antony's stay in Alexandria, and here the family connection is much more tangential. I will start with the latter, following the chronology of the *Life*.

Plutarch introduces a friend of his grandfather Lamprias, named Philotas from Amphissa, a town in Phokis.[43] While this Philotas was studying to be a doctor in Alexandria, he struck up friendships with one of the royal cooks, and, notably, with Antony's son by Fulvia, Antyllus.[44] The cook invites Philotas to come and look at the extravagant preparations for a royal supper for Antony and Cleopatra. When Philotas remarks that they must be expecting a lot of guests, the cook explains that the dinner party will only be twelve people. Large amounts of food are being prepared on a staggered schedule, because when Antony may want to eat is unpredictable, so fresh and delicious meals have to be kept ready at all times (*Ant.* 28.2–4). The anecdote, though it comes across as humorous and light-hearted, is also a clear illustration of Antony's excessive, unrestrained lifestyle, and as such it fits into the apotreptic narrative of the *Life* as a whole.

The other Philotas anecdote is similarly lighthearted, but has a threatening undertone. Plutarch writes that Philotas became one of Antyllus' companions, and dined with him whenever he did not eat with his father. On one occasion, in appreciation for a witty quip Philotas made, Antyllus gifts him all the golden goblets that are on the table. Philotas initially thinks Antyllus does not have the power to give the goblets away, because he is so young, but a while later one of the slaves brings him the cups stuffed into a bag. The slave tells him that because

---

[42] Duff 1999, 60–62; cf. Pelling 1988, 10–18. On the connection between audience emotions and moral judgment in historiography see Damon 2017, 185–186.
[43] A Delphic inscription (*SEG* 1.181) mentions a Philotas of Amphissa who is a doctor, and spent much time in Delphi, as did Plutarch's grandfather, cf. Flacelière and Chambry 1977, 125; Pelling 1988, 195.
[44] The events probably date to 40–35 BCE, taking into account the reference to the Perusine war at *Ant.* 28.1 and Antyllus' birth around 47/46 BCE, cf. Pelling 1988, 196.

Antyllus is Antony's son he *does* have the right to make the gift, but Philotas should still be cautious:

> Do take my advice and exchange all of them with us for money. His father might perhaps miss some of the ones that were made long ago and are highly valued for their craftsmanship.[45]

This anecdote again shows the – from Plutarch's point of view – lamentable decadence of Antony's life in Egypt. Yet it also suggests that associating with the likes of Antony, or even just his son, carries risks. Philotas' impulse to keep his distance was sensible, and the savvy slave offers a pragmatic solution for accepting the gift without potentially incurring Antony's reproach.

Plutarch caps the two Philotas anecdotes saying: 'Such things, then, my grandfather used to tell me, Philotas would recount time and again.'[46] Plutarch's connection to the events is explained by the chain of repeated story telling between him and the student-doctor: Philotas, a family friend, was telling Lamprias these anecdotes all the time, and Lamprias, in turn, used to repeat these stories to Plutarch when he was still alive. The frequent repetition of the anecdotes, first by Philotas and subsequently by Lamprias, is highlighted by the imperfect verbs sprinkled throughout the passage, and, in the last sentence by the addition of 'time and again'.[47]

The Philotas anecdotes increase the liveliness of Plutarch's account of Antony's time in Alexandria, and being able to cite a family friend as a source strengthens their reliability. We cannot really say, however, that Plutarch is boasting about this connection with Antony. In the anecdotes Philotas is shown interacting with cooks and slaves, and he witnesses Antony's extravagance through their eyes. This specific perspective is reduplicated via Lamprias and Plutarch all the way down to the reader. The audience becomes eyewitness to Antony's Alexandrian adventures alongside Philotas. Together with him we are puzzled by Antony's dinner arrangements, and cautious about his son's generosity. In trying to maintain his role as observer rather than participant Philotas is very much like the reader, while Lamprias and Plutarch follow Philotas' example by passing on these playful yet moralizing anecdotes to readers for their edification.

---

45 *Ant.* 28.7: ἐμοὶ μέντοι πειθόμενος πάντα διάμειψαι πρὸς ἀργύριον ἡμῖν· ἴσως γὰρ ἂν καὶ ποθήσειεν ὁ πατὴρ ἔνια τῶν παλαιῶν ὄντα καὶ σπουδαζομένων κατὰ τὴν τέχνην ἔργων.
46 *Ant.* 28.7: ταῦτα μὲν οὖν ἡμῖν ἔλεγεν ὁ πάππος ἑκάστοτε διηγεῖσθαι τὸν Φιλώταν.
47 *Ant.* 28.3: διηγεῖτο; 28.4: ἔλεγε; 28.7: ἔλεγεν, ἑκάστοτε διηγεῖσθαι.

We now move to the battle of Aktion, and its repercussions in Boeotia at the time. In his narrative of Aktion and its aftermath Plutarch cites Augustus' *Autobiography* (*Ant.* 68.1), while also relying on the oral history handed down in his family. He describes how, in spite of Antony and Cleopatra abandoning the fight early on, Antony's navy held out for seven more days. But, after the general Canidius flees, the troops surrender to Octavian, with the following consequences:

> After making a settlement with the Greeks, he [Octavian] distributed the grain that was left after the war among the cities; these were in a bad state, and had been stripped of money, slaves, and pack animals. My great-grandfather Nikarchos used to tell how all the citizens were forced to carry on their shoulders a set measure of wheat down to the sea at Antikyra, and how they were urged on by the whip. Having carried one load like this, he said, the second had already been measured out, and they were just about to carry it down, when word was brought that Antony had been defeated, and that the city [Chaironeia] had been saved. Immediately the overseers and soldiers of Antony fled, and the men divided the grain among themselves.[48]

Plutarch's great-grandfather Nikarchos was probably already dead when Plutarch was born, who must have heard this story from his grandfather Lamprias instead.[49] Nikarchos and his fellow Chaironeians had to bring grain from the city all the way down to Antikyra, which is almost 25 km as the crow flies, through mountainous terrain. From Antikyra it would have been shipped, presumably, to Antony's troops at Aktion.

Just as with the Philotas anecdotes Plutarch emphasizes the repeated telling of this story with an imperfect verb (διηγεῖτο). He assumes that the reader will understand that Plutarch's grandfather Lamprias, whom we encountered as a storyteller earlier in the *Life*, passed on this narrative from Nikarchos to Plutarch. It inserts a vivid account of the extensive human suffering Antony and his troops inflicted on the local population during the civil war into Plutarch's account of Aktion. While the Philotas anecdotes showed Antony's faults in a light-hearted way, Nikarchos' story displays the dire consequences. By referring to the

---

48 *Ant.* 68.4–5: καὶ διαλλαγεὶς τοῖς Ἕλλησι τὸν περιόντα σῖτον ἐκ τοῦ πολέμου διένειμε ταῖς πόλεσι πραττούσαις ἀθλίως καὶ περικεκομμέναις χρημάτων, ἀνδραπόδων, ὑποζυγίων. ὁ γοῦν πρόπαππος ἡμῶν Νίκαρχος διηγεῖτο τοὺς πολίτας ἅπαντας ἀναγκάζεσθαι τοῖς ὤμοις καταφέρειν μέτρημα πυρῶν τεταγμένον ἐπὶ τὴν πρὸς Ἀντίκυραν θάλασσαν, ὑπὸ μαστίγων ἐπιταχυνομένους· καὶ μίαν μὲν οὕτω φορὰν ἐνεγκεῖν, τὴν δὲ δευτέραν ἤδη μεμετρημένοις καὶ μέλλουσιν αἴρεσθαι νενικημένον Ἀντώνιον ἀγγελῆναι, καὶ τοῦτο διασῶσαι τὴν πόλιν· εὐθὺς γὰρ τῶν Ἀντωνίου διοικητῶν καὶ στρατιωτῶν φυγόντων διανείμασθαι τὸν σῖτον αὐτούς.
49 Flacelière and Chambry 1977, 168.

Chaironeians as 'citizens', whipped by Antony's men, Plutarch underlines the grave injustice of Antony's actions.

This particular narrative fits into a larger context in the *Life*, whereby Plutarch contrasts Antony's ostentatious philhellenism with the suffering he caused to the Greeks.[50] Such a message, however, need not cater specifically to a Greek audience.[51] Rather, it continues the theme from the *Lives of Lysander and Sulla*: seemingly good ambition can lead to bad outcomes. The personal element in Plutarch's account of Aktion heightens the emotional appeal of this episode, but it makes it no less relevant to the general readership, as it clearly recalls the introduction of the *Lives of Demetrios and Antony*: Antony's strong enthusiasm for Greek culture and learning could have been a major virtue, to which his disregard for the plight of the Greeks of his own time sadly stands as the corresponding, major fault.

5 Plutarch on Otho in Italy

With the *Life of Otho* we have come down to events that took place in Plutarch's lifetime. The circumstances of Otho's reign date to the author's early twenties. The *Life of Otho* is unusual within Plutarch's biographical project for several reasons. It is not part of the *Parallel Lives*, but belongs to the *Lives of the Caesars*, of which the only other preserved biography is the *Life of Galba*. Further, it does not provide a full biography of Otho, but describes only the events of 68/9 CE, also known as the Year of the Four Emperors, and as such is the immediate sequel to the *Life of Galba*. In the preserved *Lives of the Emperors* Plutarch dispenses, for the most part, with the kind of anecdotal material used in his *Parallel Lives* to elucidate the character traits of his subjects. An important question, then, is what the goal might be of these *Lives*, since Plutarch clearly did not aspire for them to be close biographical portraits.

The introduction to the *Life of Galba* opens by discussing the paramount importance for an army to be made up of obedient and courageous soldiers, whose noble nature blends gentleness with aggressiveness. Plutarch continues:

---

50 Antony as philhellene: *Ant.* 2.7–8, 23.2 (though with foreboding), 33.7–34.1, 57.1–2. Antony inflicting suffering on Greeks: *Ant.* 62.1, 64.1–2, 67.2–3.
51 On the audience of the *Lives* consisting of elite Greeks and Romans see Stadter 2014, 45–55.

Many instances of suffering, but particularly by those that befell the Romans after Nero's death bear witness, and show by example that nothing is more fearful in an empire than a military force governed by uneducated and irrational impulses.[52]

If we take this passage as programmatic, as many commentators have done, the *Lives of Galba and Otho* appear to have a much more specific thematic focus than the *Parallel Lives*: armies and their commanders.[53] Plutarch's *Life of Otho*, in spite of its brevity and the short amount of time covered, presents his reign as a neat arc, precisely with respect to Otho's relationship to his soldiers. Initially, Otho tries to appease the men. He frees Galba's general Celsus (*Oth.* 1), arrests the hated Tigellinus (*Oth.* 2), and negotiates his position vis-à-vis the legacy of Nero (*Oth.* 3). But very quickly the soldiers start to follow their own agenda. A number of them march on Rome, and storm a dinner party that Otho is hosting for the senate. They claim to suspect, perhaps insincerely, the senators of fomenting resistance against Otho, and threaten to kill them (*Oth.* 3.2–6). The emperor has much trouble restraining his soldiers, but succeeds after 'many exhortations, entreaties, and tears'.[54] Swayed by bad advice, the impatience of the soldiers, and his own nervousness Otho engages Vitellius in battle too quickly; this bad decision is compounded by Otho's poor skills in managing the troops in the field, and his men are beaten (*Oth.* 8–12). Once defeated, Otho conducts the peace agreement and the transition of power to Vitellius admirably and honorably, and, by now, resigned to his death, receives moving expressions of loyalty and affection from his soldiers (*Oth.* 15–18).

Plutarch's *Life of Otho* is presented almost as a ring composition: Otho starts out trying to fulfill his role of emperor well, and, after he has failed, manages to display virtue in his defeated position until the end of his life. This structure shows that, even though the generic differences between the *Parallel Lives* and *Lives of the Caesars* are stark, Plutarch remains invested in the ethical appeal of his writings also in the *Life of Otho*. Showing fortitude and composure in adverse circumstances is a virtue that has a universal applicability, and would have been easily recognizable as such to Plutarch's readers.

---

52 *Galba* 1.3: ἄλλα τε πάθη πολλὰ καὶ τὰ Ῥωμαίοις συμπεσόντα μετὰ τὴν Νέρωνος τελευτὴν ἔχει μαρτύρια καὶ παραδείγματα τοῦ μηδὲν εἶναι φοβερώτερον ἀπαιδεύτοις χρωμένης καὶ ἀλόγοις ὁρμαῖς ἐν ἡγεμονίᾳ στρατιωτικῆς δυνάμεως.
53 Ash 1997, 189–192; cf. Georgiadou 2014, 251–266; De Blois 2014, 267–278; Stadter 2014, 56–69.
54 *Oth.* 3.7: πολλὰ παρηγορήσας καὶ δεηθεὶς καὶ μηδὲ δακρύων φεισάμενος.

The autobiographical episode in the *Life of Otho* is wedged in between Plutarch's narrative of the defeat of Otho's men and the moving account of his final demise. I cite it at some length, to illustrate its position within the narrative:

> This is how most of those who were present report the battle to have happened, although they themselves admit that they do not know the details clearly because of the disorder and unevenness of the event. At a later time, when I was traveling through the plain with Mestrius Florus, a man of consular rank who was with Otho then, not through conviction but through necessity, showed me an old temple, and he related that when he came up to it after the battle he saw a pile of corpses so high that the ones on top touched the pediments. He said that he could not find the reason for this himself nor learn it from someone else. In civil wars, whenever a rout happens, it makes sense that there are more casualties, because no one is taken alive since there is no use for captives, but why they are heaped up and gathered like that is not easy to explain.[55]

Immediately after this passage Plutarch narrates how Otho finds out about the battle through a vague rumor, and only later receives eye witness accounts from wounded soldiers (*Oth*. 15.1). This moment in the *Life of Otho* clearly thematizes the difficulty of obtaining detailed, reliable information about a battle, even and perhaps especially for contemporaries. Otho's lack of information emphasizes his lack of control over what is happening, while the disparity between the account of the battle immediately prior to this passage and Florus' report confirms that those who participated, indeed, did not know the details. While according to them many of Otho's men went over to Vitellius' side in a peaceful and friendly manner (*Oth*. 13.5–7), Florus' account shows that there were in fact very many casualties.

Mestrius Florus was a very close friend of Plutarch's. He would go on to be consul under Vespasian, and later on proconsul of Asia; he procured citizenship for Plutarch, and, as we read in this passage, travelled with him through northern Italy right after the civil wars of 69 CE.[56] Plutarch's inclusion of this anecdote illustrates elegantly how the landscape can become a carrier of memory. Florus'

---

[55] *Oth*. 14: οὕτω μὲν οἱ πλεῖστοι τῶν παραγενομενων ἀπαγγέλλουσι γενέσθαι τὴν μάχην, οὐδὲ αὐτοὶ σαφῶς ὁμολογοῦντες εἰδέναι τὰ καθ' ἕκαστα διὰ τὴν ἀταξίαν καὶ τὴν ἀνωμαλίαν. ἐμοὶ δὲ ὕστερον ὁδεύοντι διὰ τοῦ πεδίου Μέστριος Φλῶρος, ἀνὴρ ὑπατικὸς τῶν τότε μὴ κατὰ γνώμην, ἀλλ' ἀνάγκῃ μετὰ τοῦ Ὄθωνος γενομένων, νεὼν ὄντα παλαιὸν ἐπιδείξας διηγεῖτο μετὰ τὴν μάχην ἐπελθὼν ἰδεῖν νεκρῶν σωρὸν τηλικοῦτον ὥστε τοὺς ἐπιπολῆς ἅπτεσθαι τῶν ἀετῶν, καὶ τὴν αἰτίαν ἔφη ζητῶν οὔτε αὐτὸς εὑρεῖν οὔτε παρ' ἄλλου του πυθέσθαι. θνήσκειν μὲν γὰρ παρὰ τοὺς ἐμφυλίους πολέμους, ὅταν τροπὴ γένηται, πλείονας εἰκός ἐστι, τῷ μηδένα ζωγρεῖν, χρῆσθαι γὰρ οὐκ ἔστι τοῖς ἁλισκομένοις, ἡ δ' ἐπὶ τοσοῦτο σωρεία καὶ συμφόρησις οὐκ ἔχει τὴν αἰτίαν εὐσυλλόγιστον.
[56] Jones 1971, 48–49; Stadter 2014, 21–44.

memory is triggered by seeing the temple,[57] and this prompts him to share his story with Plutarch. At the same time this short vignette encapsulates how hard it is to come to *know* and subsequently *explain* the details of historical events. As in the quasi autobiographical passages already discussed Plutarch's connection to the past is not necessarily a flattering one. Even though Plutarch emphasizes Florus' involuntary involvement with Otho, the reader is still receiving the story through the eyes of the 'losers'. Another continuity has by now also emerged quite clearly: when Plutarch or a relative appears in the *Lives* there often follows an illustration of the high human toll of war. In the *Life of Sulla* and *Life of Antony* this cost is explained by excessive ambition (Sulla) and complete moral failure (Antony), and underlines the ethical warning of these respective *Lives*. In the *Life of Otho* the reader is made to sit next to Plutarch as he hears about the horrors of the battle from Florus, which contribute to the overall message of the work about the danger of weak commanders and unruly soldiers.

Plutarch ends the *Life of Otho* with a description of Otho's tomb in Brixillum, which, he writes, he saw when he was there. The monument is small and has a modest inscription, such that it will not arouse jealousy (*Oth.* 18.1). Plutarch then goes on to cite the inscription: 'To the underworld spirits of Marcus Otho.'[58] Plutarch's remarks fit with the idea of a ring composition in which Otho is depicted in a positive light only at the beginning and end of the *Life*. The theme of jealousy is quite appropriate to the Year of the Four Emperors, where suffering was caused by disobedient armies and a revolving cast of insignificant pretenders to the emperorship vying among each other for power.

6 Conclusion: Communicative Memory, Universal History

The chronological progression through quasi autobiographical and autobiographical moments in Plutarch's *Parallel Lives* brings to mind Assman's influential distinction between 'communicative memory' and 'cultural memory'. According to Assman's definition 'communicative memory' reaches back between eighty and a hundred years; it is constituted by lived experience and by oral

---

[57] Perhaps the temple of Castor near the battle site in Bedriacum, Hardy 1890, 264.
[58] There is a problem with the text here, which cites the inscription as 'for the pointing out (δηλώσει) of Marcus Otho'; this is a very unlikely Greek rendering of Latin *memoriae*. I follow Hardy (1890, 274) in supporting the emendation δαίμοσι as a translation of *Dis Manibus*.

transmission in informal settings by non-specialists. 'Cultural memory', in contrast, reaches back much further in time, to a mythical, primeval age; in oral societies it is handed down through rituals, performances, and monuments, typically in organized, formal settings by specialized tradition bearers. In literate societies rituals and monuments are supplemented as bearers of cultural memory by written, canonized text (poetry, historiography, philosophy etc.).[59]

Assman notes that in some societies, like ancient Egypt, the distinction between communicative and cultural memory can be very sharply drawn, while in other societies the two categories should be understood as operating on a sliding scale.[60] If we put Plutarch's *floruit* around 80 CE, the events of Sulla's campaigns in the First Mithridatic War ought to fall entirely outside of the range of communicative memory, while the stories of Antony at Aktion almost fall within it. The Year of the Four Emperors is, of course, recent for Plutarch, and therefore clearly communicative memory.

In the *Life of Sulla* Plutarch includes as narrative elements connected to himself the armor of killed Mithridatic soldiers from Orchomenos, the inscriptions set up by Sulla in and near Chaironeia, and stories being told about the events by Boeotians. The inscriptions mentioned can easily be categorized as bearers of cultural memory, because of their authorized and monumental nature. The Boeotians' stories (about the oracles) ought to be categorized as communicative memory, while the found armor is actually quite difficult to analyze properly: even if they are objects, just like monuments, they are clearly unauthorized, and they become meaningful with respect to memory only once they are explicitly connected in (oral) narrative to the battle. The autobiographic elements in the *Life of Antony* are, once again, easily recognized as examples of communicative memory: they are personal stories handed down across generations within Plutarch's family. The *Life of Otho* shows how the landscape itself, when connected with oral narrative, can be imprinted with memory; secondly, Otho's grave is included as a monument, typically a bearer of cultural memory, even though the events are easily within reach of communicative memory as well.

The passages that I have focused on in this chapter illustrate clearly that cultural and communicative memory in this case indeed exist on a sliding scale: Plutarch's family narratives reach back further than they 'should', while even the recent past could already be monumentalized in (Roman) Greece. In reading Plutarch's *Lives*, however, we are always already handling a bearer of cultural memory: it is a work of historiography composed by a specialist. When Plutarch

---

[59] Assman 2011 [1992], 15–110.
[60] Assman 2011 [1992], 40–41.

includes materials drawn from communicative history, like the stories circulating in his family or among locals, his roles of specialist and non-specialist become intertwined. By virtue of including these stories in his historiography Plutarch causes them to become codified and canonized. Plutarch's autobiographical moments in the *Lives* can be read as, what Whitmarsh has called, 'discursive resistance': they temporarily displace the narrative of inevitable, all-encompassing empire by means of hyperlocal micro-history.[61]

As I discussed in the introduction to this chapter, in historical studies 'memory' to an important degree has been defined in opposition to 'history': if memory is about experience, history is about theory and analysis; memory belongs to in-groups, history is created by outsiders for a universal audience; memory is about continuity between past and present, history is about development and change. The quasi autobiographical passages that I have studied in this chapter show how memory and history are blended together by Plutarch in his biographical project. He uses in-group memory (of his native region and his family) and presents it to a universal audience, switching from being an insider non-specialist to an outsider specialist by including these moments in his historiography. Plutarch seeks to re-create experience through narration, but frames these experiences in an analytical framework, and encourages his audiences to mimic his own intellectual engagement with the events of his protagonists' *Lives*. Finally, he breaks down the 'memory as continuity' and 'history as change' antithesis: his ethical program and insistence on the moral applicability of events of the past impose continuity on the gulf between himself and his readers, on the one hand, and his radically other protagonists on the other.

The autobiographical moments in the *Parallel Lives* are emphatically not about particularizing the experience of the past, as many modern approaches seek to do in an attempt to unlock access to history for modern individuals. Plutarch intrudes into the *Lives* if he has relevant material stemming from his personal connections or experiences to add. His intrusions occur often in sections describing the individual, human toll of wars. Consequently, these moments are not about highlighting his family's or his own achievements, but rather about showcasing the perennial, tangible risk of bad leaders, and the vital need for good ones. By enmeshing this material of his own within his intersubjective, ethically universal project of biography Plutarch shows that even in his moments as Chaironeian, as grand-son, or great-grandson, he is still first and foremost showing us, for our edification, the lives of others.

---

61 Whitmarsh 2013, cf. Ursin 2019, 266–272.

Bibliography

Ankersmit, Frank (2005), *Sublime Historical Experience*, Stanford, CA.
Ash, Rhiannon (1997), "Severed heads: individual portraits and irrational forces in Plutarch's *Galba* and *Otho*", in Judith Mossman (ed.), *Plutarch and His Intellectual World*, Swansea, 189–214.
Assmann, Jan (2011) [1992], *Cultural Memory and Early Civilization. Writing, Remembrance, and Political Imagination*, Cambridge.
Badian, Ernst (1976), "Rome, Athens, and Mithridates", *American Journal of Ancient History* 1, 105–128.
Berliner, David (2005), "The Abuses of Memory: Reflections on the 'Memory Boom'", *Anthropological Quarterly* 78, 197–211.
Carr, David (2014), *Experience and History: Phenomenological Perspectives on the Historical World*, New York.
Camp, John/Ierardi, Michael/McInerney, Jeremy/Morgan, Kathryn/Umholtz, Gretchen (1992), "A Trophy from the Battle of Chaironeia of 86 BC", *American Journal of Archaeology* 96, 443–455.
Chrysanthou, Chrysanthos S. (2018), *Plutarch's* Parallel Lives: *Narrative Technique and Moral Judgement*, Berlin.
Damon, Cynthia (2017), "Emotions as a Historiographical Dilemma", in Douglas Cairns/Damien Nelis (eds), *Emotions in the Classical World: Methods, Approaches, and Directions*, Stuttgart, 177–194.
De Blois, Lukas (2014), "Plutarch's *Galba* and *Otho*", in Mark Beck (ed.), *A Companion to Plutarch*, Malden, MA, 267–277.
De Boose, Johan (2018), *Vloekhout*, Amsterdam.
Duff, Tim (1997), "Moral ambiguity in Plutarch's *Lysander-Sulla*", in Judith Mossman (ed.), *Plutarch and His Intellectual World*, Swansea, 169–188.
Duff, Tim (1999), *Plutarch's Lives. Exploring Virtue and Vice*, Oxford.
Eckert, Alexandra (2016), *Lucius Cornelius Sulla in der antiken Erinnerung. Jener Mörder, der sich Felix nannte*, Berlin.
Flacelière, Robert/Chambry, Emile (1971), *Plutarque Vies. Tome VI*, Paris.
Flacelière, Robert/Chambry, Emile (1977), *Plutarque Vies. Tome XIII*, Paris.
Georgiadou, Aristoula (2014), "The Lives of the Caesars", in Mark Beck (ed.), *A Companion to Plutarch*, Malden, MA, 251–266.
Grethlein, Jonas (2013), *Experience and Teleology in Ancient Historiography: 'Futures Past' from Herodotus to Augustine*, Cambridge.
Grigoropoulos, Dimitris/Di Napoli, Valentina/Evangelidis, Vasilis/Camia, Francesco/Rogers, Dylan/Vlizos, Stavros (2017), "Roman Greece and the 'Mnemonic Turn', Some Critical Remarks", in Tamara M. Dijkstra/Kuin, Inger N.I./Moser, Muriel/Weidgenannt, David (eds), *Strategies of Remembering in Greece Under Rome (100 BC–100 AD)*, Leiden, 21–35.
Hardy, Ernst George (1890), *Plutarch's Lives of Galba and Otho*, London.
Jones, Christopher P. (1971), *Plutarch and Rome*, Oxford.
Kountouri, Elena/Petrochilos, Nikolaos/Zoumbaki, Sophia (2018), "The Tropaion of Sulla over Mithridates VI Eupator: A First Approach", in Valentina Di Napoli/Francesco Camia/Vasilis Evangelidis/Dylan Rogers/Stavros Vlizos (eds.), *What's new in Roman Greece?: Recent work on the Greek mainland and the islands in the Roman Period*, Athens, 359–369.

Kuin, Inger N.I. (2017a), "Rewriting Family History: Strabo and the Mithridatic Wars", *Phoenix* 71, 102–118.

Kuin, Inger N.I. (2017b), "Anchoring Political Change in Post-Sullan Athens", in Dijkstra, Tamara M./Kuin, Inger N.I./Moser, Muriel/Weidgenannt, David (eds), *Strategies of Remembering in Greece Under Rome (100 BC–100 AD)*, Leiden, 157–167.

Kuin, Inger N.I. (2018), "Sulla and the Invention of Roman Athens", *Mnemosyne* 71, 616–639.

Lamberton, Robert (2001), *Plutarch*. New Haven, CT.

Marincola, John (1997), *Authority and Tradition in Ancient Historiography*, Cambridge.

Nora, Pierre (1984–1992), *Les lieux de mémoire*, 3 vols., Paris.

Nora, Pierre (1989), "Between Memory and History: Les Lieux de Mémoire", *Representations* 26, 7–24.

Pelling, Christopher (1988), *Plutarch. Life of Antony*, Cambridge.

Pelling, Christopher (2002), *Plutarch and History. Eighteen Studies*, Swansea.

Robert, Louis (1960), *Hellenica. Recueil d'épigraphie, de numismatique, et d'antiquités grecques. Volumes XI–XII*, Paris.

Runia, Eelco (2006), "Presence", *History and Theory* 45, 1–29.

Runia, Eelco (2010), "Inventing the new from the old – from White's 'tropics' to Vico's 'topics'", *Rethinking History* 14, 229–241.

Stadter, Philip A. (1992), "Paradoxical paradigms: Lysander and Sulla", in Philip A. Stadter (ed.), *Plutarch and the Historical Tradition*, London, 41–55.

Stadter, Philip A. (2014), *Plutarch and His Roman Readers*, Oxford.

Swain, Simon (1996), *Hellenism and Empire: Language, Classicism, and Power in the Greek World AD 50–250*, Oxford.

Thompson, Paul/Bornat, Joanna (2017) [1978], *The Voice of the Past: Oral History. Fourth Edition*, Oxford.

Ursin, Frank (2019), *Freiheit, Herrschaft, Widerstand. Griechische Erinnerungskultur in der hohen Kaiserzeit (1.–3. Jahrhundert n. Chr.)*, Stuttgart.

White, Hayden (1980), "The Value of Narrativity for the Representation of Reality", *Critical Inquiry* 7, 5–27.

Whitmarsh, Tim (2013), "Resistance Is Futile? Greek Literary Tactics in the Face of Rome", in Paul Schubert/Pierre Ducrey/Pascale Derron (eds), *Les Grecs héritiers des Romains: huit exposés suivis de discussions*, Geneva, 57–78.

Zadorojnyi, Alexei V. (2010), "ὥσπερ ἐν ἐσόπτρῳ: the rhetoric and philosophy of Plutarch's mirrors", in Noreen Humble (ed.), *Plutarch's Lives: Parallelism and Purpose*, Swansea, 169–196.

Ahuvia Kahane
Demos, Democracy and Method: Political Trust and the Science of Suspicion

1 Introduction

1.1 The *Logos* of Democracy

Already etymology, the "true *logos*" of words, seems to lay bare the meaning of 'democracy',[1] and (by a kind of implicit cognitive transfer) to vouch for the transparency of its constitutional principle.[2] Thus, Peter Rhodes, for example, says: "Δημοκρατία; *dēmokratía*, 'people-power', is the standard Greek term for a form of government in which power resides with the many rather than with the few (*oligarchía*) or with a single man (*monarchía*)". "The word", he adds, "could be used to characterize any kind of constitutional government as opposed to despotism, (e.g., Hdt. 4.137,2; 6.43,3), but it came to be used, in accordance with the threefold classification, of the kind of constitutional government in which power resides with the many".[3]

Democracy's *logos* is hardly so clear. In this essay, I want to revisit some of its less transparent and perhaps contradictory aspects and some elements of critical method on which our reading of these aspects depends. I shall focus my discussion on one of the canonical formulations of democracy in classical antiquity,

---

[1] See, e.g., Herzfeld 1997, 351: "The politicization of language in [modern] Greece produced a form of 'political philology' that makes etymology an important but contested item of symbolic capital and a yardstick of cultural and moral purity". The practice is, of course, ubiquitous in terms that are as different from each other in sentiment, linguistic profile, ethics, politics, history, etc. as possible: *isonomia* (Herod. 3.80; Thuc. 3.82), *auctoritas* (*Res Gestae* 28, 32), *Israel* (=Jacob. Gen. 32.27–9), Homeland, Brexit, etc.
[2] 'Natural' unpacking of this compound into its constituents, *demos* and *kratia*, suggests, by analogy, that the principle of democracy is likewise 'natural' and transparent to all. For the mechanism, see Underhill 2011.
[3] Rhodes 2011, 590 (cf. Rhodes 1988, 219). Ober 1989, 3, likewise etymologizing: "the people (*demos*) possess the political power (*kratos*) in the state". Rhodes, Ober 1989, 83 and others (Bleicken 1985; Meier 1969; Murray 1993; Raaflaub 1980; etc.; recently, e.g., *passim* in Arnason/Raaflaub/Wagner 2013) suggest that usage of the term *dēmokratía* rises with the ascent of Athens' democratic polity in the 5th century, perhaps with Ephialtes' reforms (462/1 BCE). Objections (e.g., Hansen 1986) sometimes downplay the social and political contexts of discourse.

https://doi.org/10.1515/9783110627305-010

Pericles' Funeral Oration in the second book of Thucydides' *Histories*. The Funeral Oration has, of course, attracted a vast body of comment from almost every student of Thucydides, ancient history and politics. My objective is not to survey such scholarship, let alone the work on ancient democracy.[4] Rather, I want to concentrate on three politically and methodologically significant readings of the Oration: the first by A.W. Gomme, a historical and philological *locus classicus* that will help us to identify an underlying terms of engagement and their contradictory potential,[5] the second by Josiah Ober, a historian and political theorist whose perspective will rephrase the problem in more-recent critical framework of ideology and knowledge,[6] and finally, by philosopher Jacques Rancière, a pivotal contemporary student of democracy, history and political philosophy.[7] With the help of these readings, I shall try to bind critical method to a revised and different figuration of the elements of democratic politics as they are presented in Thucydides. Pericles, I will argue, accurately represents Athenian democracy as it is, and especially its contradictory but necessary state of private and public, the governable and the ungovernable.

1.2 Method, Ideology, and History

The views we are about to consider belong to different eras of critique and thought and they differ significantly in method and approach. Yet they also converge with regard to some essential readings and critical observations on 'the text itself', one might say. Such divergence and convergence, as I will later explain in detail, define our own method, which argues for a coherent principle without the need for unity. This principle can help us accommodate some basic yet contradictory characteristics of the distribution and representation of power and knowledge and the definition of both *demos* and *kratê* in the idea of democracy in the Oration. My discussion, I should stress, is an attempt to characterize a particular feature of ancient democratic discourse and democracy in a more general

---

[4] Essential survey of views of the Oration in Hornblower 1991, 292–316; Rusten 2004; Rusten 2009. Useful annotated bibliography on Pericles in Wallace 2016. Recent views of ancient democracy and bibliography in Rhodes 2015; Arnason, Raaflaub *et al.* 2013; Ober 2008, etc.
[5] Gomme 1973; later discussion in Harris 1992; Andrews 2004; Andrews 2004; Winton 2004; Hansen 2008; Connor 2018; also in items in Wallace 2016.
[6] Conveniently in Ober 1993 but formulated in his many other publications.
[7] Rancière 1996 (French: 1992) with reference to, e.g., Rancière 2003, Rancière 2004, Rancière 2010.

sense, not to explore the historical reality which lies behind the words or the relations between such reality and Thucydidean discourse. I will, nevertheless try to historicize a few significant features of scholarly and political positions and especially, inspired by the critical sources, some fundamental questions of the relation between merit on the one hand and broad inclusion on the other, freedom on the one hand and effective government on the other. The question of merit and inclusion, I will argue, points to important 'isomorphic' principles of politics, philology and philosophy which can guide our understanding of historical perspective and the relation between the classical past, ideological positions and modernity.

2 A Divided *Demos*

2.1 Gomme on the Oration

Let us first look again at one particularly famous passage which lies at the heart of the Pericles' speech and consider some of the underlying tensions of language and political principle it contains (Thuc. *Hist.* 2.37.1–3):

> Χρώμεθα γὰρ πολιτείᾳ οὐ ζηλούσῃ τοὺς τῶν πέλας νόμους, παράδειγμα δὲ μᾶλλον αὐτοὶ ὄντες τισὶν ἢ μιμούμενοι ἑτέρους. καὶ ὄνομα μὲν διὰ τὸ μὴ ἐς ὀλίγους ἀλλ' ἐς πλείονας οἰκεῖν δημοκρατία κέκληται· μέτεστι δὲ κατὰ μὲν τοὺς νόμους πρὸς τὰ ἴδια διάφορα πᾶσι τὸ ἴσον, κατὰ δὲ τὴν ἀξίωσιν, ὡς ἕκαστος ἔν τῳ εὐδοκιμεῖ, οὐκ ἀπὸ μέρους τὸ πλέον ἐς τὰ κοινὰ ἢ ἀπ' ἀρετῆς προτιμᾶται, οὐδ' αὖ κατὰ πενίαν, ἔχων δέ τι ἀγαθὸν δρᾶσαι τὴν πόλιν, ἀξιώματος ἀφανείᾳ κεκώλυται. ἐλευθέρως δὲ τά τε πρὸς τὸ κοινὸν πολιτεύομεν καὶ ἐς τὴν πρὸς ἀλλήλους τῶν καθ' ἡμέραν ἐπιτηδευμάτων ὑποψίαν, οὐ δι' ὀργῆς τὸν πέλας, εἰ καθ' ἡδονήν τι δρᾷ, ἔχοντες, οὐδὲ ἀζημίους μέν, λυπηρὰς δὲ τῇ ὄψει ἀχθηδόνας προστιθέμενοι. ἀνεπαχθῶς δὲ τὰ ἴδια προσομιλοῦντες τὰ δημόσια διὰ δέος μάλιστα οὐ παρανομοῦμεν, τῶν τε αἰεὶ ἐν ἀρχῇ ὄντων ἀκροάσει καὶ τῶν νόμων, καὶ μάλιστα αὐτῶν ὅσοι τε ἐπ' ὠφελίᾳ τῶν ἀδικουμένων κεῖνται καὶ ὅσοι ἄγραφοι ὄντες αἰσχύνην ὁμολογουμένην φέρουσιν.[8]

> We live under a form of government which does not emulate the institutions of our neighbours; on the contrary, we are ourselves a model which some follow, rather than the imitators of other peoples. It is true that our government is called a democracy, because its administration is in the hands, not of the few, but of the many; yet while as regards the law all men are on an equality for the settlement of their private disputes, as regards the value set on them it is as each man is in any way distinguished that he is preferred to public honours, not because he belongs to a particular class, but because of personal merits; nor, again, on

---

[8] Text: Jones and Powell. Transl.: Thucydides 1919, with alterations, or as otherwise stated.

> the ground of poverty is a man barred from a public career by obscurity of rank if he but has it in him to do the state a service. And not only in our public life are we liberal, but also as regards our freedom from suspicion of one another in the pursuits of every-day life; for we do not feel resentment at our neighbour if he does as he likes, nor yet do we put on sour looks which, though harmless, are painful to behold. But while we thus avoid giving offence in our private intercourse, in our public life we are restrained from lawlessness chiefly through reverent fear, for we render obedience to those in authority and to the laws, and especially to those laws which are ordained for the succour of the oppressed and those which, though unwritten, bring upon the transgressor a disgrace which all men recognize.

Already A.W. Gomme, commenting on this passage, recognized that beneath its seemingly direct address lie fundamental divisions. Grammar itself here is inseparable from crucial lexical, semantic, political and philosophical problems[9] – problems which we, nevertheless, need to format further.

"The main δέ-clause (μέτεστι δέ, κ.τ.λ.)", says Gomme in a comment that has engendered a broad scholarly discussion, "must either qualify or more closely define the μέν-clause. Such qualification or definition being necessary because of the inevitable ambiguity of the word δημοκρατία". Gomme explains:

> This ambiguity arises from the two common meanings of δῆμος, *the whole people, the state, the populous*, and *the masses*, in effect, *the poor, populares* (as in 65. 2); so that δημοκρατία can mean either simply majority rule in a state where all citizens have the vote (cf. Athenagoras' statement vi. 39. 1 ἐγὼ δέ φημι πρῶτα μὲν δῆμον ξύμπαν ὠνομάσθαι, ὀλιγαρχίαν δὲ μέρος ; and Alkibiades, v. 89. 6, ἡμεῖς δὲ τοῦ ξύμπαντος προέστημεν) or the consistent domination of the state by the masses—the vulgar and ill-educated, as, for example, the Old Oligarch understood democracy.[10]

The question, then, is about the semantics of a common word and its elements, but also, guided by grammatical structure itself, about two sharply divided polit-

---

9 See above, n. 4; also, e.g., Ober 1989, 4 n. 2, on *demos*, outlining seminal views in Vlastos 1964; Whitehead 1986; de Ste Croix 1954/5; Raaflaub 1986; Sealey 1974, 1986; more recently Rhodes 2016; Mossé 2013; Kallet 2003; etc. However, at issue, as we have indicated at the beginning of this essay and as we will discuss further below, is not the etymology or even the semantic range of the word, but the oppositional structure of such semantics and its political and methodological implications. Hornblower 1991, 298–299 cites Loraux's (1986a, Ch. iv) work and Goldhill 1986, 63, neither of which focus the contradiction *qua* contradiction. Hornblower ultimately seems to draw on Hansen 1986 and does not engage with the problem which Gomme so clearly flags.
10 Gomme 1973 vol. I, 107–108. See Harris 1992 with reference to essential comments by Oliver 1955; de Romilly 1962; Vlastos 1964; Grant 1971; de Ste Croix 1972; Hansen 1974; Hansen 1978; Ostwald 1986; Sealey 1986; Meier 1990; Raaflaub 1990 and others; see also Rusten 2004; Andrews 2004; Winton 2004; Hansen 2008; Connor 2018.

ical principles: *majority rule* versus *domination by the masses – the poor, the vulgar and ill-educated*.¹¹ The essential distinction in this passage, then, is *not* between "any kind of constitutional government as opposed to despotism" and "constitutional government in which power resides with the many". Rather, Pericles and Thucydides here seem to mark a salient political distinction, one familiar to us, in slightly different form, from, e.g., the Platonic critique of democracy. Plato, of course, does not mask his preferences, as his many different classical readers and as philosophers as different as Karl Popper and Leo Strauss all acknowledge.¹² In essence, the words of the Oration distinguish rule by those of the people who are in some way deemed qualified to guide the state and rule of the *ochlos*,¹³ and those who may not be qualified to do so, everyone, the poor and the uneducated.¹⁴ This divide of principle, as Gomme himself stressed, has direct

---

11 Cf. Dahl's 'Strong Principle of Equality'/'the Principle of Equal Consideration of Interests' (1989, 30–31): "The members believe that no single member, and no minority of members, is so definitely better qualified to rule that the one or the few should be permitted to rule over the entire association. They believe, on the contrary, that all the members of the association are adequately qualified to participate on an equal footing with the others in the process of governing the association" (also Dahl 1989, 55, 85–86, 167; Dahl 2006). Discussions in Ober and Hendrick 1996, esp. Morris 1996; Cartledge 1996; also in Robinson 2004. Useful comments in Ober 2018, 145.
12 For Strauss and Popper see, e.g., Monoson 2000 and briefly Saxonhouse 2009 with discussion further below.
13 The term *ochlos* is philosophically important in Rancière's work. See definition and references by Rockhill in his glossary at the end of Rancière 2004, 88.
14 Gomme's comments have, of course, engendered many subsequent discussions. See, e.g. Vlastos 1964; Loraux 1986a, 186–188, all of whom are aware of the contradiction between the terms proposed but many, in different ways, mitigate their essential state of contradiction. Ober 1989, 158–159: "In order to function as a citizen, and certainly in order to carry out the responsibilities of many of the magistracies, the Athenian citizen needed a basic command of letters. On the other hand, it seems unlikely that many Athenians were fully literate in the sense that they read easily and frequently, for pleasure and instruction. Books were relatively speaking, rare and expensive. Although books were no longer exotic by the later fifth century, they were probably still, for the most part, the possessions of the educated elite, and Athenian political culture remained at its heart an oral culture. Thus, in the Funeral Oration (Thuc. 2.40.2) Pericles emphasized that the Athenians made good political decisions because they believed that speeches *(logoi)* were not a hindrance to action, but rather they regarded it as a disgrace not to be well instructed by public debate before engaging in action. Even if the common Athenian citizen was not fully literate, he was widely exposed to the products of literary culture. The state-subsidized performances at the Panathenaic festival and the festival of Dionysus exposed the average citizen to poetry, music, and dance ... He might also attend various public readings, such as the ones Herodotus reputedly gave of his *Histories*. The average Athenian had no doubt gained at least a passing acquaintance with the stories of Homer and the myths and legends associated with Athenian antiquity. Much would have been learned from his parents and relatives, much

implications for the practice of democracy. Rule by the masses, for example, "might be secured either by united and consistent action by the poor majority without alteration of the laws of the normal Greek democratic state" or it could be achieved "by an extension to the extreme limit of the use of the lot in elections to office". The fundamental point, nevertheless, reaches to the very heart of politics:

> Instead of the principle 'everyone must have equal opportunity to prove himself worthy of office, or of giving advice to the state', we should have 'everyone is as good as his neighbour, and therefore anyone can advise and everyone should hold office in his turn'.[15]

Beneath the surface of the common-noun (ὄνομα) 'democracy', behind its transparent and in this sense 'common' etymological elements which all can understand and the open (κοινός) political principle which the noun itself seems to enact,[16] lie substantive ideological divisions, potential threats to constitutional order and good governance, and contradicting forces of exclusion and inclusion.

Such contestable elements of ideology are not fully disclosed in the Oration. But that is hardly surprising. As Fredric Jameson among others rightly reminds us:

> Every universalizing approach ... will from the dialectical point of view be found to conceal its own contradictions and repress its own historicity by strategically framing its perspective so as to omit the negative, absence, contradiction, repression, the *non-dit*, or the *impensé*.[17]

Democracy's hegemony – we shall have more to say on this point further below – often rests precisely on constructive ambiguity and on the elision of exclusion (of those deemed not worthy of rule, the mob) on the one hand and risks of inclusion (of the uneducated mob) on the other.

Yet, as Gomme persuasively argues, it is the very grammar of Thucydides' speech and the structure of its μέν and δέ clauses, the conventional material rules of construction of Greek, that should lead us to Pericles' meaning: first, "the general democratic principle of equality before the law of all citizens as individuals", and then, as Gomme saw it, an important modification stating, κατὰ τὴν ἀξίωσιν, that "for public affairs there is not complete equality (since in fact everyone is *not*

---

picked up casually in the course of listening to others, perhaps especially to the elders of his deme".
15 Gomme 1973, 108. Hornblower 1991 does not expand on this point.
16 But the term, by most accounts, is a late introduction concomitant with the rise of a democratic regime. See above, n. 3.
17 Jameson 1981, 109–110.

as good as his neighbour), but ἀξίωσις, ἀρετή determines election to office".[18] Thus, "since ἀξίωσις, if not ἀρετή, so often accompanies wealth, ... no poor man is barred from serving the state by his obscurity".[19] Crucially, in Pericles' mouth the words οὐκ ἀπὸ μέρους τὸ πλέον ἐς τὰ κοινὰ ἢ ἀπ' ἀρετῆς προτιμᾶται must mean "not from a section of the citizens but from all according to merit".[20] Democracy offers us an uneasy balance of opposing principles.[21]

2.2 Changing the Question

Gomme, let me suggest, identifies the problem with both philological acumen and political precision. Yet, looking at democracy in essence as a "form of constitutional government" and asking what are the criteria for election to office, he defers some of the underlying force of this opposition of principles in a manner that, we might add, also marks his position in the history of modern thought and especially in relation to more-recent phenomenological readings of power and politics.[22]

---

18 Gomme 1973, 108. The bibliography on ἀξίωσις (cf. also Thuc. 3.82) is substantial. See Loraux 1986b; Frazier 2001; Allison 2001 ('worth' is an economic term); Musti 1995; Hornblower 1991, 301– discussion of related ἀξίωμα and its links to Augustan *auctoritas*. There is an important modern discussion of this latter concept (e.g., Rancière 1996; Agamben 2005 and Derrida 1992) which exposes pertinent paradoxes of 'sovereignty' and the 'force of law' (*sic* – underscoring the transcendence of the juridical principle, see further below, on the 'ungovernable'), which the limited scope of this essay prevents us from discussing.
19 Gomme 1973, 108.
20 Gomme 1973, 108. Ober 1991, 194: "The importance to the democratic form of government of the disjunction of property ownership from political participation was underlined by Pericles in the Funeral Oration (Thuc. 2.37.1). Pericles states that one of the reasons the Athenian form of government was imitated widely was because no citizen with something worthwhile to contribute was excluded by his poverty (*kata penian*) from participation in the decision-making process". Cf. Athenagoras (Thuc. 6.39.1) who suggests the rich are best guardians of wealth but the many are best judges of what is right for the state; Lysias (34) on democracy without property distinctions; Isocrates (*Panegyricus* 4.105) on rule of the many and on not being barred from political office by poverty. As we shall see, such positions require further qualification.
21 The relationship between wealth and merit is, in fact, significantly more complex if we allow (see Allison 2001) that ἀξίωσις is in essence a financial/banking metaphor.
22 See Said 1972 (but not specifically on Gomme); also (somewhat limited) Gurd 2010; Gurd 2015.

Democracy is, to be sure a "form of government".[23] Yet a polity, as already Thucydides' use of the Greek term πολιτεία suggests, is not simply a constitutional order of administration, civic institutions, offices and laws.[24] Rather, as many modern students of politics and power, history and historiography, social historians and students ideology (among them, in different ways, Gramschi, Althusser, Foucault, Bourdieu, Jameson and many students of antiquity) stress, it should be seen as a wider embodiment of enacted truths, a regime of historicized knowledge and cognition that marks the deeper character of specific forms of political power and particular states of the being and consciousness of political 'subjects'.[25]

Thus, rather than asking, for example, "who or which group is marked by the word *demos* as it is used in Pericles' Oration and what are this group's rights?" we might ask, with a slight shift in focus, "what are the states of knowledge and the conditions of truth that define the semantic and political regimes embodied in our terms *demos* and *democracy* and which characterize its historical meaning and the idea of democracy in Pericles' Funeral Oration?"

3 From Social Structures to Structures of Knowledge

3.1 Ober on the Oration

The Funeral Oration is a central piece of evidence in the debate over democracy in the ancient Greek world. Not least since, as, for example Loraux, Ostwald, Ober

---

[23] For this approach, earlier pursued, e.g., under the heading *Staatsaltertümer*, see Busolt 1920/6; more recently, e.g., Hansen 1999. Scholars like Sealey (1967) and Bicknell (1972) focused on individuals; Davies (2003) famously argues for a polity governed, not by democratic ideals but by ad-hoc responses to contingent circumstances. This is important, but fails to acknowledge that any action taken, whether conscious or not, is taken by 'subjects' that are part of a culture, a society, and thus a set of cultural beliefs, norms, expectations, etc. See further below.

[24] Loraux 1986a, 173 on II.36.4: "At the beginning of his oration Pericles distinguishes between the constitution (*politeia*), on the one hand and the practice (*epitedeusis*) and spirit (*tropoi*) of Athens". See also Bordes 1982, 13; Harte and Lane 2013.

[25] Foucault 1979; Foucault 1980; Althusser 2014; in relation to ancient history, Hartog 2016, etc.; with a focus on the study of ancient democracy, e.g., Ostwald 1986; Ober 1993 (below); Mossé 2013; throughout in Arnason/Raaflaub/Wagner 2013. Admittedly, the word 'regime' can also be used as a synonym of government ('the regime of the Four Hundred', etc.).

and others suggest, "no systematic defence of democracy – no democratic theory – survives from an Athenian pen".[26] Pericles' speech must, Ober points out, be viewed against the background of the hegemony of Athenian democracy – the rule of the *demos* - and its dominance over political knowledge. We might slightly rephrase this to suggest that the knowledge that defines discursive representation and the medium of speech is equally the substance of politics itself. Thus, as Ober says, democracy's dominance forces observers and critics, including those within the Athenian polity, like Thucydides himself, "to find a way of knowing about the world of political affairs that would not be colonized by the hegemonic tendencies of democratic discourse".[27]

"Thucydides", Ober explains, "knew that Athenian democracy was based on open deliberation and voting and recognized this as a distinctive way of gaining knowledge about the world and acting upon that knowledge". Yet it depended – here Ober appeals directly to work by Michel Foucault and other contemporary critics[28] – "on socially and politically constructed 'regimes of truth' that we may call 'democratic knowledge'". Democracy in Athens entailed, not simply institutional practice, but, perhaps more fundamentally, certain implicit assumptions and information which "citizen-participants" accepted and lived by, and "on the basis of which they cast their votes".[29] It is against the background of such implicit assumptions and as an attempt to overcome them, Ober proposes, that Thucydides' historiographic critique and his representation of Pericles' speech is set.

3.2 Between Exclusion and Inclusion

Analysing the Oration, helped along by Gomme's philological and philosophical lines of argument,[30] albeit with an added epistemological/hermeneutic perspective, Ober notes that "Pericles' Athens is divided into two interest groups – the few and the many – and the πολιτεία is called a democracy because it favours one group rather than the other". He nevertheless stresses: "the ... two clauses of the

---

26 Ober 1993, 81. Likewise, famously, Loraux 1986a Ch. 4.
27 Ober 1993, 1. Ober stresses: "From the late fifth to the late fourth century B.C., democratic ideology was in a sense hegemonic: It so thoroughly dominated the Athenian political landscape that formal democratic theory was otiose".
28 See Ober 1993, 82 n. 2.
29 Ober 1993, 81.
30 Openly acknowledged, p. 95 n. 21. See also above, n. 14.

passage, which should explain and clarify the referent πολιτεία, are spectacularly antithetical".[31]

Here, in a reformulation of Gomme's argument is precisely the tension between inclusion and exclusion bound within the single, seemingly unproblematic term. The passage points to a general open regime wherein the individual is not excluded by poverty and obscurity from service. Yet the system is not so radically equal as to disregard individual merit. This system "denies the priority of pre-established class orders (οὐκ ἀπὸ μέρους) and gives priority to individual good reputation (εὐδοκιμεῖ)". In other words, it offers "equality before the law for all, and individual merit in public service". Yet Ober very precisely articulates the difficulty and makes it clear that we are dealing with two opposing political principles, and not with two grades on a scale:

> The passage does not clarify what happens if there is a conflict between the perceived interests of the groups or between the equality of all and the merit of individuals. Can a political balance based on such a complex set of contrasts hold up under stressful circumstances of a long, hard war?[32]

3.3 *Logoi* and *Erga*

It is, as Ober proposes, in the Oration's next section that Pericles explains how this conflict between "group-interest oriented government and individual merit" is managed in Athens. As Pericles says (2.40.2–3, Ober's translation and supplements):

> καὶ οἱ αὐτοὶ ἤτοι κρίνομέν γε ἢ ἐνθυμούμεθα ὀρθῶς τὰ πράγματα, οὐ τοὺς λόγους τοῖς ἔργοις βλάβην ἡγούμενοι, ἀλλὰ μὴ προδιδαχθῆναι μᾶλλον λόγῳ πρότερον ἢ ἐπὶ ἃ δεῖ 2.40.3 ἔργῳ ἐλθεῖν. διαφερόντως γὰρ δὴ καὶ τόδε ἔχομεν ὥστε τολμᾶν τε οἱ αὐτοὶ μάλιστα καὶ περὶ ὧν ἐπιχειρήσομεν ἐκλογίζεσθαι· ὃ τοῖς ἄλλοις ἀμαθία μὲν θράσος, λογισμὸς δὲ ὄκνον φέρει.

> We ourselves can [collectively] judge rightly regarding affairs, even if [each of us] does not [individually] originate the arguments; we do not consider words [λόγους] an impediment to action [ἔργοις], but rather [regard it] essential to be previously instructed [προδιδαχθῆναι] by speech [λόγῳ] before embarking on necessary action [ἔργῳ]. We are peculiar also in that we hold that we are simultaneously persons who are daring and who debate what they will put their hands to. Among other men ignorance [ἀμαθία] leads to rashness while seasoned debate [λογισμός] just bogs them down.

---

31 Ober 1993, 95.
32 Ober 1993, 95.

"This passage", Ober says, "is virtually a definition of democratic knowledge and its relation to enactment and action". The Athenians, he adds:

> recognize that not everyone is equally capable of coming up with plans (this will be the job of the individual political leader), but many can participate in the decision (as assemblymen). So far so good, but in the next clause, it becomes clear that the Athenians are proud of making policy on the basis of λόγοι" and, crucially, "that they reject the existence of a hierarchy between λόγοι and ἔργα.[33]

Ober's argument (which depends on a wider analysis, the details of which are familiar and too long to recount here) is nevertheless precisely that this "virtual definition of democratic knowledge" is what is being questioned by Thucydides, who sharply distinguishes his own view from such democratic principles:

> Thucydides considers untested and competing λόγοι to be a very dubious basis for understanding reality, and he elevates ἔργα above λόγοι in his hierarchy of explanatory values.[34]

It is, Ober argues, precisely the value of ἔργα, "facts", that Pericles implicitly underlines in his speech and which Thucydides promotes as his route to truth, primarily in the form of his own historical method and his analysis of democratic Athens' downfall. The Funeral Oration itself, claims Ober, calls Athens' exceptional democratic principle into question, first by exposing the difficulties in affecting a "seamless mix of the interests of the few, the many and the individual" and also because of the difficulty of "employing public speeches to plan deeds". Thus, Ober says,

> Pericles' role as a statesman mimics that of Thucydides as historian — the hard work of fact-sifting and interpretation is done in advance by the expert, rather than being left to the assemblyman or reader.[35]

3.4 Politics, History and the *Non Dit*

Ober's analysis here beautifully proposes to cut through the knot of the problem of democracy, its regimes of truth and silenced tensions between the privileged few who possess knowledge and the uneducated masses. He is suggesting that

---

[33] Ober 1993, 96–97.
[34] Ober 1993, 96.
[35] Ober 1993, 97. Rephrasing in effect the tension to which Gomme originally points. See 95, n. 21.

Thucydides conflates (with a kind of 'Pindaric' bravado, we might almost say)[36] the practice and knowledge of political leaders and their privileged expertise at understanding actions and facts, embodied in the person of Pericles, with a parallel methodological argument about the expert practice and reflective knowledge of the writer, embodied by Thucydides in the person of himself and his skill in interpreting the historical facts.[37]

Regardless of whether we do or do not accept this argument about the Thucydidean reformulation of the hierarchy of λόγοι and ἔργα and the privilege of the latter, it should be clear that Thucydides, precisely *qua* historian – and no matter what his relationship to facts or his method of approaching them – is, in fact, a writer, a man whose primary element is λόγος.[38] It may well be that, as Thucydides suggests (2.65), the death of Pericles and the loss of his singular expertise precipitated the misjudged actions of democracy and the *demos* and the downfall of Athens which might otherwise have been averted.[39] We can reasonably espouse this view and the argument about Thucydides' critique of the history of his time. We should have little room to doubt that *our* understanding of the fateful progress of the Peloponnesian war and its causes are heavily inflected by Thucydides' historical narrative. Yet, whatever the historical reality and historiographic perspective behind Pericles and Thucydides, both men are, paradoxically though in the most practical way, first and foremost *de facto* figures in a dramatic λόγος – since the immediate object we today have to hand is the material text of the *Histories* – and through this text to figures of historical ἔργα. Put otherwise (in terms of the ontology of phenomenology), the historicity of history is heavily dependent on the mediation of historiography.[40] This, I should stress, is not simply an abstracted philosophical principle. Pericles, and Thucydides, and perhaps Ober himself as the proponent of the argument for hierarchy and the truth of 'merit', seem to enact a unity of thought and action which contradicts, – or must at least necessitate a re-definition the dichotomy of λόγος and ἔργον which is fundamental to the argument for the privilege of merit and thus also for

---

36 For Pindar, see the long discussion following Kurke 1991. For Thucydides and Pindar, see Hornblower 2004

37 For a different view, see Grethlein 2013, who interestingly tries to argue for "democratic features" of Thucydides' criticism.

38 The methodological shift is by now long in the history of Thucydidean scholarship. See, e.g., Connor 1977.

39 For the death of Pericles and the downfall of Athenian democracy, see recently Azoulay 2014, 127–136.

40 For a discussion of the philosophical elements of this historiographic position see, e.g., Tucker 2004 and overviews in Tucker 2009.

the foundation of Thucydides' critique of Athenian democracy. Ober's argument, built on the foundation of a phenomenological approach to history, is challenged precisely by its phenomenological foundations, by the underlying *non-dit* of his method.

Furthermore, if we allow this challenge, we must also allow that Thucydides, *qua* historian, and Ober *qua* political philosopher and historical commentator, seem – despite a close reading of the state of 'democratic knowledge' – to defer the very question "what is democratic knowledge". They characterize the problem of its dubious mix of deliberation and action, of inclusive and exclusive principles as unworkable and therein gain remarkably traction and important insights, but are themselves methodologically dependent on this very same mix. This argument, let me suggest, takes us back to the question that has dogged us from the start, namely the question: what is the relation between "group-interest oriented government and individual merit" and between radical equality and the privilege of distinction which seems to lie at the heart of the Funeral Oration and its presentation of the democratic principle.

4 Equality and Merit

4.1 Freedom

In what follows, then, I want to ask the question again while trying to avoid its deferral, both politically and in terms of essential method. It is clear, it seems to me, that, despite what we have seen so far, a hermeneutic of the problem needs to keep equality and merit together. Yet in order to address the essential political and methodological complications of the problem, we must reconfigure the relation between these elements of democracy. Here, I propose to do so with the aid of another recent student of political discourse and thought, philosopher Jacques Rancière.[41]

The tension between those who possess skilled knowledge and the uneducated masses can, let me suggest, indeed as the Oration itself makes clear, be rephrased in terms of the question of freedom: who is free to act and whose freedom

---

[41] Rancière's work is one of the most prominent influences on general democratic thinking today. See, e.g., Genel and Deranty 2016; Rockhill and Watts 2009. Rancière, perhaps because of the contents of his position, is only infrequently discussed within the discipline of classics and ancient history; see, however, O'Gorman 2018; Kahane 2007; as far as I am aware, there are no references within this discipline to his comments on the Funeral Oration.

to act is defined, guided and constrained by political agents whose understanding is assumed to be superior and thus, for example, assumed to be conducive to the success of the commonwealth. The distance between complete freedom for all and freedom only for some is, as we have seen, acknowledged by Gomme, Ober, and many other students of the Funeral Oration and of Athenian Democracy. Guided, not least by Thucydides' own judgement of Pericles (2.65) and perhaps by what we might regard as 'common sense', we are forced into an antithetical relation between equality and political wisdom. As Donald Kagan, for example, says in the concluding paragraphs of *The Fall of the Athenian Empire*:

> ...the Athenian experience in the Peloponnesian War suggests that in warfare democracies, where everything must be debated in the open and relatively uninformed majorities persuaded, may find it harder to adjust to the necessities of war than other, less open societies. Perhaps that is what Thucydides had in mind when he connected the Athenian defeat with the death of Pericles, who alone among Athenian politicians could persuade the people to fight in a way contrary to their prejudices and experiences.[42]

Democracies, we assume almost as a matter of course, are governed by open debate and relatively uninformed majorities. As Kagan and many others suggest, truly democratic regimes are less well-equipped to "adjust to the necessities of war than other, less open societies". The practical constraints of persuading majorities and thus of democratic decision-making, for example in times of war, are indeed self-evident. Such assumptions nevertheless foreclose the fundamental question of political equality and freedom. To begin with, even in practical terms, it may be somewhat difficult to prove is that swift and decisive political action on the authority (*auctoritas*, ἀξίωσις, ἀξίωμα, etc.)[43] of a single decision-maker or closed group leads reliably to political success or can avert political disaster. Indeed, at least some historical examples may argue to the contrary. Furthermore, hegemonic regimes have always been content to rationalize the exclusion, whole or partial, of political agency from some social groups, such as women, slaves, persons of colour or the poor on the basis of necessity and claims about the diminished capacity for political agency of those groups.[44] Thus, again, an implicit

---

[42] Kagan 1987, 426. For an evaluation of Pericles in the War, see, e.g., Kagan 2005.
[43] See above, n. 19, Hornblower 1991, 301 and the modern debate, one of whose fundamental conclusions is revolves around the paradox of the sovereign who has no law (Derrida, Agamben and the 'force of law').
[44] Senator John C. Calhoun, political theorist, vice-president of the United States (1825–1832) and outspoken advocate of slavery held that "if he could find a Negro who knew the Greek syntax, he

requirement of ἀρετή and ἀξίωσις (especially if the latter is, as Alison has argued, a banking metaphor and thus within the semantic field of 'wealth')[45] merely defers the engagement with the true problem of democracy.

4.2 The Public and the Private

In the section entitled, 'The Reign of the Many' in *On the Shores of Politics*, one of Jacques Rancière's many works on politics and the political, following extended discussions of Plato and Aristotle (which we will not here consider), Rancière finally turns to the that "founding text of democracy's reflection on itself"[46] and to Pericles' Funeral Oration. Rancière says:

> This speech immediately proposes a concept of freedom which treats it as the unity of two ideas: a particular idea of the *public* and a particular idea of the *private*. In the words that Thucydides puts in his mouth, Pericles says something like this: in public we conduct the affairs of the city; as for the private, as for the affairs of the individual, we leave those things to be handled as each person sees fit.[47]

This is an accurate paraphrase,[48] but it is worth looking again at Thucydides' text (2.37.2–3):

> ἐλευθέρως δὲ τά τε πρὸς τὸ κοινὸν πολιτεύομεν καὶ ἐς τὴν πρὸς ἀλλήλους τῶν καθ' ἡμέραν ἐπιτηδευμάτων ὑποψίαν, οὐ δι' ὀργῆς τὸν πέλας, εἰ καθ' ἡδονήν τι δρᾷ, ἔχοντες, οὐδὲ ἀζημίους μέν, λυπηρὰς δὲ τῇ ὄψει ἀχθηδόνας προστιθέμενοι. ἀνεπαχθῶς δὲ τὰ ἴδια προσομιλοῦντες τὰ δημόσια διὰ δέος μάλιστα οὐ παρανομοῦμεν, τῶν τε αἰεὶ ἐν ἀρχῇ ὄντων ἀκροάσει καὶ τῶν νόμων, καὶ μάλιστα αὐτῶν ὅσοι τε ἐπ' ὠφελίᾳ τῶν ἀδικουμένων κεῖνται καὶ ὅσοι ἄγραφοι ὄντες αἰσχύνην ὁμολογουμένην φέρουσιν.

> And not only in our public life are we liberal, but also as regards our freedom from suspicion of one another in the pursuits of every-day life; for we do not feel resentment at our neighbour if he does as he likes, nor yet do we put on sour looks which, though harmless, are painful to behold. But while we thus avoid giving offence in our private intercourse, in our

---

would then believe that the Negro was a human being and should be treated as a man" (Greenwood 2011, 163; Kahane 2011, 414–415. Source: Crummell 1898, 10–11. Discussion in Gates 1987, 21).
45 Allison 2001.
46 Already this characterization suggests a difference relative to, e.g., Ober, since it does seem to take the Funeral Oration as an expression of political theory rather than as a complex attempt to evade the colonizing hegemony of "democratic knowledge".
47 Rancière 1996, 40.
48 See below, Appendix on Paraphrase.

public life we are restrained from lawlessness chiefly through reverent fear, for we render obedience to those in authority and to the laws, and especially to those laws which are ordained for the succour of the oppressed and those which, though unwritten, bring upon the transgressor a disgrace which all men recognize.

Here, already Gomme again in his commentary identifies the fundamental principle: there is majority rule but "no tyranny by the majority over individuals, either in public or in private affairs".[49] But where Gomme, Ober, Kagan and others see a plain contradiction that requires choosing one option or the other, Rancière sees a single principle and, perhaps not surprisingly (when viewed within the contexts of the history of ideas in the 20th and 21st century), what we might describe as the principle of the principle, a meta-principle. He says:

> The concept of freedom unifies the private and the public, then, but it unifies them in their very separateness ... the democratic political subject has a shared domain in the very separateness of a way of life characterized by two great features: the absence of constraints and the absence of suspicion [ὑποψία].[50]

This "absence of suspicion" (ἐλευθέρως ... ἐς τὴν ... ὑποψίαν[51]) is the political corollary – formulated by Rancière but not in the actual Greek as a negation – in the realm of private life, of the obedient trust which the Athenians place in those in public authority and in their common laws (τῶν τε αἰεὶ ἐν ἀρχῇ ὄντων ἀκροάσει καὶ τῶν νόμων), between the many and the smaller group who actually makes the decisions. We need not, of course, accept this portrait of democracy as a true account of historical circumstances (Rancière here reminds us, among other things, of Loraux' critique of the Thucydidean presentation).[52] But Thucydides' words do, Rancière stresses, point to the essential "sporadic character" of democ-

---

49 Gomme, 111. Edmunds and Martin 1977, 193 rightly recognize the contradictions: "The adverb in 2.37.2 sums up the description of the Athenian constitution that Pericles has just given in 2.37.1. This description is quite paradoxical, in that it presents democracy as a mixture of democracy and aristocracy". Cf. Hornblower 1991, 301.
50 Rancière 1996, 41.
51 Accepting the text, against Reifferscheid and Gomme (*ad loc.* 111), following Connor 1984; 180 n. 58, Hornblower 1991, 301, etc.). The meaning is undoubted, but we should allow for the emphasis of this somewhat unusual construction, ἐλευθέρως δὲ τά τε πρὸς τὸ κοινὸν πολιτεύομεν, καὶ ἐς τὴν πρὸς ἀλλήλους τῶν καθ' ἡμέραν ἐπιτηδευμάτων ὑποψίαν, "we conduct our public life in a free way, indeed also in respect of suspiciousness in our day-to-day transactions with others". The absence of suspiciousness is, in the construction, the substance of the citizens' political freedom.
52 See Loraux 1986a, esp. 172–220.

racy, that element of inconsistency which opponents and proponents of the argument alike have recognized and which, indeed, both proponents and opponents of democracy more generally have stressed. Plato, for example, in Book VIII of the *Republic* famously mocks the political system in which a man might one day listen to the flute, then fast, then take exercise, then lie idle, take part in politics, then in philosophy, fight, then abandon warfare.[53] For Plato, "democracy is the regime of multiple accommodations".[54] More constructively perhaps, for Aristotle, advocate of complex mixed regimes, in Book IV of the *Politics*, for example, both oligarch and democrat should see their own preferred principles within the regime.[55] Thus, "democracy – the power of the *demos*", Rancière concludes, "is not synonymous with some principle of unity and ubiquity". It is, rather "a style of life which gives private and public their due".[56]

4.3 *Demos* and *Kratein*

In different ways, many readers of Athenian democracy of different dispositions, ancient and modern, do acknowledge what is, in fact, openly stated in the Oration: that democracy is a regime of "multiple accommodations". The question, as Kagan, for example, implies at the end of *The Downfall of the Athenian Empire* (see above) or as Ober puts it in his argument for Thucydides' critique, is whether "a political balance based on such a complex set of contrasts hold up under stressful circumstances of a long, hard war?"

Kagan's and Ober's characterization of Thucydides' position suggest an answer in the negative.[57] Decisive governance through the rigors of war demands

---

53 *Republic* VIII 561c: Οὐκοῦν, ἦν δ' ἐγώ, καὶ διαζῇ τὸ καθ' ἡμέραν οὕτω χαριζόμενος τῇ προσπιπτούσῃ ἐπιθυμίᾳ, τοτὲ μὲν μεθύων καὶ καταυλούμενος, αὖθις δὲ ὑδροποτῶν καὶ κατισχναινόμενος, τοτὲ δ' αὖ γυμναζόμενος, ἔστιν δ' ὅτε ἀργῶν καὶ πάντων ἀμελῶν, τοτὲ δ' ὡς ἐν φιλοσοφίᾳ διατρίβων. πολλάκις δὲ πολιτεύεται, καὶ ἀναπηδῶν ὅτι ἂν τύχῃ λέγει τε καὶ πράττει· | κἄν ποτέ τινας πολεμικοὺς ζηλώσῃ, ταύτῃ φέρεται, ἢ χρηματιστικούς, ἐπὶ τοῦτ' αὖ, καὶ οὔτε τις τάξις οὔτε ἀνάγκη ἔπεστιν αὐτοῦ τῷ βίῳ, ἀλλ' ἡδύν τε δὴ καὶ ἐλευθέριον καὶ μακάριον καλῶν τὸν βίον τοῦτον χρῆται αὐτῷ διὰ παντός.
54 Rancière 1996, 42.
55 *Politics* IV 1294b: δεῖ δ' ἐν τῇ πολιτείᾳ τῇ μεμειγμένῃ καλῶς ἀμφότερα δοκεῖν εἶναι καὶ μηδέτερον, καὶ σῴζεσθαι δι' αὑτῆς καὶ μὴ ἔξωθεν, καὶ δι' αὑτῆς μὴ τῷ πλείους [ἔξωθεν] εἶναι τοὺς βουλομένους (εἴη γὰρ ἂν καὶ πονηρᾷ πολιτείᾳ τοῦθ' ὑπάρχον) ἀλλὰ τῷ μηδ' ἂν βούλεσθαι πολιτείαν ἑτέραν μηθὲν τῶν τῆς πόλεως μορίων ὅλως.
56 Rancière 1996, 43.
57 As does, for example, from a different perspective, Leo Strauss; see Saxonhouse 2009, 733: "Strauss too may see in Plato the model antidemocrat, but he does not 'break with the habit of

the firm direction of clear individual expertise. Rancière too necessarily allows for these important reservations, yet he takes a very different position which replicates and embodies precisely the fundamental principles of democratic diversity.

> Thucydides was well aware that the question of politics was indivisible from that of whether democracies were governable. But he also knew that this question is invariably already settled, that democracies are always both governed and ungovernable – indeed governed inasmuch as they are ungovernable.[58]

Those familiar with Rancière's political philosophy will recognize here the essence of his wider positions. But it is worth, for the sake of clarity, to briefly invoke them as they appear in his own text. "There is politics, the art and science of politics", Rancière says, "because there is democracy":

> Politics is encountered as already present in the factuality of democracy, in the very strangeness of the combination of words which joins the unassignable quantity of the *demos* to the indefinable action of *kratein*.[59]

If this seems a startling argument, we should remind ourselves that, as we have seen above, already A.W. Gomme's position, uttered from a traditional philological perspective on the text, exposes exactly this "unassignable quality of the *demos*" in the form of its double meaning (as attested by essential references within

---

deference', as Popper urged. Strauss's detractors would argue that he finds in the *Republic* a model of elite rule over the many, a model worthy of emulation in these chaotic times. Whether this portrayal of Strauss is accurate or not, Strauss does not find in Plato the origins of totalitarianism as does Popper; rather, he finds resistance to totalitarianism in the resources provided there that are necessary to protect the liberal modern world from drowning the individual in the maw of mediocrity and unthinking lives".

58 Rancière 1996, 94.

59 Rancière 1996, 94. See, with wider references, the entry 'Politics (*La Politique*) in Rockhill's glossary in Rancière 2004, 90: "If politics has no proper place or predefined subjects for Rancière, this does not mean that everything is political. In its strict sense, politics only exists in intermittent acts of implementation that lack any overall principle or law, and whose only common characteristic is an empty operator: **dissensus**. The essence of politics thus resides in acts of **subjectivization** that separate society from itself by challenging the natural order of bodies' in the name of **equality** and polemically reconfiguring the **distribution of the sensible**. Politics is an anarchical process of **emancipation** that opposes the logic of **disagreement** to the logic of the **police**" (items in **bold** indicate technical terms in Rancière's thought, further defined in the glossary. AK). It is precisely those "acts of implementation that lack any overall principle or law" that constitute both democracy and politics, as Rancière understands them.

the Thucydidean text itself). Similarly "the indefinable action of *kratein"* is precisely the recognition which rests at the base of Ober's analysis. Rancière, in this sense, follows traditional lines of reading, yet this leads him to a rather different conclusion whose essence is a fundamental juxtaposition of surplus and lack:

> The primary unsettling fact in this juxtaposition is not that the people are too ignorant for matters which demand knowledge, too fickle for matters which demand stability, too excitable when prudence is called for or too petty when grandeur is required. Rather, it is that the people are always more or less than they are supposed to be: the majority instead of the assembly, the assembly instead of the community, the poor instead of the city, applause instead of agreement, pebbles counted instead of a firm decision taken. Reaching a decision by totting up pebbles and the bemoaning of stupidity of majorities are the small change of that 'one too many', that divergence from itself, which constitutes the *demos* as such. The people are at once disproportionate and anarchic.

Rancière (in a somewhat 'philological' mood) immediately explains:

> Language bears witness to this: there can be no *arche* corresponding to the *demos* as subject, no way of ruling according to some inaugural principle; there is only a *–cracy* – a manner of prevailing. Prevailing because one is the best, say Pericles' admirers Thucydides and Callicles; prevailing because one prevails, retorts his detractor Plato. The *–cracy* of the best – of the *kreitton* – is no quality, no definable expertise, but rather the sheer extra weight borne by the one best able to submit to the dictates of his own desire, who prevails among the people; for he who gives the people the greatest number of arsenals, the greatest number of colonies and the greatest sense of their own importance, is the one who receives the most power [[95]] from them in return. The 'one too many' of democracy here allows itself to be reduce to the 'more, always more' of unsatisfied desire, of the economic imperialism that turns democracy into the child of oligarchy and the mother of tyranny.[60]

This, then, is Rancière's revised philosophical argument for democracy. Strangely perhaps, yet as we have seen, it is based on readings of the text which, in their literal sense, many influential earlier readers accept. Rancière does not take liberties with Thucydides' words. Yet his conclusions diverge from those of some of his predecessors. Democracy, is a regime *"governed by the judicious use of its own un-governability"* which is precisely, in Rancière's political philosophy, the purpose of politics itself: *"leading the community harmoniously through discord itself, through the impossibility of the people being equal to themselves"*.[61]

---

60 Rancière 1996, 94.
61 Rancière 1996, 95.

4.4 Democracy's Regime of Truth

Reading Thucydides in this manner, we must also recognize that Rancière's argument is a reformulation, at once both conformant and subversive – and thus enacting in its own substance and practice of the democratic principle of diversity – of "democratic knowledge" and of democracy's "regime of truth". We are in a world which deploys a 'Foucauldian' epistemological perspective but which nevertheless alters its ontology, since such knowledge is now defined precisely as the essential absence (essential because it embraces explicit structural non-agreement) of a single, expert authoritative point of view or argument.[62] This, then, is a "non-regime" of truth which, quite in opposite to the idea of resolving the relations between *logos* and *ergon* through hierarchy and expertise, maintains the unresolved tension of these elements as a matter of political principle, as the very substance and goal of politics.[63]

This last position, we should add, allows us to put aside the paradoxes which emerge from a hierarchical arrangement of such relations in a claim with regard authority and truth, since there is no longer any problem with the presentation of a historian's argument about *erga* in discursive *logos* form. What's more, the explicit presence of the unresolved 'democratic' political relations between *logos* and *ergon* in Thucydides' histories serves as an empirical παράδειγμα (*Hist.* 2.37.1.2 παράδειγμα δὲ ... αὐτοὶ ὄντες ...) that this "non-regime" can, *pace* Ober's argument, be stated by- and from within the hegemonic framework of democratic knowledge, knowledge that, paradoxically and despite the catastrophic outcome of the Peloponnesian war, allows, openly and as a matter of principle, for a diversity of positions. "Democratic knowledge" redefined does, we might agree, "colonize" the discourse and our ways of knowing about the world of political affairs. But it does so in a manner that alters the conventional meaning of both democracy and knowledge and which thus, to borrow the words of Pericles himself, allows for expression in a "free manner" (ἐλευθέρως).

What's more, not only are such freedom and the principle of diversity it embodies capable of being stated openly, and thus democratically, within the discourse, but, as we have seen, they are also embedded at the very surface of the language of the speech, in its *men... de...* syntactic and rhetorical structure, in the multiple and incompatible semantics of the common-noun *demos*, in the contrast between public and private, and indeed, in the word *demokratia* itself, and its

---

[62] For Rancière and Foucault, see Biesta 2008.
[63] See above, n. 58.

transparent etymology, which we can now re-define using, strangely (but following, e.g., the Aristotelian principle of mixed regimes outlined above) exactly the same words used by Peter Rhodes, "people-power". Democracy is indeed – we can now call upon Peter Rhodes' definition again – "the standard Greek term for a form of government in which power resides with the many". Yet democracy is also, we must now conclude, a form of government in which, as Rancière argues, the ontological and political constitution of the "many" is inherently, irreducibly diverse, both more-than and less-than itself.

Did Thucydides agree with this position? Did Pericles, or Pericles as he is portrayed by Thucydides agree with this position? These are questions require a discussion which lies well beyond the limited scope of this essay. What, let me suggest, is nevertheless clear is that whatever the answers, they can all be comfortably accommodated within the definition of democracy which is presented above. Did the Athenian state bring about its own demise through the application of such democratic principles? Was the *demos* "too ignorant for matters which demand knowledge, too fickle for matters which demand stability, too excitable when prudence is called for or too petty when grandeur is required", as Rancière acknowledges? Was the Athenian *demos* thus not capable, after the death of Pericles, of defending the State against the very great pressures of its circumstances in the fifth century? These are questions that require further separate consideration elsewhere. What we can again say, however, is that the principle of political diversity which we have outlined above precludes a single, expert answer. This is true first, because there can be no single answer as to the responsibility of such plurality for historical action and second, because it is impossible to say with certainty whether any single man's *axiôma* – what in Rome and in more general debates over sovereignty and political authority ranging from Theodor Momsen to Carl Schmitt and Giorgio Agamben is presented as the problem of *auctoritas* – would have saved Athens from itself.[64]

5 Postscript

There remains, it seems to me, at least one more rather large question in the wake of our discussion, to which, let me nevertheless suggest by way of an afterword, it might be possible to provide at least a guiding response. The question, then, is: are we being foolishly utopian, idealistic and indeed naïve in believing that the

---

[64] See above, n. 42.

argument for ancient democracy is, in fact, openly stated as a kind of compact 'theory of democracy' in the Funeral Oration, in believing that we can hear a genuine democratic voice in Pericles' speech?

The response, let me suggest, has two closely enmeshed elements, one methodological the other political. The democratic principle as we have tried to read it in the Oration and as Rancière stresses, is characterized by a freedom from *hypopsia*, by an absence of suspicion. This principle, as Rancière notes, is nevertheless antithetical to key elements in modernity's general methodological outlook. Indeed, 'suspicion' is so fundamental, so internalized in our critical practice that many of us will have not taken account of it.

> Suspicion in Thucydides' Greek is called *hypopsia*: looking underneth. What characterizes democracy for Thucydides is the rejection of this looking underneath is something which the social theorists of the modern age elevate, by contrast [to Thucydides and the Funeral Oration, as Rancière reads them], to the rank of a theoretical virtue, an appropriate means of apprehending, beneath the appearance of commonality, a truth which belies it.[65]

The open structure of democracy's political cognition as it is presented in the Funeral Oration, this argument suggests, is directly at odds with the structure of critical suspicion. Rancière is, of course, here making a statement on a very large historical and philosophical scale. Yet its fundamentals are, let me suggest, in plain sight, as indeed must be if the principle is true. In the Oration, Pericles does (notwithstanding formal textual difficulties that do not affect the meaning)[66] state clearly that Athenian democracy is based on an absence of suspicion. Equally clearly, if in direct contrast, we can see that suspicion as the "appropriate means of apprehending, beneath the appearance of commonality, a truth which belies it" underpins, for example, most of the scholarly sources which we have invoked in this essay: Gomme's philological analysis identifies the underlying double meaning of *demos* and its possible threats; Ober's discussion of ideology identifies democracy's regime of truth and the underlying knowledge whose colonizing silence Thucydides tries to overcome; and, indeed Fredric Jameson too, whose classic analysis we have briefly cited, underscores the *non-dit* principle of ideology.

Yet, have we not emphasised throughout this essay and our reading of the sources – guided by Rancière's approach – the open meaning of democracy's multiple accommodations, marked by the very rhetoric, grammar and semantics of the text?

---

[65] Rancière 1996, 41.
[66] See above, n. 50.

This overlap of method and politics, whose consideration would easily overrun even a very long book, is characteristic of many other seminal political and methodological debates, both ancient and modern. Thus, to give one brief example, consider Plato's critique of democracy in the *Republic* and two of its opposing methodological and political interpreters, Karl Popper on the one hand and Leo Strauss on the other. Popper famously marked Plato as an enemy of the "open society". As Arlene Saxonhouse, for example, notes in a recent discussion, Popper read the *Republic* as "a blueprint ... for a closed society". Leo Strauss, in contrast, so it is often suggested, saw the Platonic argument "as a proposal for the rule of the elite".[67] Notwithstanding many disagreements over these two opposing readings and their politics, each separately and both in relation to each other, were genuine efforts to address the threat of the atrocities of the first half of the twentieth century. Popper; wanted "to break with the habit of deference to great men", Strauss, in many ways, advocated it.[68]

Yet these readings are equally a matter of basic methodological divisions. As Saxonhouse rightly stresses, "Popper read Plato straight-on, where the words of the dialogue [the *Republic*] put into the mouth of Socrates are those of Plato and reveal Plato's ideal political system". "One need only glance briefly at Plato's *Republic*", she says, "to find ready support for such a view". In contrast, she adds, "Straus's methodology refuses to make the speech of the dialogues the philosophy of Plato". Attending to the examples of medieval Arabic authors commenting on Plato who emphasised the dialogic form of Plato's work, Strauss encouraged his own readers to read the dialogues "by paying attention to the character of the interlocutors ...". She explains:

> Strauss' fascination with medieval political thought, the Talmud, the mystical writings of the Cabala fostered the interest in hidden meanings in texts and the theory of reading between the lines, suggesting that an examination of silences and contradictions barely noticeable to the casual reader might reveal hidden meaning in the texts.[69]

Neither method, nor ideology nor indeed the politics that accompany such approaches are monolithic structures, and it would be methodologically, ideologically and indeed politically reductive to try to argue for such monoliths or to expect to arrange them within a single critical hierarchy. Perhaps ultimately that is part of the point of our essay. There is, let me stress, something of a contrast or at

---

67 Saxonhouse 2009, 732.
68 Above, n. 56.
69 Saxonhouse 2009, 733.

least a tension here, between, on the one hand what we might call the hermeneutics of suspicion and, on the other hand critique based – philosophically and methodologically – on trust. This tension is inflected by philosophical perspectives and political orientation and by history as well.[70] Is the position of trust and diversity reflected, in our debate at least, by Rancière's position too utopian to be taken seriously? That, it seems to me, is a matter of historical judgement and ethical outlook. Have different cultures, amongst them, prominently, Athens in the classical era but also many modern cultures and societies believed in the superiority, authority and expertise of, say, one gender over those of another, of one class of persons over others, of one race, culture or consciousness over others, of certain professions and technologies over others? It would be impossible to suggest otherwise. Athenian citizenship excluded all but adult males of Athenian parentage.[71] But should we try to challenge such exclusive structures? Probably. This may involve, in part, trying to re-read some of our ancient texts.

6 Appendix: Hermeneutics, Paraphrase and 'the Text'

Like Foucault's work, which so frequently engages with Greco-Roman antiquity and provides such a steady methodological frame of reference for so many scholars of antiquity, Rancière's work too frequently engages with Greece and Rome and with questions of historicity and the material substance of historical sources and texts.[72] In *Les Mots de l'histoire: Essai de poétique du savoir* (1994. English: *The Names of History*, 2014), for example, Rancière considers, among other discussions, the possibility of attending to the voices of the non-aristocratic soldiers in Tacitus' historical account in the *Annales* of the Panonian revolt.[73] Rancière attempts to reach beyond the veil of Tacitus' Patrician epistemic and discursive habit to the voice of the *populus*. But he does so by examining the surface of language – its *'aesthetic'* qualities, as Rancière often puts it, its "distribution of the sensible", or rather to the *politics of aesthetics*. In *Les mots de l'histoire* he does so

---

70 For 'trust' in the context of democracy, see, e.g., Mara 2001.
71 See, e.g., Roberts 1994.
72 For Rancière and antiquity, Mecchia 2009; papers from the workshop 'Reading Rancière Reading the Classics' (organizers, E. O'Gorman and A. Kahane, London 2017) are in preparation for publication. For Rancière and Foucault see Biesta 2008.
73 Rancière 1994, 25–26. Cf. also his comments on Thersites in the *Iliad* and comments in Kahane (forthcoming).

by looking at Tacitus' use of *oratio obliqua* – a mode of speech that properly 'belongs to no one' and in whose interstices we can thus try to reach to history itself as a "regime of truth" and to listen to those who, like the rabble-rousing Percennius, are excluded from knowledge and have no right to speak.[74]

Nevertheless, unlike Foucault, whose title *Les Mots el les choses* is echoed in Rancière's title *Les Mots de l'histoire*, Rancière's work is less concerned with historical 'excavation' (an 'archaeology') and more with the phenomenology of politics and truth. Rancière often invokes ancient sources like Tacitus, Plato or Thucydides and Pericles' Funeral Oration, but likewise staples of modernity such as Durkheim and Mauss, Michelete and Febvre, Marx, Bourdieu and others through the trope of 'paraphrase'.[75] Such paraphrase frequently looks to antiquity as an accessory to ethical discussion rather than as historical object in its own right. Yet paraphrase, – as I hope I will have demonstrated in this essay using deliberately extended quotations from 'the texts themselves', is not the enemy of history. As even a quick read in, e.g., Loraux' sweeping survey of readings of the Pericles' Funeral Oration in *The Invention of Athens* demonstrates, it is, practically and inevitably the substance of history, or at least, *secundum* Loraux, if we are to judge by the diverse practice of German philosophy, English empiricism and other historical strands of thought.[76] More generally, paraphrase should be viewed from the perspective of hermeneutics (or indeed reception, which now has such purchase among students of classical antiquity) as a historically committed antidote to positivism.[77] Indeed, precisely if we accept that truth is only possible within the realm of the historical consciousness of subjects and the fragility of time and place, we have every reason to return to 'the text itself' and to a philological reading of the sources.[78] *Ipso facto*, our attention to the historicity of political regimes should prevent us from reading the ancient sources, in our case Pericles' Funeral Oration, with a view to some external substance rather than through the constraints, indeed, the historical *advantages* of philological method.

---

74 Rancière 1994, 89, 96.
75 See Swanson 1963.
76 See Loraux 1986a, 5–10.
77 Discussion, e.g., in Tucker 2004; Koselleck 2004. With reference to antiquity, Hartog 2016; Grethlein 2010; etc.
78 Koselleck 2004; philosophically, Gadamer 2007; etc.

Bibliography

Agamben, Giorgio (2005), *State of Exception*, Chicago, IL.
Allison, June W. (2001), "*Axiosis*, the New *Arete*: A Periclean Metaphor for Friendship", *Classical Quarterly* N. S. 51, 53–64.
Althusser, Louis (2014), *On the Reproduction of Capitalism: Ideology and Ideological State Apparatuses*, London.
Andrews, James A. (2004), "Pericles on the Athenian Constitution (Thuc. 2.37)", *American Journal of Philology* 125, 539–61.
Árnason, Jóhann Páll/Raaflaub, Kurt A./Wagner, Peter (eds) (2013), *The Greek Polis and the Invention of Democracy: A Politico-Cultural Transformation and its Interpretations*, Chichester.
Azoulay, Vincent (2014), *Pericles of Athens*, Princeton, NJ.
Bicknell, Peter J. (1972), *Studies in Athenian Politics and Genealogy*, Athens.
Biesta, Gert (2008), "Toward a New "Logic" of Emancipation: Foucault and Rancière", *Philosophy of Education*, 169–77.
Bleicken, Jochen (1985), *Die athenische Demokratie*, Stuttgart.
Bordes, Jacqueline (1982), *Politeia dans la pensée grecque jusqu'à Aristote*, Paris.
Busolt, Georg (1920/6), *Griechische Staatskunde*, Munich.
Cartledge, Paul (1996), "Comparatively Equal", in Josiah Ober and Charles Hedrick (eds), *The Athenian Revolution: Essays on Ancient Greek Democracy and Political Theory*, Princeton, NJ, 175–85.
Connor, W. Robert (1977), "A Post Modernist Thucydides?", *Classical Journal* 72, 289–98.
Connor, W. Robert (1984), *Thucydides*, Princeton, NJ.
Connor, W. Robert (2018), "Pericles on Democracy: Thucydides 2.37.1", *Classical World* 111, 165–75.
Crummell, Alexander (1898), "The Attitude of the American Mind Toward the Negro Intellect", *Occasional Papers of the American Negro Academy* 3, 8–19.
Dahl, Robert A. (1989), *Democracy and its Critics*, New Haven, CT.
Dahl, Robert A. (2006), *A Preface to Democratic Theory* (Expanded Edition), New Haven, CT.
Davies, John K. (2003), "Democracy Without Theory", in Peter Derow and Robert Parker (eds), *Herodotus and His World: Essays from a Conference in Memory of George Forrest*, Oxford, 319–35.
de Romilly, Jacqueline (1962), *Thucydide: La guerre du Péloponnese*, Paris.
de Ste Croix, G.E.M. (1954/5), "The Character of the Athenian Empire", *Historia* 3, 1–41.
de Ste Croix, G.E.M. (1972), *The Origins of the Peloponnesian War*, London.
Derrida, Jacques (1992), "Force of Law: The 'Mystical Foundation of Authority", in Drucilla Cornell/Michael Rosenfeld/David Gray Carlson (eds), *Deconstruction and the Possibility of Justice*, London, 3–67.
Edmunds, Lowel/Martin, Richard P. (1977), "Thucydides 2.65.8: ΕΛΕΥΘΕΡΩΣ", *Harvard Studies in Classical Philology* 81, 187–93.
Foucault, Michel (1979), *The History of Sexuality Vol. I*, London.
Foucault, Michel (1980), *Power/Knowledge*, New York, NY.
Frazier, Françoise (2001), "Prestige et autorité de l'homme d'État chez Thucydide", *Ktèma* 26, 237–56.

Gadamer, Hans-Georg (2007), "Classical and Philosophical Hermeneutics", in Richard E. Palmer (ed.), *The Gadamer Reader: A Bouquet of Later Writings*, Evanston, IL, 41–71.
Gates Jr, Henry Louis (1987), *Figures in Black: Words, Signs, and the Racial Self*, Oxford.
Genel, Katia/Deranty, Jean-Phillipe (eds) (2016), *Recognition or Disagreement: A Critical Encounter on the Politics of Freedom, Equality and Identity*, New York.
Goldhill, Simon (1986), *Reading Greek Tragedy*, Cambridge.
Gomme, Arnold W. (1973), *A Historical Commentary on Thucydides*, Oxford.
Grant, J.R. (1971), "Thucydides 2.37.1", *Rheinisches Museum* 109, 108–20.
Greenwood, Emily (2011), "The Poetry of Phyllis Wheatley", in Edith Hall/Richard Alston/Justine McConnell (eds), *Ancient Slavery and Abolition: From Hobbes to Hollywood*, Oxford.
Grethlein, Jonas (2010), "Beyond Intentional History: A Phenomenological Model of the Idea of History", in Lin Foxhall/Hans-Joachim Gehrke/Nino Luraghi (eds), *Intentional History*, Stuttgart, 327–42.
Grethlein, Jonas (2013), "Democracy, Oratory, and the Rise of Historiography in Fifth-century Greece", in Jóhann Páll Árnason/Kurt A. Raaflaub/Peter Wagner (eds), *The Greek Polis and the Invention of Democracy*, Malden, MA, 126–43.
Gurd, Sean Alexander (ed.) (2010), *Philology and its histories*, Columbus, OH.
Gurd, Sean Alexander (2015), "Philology and Greek Literature", Retrieved 09/07/2019, 2019, from https://www.oxfordhandbooks.com/view/10.1093/oxfordhb/9780199935390.001.0001/oxfordhb-9780199935390-e-65?print=pdf.
Hansen, Mogen Herman (1974), *The Sovereignty of the People's Court in Athens in the Fourth Century B.C. and the Public Action against Unconstitutional Proposals*, Odense.
Hansen, Mogens Herman (1978), "*Nomos* and *Psephisma* in Fourth-Century Athens", *Greek Roman and Byzantine Studies* 20, 27–53.
Hansen, Mogens Herman (1986), "The Origin of the Term Democratia", *Liverpool Classical Monthly* 11, 35–6.
Hansen, Mogens Herman (1999), *The Athenian Assembly in the Age of Demosthenes* (1st ed. 1987), London.
Hansen, Mogens Herman (2008), "Thucydides' Description of Democracy (2.37.1) and the EU-Convention of 2003", *Greek, Roman, and Byzantine Studies* 48, 15–26.
Harris, Edward M. (1992), "Pericles' Praise of Athenian Democracy Thucydides 2.37.1", *Harvard Studies in Classical Philology* 94, 157–67.
Harte, Verity/Lane, Melissa (eds) (2013), *Politeia in Greek and Roman Philosophy*, Cambridge.
Hartog, François (2016), *Regimes of Historicity: Presentism and Experiences of Time*, New York, NY.
Herzfeld, Michael (1997), "Political Philology: Everyday Consequences of Grandiose Grammars", *Anthropological Linguistics* 39, 351–75.
Hornblower, Simon (1991), *A Commentary on Thucydides, Vol. I*, Oxford.
Hornblower, Simon (2004), *Thucydides and Pindar. Historical Narrative and the World of Epinikian Poetry*, Oxford.
Jameson, Fredric (1981), *The Political Unconscious: Narrative as a Socially Symbolic Act*, Ithaca, NY.
Powell, John Enoch/Stuart-Jones, Henry (eds.) (1942), *Thucydides, Historiae*, Oxford.
Kagan, Donald (1987), *The Fall of the Athenian Empire*, Ithaca, NY.
Kagan, Donald (2005), "Perikles as General", in Judith M. Barringer/Jeffrey M. Hurwit (eds), *Periklean Athens and its Legacy: Problems and Perspectives*, Austin, TX, 1–9.

Kahane, Ahuvia (2007), "Disjoining Meaning and Truth: History, Representation, Apuleius' Metamorphoses and Neoplatonist Aesthetics", in J.R. Morgan/Meriel Jones (eds), *Philosophical Presences in the Ancient Novel*, Groningen, 245–69.

Kahane, Ahuvia (2011), "Postscript: Slavery, Abolition, Modernity, and the Past", in Edith Hall/Richard Alston/Justine McConnell (eds), *Ancient Slavery and Abolition: From Hobbes to Hollywood*, Oxford, 409–23.

Kahane, Ahuvia (forthcoming). "The Politics of the Formula", in Phiroze Vasunia (ed.), *The Politics of Literary Form*, Oxford.

Kallet, Lisa (2003), "*Demos Tyrranos*: Wealth, Power, and Economic Patronage", in Kathryn A. Morgan (ed.), *Popular Tyranny: Sovereignty and its Discontents in Ancient Greece*, Austin, TC, 117–53.

Koselleck, Reinhart (2004), *Futures Past: On the Semantics of Historical Time*, New York, NY.

Kurke, Leslie (1991), *The Traffic in Praise: Pindar and the Poetics of Social Economy*, Ithaca, NY.

Loraux, Nicole (1986a), *The Invention of Athens: The Funeral Oration in the Classical City*, Cambridge, MA.

Loraux, Nicole (1986b), "Thucydide et la sédition dans les mots", *Quaderni di storia* 12, 95–134.

Mara, Gerald M. (2001), "Thucydides and Plato on Democracy and Trust", *The Journal of Politics* 63, 820–45.

Mecchia, Giuseppina (2009), "The Classics and Critical Theory in Postmodern France: The Case of Jacques Rancière", in Gabriel Rockhill/Philip Watts (eds), *History, Politics, Aesthetics: Jacques Rancière*, Durham, NC, 67–82.

Meier, Christian (1969), "Die Entstehung des Begriffe 'Demokratie'", *Politische Vierteljahresschrift* 10, 535–75.

Meier, Christian (1990), *The Greek Discovery of Politics*, Cambridge, MA.

Monoson, Sara S. (2000), *Plato's Democratic Entanglements: Athenian Politics and the Practice of Philosophy*, Princeton, NJ.

Morris, Ian (1996), "The Strong Principle of Equality and the Archaic Origins of Greek Democracy", in Josiah Ober/Charles Hedrick (eds), *Demokratia: A Conversation on Democracies, Ancient and Modern*, Princeton, NJ, 19–48.

Mossé, Claude (2013), *The Demos's Participation in Decision-Making: Principles and Realities*, Chichester.

Murray, Oswyn (1993), *Early Greece*, Cambridge, MA.

Musti, Domenico (1995), "Ἀξίωσις, ἀξίωμα nel linguaggio di Pericle (Th. II 37, 1)", *Quaderni dell'Istituto di Archeologia e Storia antica* 5, 11–6.

O'Gorman, Ellen (2018), "The Noise and the People: Popular Clamor and Political Discourse in Latin Historiography", in Sebastian Matzner/Stephen Harrison (eds), *Complex Inferiorities The Poetics of the Weaker Voice in Latin Literature*, Oxford, 129–48.

Ober, Josiah (1989) *Mass and Elite in Democratic Athens: Rhetoric, Ideology and the Power of the People*, Princeton, NJ.

Ober, Josiah (1993) "Thucydides' Criticism of Democratic Knowledge", in Ralph M. Rosen/Joseph Farrell (eds), *Nomodeiktes: Greek Studies in Honor of Martin Ostwald*, Ann Arbor, MI, 81–98.

Ober, Josiah (2008), "What the Ancient Greeks Can Tell Us About Democracy", *Annual Reviews of Political Science* 11, 67–91.

Ober, Josiah (2018), *DEMOPOLIS: Democracy before Liberalism in Theory and Practice*, Cambridge.

Ober, Josiah/Hedrick, Charles (eds) (1996), *Dêmokratia: A Conversation on Democracies, Ancient and Modern*, Princeton, NJ.
Oliver, James H. (1955), "Praise of Periclean Athens as a mixed constitution", *Rheinisches Museum für Philologie* 98, 37–40.
Ostwald, Martin (1986) *From Popular Sovereignty to the Sovereignty of Law*, Berkeley, CA.
Raaflaub, Kurt A. (1980), "Zum Freiheitsbegriff der Griechen. Materialien und Untersuchungen zur Bedeutungsentwicklung von *eleutheros/eleutheria* in der archaischen und klassischen Zeit", in E.C. Welskopf (ed.), *Soziale Typenbegriffe im alten Griechenland und ihr Nachleben bis in die modernen Sprachen IV*, Berlin, 180–405.
Raaflaub, Kurt A. (1986), "Democracy, Oligarchy, and the Concept of the Free Citizen' in Late Fifth-Century Athens", *Political Theory* 11, 517–44.
Raaflaub, Kurt A. (1990) "Perceptions of Democracy in Fifth-Century Athens", *Classica et Mediaevalia Dissertationes* 40, 33–70.
Rancière, Jacques (1994), *The Names of History: On the Poetics of Knowledge*, Minneapolis, MN.
Rancière, Jacques (1996) *On the Shores of Politics*, London.
Rancière, Jacques (2003), *The Philosopher and His Poor*, Durham, NC.
Rancière, Jacques (2004), *The Politics of Aesthetics*, London.
Rancière, Jacques (2010), *Dissensus: On Politics and Aesthetics*, London.
Rhodes, P.J. (2015), "Directions in the Study of Athenian Democracy", *Scripta Classica Israelica* 34, 39–48.
Rhodes, P.J. (1988), *Thucydides, History II*, Warminster.
Rhodes, P.J. (2011), "Demokratia", in Hubert Cancik/Helmuth Schneider/Christine F. Salazar (eds), *Brill's New Pauly*, Leiden, 1, 510.
Rhodes, P.J. (2016) "Demagogues and *Demos* in Athens", *Polis* 33, 243–64.
Roberts, Jennifer T. (1994) *Athens on Trial: The Antidemocratic Tradition in Western Thought*, Princeton, NJ.
Robinson, Eric W. (ed.) (2004), *Ancient Greek Democracy: Readings and Sources*, Malden, MA.
Rockhill, Gabriel/Philip Watts (eds) (2009), *Jacques Rancière: History, Politics, Aesthetics*, Durham, NC.
Rusten, Jeffrey S. (ed.) (2009), *Thucydides*, Oxford.
Rusten, Jeffrey S. (2004), "Pericles in Thucydides", in Aurelio Pérez Jiménez/José Ribeiro Ferreira/Maria do Céu Fialho (eds), *O retrato literario e a biografia como estratégia de teorização política*, Málaga, 9–21.
Said, Edward W. (1972), "Michel Foucault As an Intellectual Imagination", *Boundary* 2, 1–36.
Saxonhouse, Arlene (2009), "The Socratic Narrative: A Democratic Reading of Plato's Dialogues", *Political Theory* 37, 728–53.
Sealey, Raphael (1967), *Essays in Athenian Politics*, New York, NY.
Sealey, Raphael (1974), "The Origins of *Demokratia*", *California Studies in Classical Antiquity* 6, 253–95.
Sealey, Raphael (1986), *The Athenian Republic: Democracy or Rule of Law?*, University Park, PA.
Swanson, Donald C. (1963), *A Formal Analysis of Petronius' Vocabulary*, Minneapolis.
Tucker, Aviezer (2004), *Our Knowledge of the Past*, Cambridge.
Tucker, Aviezer (ed.) (2009), *A Companion to the Philosophy of History and Historiography*, Malden, MA.
Underhill, James W. 2011. *Creating Worldviews: Metaphor, Ideology and Language*, Edinburgh.

Vlastos, Gregory (1964) "ΙΣΟΝΟΜΙΑ ΠΟΛΙΤΙΚΗ", in Jürgen Mau/Ernst Günther Schmidt (eds.), *Isonomia: Studien zur Gleichheitsvorstellung im griechischen Denken*, Berlin, 1–35.
Wallace, Robert W. (2016), Pericles. Oxford Bibliographies Online, https://wwwoxfordbibliographies com/view/document/obo-9780195389661/obo-9780195389661-0212xml.
Whitehead, David (1986), *The Demes of Attica, 508/7-ca. 250 B.C.*, Princeton, NJ.
Winton, Richard I. (2004), "Thucydides 2, 37, 1: Pericles on Athenian Democracy", *Rheinisches Museum für Philologie* 147, 26–34.

Part III: **Antiquating Modernity**

Salvatore Tufano
Walter Benjamin and Greek Historiography

> Möchtest du, Gerhard, für die Erinnerungen deiner Jugend eine Kammer in dieser Arche finden, die ich gebaut habe als die faschistische Sintflut zu steigen begann.
> Walter Benjamin, Januar 1937.[1]

In a review article published in a collection of essays on the definition of "classics",[2] Walter Benjamin writes that "a treatment of antiquity with nothing to say on slavery cannot lastly count as conclusive".[3] This comment shows the actual extent of a study of Benjamin's engagement with the Classics, which has to take into consideration his non-systematic treatment of the field. We currently lack a comprehensive work on this engagement, and the present study attempts at providing a first essay in the field. The complexity of the goals is a direct consequence of Benjamin's various interests and intellectual activity: how are we to judge, for instance, his use of Greek and Roman authors in his literary essays? Is there a connection between his philosophy of history and the one underlying Classical Greek historiography of the Fifth Century BC?[4]

Starting from these questions, this investigation on the legacy of Greek historiography and philosophy of history in Walter Benjamin undertakes two tasks: first of all, I evaluate the role of Greek and, more generally, Classical authors in the development of Benjamin's thought (Section 1). This first section provides a broad perspective on the formation of the philosopher and on his use of quotes

---

[1] "May you, Gerhard, find a chamber in this ark which I built when the Fascist flood was starting to rise for the memories of your youth" (tr. in Eiland/Jennings 2014, 536.) Dedication by Walter Benjamin to Gerschom Scholem of a copy of *Deutsche Menschen*, published with the pseudonym Detlef Holz in Switzerland in November 1936 (Deutsches Literaturarchiv, in Wizisla 2007, 60; see shortly on the volume Eiland/Jennings 2014, 536.) On the double meaning of the word *Arche*, which refers both to the biblical 'ark' (more commonly *Kasten* in German) and to the Gk. ἀρχή, see Schöne 1986; Britt 2014, 92–93; Eiland/Jennings 2014, 538.
[2] *GS* 3.290–4,
[3] "[E]ine Betrachtung der Klassik, die von der Sklaverei nichts zu sagen weiß, kann am Ende doch nicht als abschließend gelten" (ibid. 294.)
[4] I would like to thank the editor of the volume for the useful comments I received and Dr. Guilherme Vilaca Vasconcelos for his precious observations and advices on this piece. The quotes from the works of Walter Benjamin generally refer to the complete edition of his works, the *Gesammelte Schriften*, here mentioned as *GS* (Benjamin *GS*.) However, I chose to refer to later translations and commentaries with the year of their appearance, given the complexity of the textual tradition of the specific text under scrutiny in Section 3. Translations are mine unless otherwise noted.

from Classical authors; moreover, it follows a traditional approach in reception studies, consisting in the actual evaluation and recovery of Classical literature in later authors. The second section partially draws on this same methodology, since it concentrates on a specific use of an author, Herodotus, in the essay written by Benjamin on the Russian writer Nikolaj Leskov (1936): this work is therefore taken as a case study of the commitment of the author with Greek historiography (Section 2).

Finally, since the theses *On the Philosophy of History* were the last work written by Benjamin a few months before his suicide, I chose to concentrate on this text, as a paradigmatic and systematic exposé of the philosophy of history of the author: this final investigation juxtaposes and compares three particular theses, whose tenets allow a productive comparison with Greek historiography (Section 3.)

A methodological caveat stems from the need to circumscribe the field of *comparanda*. The extant corpus of Greek historiography is here limited to Herodotus' and Thucydides' *Histories*, since, starting from a consideration of Benjamin's works, these were the only two authors who allow an actual comparison. Thenceforth, this comparison follows two approaches: while some points of contact between Greek historiography and Benjamin's observations can be ascribed to a direct knowledge of the original texts, other parallels are suggested in the spirit of contrasting and documenting a dialogue between reconcilable ancient and modern philosophies of history.

1 Walter Benjamin's Interest in the *Altertumswissenschaft*

Cursory remarks in Walter Benjamin's writings indicate a high degree of appreciation of ancient Greek: he was aware of the dogma of the absolute superiority of ancient Greek[5] and frequently referred, in his writings, to ancient Greek authors and myths. He had studied Greek and Latin in secondary school and had almost failed the final exam (*Abitur*), for his poor performance when translating from

---

[5] Review to J.J. Bachofen, *Griechische Reise* (Heidelberg 1927) = Benjamin *GS* 3.88–94, tr. E. Leslie and E. Truskolaski in Benjamin 2016, 142. "From the Greek language is inherited its musical instrumentation. Today there is no author who approaches the Germano-Greek inclination to composite words more freely and with more understanding than this one [Franz Hessel]" (1927= Benjamin *GS* 3.82–4; tr. E. Leslie in Benjamin 2016, 107.)

Greek. He passed thanks to the oral examination.⁶ The reflection of Benjamin, also in texts of a private nature, on words such as θεωρία, κοινός and οὖτις,⁷ and a relative frequency in the use of classical mythology confirm what was perhaps more than a basic grasp of the field.⁸ In an allegorical short tale written when he was probably nineteen, *Schiller und Goethe. Eine Laienvision* ("Schiller and Goethe. A Layman's Vision"),⁹ the entrance to a dreamy landscape of ancient and modern literates is characterized by:

A black gate. In the uncontrollable twilight, its pillars appeared like Doric columns, *Iliad* on the one, *Odyssey* on the other.¹⁰

At a reading club which had started in 1908,¹¹ a few years before the *Abitur* of 1911, Benjamin apparently enjoyed reading aloud Pindar, a poet he would recite from heart even in later years.¹² Pindar would indeed inspire what Benjamin describes as his first philosophical essay, *Reflections on Nobility* (*Gedanken über den Adel*.)¹³ In the same years, he wrote a critical essay on *Socrates*, where Socrates is blamed for an unduly sexualisation of philosophy,¹⁴ this being one of his first and

---

6 Eiland/Jennings 2014, 29.
7 On the *Abitur*, see Eiland/Jennings 2014, 29. Θεωρία: in a letter to Wyneken, 1915 (Benjamin 1994, 76); κοινός: in a radio talk on Bertolt Brecht (Benjamin *GS* 2.662: "the Greek root κοινός – the general, what concerns everything, what belongs to everybody"); οὖτις is the definition used twice for Herr Keuner, a character invented by Brecht (Benjamin *GS* 2.523 and 7.655; on the context of these observations, see Wizisla 2004, 182.)
8 Here are a few examples: he comments on Τύχη as a loony goddess for the collectors (Benjamin *GS* 1.158; 3.237); he refers to Platonic and Menander mask-wearers in a review-article (Benjamin *GS* 3.82–4); he recognizes a "Plutarchische Linie" in the anachronisms of a book by Max Kommerell (Benjamin *GS* 3.256); he defines the coin-operated automatic scales the modern γνωθι σεαυτον [*sic*]» (Benjamin *GS* 5.1025) (in another curious short note, he writes "Caissière als Danae": *GS* 5.133.) The presence of classical mythology in the different works would also deserve a systematic attention which cannot be paid here: the author oscillates from a standard use of ancient myths, as in his use of the motif of Odysseus as traveller *par excellence* (see the "Welti's Moonlit Night", the transcript of a dream, tr. in Benjamin 2016, 55–56), as well as combining figures of the Greek myth such as Niobe with disturbing and contrasting parallels, as a series of statues he saw in Sweden (Benjamin *GS* 4.383–7.) A study which would we ascribe today to the field of the reception studies, insofar as it tackles the reception of Oedipus in contemporary literature, is *Oedipus oder Der Vernünftige Mythos* ("Oedipus, or the Rational Myth": Benjamin *GS* 2.391–5.)
9 Benjamin *GS* 7.636–9.
10 Tr. S. Truskolaski in Benjamin 2016, 6.
11 Eiland/Jennings 2014, 27.
12 Scholem 1981, 8–9.
13 Benjamin *GS* 6.504.
14 Benjamin *GS* 2.129–32.

more direct commitments with the work of Plato.¹⁵ Still in his university years, he allegedly owned only two philosophical *opera omnia* in their entirety: the works of a Romantic thinker, Fritz von Baader (1765–1841), and those of Plato.¹⁶

In his first year at university, Benjamin attended a seminar on Aristotle's *Metaphysics* held by Richard Herbertz;¹⁷ however, it seems that most of his interest in ancient philosophy lay in his appreciation of Hellenistic schools, especially of stoicism,¹⁸ and he attended more than one seminar in what we would define today as 'Late Antique' studies. Furthermore, one of the last books Walter Benjamin read was an essay by Marrou on Augustine.¹⁹ Other authors of the classical antiquity which formed the backbone of Benjamin's literary and philosophical background, as explicitly recorded by him, were the Athenian playwrights of the classical period (with a special focus on tragedy and an apparently minor interest in comedy)²⁰ and Latin poets, such as Catullus and Lucretius.²¹

A vehement reply to an essay on Virgil testifies, however, to a variety and depth of knowledge which alludes to a knowledge of the poet, possibly beyond a scholastic commitment.²² Benjamin wrote a *Catalogue of Read Books* (*Verzeichnis*

---

15 On Benjamin's view of friendship as grounded on the Platonic *philia*, and on his reading of the *Symposion*, cf. Eiland/Jennings 2014, 41 and 85. On his essay On Platonic Love, cf. da Costa 2011.
16 Eiland/Jennings 2014, 81.
17 See Eiland/Jennings (2014, 100), to which I refer in general for a profile of the *curriculum studiorum* of Walter Benjamin. Following Scholem (1981, 28), however, we may not want to stress too much the sheer relevance of the contents of the courses attended by the two friends: "I cannot recall either of us ever speaking of our university teachers with enthusiasm, either then or later; if we had praise for any of them, they were eccentrics and outsiders – for example, one of Benjamin's teachers, the philologist Ernst Lewy [...]. We did not take the philosophy teachers very seriously; perhaps we were too presumptuous in this. I was very disappointed in Ernst Cassirer's course on Greek philosophy before Plato".
18 This may result from Benjamin's reactivation and reflection on the Stoic concept of ἀποκατάστασις, although his use of the word in his philosophy of history also draws on the ancient re-reading of the concept (see Eiland/Jennings 2014, 659–60); the weight of Origen on the theses *On the Concept of History* is illuminated by Jennings 2016.
19 Benjamin wrote a review of *Saint Augustin et la fin de la culture antique* (Paris 1938) which was not published in his lifetime (*GS* 3.587–9; in 1940, he wrote to Karl Thieme, suggesting this read: ibid. 740.)
20 On Benjamin and Greek tragedy, see Vandevoordt 2014 and Billings 2015.
21 He is reading Tibullus and Propertius and ordered a translation of Catullus in late March 1918 (Benjamin 1994, 122); he recalls reading Lucretius in Ibiza, in 1936, with great joy (Benjamin 1994, 464).
22 Benjamin *GS* 3.315–22. In this review article on T. Haecker's *Vergil. Vater des Abendlandes* (1931), appeared in February 1932, Benjamin accuses the author of reading the poet as a Christian

der gelesenen Schriften), which enumerates more than 1700 books read by the philosopher between 1911 (when he was 19) and his last months (we miss nos. 1–461).[23] Yet, it has been proved that there are items he actually read and did not choose to quote here, as in the case of some books by Karl Kraus. Furthermore, Tiedemann and Schweppenhäuser, the editors of this material, underlined how this inventory exhibits a Benjamin as historiographer of his own education.[24] It is entirely possible, in other words, that some readings were omitted on purpose. While he had a profound interest in classical theatre, from this list it would appear that he had only read part of Wilamowitz's *Einleitung in die Tragödie* and Körte's book on comedy.[25] Besides, he carefully read the *Götternamen* by Hermann Usener (1896), when he was writing his *Habilitationsschrift* on the German *Trauerspiel*.[26]

There are therefore reasons to infer that, although authors as Herodotus and Thucydides are absent in the aforementioned list, Benjamin had more than a vague knowledge of their writings and thinking. His classical education lay behind his participation in the youth movement, for which he wrote an important essay, *Unterricht und Wertung* ("Lesson and Evaluation", 1913–1914), which anticipates some of his later views on the philosophy of history.[27] Therein, he denied any truth to a linear evolution of history. If a relationship exists between past events and the present, this has not to be found in a direct connection. History presents itself as a juxtaposition of single moments of time, later on defined as 'burning points' (*Brennpunkt*).[28] It is thus important to recognize the consistency

---

voice. A further example may be represented by his quote of Pliny the Younger's letter on the death of his uncle Pliny the Elder (Plin. *Ep.* 6.20.6–9 and 11–17), during a radio show held on 8.9.1931 on the *Untergang von Pompei und Herculanum* ("The Fall of Pompeii and Herculanum"): *GS* 7.214–20; here, he wrongly locates the Minotaur in Thebes at 214, rather than in Crete.)
23 Benjamin *GS* 7.437–76.
24 See Benjamin *GS* 7.724.
25 Benjamin *GS* 7.445; 659: "A<lfred> Körte: Die griechische Komödie <Leipzig 1914>"; ibid. 455: 936) "<Ulrich von> Wilamowitz <–> Moellendorff: Einleitung in die griechische Tragödie <Berlin 1907> (zum Teil)".
26 The book is no. 888 in the *Verzeichnis*; cp. Eiland/Jennings 2014, 183–4.
27 Benjamin *GS* 2.35–9. For a fuller discussion of the evolution of philosophy in Benjamin's lifetime, see Fenves 2011.
28 The word occurs in his writing *Das Leben der Studenten* ("The Life of the Students": 1915.) "He speaks here of a situation where history lays suspended as in a focal point (*Brennpunkt*), as from time immemorial in the utopical images of the thinkers" (Benjamin *GS* 2.75).

displayed throughout the evolution of his thoughts on these matters, finally leading to his theory of historical materialism.[29] Incidentally, this evolution seems to minimize the weight of the criticisms by more than a friend on the impact and the bad influence exerted by Berthold Brecht after the beginning of their friendship in 1929.[30]

This brief consideration of the relevance of classical studies in the formation of Walter Benjamin allows us to ground our investigation in a concrete ground. His knowledge of a variety of classical sources and of a few relevant pieces of secondary scholarship makes Benjamin an intellectual to whom Classics continued to matter, all throughout his life. Independently of the subject on which he was writing, Benjamin uses a number of references which are often cursory, as seen in this perspective. However, there is an important exception to this picture, consisting in his use of Herodotus in an essay written on a Russian writer, Nikolai Leskov.

2 Herodotus as a Storyteller

On est philologue, ou on ne l'est pas.[31]

Der Erzähler. Betrachtungen zum Werk Nikolai Lesskows (*The Storyteller. Observations on the Work of Nikolai Leskov*), published in 1936, summed up and revised a series of essays and notes on narratology, which Walter Benjamin had been writing since the beginning of the decade.[32]

According to Benjamin, a real, proper narration does not require giving an answer or an explanation to the story: [t]he novel, as a literary form dependent on the invention of printing, is born in the dissolution of the oral tradition and of

---

29 Cf. Wizisla 2004, 273. Benjamin introduces the theses *On the Concept of History* to Theodor W. Adorno as a "precise step of my reflections on the continuation of "Baudeilaire"" (Paris, 7.5.1940; Br. 93; Adorno 1994, 424–434; cf. Benjamin 2010, 189: "It thus results once again that the theses have become a *work in progress* [in Engl. in the or.], and the history of their development can apparently be traced back to the mid-30s".) The essay *Über einige Motive bei Baudelaire* had been published in the «Zeitschrift für Sozialforschung» in 1939, printed in early 1940 (Eiland/Jennings 2014, 657.)
30 The story of ups and downs in the relationship between Brecht and Benjamin is analyzed by Wizisla 2004.
31 Benjamin 1994, 596. Cf. Miller 2007, 348–349.
32 Benjamin *GS* 2.438–65.

the artisanal community it served,³³ He held that the best storyteller must have experienced the world and entertained a relationship with real life. The novel as a long narration, the information as a genre where an explanation is compulsory (in newspapers, for instance), and the end of craftsmanship have caused the death of the proper narrative. Nikolaj Leskov (1831–1895) was still a great writer, a good *Erzähler*, and therefore the comparison with Herodotus aims to show how an ancient example might have been suitable for him. The example taken from Herodotus presents how a real *Erzählung* ("chronicle")³⁴ never really ends with a full explanation, but leaves space for various interpretations:

> Leskov was grounded in the classics [*die Schule der Alten*]. The first storyteller [*Erzähler*] of the Greeks was Herodotus. In the fourteenth chapter of the third book of his *Histories*, there is a story [*Geschichte*] from which much can be learned. It deals with Psammenitus. After the Egyptian king Psammenitus had been vanquished and captured by the Persian king Cambyses, Cambyses was bent on humbling his prisoner. He ordered that Psammenitus be placed on the road that the Persian triumphal procession was to take. And he further arranged that the prisoner should see his daughter pass by as a maid going to the well with her pitcher. While all the Egyptians were lamenting and bewailing this spectacle, Psammenitus stood alone, mute and motionless, his eyes fixed on the ground; and when presently he saw his son, who was being taken along in the procession to be executed, he likewise remained unmoved. But when he subsequently recognized one of his servants, an old, impoverished man, in the ranks of the prisoners, he beat his fists against his head and gave all the signs of deepest mourning. This tale shows what true storytelling is [*wie es mit der wahren Erzählung steht*]. The information [*Information*] does not survive the moment in which it was new. It lives only at that moment [...]. A story [*Erzählung*] is different. It does not expend itself. It preserves and concentrates its energy and is capable of releasing it even after a long time. Accordingly, Montaigne referred to this Egyptian king and asked himself why he mourned only when he caught sight of his servant. Montaigne answers: "Since he was already over-full of grief, it took only the smallest increase for it to burst through its dams". Thus Montaigne. But one could also say: The king is not moved by the fate of those of royal blood, for it is his own fate. Or: We are moved by much on the stage that does not move us in real life; to the king, this servant is only an actor. Or: Great grief is pent up and breaks forth only with relaxation; seeing this servant was the relaxation.

Herodotus offers no explanations. His report is utterly dry [*der trockenste*]. That is why, after thousands of years, this story from ancient Egypt is still capable of provoking astonishment and reflection.³⁵

---

33 Eiland/Jennings 2014, 530.
34 Fenves 2011, 237: "The chronicle is distinguished from other modes of historiography in that it "chronicles" occurrences without any intention of determining how they follow from one another, much less how one epoch is related to another".
35 tr. from Eiland/Jennings 2002, with minor modifications.

Psammenitus' wise reply to a counsellor is explained differently by Benjamin, after quoting Montaigne, who had mentioned the story in his *Essais*. Benjamin offers a variety of interpretations, none of which, however, seems to take into serious account the letter of the original text of Herodotus.[36] Indeed, Herodotus continues the episode and remembers the famous answer given by Psammetichus on the sadness of the old age, which echoes a well-known popular motif, recorded at least from Bacchylides (F 2 S.-M.) and, most notably, parallel to the encounter between Solon and Croesus in the *Histories* (Hdt. 1.86–90). In Herodotus, the episode represents a didactic chapter, because it provides the audience with an important lesson: this rests on important historical background (the parade of the prisoners, the hard resistance of the last pharaoh) and on literary *topoi*, such as the motif of the wise counselor.[37] Is it possible that Benjamin actually ignored the final part of the story? The answer is negative, as the consideration of further materials proves.

We have two notes, belonging to the preparatory materials for essays and articles on narratology,[38] whence it is clear that Benjamin had actually looked for the passage in Herodotus. Despite these, it must be ascertained, as the documents confirm, that the same Montaigne had presented the end of the story in good faith (another fact of which Benjamin was aware):

Psammenitus' answer: "Son of Cyrus" (but there is only an ambassador before him), "the misfortunes, which have affected my family, are too big to be wept over; but the sad fate of a friend, who has fallen prey to the squalor on the threshold of old age, whereas he once had a strong position, seemed to me worthy of tears", Herodotus III, 14.

Hessel's exegesis: The fate of the royals does not concern the king, because it is his own [*sein eignes*].

---

[36] Hdt. 3.14.7–10 (tr. R. Waterfield): When Psammenitus saw him, he let out a loud groan, called out his friend's name, and struck his head in distress. Now, the guards who were there brought back to Cambyses a report of Psammenitus' reaction to each procession out of the city, and Cambyses was so surprised at Psammenitus' behaviour that he sent a messenger to him with the following query: 'Your master Cambyses wants to know, Psammenitus, why the sight of your daughter being humiliated and your son being taken to his death did not move you to protests and tears, whereas a beggar who, he has been informed, is not related to you at all did receive this mark of respect from you.' To this question, Psammenitus replied: 'Son of Cyrus, my personal troubles are too immense to cry over, but when a friend on the threshold of old age has lost a fortune and happiness, and been reduced to beggary, his sorrow calls for tears".

[37] Asheri *ad loc.* in Asheri *et al.* 2007.

[38] Benjamin–Archiv, Ms 1711 (=Benjamin *GS* 3.1011–2; *paralipomenon* to the *Kleine Kunst–Stücke*, 1932 (?).

Benjamins'exegesis: The pain appears more frequently for a reason, which is less profound than its original cause. It is a huge cap on a small pot. It can even avoid the reason and put up with the impulse. Such is the impulse, which brings the first tears to Proust's eyes after the death of his beloved grandmother –the gesture of his bending down, to undo the shoelace.

Asja's exegesis: Much of what concerns us on the stage, does not concern us in real life; this old man ist just an actor, for the king.

Montaigne's exegesis: "Ce fut, qu'hant d'ailleurs plein et combte de tristesse, la moindre surcharge brisa les barrieres de la souffrance [original: patience]".

Note by Martin-Guelliot: "Si Psammenitus avait vécu de nos jours, tous les journaux nous auraient appris qu'il préférait son domestique à ses enfants".[39]

Stefan Bub (2006) showed that this voluntary omission of the end of the story and the interest in this passage were shared by Ernst Bloch and other friends of Benjamin: according to Bub, who focused especially on the implications of the presence of Proust in the so-called 'Benjamin's *Auslegung*', a sort of 'collective realm of experience' [...] adheres to the re-narrating, and thereby spreading again and interpreting, committal with Herodotus in the circle of Benjamin and Bloch.[40] This observation is confirmed by another handwritten note, where the ideas shared by Walter Benjamin's son Stefan and his sister Dora are added to the aforementioned witnesses.[41]

Moreover, if we try to concentrate on written references, the only one we are explicitly given by the author is a note by René-Martin Guelliot. The former director of *Le Spectateur* had been quoted by Jean Paulhan in a peculiar article on *La nouvelle revue française* (1928), assembled around a series of alleged conversations between Paulhan and Guelliot. According to Paulhan:

---

[39] Paulhan 1928, 696; *ibid.* 695: "I will try to recall here the intention of my friend, with no great misrepresentation. As far as the examples he would usually quote are concerned, I might have forgotten them. I will happen to suggest new ones: an example is mostly worthy the reflections it elicits. [Je m'efforcerai de rappeler ici, sans trop les déformer, les propos de mon ami. Pour les exemples qu'il avait coutume de citer, je peux les avoir oubliés. Il m'arrivera d'en proposer de nouveaux un exemple ne vaut guère que par les réflexions qu'il provoque]".

[40] Bub 2006, 50 (my tr.).

[41] Benjamin–Archiv, Ms 1710 (=Benjamin *GS* 2.1288): [...] 6) Stefan [Benjamin]: weil der Soldat tm a h r [Wort aus der Kindersprache?] war (Erklärung: tapferer) Zur Erklärung von Montaigne: er erklärt das genial natürlich und unabhängig. Nach seiner Erklärung könnte auch der Sohn zuletzt kommen. Er achtet die Pointe für nichts. 7) Dora [Benjamin] (eigentlich Andre Gide) [:1 es gehört dazu ["6) Stefan [Benjamin]: because the soldier was *tm a h r* [children's language?] (Explanation: brave) On the explanation of Montaigne: he explains it in a natural and independent way. In his explanation, even the child may come last. He does not care at all about the punchline. 7) Dora [Benjamin] (properly Andre Gide) [:1 it is required".]»

> Confrontations, poems or marketing imply way more arguments and rationales which we can possibly record, or even be aware of. Their resource escapes our understanding.[42]

The observation by Guelliot comes from the first conversation between the two men, whose title is "La tristesse de Psammenitus". These few pages start with a quote from Montaigne and it does not seem unreasonable to suggest that it was this reading, which might have elicited Benjamin's interest, both for the choice of the passage in Herodotus and for its use.[43] The philosopher gives a distorted representation of Herodotus, but it cannot be denied, as Paulhan had written in his article, that an example is only worthy for the reflections which it elicits [un exemple ne vaut guère que par les réflexions qu'il provoque].

The dehistoricisation of the historical episode does not change its didactic character: even if we do not hold that Benjamin ignored Herodotus at all, it is reasonable to infer that this article by Paulhan was one of the first springs of interest feeding Benjamin's focus on *trocken* narrative,[44] which is the only cultural medium able to resist with the passage time.

I would therefore contend that Benjamin's deliberate omission of the act of judgement[45] by Psammenitus consciously opens space for a new use of this historiographical item, letting history speak for itself, with its nude facts, under no influence of the so-called 'eye of the winners'. This eye is represented, here, by Herodotus, as a writer of a historiography which has always been written by the winners, by the predominant acting eyes of judgements. On the other side, we learn from *On the Concept of History* that Benjamin opposes to universal history as a list of cumulating moments, the idea that history might be written and understood only in the *Jetztzeit*, in that "now-time" which constitutes the concentration of event and meaning.[46]

---

42 Paulhan 1928, 694 ([L]a dispute, le poème ou l'annonce mettent en jeu bien plus d'arguments et de raisons que nous ne sommes capables d'en retenir, ou seulement d'en com prendre. Leur ressource nous échappe.)

43 Ibid. 696–7.

44 The use of the adj. *trocken* is noteworthy, as it also occurs in a digression of a short tale, *Das Taschentuch* (*The Handkerchief*), where the author repeats the same arguments: Should not we commend the elders who left the events, so as to say, in a dry manner [*die das Geschehen sozusagen trocken legten*], for the fact that they drained off every psychological foundation and every meaning?» (Benjamin *GS* 4.743.)

45 Vardoulakis 2010, 162.

46 Eiland/Jennings 2014, 660–1: "All such efforts at enshrining, and hence reifying, the events of the past presuppose just that empty homogeneous continuum that is shattered in the monadically concentrated "now-time" (*Jetztzeit*) of the dialectical image and its "tiger's leap" into "the thickets of long ago".

This *Jetztzeit*, the idea that, no matter what Herodotus wrote, an 'incomplete' brick of his *Histories* might be enough to shed light on the anonymous characters of the past, takes us back to a thesis I will be now dealing with, the Third one, where it is said that history is accessible only to a redeemed mankind. "The past flies away (*huscht vorbei*) (Th. V)", and if we look for its salvation (*Rettung*: Ms 448 *ad* V), we must allow for a deliberate redefinition and cutting of our sources.

This analysis of the way in which Benjamin arrived at Herodotus shows two things: on the one side, he might have used an intermediate source to delve in the ancient text, and this sets his commitment with Greek historiography on a more direct, straightforward line. On the other side, the original treatment of ancient historiography reflects Benjamin's own philosophical agenda and thus represents an interested reading in the past. This selective approach to the texts is also demanded by Benjamin's specific philosophy of history, which places at the centre the 'now-time.' We will therefore now move to the text which, in its theses, most clearly expresses this view. It will also be a final step in our comparison of ancient historiography and thought, in line with Benjamin's own commitment with the same theories.

3 *Über den Begriff der Geschichte* in Its Context

> Pausanias schrieb seine Topographie von Griechenland 200 n.Chr. als die Kultstätten und viele der anderen Monumente zu verfallen begannen.[47]

Bertolt Brecht received the sad news of the suicide of Walter Benjamin (26.9.1940) in Santa Monica, only almost a year after the tragic episode. In reconnaissance of the great friendship which had bound them, he said that Benjamin had been the first real loss that Hitler had caused to the German literature.[48] Between July and September 1941, he wrote four epitaphs out of the grief.[49] Among them, *Zum Freitod des Flüchtlings W.B.* ("On the Suicide of the Refugee W.B".) represents a convenient starting point to understand Benjamin's personal situation when he wrote in almost three months, in the beginning of 1940, his theses *On the Concept of History*:

---

[47] "Pausanias wrote his topography of Greece in 200 CE, when the sanctuaries and many other monuments started to lapse": Benjamin *GS* 5.133.
[48] Arendt 1971, 21.
[49] On these four poems, see Wizisla 2004, 276–287.

> I'm told you raised your hand against yourself Anticipating the butcher. After eight years in exile, observing the rise of the enemy Then at last, brought up against an impassable frontier You passed, they say, a passable one. Empires collapse. Gang leaders Are strutting about like statesmen. The peoples Can no longer be seen under all those armaments. So the future lies in darkness and the forces of right Are weak. All this was plain to you When you destroyed a torturable body.[50] (tr. C. Shuttleworth.)

As E. Wizisla observed,[51] the effect of the poem rests on contradictions and paradoxes: this *Zukunft in Finsternis*, a 'future in darkness' doomed by the current success of the Axis powers in 1941, reminds us of the *Angelus Novus*, the well-known metaphor at the centre of the theses of Benjamin's *On the Concept of History* and inspired to him by his beloved painting by Paul Klee.[52] It cannot surprise us that the growth of interest in this subject by Walter Benjamin was a direct consequence of the gruesome events of his late life, from the forced exile of 1933, explicitly recalled by Brecht in the poem, to the Molotov – von Ribbentrop Pact (1938), that seemed to operate in history that gradual refusal of historical Marxism, a phenomenon starting in Benjamin's thought immediately after the travel to Russia to meet one of the loves of his life, the actress Asja Lacis, between 1927 and 1928.[53]

In the words of the Eighth Thesis, still redolent with the disdain for the initial position of the German Marxists, who had considered the rise to power of Hitler as a necessary stage towards the final revolution:

> The tradition of the oppressed teaches us that the "state of emergency" (*Ausnahmezustand*) in which we live is not the exception but the rule. We must attain to a conception of history that accords with this insight. [...] [I]t is our task to bring about a real state of emergency, and this will improve our position in the struggle against fascism. (tr. M.W. Jennings.)

The philological study of the text has now detected the different stages through which Benjamin came to a final, yet textually instable version of his *Über den Begriff der Geschichte* only in the very last months of his life, in the spring of 1940. The best witnesses of the text testify to the ongoing rewritings and order of these

---

50 Benjamin 2010, 168–172.
51 Wizisla 2004, 284.
52 Benjamin bought the monoprint in April 1921 (Eiland/Jennings 2014, 138–139) and it followed all his different accommodations, in his lifetime. The monoprint was inherited by Scholem and it is now in the Israel Museum of Jerusalem.
53 A philological introduction to the complex tradition of this text is offered by Bonola/Ranchetti (Benjamin 1997, 5–19) and Raulet (Benjamin 2010, 161–208, the critical edition, followed in the text).

theses, which were meant as a theoretical prelude to the great study on Baudelaire, according to the very last research on the text, sprouting up with the recent critical edition by Gérard Raulet of *Werke und Nachlaß*.[54] These aphorisms only rarely refer directly to historical events or turning points in history, with a few notable exceptions, such as the European period between 1830 and 1848[55] and the honors the revolution paid to Roman history.[56] By and large, it would seem, however, that ancient history and historiography, in themselves often pivotal, in their distorted shadows, in the formation of the ideology of the fascisms in Europe,[57] did not make their way in Benjamin's theory of history. Yet, it can be claimed that the distance is not so straightforward as it might seem.

This contrast between a ruling eye of the historian and of the observer and the naked, invisible eyes of the subjects of history, as well as the importance assumed by the *Jetztzeit* as the chronological perspective necessary to build a feasible and meaningful history, are among the main themes of Benjamin's theses on the philosophy of history, forming a unity of thought. If there is a difference in the relationship between Benjamin and classical historiography articulated in his work on Leskov and the one displayed in *On the Concept of History*, then it lies in the more explicit expression of his views on the philosophy of history in the second work. The theses are a long work in progress and often need to be understood, with the help of the notebooks which we possess today.

For a study on the role of ancient history in Benjamin, we must stress his knowledge of Eduard Meyer's leaflet on the theory of history.[58] A long quote from this text, focusing on the possible interconnection between the persistence of slavery and Christian religion, is present in the *Konvolut III* of the materials pertaining to the philosophical treatise.[59] As Meyer wrote in this essay, absent in the afore-mentioned *Verzeichnis der gelesenen Schriften*:

> [T]he Christian Middle Ages start with unity [*mit der Einheit*] and, despite all the destroying elements, has at least preserved, though limited to Christianity, the idea, inherited from

---

54 Benjamin 2010.
55 *Vormärz* (Th. XI.)
56 Th. XIV.
57 Bonola and Ranchetti (1997, 47 n. 35) hint at a convergence between the recognition of the Roman model in the French Revolution with the essay by Marx on Louis Bonaparte (*Der 18te Brumaire des Louis Napoleon*, 1852.) In general on classical ideologies and European fascisms, see Canfora 1980 and Chapoutot 2008.
58 Meyer 1902; 1910.
59 Benjamin 2010, 146. Cf. the quote in the beginning of the Introduction, which confirms the long trends in Benjamin's interests.

antiquity, of a unity of the mankind [*Einheit des Menschengeschlechts*]: for the first time, within its space, it gave new shape to the nations.⁶⁰

This positivistic theory is seriously criticised by Benjamin in a series of notes referred to a thesis (XVIIa), where the idea of an empty and homogeneous time is contrasted with the epistemological and revolutionary potential of a single moment (*Augenblick*, not that dissimilar, here, from *Jetztzeit*):

> [...] The historical materialist approaches a historical object only where it confronts him as a monad. In this structure he recognizes the sign of a messianic arrest of happening, or (to put it differently) a revolutionary chance [*seine revolutionäre Chance*] in the fight for the oppressed past (tr. H. Zorn.).⁶¹

There is therefore a serious risk in every effort of dehistoricization and decontextualization: these are ahistorical processes, in Benjamin's view, which are transparent from Meyer's work. As Benjamin writes, on a manuscript found in the aforementioned *Konvolut III*: Identifying oneself with what has been lastly serves to actualize it. Not apropos tending to do so goes quite well with a positivistic conception of history (as one can see in Eduard Meyer).⁶² More generally, the theses III- VII rebut the biases of historicism: Meyer, along with figures like Droysen and Ranke with his *wie es gewesen sei*, could not enter the pantheon of Benjamin's models (it is indeed surprising how this name prevailed, instead of the more popular Meinecke, author in 1936 of the influential *Die Enstehung des Historismus*.)⁶³ The historical materialism of Benjamin refuses the idea of a linear process and suggests that a comprehension of the historical events only results from the refusal of this historicist principle.

Lastly, one should be aware of an indirect consequence in our recognition of the study of Meyer's leaflet: Meyer had founded his theory and his opposition to the mechanical determinism in history on a profound knowledge and direct use of Thucydides.⁶⁴ This use cannot have escaped the attention of Benjamin when

---

60 Meyer 1910, 202.
61 Bonola/Ranchetti (in Benjamin 1997, 145): "In his theses, Benjamin peculiarly adopts the notion of 'moment' [*attimo*], to underline the dramatic urgency which characterizes the revolutionary situation, and, thus, to show that the revolution demands an utter timeliness".
62 Benjamin 2010, 151.
63 On Benjamin's early rejection of historicism, see Benjamin GS 5: 578 and Eiland/Jennings 2014, 43–4. One should remember here that the criticisms to Leopold von Ranke also embodied the criticism to a philological approach which had looked as superseded since Nietzsche (cf. Miller 2007, 348–349 and 359); on von Ranke's philological method, see Tessitore 2009, 68–79 and Fantasia in Piovan 2018, 169 on his legacy.
64 On the relevance of Thucydides for the development of Meyer's essay, see Piovan 2018, 36–37.

he was reading Meyer, so that an indirect presence of Thucydides in Benjamin's mindset, which goes beyond the parallels suggested in the next observations. I will now focus on three theses, in order to check whether Benjamin's viewpoint can actually find classical precedents.

The Third thesis centers on the chronicler, *der Chronist*, who knows that we need to take into account all the events (*Ereignisse*), for the past to be in the hands of a redeemed mankind:

> The chronicler [*Der Chronist*], who recounts events, without distinguishing between great and small ones [*ohne grosse und kleine zu unterscheiden*], thereby takes into account the truth, that nothing which has ever happened is to be assumed as lost to history. Sure, the past can only pass into the possession of a redeemed mankind [*der erlösten Menschhheit*]. Said another way: only for a resurrected mankind would its past, in each of its moments, be citable. Each of its lived moments becomes a *citation à l'ordre du jour* – whose day is precisely that of the Last Judgement (tr. M.W. Jennings.).

The *citation à l'ordre du jour* is a military expression, which refers to the habit of mentioning a memorable event in the diary, at the end of the day: the fact that every instant becomes memorable, part of a history, overcomes the longing for a never-ending list with which universal history was obsessed, substituting it with an ongoing, selective process. The past carries with it a messianic power, insofar as every moment can help to redeem – *erlösen* – the mankind: each of its lived moments becomes a *citation à l'ordre du jour*. The historian must actually be a chronicler, because, as we have seen in the case of the Herodotus-*Erzähler*, history cannot coexist with an interpretation: it cannot and must not distinguish between great (*grosse*) and small (*kleine*) events. Now, despite the fact that this contraposition might seem general and topical, there are at least two paramount passages, in Herodotus and in Thucydides, which seem to predate this use in methodological terms.

The first one actually opens the *spatium historicum* covered by Herodotus' *Histories* when he introduces Croesus' campaigns against the Greek colonies in Asia Minor, in the middle of the Sixth Century B.C. It is one of the few passages with a strong authorial voice in Herodotus, expressed through the recourse to the first singular pronoun and meant to emphasise the transition from the mythical period, dealt through the reciprocal abductions between Asians and Greeks, to the historical period, directly covered in the work.[65] These are Herodotus' words:

---

65 On the reasons underlying this emphasis, see Dewald 1987, 168; Marincola 1997, 8; Asheri in Asheri *et al.* 2007 *ad loc.*

> I will talk about the man who, to my certain knowledge (οἶδα), first undertook criminal acts of aggression against the Greeks. I will show who it was who did this (τοῦτον σημήνας), and then proceed with the rest of the account. I will cover minor and major human settlements equally (ὁμοίως μικρὰ καὶ μεγάλα ἄστεα ἀνθρώπων), because most of those which were important in the past have diminished in significance by now, and those which were great in my own time were small in times past (tr. R. Waterfield.).

This reversal of fortune, a recurrent motif in the *Histories*, is related to a cyclical view of history, not directly pertinent if we compare it to the aoristic philosophy of time which is in action in Benjamin. Still, it is fair to suggest that this combination of dimensions, the big and the small, with their role on the knowledge of the historical liabilities, invites prudence in dismissing the parallel. The attention which Benjamin paid to Herodotus demonstrated by the Psammetichus episode might invite us to suppose a deeper influence of these gnomic sections, towards the creation of a different, even though similar at first stance, historical method.

The passage in Thucydides (1.10), whose fortune in Benjamin and, more generally, in the German formation of the period is less documented,[66] seems to point to the same direction. This chapter of the *archaiologia* in the First Book deals directly with the comparison between the dimensions of two cities in different times, since we cannot put on the same level diverse historical experiences:

> The fact that Mycenae was a small place (μικρὸν ἦν)— or that the buildings of any town of that period do not now seem very impressive (μὴ ἀξιόχρεων)— would not be a valid argument (τις σημείῳ χρώμενος) for doubting the scale of the expedition as related by the poets and maintained in the tradition. [...] I think that there would be much unbelief in posterity, long afterwards, in their past power (τῆς δυνάμεως προελθόντος), judging from their present fame (πρὸς τὸ κλέος αὐτῶν εἶναι) (tr. M. Hammond, with modifications.).

This single chapter of the whole section of the book, in itself both a methodological premise and a homage to Homer, singles out, as Kallet wrote, the importance of the "visual" in Thucydides' approach, even though the lexicon of the 'proof' (σημεῖον, partly reminiscent of the σημαίνω in Herodotus) adds a theoretical nuance, important for the general argument.[67] In particular, L. Kallet observed that

---

66 The revival of interest in Thucydides, in Germany, is profoundly associated with the appreciation of his method in the historicist school (see Piovan 2018, 23–47 and Murari Pires 2006 on this 'apotheosis of Thucydides' (ibid. 811.)). It is however reasonable to claim that the fortune of Thucydides after Ranke had not sensibly suffered, in Germany, in the new century: see an overview in Muhlack 2011 and Meister 2015. As far as Herodotus is concerned, one can recall here the observation, already by Muhlack 2011, that after the 19th century Herodotus can be praised only at the expense of Thucydides, or vice versa» (Morley 2016, 144.)
67 Kallet 2006.

[Thucydides] invites his reader to try his hand at the kind of analysis the historian himself earlier performs.⁶⁸ Here, the reader is quite easily identifiable with the τις σημείῳ χρώμενος, the one who is able to profit from the evidence but, at the same time, knows that external dimensions cannot be enough, that *opsis* might shed illusory light on the dimensional scale of the past. We cannot conclude that Benjamin might have actually been inspired or influenced by these famous chapters, but the internal echoes suggests a productive parallel in the revaluation of the dimensional side of a historical *Ereignis*: when the single historical event is not seen as part of a process, but as a synchronic object of knowledge, it can be fully understood.

The Thesis VIIa apparently espouses the position of historical materialism versus the empathy implied by the historicism, here symbolized by the recourse to Fustel de Coulanges (1830–1889). A closer reading of the famous, final aphorism, which presupposes an identity between a document of culture and a document of barbarism, might instead indicate a more nuanced position, as the scholarship has generally been prone to accept:

> Consider the darkness and the great cold, In this vale resounding with mystery.
>
> Brecht, *The Threepenny Opera*

Addressing himself to the historian [*dem Historiker*] who wishes to relive an era, Fustel de Coulanges recommends that he blot out everything he knows about the later course of history. There is no better way of characterizing the method which historical materialism has broken with. It is a process of empathy [*ein Verfahren der Einfühlung.*] [...] The nature of this sadness becomes clearer if we ask: With whom does historicism actually sympathize? The answer is inevitable: with the winner. And all rulers are the heirs of prior conquerors. Hence, empathizing with the winner invariably benefits the current rulers [*Die Einfühlung in den Sieger kommt demnach den jeweils Herrschenden allemal zugut.*] The historical materialist knows what this means. Whoever has emerged victorious participates to this day in the triumphal procession in which current rulers step over those who are lying prostrate. According to traditional practice, the spoils are carried in the procession. They are called 'cultural treasures' [*Kulturgüter*], and a historical materialist views them with cautious detachment. [...] They owe their existence not only to the efforts of the great geniuses who created them, but also to the anonymous toil [*der namenlosen Fron*] of others who lived in the same period. There is no document of culture which is not at the same time a document of barbarism [*Es*

---

68 Kallet 2006, 361.

ist niemals ein Dokument der Kultur, ohne zugleich ein solches der Barbarei zu sein.] And just as such a document is never free of barbarism, so barbarism taints the manner in which it was transmitted from one hand to another. The historical materialist therefore dissociates himself from this process of transmission as far as possible. He regards it as his task to brush history against the grain (tr. from M. Jennings 2002, with minor modifications).

This chapter was read under the lens of the overall, constant reflection by Benjamin on tradition and its technical means, a theme that was often of the utmost interest for our philosopher.[69] Not only was he going to become, with his *Das Kunstwerk im Zeitalter seiner technischen Reproduzierbarkeit* (1936), among the most influential sociologists of mass media, with a never-ending influence on cinema studies and, more generally, on the development of aesthetics in the decades to come; it should also be mentioned, in fact, despite Benjamin's own dismissal of this side of his activity as an Abfall aus Studien,[70] that between 1929 and 1932 Walter Benjamin held, for the FunkStunde AG and the Sudwestdeutscher Rundfunk, short radio shows for children, the *Rundfunkgeschichten* (radio stories.)[71] These pleasant tales, well-known since their edition in the *Gesammelte Schriften*,[72] but very rarely associated with the serious intellectual production of the philosopher, actually contribute to the idea that the concise and obscure framework deployed in *On the Concept of History* was the last fruit of a very long series of observations. As a storyteller himself, Benjamin recurs to the *Eingedenken*, i.e. the memory of a single event subject to historical reproduction and analysis, as opposed to the *Gedächtnis*, the reproduction of souvenirs in a series, which cannot allow us to know the past.[73]

The subjects of the radio shows, from the Berliner dialect to Naples to current toys, were, if not *a minori*, the *Kulturgüter* here presented as documents of the past, in our thesis: tradition is intertwined with memory and time, because, as the same Benjamin wrote in the essay on Leskov (XIII), Memory (*Die Erinnerung*) creates the chain of tradition (*die Kette der Tradition*), which transmits the events (*das Geschehene*) from generation to generation. We can see how the estimation of the nature of the medium, the (oral) memory, has had consequences on the judgment of the outcome of the historical process. This *Kette der Tradition*, as a

---

[69] Simay 2005.
[70] Benjamin *GS* 7.853.
[71] See a translation and a commentary in Benjamin 2014.
[72] *Hörmodelle* (Benjamin *GS* 4.627–720) and *Radiofunkgeschichten* (Benjamin *GS* 7.68–249.)
[73] Cp. Vardoulakis 2010, 157.

matter of fact, is identical with an accumulation of documents of barbarism, because they come from the winners, the ones with whom the superficial historian identifies.

Was there an analogous assessment in classical historiography? Can we posit that Herodotus already shared this caution, against his sources and the process of his own *historie*? The debate on the role played in his *Histories* by the epigraphical documents led to very different assumptions, with the recent tendency of admitting a critical, if not silently skeptical, position of the historiographer in front of the documents he quotes.[74] For example, Herodotus might have been aware of the political nature underlying public inscriptions.[75] Eventual omissions or variances might betray an imperfect quest for balance among the strands of the traditions circulating, in the middle of the Fifth Century B.C., on the Persian Wars.

More to the point, perhaps, in line with the discursive nature of ancient historiography, which circulates in an age of limited written literacy and in concurrence with other genres,[76] there are frequent mentions, in the *Histories*, of the local origin of the traditions accepted in the main storyline.[77] How much these attributions really are local is debated. It could also be posited that the focus on the local provenance of these sections of the *Histories*, from the Egyptian book to the problematic chapter on the human sacrifice in the Seventh Book (Hdt. 7.197.2),[78] might imply the community where these versions were accepted or deemed as acceptable.[79] From another point of view, Herodotus would be suggesting a clear distinction between the universal eye of the historian and the single, diverse strands interspersed in the narrative.[80]

The anonymous characters seen by Benjamin as the veiled and unattainable sources, nevertheless, are already present to the authorial voice in Herodotus, as is shown by a telling remark in the Seventh Book (152.3), focused on the serious possibility that it were the Argives who elicited Xerxes' benevolence and that they willingly stayed neutral, in the last phase of the wars. Herodotus must (ὀφείλω) believe in what he hears: it is not his job to reject what circulates around a fact

---

[74] See as starting points West 1985; Corcella 2003; Fabiani 2003. It is also claimed that there reasons to believe Herodotus may have hidden actual documentary sources, "documenti nascosti nelle pieghe del racconto" (Porciani 2016, 110).
[75] Corcella 2003.
[76] See Thomas 2000 and Grethlein 2010.
[77] In general on the impact local traditions in Herodotus, see Luraghi 2001b.
[78] See on this problematic tradition Vannicelli 2017, 542.
[79] Luraghi 2001b.
[80] Goldhill 2010.

and has come down to his ears.[81] His is a historiography still ambivalent between hearsay and evidence, with a penchant for allowing every oral source, in order not to lose any witness, a cultural product – a *Kulturgut*, Benjamin would say – on the theme of his research. Even when Herodotus seems to perceive the paradoxical aspect of the details he is reporting, as in the Second Book, he sticks to the general end that παρὰ πάντα λόγον, along his whole account, he will stay faithful to τὰ λεγόμενα.[82] We could not possibly say how much Benjamin would have appreciated this sense of moral duty and the inclination towards a complete history and a complete time, in Herodotus, in contrast with the fallacies of the continuum denounced, for instance, in the sixteenth Thesis of *On the Concept of History*. What certainly surprises the contemporary reader is that both Herodotus and Benjamin lived in ages where technological change was in process: from an aural culture to a semi-literate one in Herodotus, who seems anxious to accept what is being said as a peculiar part of the covenant he signs with his listener/reader; in Benjamin, from blind faith in a writable, understandable history to a history of moments in their reciprocal isolation. He perceives the cultural nuance they convey through the media which document them.

In the essay on Leskov, Walter Benjamin introduces a clear dichotomy between two kinds of memories, which might be of some help, in the understanding of the last Thesis (XV) under scrutiny:

> What characterizes revolutionary classes at their moment of action is the awareness that they are about to make the continuum of history explode. The Great Revolution [wanted to be a new Rome and] introduced a new calendar. The initial day of a calendar presents history in time- lapse mode [*ein historischer Zeitraffer*]. And basically it is this same day that keeps recurring in the guise of holidays, which are days of remembrance [*Tage des Eingedenkens*]. Thus, calendars do not measure time the way clocks do; they are monuments of a historical consciousness [*Monumente eines Geschichtsbewusstseins*] of which not the slightest trace has been apparent in Europe, it would seem, for the past hundred years. In the July Revolution an incident occurred in which this consciousness came into its own. On the first evening of fighting, it so happened that the dials on clocktowers were being fired at simultaneously and independently from several locations in Paris. An eyewitness,

---

[81] Hdt. 7.152.3, tr. R. Waterfield: I [ἐγὼ δέ] am obliged [ὀφείλω] to record the things I am told [τὰ λεγόμενα], but I am certainly not required to believe them—this remark [τοῦτο τὸ ἔπος] may be taken to apply to the whole of my account [ἐς πάντα τὸν λόγον].» On the apparent neutrality of this judgment, which must however be read in line with the opinions expressed elsewhere by the author on the policies of Argos, see Vannicelli 2017, 481.

[82] Hdt. 2.123,1, tr. R. Waterfield: "My job [ἐμοί ... ὑπόκειται], throughout this account [παρὰ πάντα λόγον], is simply to record whatever I am told by each of my sources [τὰ λεγόμενα ὑπ' ἑκάστων.]".

who may have owed his insight to the rhyme, wrote as follows: "Qui le croirait! on dit, qu'irrités contre l'heure,/ De nouveaux Josués, au pied de chaque tour,/ Tiraient sur les cadrans pour arrêter le jour [Who would believe it! It is said that, incensed at the hour,/ Latter-day Joshuas, at the foot of every clock tower,/ Were firing on clock faces to make the day stand still.]".[83]

The novel (*der Roman*), therefore, seems to represent a convenient mould for history. This Thesis on the importance of the calendar and of its first day seems to strengthen the opinion that a real historian has to explain and, therefore, needs to use *Eingedenken*, remembrance, and not just *Gedächtnis*, as Herodotus did. In particular, in the *On the Concept of History*, we read (Th. XV) that this same day [i.e., the initial day of the calendar] [...] keeps recurring in the guise of holidays, which are days of remembrance [*Tage des Eingedenkens*]. This *Eingedenken*, "souvenance" in the French translation made by the same Benjamin,[84] forces us to think in a critical way about the past; this "historical consciousness" (*Geschichtsbewusstsein*), worryingly disappeared in Europe, is a consequence of a purportedly constructed calendar.

In this idea of a temporality of time, in other words, as K. Clarke wrote, of time as a more broadly constructed and socially reflective phenomenon,[85] Walter Benjamin shows an awareness of its cultural subtext, which is a notorious feature of the Thucydides' *History*, as pointed out in the second chapter of the second book:

> The Thirty Years Treaty agreed after the conquest of Euboea lasted for fourteen years. In the fifteenth year, when Chrysis was in her forty-eighth year as priestess at Argos, Aenesias was ephor in Sparta, and Pythodorus had two more months of his archonship in Athens, in the sixth month after the battle at Potidaea, and at the beginning of spring, in the first watch of the night an armed force of slightly over three hundred Thebans entered Plataea (*Thuc.* 2.2.1, tr. M. Hammond).

The accumulation of chronological frames forms a string whose internal and external grounds have been firmly established by the scholarship: on the one side, it responds to internal methodological issues, such as the need to clarify the soundness of the new chronographical criterion of narrating by summers and

---

83 Tr. from Eiland/Jennings 2002, with minor modifications.
84 C'est encore ce jour, le premier d'une chronologie, qui est |évoqué et même| figuréx, sinon évoqué, par les jours fériés qui, eux tous, sont aussi bien des jours initiaux que des jours de souvenance» (Benjamin 2010, 66).
85 Clarke 2008, 27.

winters and to signal the importance of the moment, with a list of powerful effect.[86] On the other side, this momentum of *gravitas* exhibits an implicit hint at Hellanicus, the only historiographer quoted by name by Thucydides in his work, profoundly interested in chronological issues with his *Priestesses of Hera*[87] and, really not that incidentally, given the explicitly mention of this second book by Thucydides, with his *Atthis*.[88]

The Athens of the first two decades of the Peloponnesian War was deeply imbued with questions about systems of time and a need for clarification among the disparate calendars, in use in the single *poleis* involved by the conflict.[89] Sure, it was more than a result of the debate on the war and the sophistic movement, in its inner variety and absence of a unity of thought, proves that more than one intellectual, from Hippias to Protagoras, participated to this debate about the rightfulness and the choice of a chronological criterion. Given the fragmentary nature of what we know about Hellanicus and his local histories, it is ultimately hard to gauge how systematic was his recourse to an annalistic frame, so much so, that there seems to spread a growing appreciation of the possibility that local historiography, in Greece, was not always and regularly a horographically determined genre.[90] If local historians did not regularly adopt this scheme, is it fair to conclude that here Thucydides was necessarily engaging in a direct allusion to Hellanicus?

The same doubt might arise if we briefly reconsider another vexed chapter in the Fifth Book of Thucydides' *History* (20.1), which might be considered 'programmatic' in the way it aims at justifying the seasonal texture of the *Histories*:

> This treaty was concluded at the end of winter, just at the beginning of spring, immediately after the City Dionysia: ten years, with the addition of a few days, had passed since the invasion of Attica and the beginning of the year. People should calculate the actual periods of time [σκοπείτω δέ τις κατὰ τοὺς χρόνους]; they should not rely on lists of archons or other officials whose names may be used in different cities to mark the dates of past events. For such methods of calculation are inaccurate [οὐ γὰρ ἀκριβές ἐστιν] in that they leave it unclear whether an event occurred in the beginning, in the middle or at some other point, of a magistrate's term of office (5.20.1, tr. S. Hornblower).

---

86 See Fantasia 2003, 225.
87 Cf. Fantasia 2003, 225 and Pownall 2016 *ad BNJ* 4 F 74.
88 The relationship between the *Atthis* of Hellanicus and Thucydides represents a troublesome issue, which cannot be full readdressed here: see, with further scholarship, Ottone 2010 and Pownall 2016.
89 Cf. Möller 2001.
90 Cf. Thomas 2014a; Thomas 2014b; Tufano i.p.

Apart from being careful to choose a system which is precise, ἀκριβές, Thucydides seems particularly interested in acknowledging the limits of the use of the eponymous calendars, the most common system in the *poleis* at that time: they should not rely on lists of archons or other officials whose names may be used in different cities to mark the dates of past events. He probably aimed at a chronological system which was readily comprehensible and meaningful to the inhabitants of more than one polis;[91] he was also aware of the political danger of letting the reader imprisoned in a calendar, locally and possibly parochially limited.

A calendar, with all its mechanics and meanings, is strictly related to an epoch: that is why to narrate a war you had better, for Thucydides, think of summers and winters; that is why, during the French Revolution which led to the dethronement of Charles X and saw itself as a new Rome (an original addition by Benjamin, lately erased), a new calendar was introduced, to substitute the previous one. To return now to the final anecdote in the thesis *On the Concept of History*, with the destruction of the clocks, as Benjamin makes clear in other preparatory notes for the *Arcades Project*, focuses on the sole act of vandalism perpetuated by the people against the public monuments:[92] the annoyed Joshua refers to the chapter of the first historical book of the *Bible*, where the King of Israel asks the God for help in his battle against the Amorites:

On the day the Lord gave the Amorites over to Israel, Joshua said to the Lord in the presence of Israel: "Sun, stand still over Gibeon,/ and you, moon, over the Valley of Aijalon./ So the sun stood still,/ and the moon stopped,/ till the nation avenged itself on its enemies," as it is written in the *Book of Jashar*. The sun stopped in the middle of the sky and delayed going down about a full day (*Joshua* 10: 12–3, tr. *NIV*.).

The passage poses many problems, from the actual origin of the verses pronounced by Joshua, which derive from a previous tradition, as is the case of many reused oracles in Greek literature, to the meaning of the standstill of the sun and the moon, expressed by a verb, *dmm*, which in Hebrew might mean "stand still" or "be silent", i.e. an eclipse of the corpses.[93] The most economical explanation, though, sees this appeal to God, despite its almost clear remnants of a devotion to the stars, as a request for more time. God would have allowed a longer period for fighting, represented by the slowing down of the alternation between the daylight and the moonlight. It does not surprise us much that Benjamin condenses, even in this example, an important lesson he wants to convey, the one on the

---

91 Clarke 2008, 95.
92 Benjamin *GS* 5.895.
93 See Nelson 1997, 142.

political backside of time systems and on their maneuverability. This is what Thucydides, too, might have intended in his chapter: a convergence, once again, between philosophies of history very far in their premises, but close in their external appearances.

4 An Open Path

As argued in the introduction, in the absence of explicit authorial admissions, we can only guess that a few pages of Herodotus and Thucydides were known to Benjamin. He had attended classes of ancient philosophy – most notably, the course on Aristotle held by Richard Herbertz in Bern in 1918 – and was certainly imbued with the main tendencies of *Altertumswissenschaft* which were spread in the German universities in the second decade of the twentieth century. By going beyond the explicit mention of these ancient authors, we suggested a different approach to this comparison, in the form of a joint analysis of a few significant tenets of Benjamin's theses on the philosophy of history, with famous passages by Herodotus and Thucydides.

Umberto Eco wrote in the introduction to the first Italian version (1962) of *The Open Work* (*Opera aperta*) that developing a problem does not mean solving it: it can just mean clarifying its terms, so as to allow a more thorough discussion.[94] A more profound and overarching investigation of the legacy of classical thought and literature in Benjamin still has to be achieved and may shed further light on the question we tried to answer in the present pages. What may be kept, in our view, is the necessity to spoil ourselves of the view of Herodotus and Thucydides as two 'ancient historiographers': to Benjamin, they were two ancient narrators, and it is through this aesthetic perspective, without a profound interest in the chronological background of the classical authors, that they might have found their way in the development of Benjamin's final thesis on the philosophy of history.

---

94 Eco 2006, 1.

Bibliography

Adorno, Theodore W. (1994), *Briefe und Briefwechsel*. Hrsg. Von Theodor W. Adorno Archiv. Band I: Theodor W. Adorno/Walter Benjamin: Briefwechsel 1928 – 1940, (Ed. Henri Lonitz), Frankfurt.
Arendt, Hannah (1971), *Walter Benjamin, Bertolt Brecht. Zwei Essays*, München.
David Asheri/Lloyd, Alan/Corcella, Aldo (2007), *A Commentary on Herodotus Books I-IV* (eds. Oswyn Murray/Alfonso Moreno), Oxford.
Benjamin, Walter (1972–99), *Gesammelte Schriften. Vols. I-VII, With Three Supplements*, (eds. Theodore W. Adorno/Gershom Scholem/Rolf Tiedemann/Herman Schweppenhäuser), Frankfurt.
Benjamin, Walter, (1994), *The Correspondence of Walter Benjamin 1910–1940*. (Edited and annotated by Theodore W. Adorno/Gershom Scholem; tr. Manfred R. Jacobson/Evelyn M. Jacobson), Chicago, London.
Benjamin, Walter (1997), *Sul concetto di storia* (Eds. Gianfranco Bonola/Michele Ranchetti), Turin.
Benjamin, Walter (2010), *Über den Begriff der Geschichte* (Ed. Gérard Raulet), Berlin.
Benjamin, Walter (2014), *Burattini, streghe e briganti. Racconti radiofonici per ragazzi (1929–1932)* (Ed. Giulio Schiavoni), Milano.
Benjamin, Walter (2016), *The Storyteller. Tales Out of Loneliness* (Tr. & ed. by Sam Dolbear/Esther Leslie/Sebastian Truskolaski), London.
Billings, Joshua (2015), "Margins of Genre: Walter Benjamin and the Idea of Tragedy", in Joshua Billings/Miriam Leonard (eds), *Tragedy and the Idea of Modernity*, Oxford, 266–84.
Biraschi, Anna M. *et al*. (2003), *L'uso dei documenti nella storiografia antica*, Napoli.
Britt, Brian (2014), "Identity and Survival in *Deutsche Menschen*", in Daniel Weidner/Sigrid Weigel (eds), *Benjamin-Studien* 3, Paderborn: 83–104.
Bub, Stefan (2006), "Die verschlossenen Samenkörner. Zu einer Herodot-Episode bei Walter Benjamin", *Poetica* 38, 437–50.
Canfora, Luciano (1980), *Ideologie del classicismo*, Turin.
Chapoutot, Johann (2008), *Le national-socialisme et l'antiquité*, Paris.
Clarke, Katherine (2008), *Making Time for the Past. Local History and the Polis*, Oxford.
Corcella, Aldo (2003), "Echi di documenti sulle guerre persiane in Erodoto", in Anna M. Biraschi, *et al*. (2003), *L'uso dei documenti nella storiografia antica*, Napoli, 125–49.
da Costa, Gilmário Guerreiro (2011), "O *páthos* da distância e da diferença", *Archai* 7, 37–42.
Dewald, Carolyn (1987), "Narrative Surface and Authorial Voice in Herodotus' *Histories*", *Arethusa* 20, 147–70.
Eco, Umberto (2006) [1962], *Opera aperta. Forma e indeterminazione nelle poetiche contemporanee*, Milano.
Eiland, Howard/Jennings, Michael W. (2002), *Walter Benjamin. Selected Writings. Volume 3. 1935–1938* (Tr. Edmund Jephcott/Howard Eiland, *et al*.), Cambridge (MA), London.
Eiland, Howard/Jennings, Michael, W. (2014), *Walter Benjamin. A Critical Life*. Cambridge (MA), London.
Fabiani, Roberta (2003), "Epigrafi in Erodoto", in Anna M. Biraschi, *et al.*, *L'uso dei documenti nella storiografia antica*, Napoli, 163–85.

Fantasia, Ugo (2003), *Tucidide. La Guerra del Peloponneso. Libro II. Testo, traduzione e commento con saggio introduttivo a cura di U.F.*, Pisa.

Fenves, Peter D. (2011), *The Messianic Reduction. Walter Benjamin and the Shape of Time*, Stanford.

Goldhill, Simon (2010), "What is Local Identity? The Politics of Cultural Mapping", in Tim Whitmarsh (ed.), *Local Knowledge and Microidentities in the Greek Imperial World*, Cambridge, 46–68.

Grethlein, Jonas (2010), *The Greeks and Their Past: Poetry, Oratory and History in the Fifth Century BCE, Cambridge*, New York.

Jennings, Michael W. (2016), "The Will to Apokatastasis: Media, Experience, and Eschatology in Walter Benjamin's Late Theological Politics", in Colby Dickinson/Stéphane S. Symons (eds), *Walter Benjamin and Theology*, New York, 93–112.

Kallet, Lisa (2006), "Thucydides' Workshop of History and Utility Outside the Text", in Antonios Rengakos/Antonis Tsakmakis (eds), *Brill's Companion to Thucydides*, Leiden, 335–68.

Luraghi, Nino (2001a), *The Historian's Craft in the Age of Herodotus*, Oxford.

Luraghi, Nino (2001b), "Local Knowledge in Herodotus' *Histories*", in *id.* (2001a), *The Historian's Craft in the Age of Herodotus*, Oxford, 138–60.

Marincola, John (1997), *Authority and Tradition in Ancient Historiography*, Cambridge.

Meister, Klaus (2015), "Thucydides in Nineteenth-Century Germany. Historicization and Glorification", in Christine Lee/Neville Morley (eds), *A Handbook to the Reception of Thucydides*, Malden (MA)/Oxford, 197–217.

Meyer, Eduard (1910), *Kleine Schriften zur Geschichtstheorie und zur Wirtschaftlichen und Politischen Geschichte des Altertums*, Halle.

Miller, Peter N. (2007), "Momigliano, Benjamin, and Antiquarianism after the Crisis of Historicism", in Peter N. Miller (ed.), *Momigliano and Antiquarianism. Foundations of the Modern Cultural Sciences*, Toronto, 334–78.

Möller, Astrid (2001), "The Beginnings of Chronography: Hellanicus' *Hiereiai*", in Nino Luraghi (ed.), *The Historian's Craft in the Age of Herodotus*, Oxford, 241–62.

Morley, Neville (2016), "The Anti-Thucydides: Herodotus and the Developments of Modern Historiography", in Jessica Priestly/Vasiliki Zali (eds), *Brill's Companion to the Reception of Herodotus in Antiquity and Beyond*, Leiden/Boston, 143–66.

Muhlack, Ulrich (2011), "Herodotus and Thucydides in the view of nineteenth-century German historians", in Alexandria Lianeri (ed.), *The Western Time of Ancient History. Historiographical Encounters with the Greek and the Roman Past*, New York, 179–209.

Murari Pires, Francisco (2006), "Thucydidean Modernities: History between Science and Art", in Antonio Rengakos/Antonis Tsakmakis (eds), *Brill's Companion to Thucydides*, Leiden, 811–37.

Nelson, Richard D. (1997), *Joshua. A Commentary*, Louisville, KY.

Ottone, Gabriella (2010), "L'Ἀττικὴ ξυγγραφή di Ellanico di Lesbo", in Cinzia Bearzot/ Franco Landucci (eds), *Storie di Atene, storia dei Greci. Studi e ricerche di attidografia*, Milano, 53–111.

Paulhan, Jean, (1928), "Carnet du spectateur", *La Nouvelle Revue Française* 182, 694–723.

Piovan, Dino (2018), *Tucidide in Europa. Storici e storiografia greca nell'età dello storicismo. Postfazione di U. Fantasia*, Milano/Udine.

Porciani, Leone (2016), "Creso, Anfiarao e la nuova iscrizione di Tebe", in Stefano Struffolino (ed.), Ἡμέτερα γράμματα. *Scritti di epigrafia greca offerti a Teresa Alfieri*, Milano, 101–12.

Pownall, Frances (2016), "Hellanikos of Lesbos", *Brill's New Jacoby* 4. Consulted online on 23 May 2019.
Rengakos, Antonios/Tsakmakis, Antonis (2006), *Brill's Companion to Thucydides*, Leiden/Boston.
Schöne, Albrecht, (1986), ""Diese nach jüdischem Vorbild erbaute Arche": Walter Benjamins Deutsche Menschen", in Stéphane Moses/ Albrecht Schöne (eds), *Juden in der deutschen Literatur. Ein deutsch-israelisches Symposion*, Frankfurt, 350–65.
Scholem, Gershom (1981), *Walter Benjamin. The Story of a Friendship* (tr. Harry Zohn), New York, NY.
Simay, Philippe (2005), "Tradition and Injunction: Benjamin and the Critique of Historicisms", in Andrew Benjamin (ed.), *Walter Benjamin and History*, London/New York, 137–55.
Tessitore, Fulvio (2009), *Introduzione a Lo storicismo*, Roma/Bari.
Thomas, Rosalind (2000), *Herodotus in Context: Ethnography, Science, and the Art of Persuasion*, Cambridge.
Thomas, Rosalind (2014a), "Local History, Polis History, and the Politics of Place, in Giovanni Parmeggiani (ed.), *Between Thucydides and Polybius. The Golden Age of Greek Historiography*, Washington (DC). Consulted online on 15 May 2019.
Thomas, Rosalind (2014b), "The Greek *Polis* and the Tradition of *Polis* History: Local History, Chronicles and the Patterning of the Past", in Alfonso Moreno/Rosalind Thomas (eds), *Patterns of the Past. Epitēdeumata in the Greek Tradition*, Oxford, 145–72.
Tufano, Salvatore (in progress), "La memoria sociale dei Beoti: una prospettiva senza Atene", *Histos*.
Vandevoordt, Robin (2014), "Unspeakable Resistance: Walter Benjamin on Greek Tragedy", *Thesis Eleven* 123, 62–79.
Vannicelli, Pietro (2017), *Erodoto. Le Storie. Libro VII Serse e Leonida*. Testo critico a cura di A. Corcella. (tr. Giuseppe Nenci), Milano.
Vardoulakis, Dimitris (2010), *The Doppelgänger. Literature's Philosophy*, New York.
West, Stephanie (1985), "Herodotus' Epigraphical Interests", *Classical Quarterly* 35, 278–305.
Wizisla, Erdmut (2004), *Benjamin und Brecht. Die Geschichte einer Freundschaft*, Frankfurt.
Wizisla, Erdmut (2007), "'Plaquette für Freunde', Widmungen für den Leser", in Barbara Hahn/Erdmut Wizisla (eds), *Walter Benjamin's 'Deutsche Menschen'*, Göttingen, 45–67.

Jerry Toner
When Augustus met Adorno: Class, Mimesis and Restoring the Past

Rome's first emperor was a man of action. His *Res Gestae* detailed the achievements of this activity, by which 'he subjected the world to Roman rule' (*Res Gestae* 1). But Augustus was not uninterested in philosophy. Suetonius tells us that he wrote 'Exhortations to Philosophy' (*Hortationes ad Philosophiam*) and that he cultivated an elegant style of writing, making it his chief aim to express his thoughts as clearly as possible. Later he became familiar in various forms of learning through association with the philosopher Areus and his sons Dionysius and Nicanor (Suet. *Aug.* 85–6, 89). Regrettably, none of his writings or details of his philosophical discussions have survived and we are left to look at his record of action to understand what Augustus was thinking. What we find, I suggest, is that Augustus' praxis can be seen to have anticipated some of the theories proposed by the twentieth-century German philosopher, Theodor Adorno. Equally, the clearer articulation these ideas received at the hands of Adorno can help us understand more exactly how Augustus managed to achieve so much.[1]

1 Adorno and Class

In his essay, *Reflections on Class Theory*, Adorno explains how class has been present throughout history and how it has allowed the exploitation of the masses by various ruling elites.[2] He opens his essay with the first line of Marx's *Communist Manifesto*: 'according to theory, history is the history of class struggles'. Both the past and the post-industrial world, he argues, share the same injustices and outbreaks of violence that result from this class system. This was no glib comparison. Adorno was familiar with the ancient world, having studied Latin and Greek as part of the traditional syllabus of the German gymnasium. But he then

---

[1] There has been considerable recent interest in Adorno's work in the English-speaking world. The best introductions are those by Wilson 2007; Jarvis 1998; O'Connor 2013. A collections of translated texts can be found in Tiedemann 2003. An excellent series of critical essays on Adorno's work can be found in Gibson/Rubin 2001. Other useful readings of Adorno's work are Witkin 2003; Schmidt 2007; Heberle 2006; Briel/Kramer 2001. His biography can be read in Müller-Doohm 2009.
[2] Adorno 2003, 93–110.

discusses how the concept of class has changed in the modern age. The shift towards monopoly capitalism, Adorno argues, established a new kind of class struggle, where ideology is used to obscure the traditional class conflict and where the masses lose consciousness of their oppression because conformity to the system comes to be seen as the sensible choice: 'the distinction between exploiters and exploited is not so visible as to make it obvious that solidarity should be their *ultima ratio*; conformity appears more rational to them'.[3]

One reason Adorno believes this has occurred is that the exploiting class, the bourgeoisie, now present a unified front which itself offers an excellent example of the benefits of class solidarity. The masses, however, do not learn or adopt the same class solidarity because the system effectively bribes them with sufficient small and short term gains that the bigger picture advantages cannot clearly be discerned. This bribery is itself only possible because of the concentration of capital in the hands of the few largest capitalists, which gives them the economic power to deliver some benefits to all. In this system, the bourgeois class is also being exploited by this ruling elite because it is only the rulers who can deliver security; what Adorno calls, 'the concession that the truly dominant owners make to those who sell themselves to them body and soul'.[4] In such a way, the ruling class 'disappears behind the concentration of capital' which itself is deployed to make the masses fall into line with their masters.

In addition, Adorno notes that the pauperization of the masses, which Marx had expected capitalism to generate, has not happened. By contrast, modern living standards for workers have risen, which has in fact resulted in a rise in the social importance of the proletariat. Workers now have more to lose than their chains: they own houses, hold modest savings and investments, and, however unequal the distribution of wealth may have become, these assets are sufficient to bind them to the system and blind them to the underlying inequalities which it has created. Instead, Adorno argues, it is social poverty that most people now suffer, a poverty which he defines as political weakness. Both the proletariat and the bourgeoisie are dominated by the capitalist system and the small cliques who control it.[5] They are unable to change or influence the system in any meaningful way despite their modest increase in wealth. Instead, people are fed the products of the culture industry and, like battery chickens, grow accustomed to their conditions of captivity. They are not violently oppressed but trapped by ideological persuasion.

---

3 Ibid. 97.
4 Ibid. 98.
5 Ibid. 104.

Though well-versed in Homer, Adorno, like many other modern theorists, has an overly simplistic view of antiquity. For him, it was a pre-industrial world where nothing fundamentally changed in the class structure: class served only to perpetuate the weakness of the exploited and extend the dominance of the exploiters.[6] As we will later see, ancient art and literature could offer Adorno inspirational examples of pre-capitalist freedom and creativity but no more than that. Looking more closely at Augustus' achievements, however, I suggest that we can see that much of Adorno's critique can in fact be applied to the first emperor's sophisticated system of government.

The most important element of this was ideology. The shift towards monopoly capitalism, in Adorno's eyes, established a new kind of class struggle, where ideology is used to obscure the traditional class conflict. The traditional view of Augustus posited a simplistic and brutal underlying reality that broadly equated to Adorno's pessimistic view of the ancient class structure. Syme saw Augustus as the initiator of a bloody military coup that had seized military power and coerced everyone into becoming the mere mouthpiece for the regime.[7] Since that somewhat blunt assessment, many Roman historians, such as Zanker and Galinsky, have seen the establishment of Augustus' imperial system as a far more subtle and complex process, one which involved the use of a blend of hard and soft power.[8] As Galinsky says, there was 'no rigid ideology' but it was an ideology none the less, which sought to legitimise and justify the new regime.[9] Above all, Augustus' regime set out to be inclusive. The shift to autocratic government was accompanied by 'an authentic involvement of much wider strata of the population'.[10] Rather than being a simple imposition of force on a cowering populace, Augustan imagery established a grammar of political relations which articulated the shared aims of all classes. Zanker has gone so far as to argue that the Augustan regime did not need to mask the reality of what it was doing because Rome, after decades of destructive and murderous civil wars, 'was generally accepting of an autocrat'. The Roman people as a whole supported the regime's aims and the stability it brought. Acquiescence cannot simply be read as support. But regardless of their underlying feelings, it is clear that the Augustan settlement created a range of incentives for ordinary Romans to support the new regime.

---

6 Ibid. 94.
7 Syme 1939.
8 See, for example, P. Zanker 1988; Galinsky 1998; Eck 2008; Levick 2010.
9 Galinsky 2005, 5.
10 Ibid. 3.

The citizens of Rome were given a stake in the system through the establishment of a new form of civic identity, one which expressed itself in a mutually beneficial arrangement of material benefits in return for political support. The *Res Gestae* are peppered with references to the benefits which Augustus gave to the Roman people. The opening description lists not only the acts that Augustus did to extend the empire but also the amounts he expended upon the state and the Roman people. The text contains details of the numerous donatives the emperor paid out to his people: 300 sesterces per man from Julius Caesar's will, three times 400 sesterces from his own pocket, as well as extra handouts of grain, and so on, all of which gifts were given to at least a quarter of a million citizens (*Res Gestae* 15). But the benefits of empire also took a non-monetary from: huge gladiatorial shows, athletic competitions, twenty-six wild beast hunts, and naval spectaculars. The total sum he paid out in cash benefits to plebs and soldiers was 600 million denarii; the total expenditure on the games was innumerable (*Res gestae*, summary 1, 4). Empire, emperor, citizens and benefits were all inextricably bound up together.

In return, it is perhaps not surprising that the people generally responded by lending their enthusiastic support for the regime. Cash, high value entertainments and grain represented considerable material benefits for the average Roman citizen to have obtained. But, as with Adorno's view of the modern proletariat, it is clear that there was also a political price to pay for these benefits. The plebs were politically pauperised, with the popular assemblies reduced to rubber-stamping talking-shops, so enervated that Augustus' successor, Tiberius, felt it safe to abolish them. As Juvenal famously complained, the Roman people had sold their votes and popular politics had been reduced from decisions concerning war and high office to mere bread and circuses (Juv. *Sat.* 10.77–81).

It is possible to see this sophisticated, complex imperial ideology as something of what Adorno termed a monopoly-controlled society that 'consumes all the energy that might be able to do things differently'.[11] Whether it was a senator supporting the emperor's candidates for magistracy, an eques bidding for an imperial contract to supply grain, or a pleb sacrificing to the imperial cult, the imperial system provided the means for individuals of all classes to improve their prospects and get something out of the system. The Roman empire became an early version of what Adorno termed a 'social totality', whereby all forms of human behaviour were determined by the interrelated social system in which they lived, which obliged them to adopt its norms for the sake of self-preservation. It

---

[11] Adorno 2003, 109.

was only the occasional free spirit, like Ovid, who was 'never really on message', who managed to express views that were not generated by the system itself.[12]

It was Augustus' skilful use of the past that was, I suggest, the key to his success in establishing this subtle, embracing ideology. Faced with the problem of having to create both an image and a reality of social unity after a long period of internal strife, Augustus could see that simple domination and ideology would never be sufficient. He needed to engage with the freedoms and traditions of republican Rome in a way that signalled that the past and present had combined to form a restored version of the past. This was a task that entailed hard, ongoing work. As Galinsky has emphasised, 'things fell into place neither automatically nor providentially after Actium and Alexandria. And how could they? The decades of disarray, amounting to almost a century, had left deep marks and fissures. A return to stability would require considerable time and always be a work in progress'.[13] It was an effort paralleled in the epic of Vergil, which celebrated the herculean labours carried out by Rome's founding father in establishing the city. Augustus set out to do nothing less than reconstruct the cultural memory.

2 Adorno's *Odyssey*

How to define and assess the process of change under Augustus has always posed a significant difficulty.[14] Did the Roman people as a whole actually believe any of this imagery, as Zanker would have us believe? Was it all just an illusion that obscured social reality, a veneer of ideology which concealed Augustus' military and financial power? Should we believe in the emperor's claim to have restored the republic? As Elder says, 'a state cannot be simply regarded as "republic" because its most powerful man does not want to look like a monarch'.[15] It is here, I think, that some of Adorno's other theories can help us understand more accurately how the Augustan process of reinventing history worked. Above all Adorno's concept of mimesis can, I believe, help us to understand how Augustus' programme worked in relation to the past. This is not the place to discuss in detail Adorno's many complicated theories concerning mimesis, but I shall outline the main points of the theory, beginning with Adorno's pessimistic view of the enlightenment.

---

12 Griffin 2005, 306.
13 Galinsky 2012, 84.
14 Galinsky 2005, 2.
15 Elder 2005, 15.

In a long excursus to the first chapter of *Dialectic of Enlightenment*, Adorno and his co-author, Max Horkheimer, famously interpret Odysseus as the archetype of the controlled and controlling personality which has come to be the norm of modern society. Published in 1947, with the authors having been forced into exile by the war, *Dialectic of Enlightenment* contained a very negative analysis of modernity: 'Enlightenment, understood in the widest sense as the advance of thought, has always aimed at liberating human beings from fear and installing them as masters. Yet the wholly enlightened earth is radiant under calamity triumphant'.[16] How is it, Adorno and Horkheimer ask, that the world of science and progress, with all its promises of liberating people from poverty, disease and ignorance, has in fact created a world where fascism thrived and weapons of mass destruction have been developed. Their conclusion is simply that the rational has become irrational.

In this analysis, the dreadful state of the post-war world had come about because of a culture of domination: the domination of nature *by* human beings and the domination of nature *within* human beings. Both of these forms of domination have resulted in some humans seeking to dominate others. The original motivation for this desire to dominate was a simple fear of the unknown: 'Humans believe themselves free of fear when there is no longer anything unknown'. Even myth posed a threat, and ancient society began the long process of demythologization which science represents. 'Enlightenment,' Adorno concludes 'is mythical fear radicalized'.[17] In such a process, any form of difference and the other comes to be seen as the enemy of progress and is at best exploited, at worst crushed. Progress has come to represent simply the degree of sophistication with which the other is taken advantage of or destroyed: capitalism is more subtle than slavery and nuclear bombs, more sophisticated than spears, but it is the same fear of others which is driving the desire to dominate them.

Adorno's solution to this is the construction of a dialectic of enlightenment, whereby self-reflection allows humans to escape from this cycle of fear-based domination.[18] Understanding that 'enlightened' thought is itself the product of a desire for self-preservation allows us the opportunity to escape from its control. The aim of thinking comes to be seen as no longer one of domination but to look for ways in which we can be reconciled to the others we fear. Many of Adorno's

---

[16] Adorno/Horkheimer 1987, 1. I have used translations from *Dialectic of enlightenment: philosophical fragments* (1987). The original can be found in Volume 5 of Max Horkheimer 1987.
[17] Ibid. 11.
[18] Ibid. 32.

later writings discuss the details of how this reconceptualization of the idea of thought can be achieved (most notably in *Negative Dialectics*).

One core part of this theory, that will become relevant to my argument here, is that of the commodification of art. In a later chapter of *Dialectic of Enlightenment*, 'The Culture Industry', Adorno argues that capitalism has turned the creation of culture into a mass industry, which has had the effect of commodifying art and reducing its autonomy.[19] Art can no longer be done for its own sake, since one of its primary aims is now saleability. Instead of representing a means of expression that could escape from society's norms and constraints, and which people could enjoy for its skill, meaning and beauty, commodified artistic productions have value only in their earning power, and it is their price which people come to mistake for artistic merit.[20] This is not to say that popular art is without any real value, but that this is largely replaced by estimations based on the financial worth of the art.

Adorno reads Homer's epic as an allegory of the dialectic of enlightenment, with the hero's voyage seen as a kind of extended business trip, 'his passions the usual affairs men fall into when they have a devoted wife at home'.[21] The epic becomes the start of humanity's journey into the process of enlightenment which, in Adorno's eyes, has actually taken it away from the truth. Odysseus is smart and successful but he is also uncompromising and unyielding. Prepared to sacrifice his men, and himself if need be, his clever strategizing represents the precursor of systematic thought. Not only does he successfully dominate the men and monsters he meets on his epic journey, but such domination becomes the primary goal of all he does.

The epic tale of the *Odyssey* therefore comes to be seen as one of the first illustrations of humanity's journey away from myth towards a mentality that seeks to control and manipulate nature. Enlightenment is nothing short of a process of regression, with art transforming into an agent of repression rather than liberation. Nothing illustrates this better, for Adorno, than the famous encounter between Odysseus and the Sirens. The Sirens represent the allure of a return to the past, to a world of myth, but Odysseus is a hero who, while tempted, remains fully focused on his end-goal and has experienced enough to know how to resist. Odysseus, tied to the mast, represents the sensitive, passive elite of the 'enlightened' world, who enjoy nature and art at a distance, and, like a modern audience

---

19 Ibid. 127.
20 Ibid. 128.
21 Comay 2000, 21.

at a classical concert (the image is Adorno's), is able only to nod its head in response to the attractiveness of the past. By contrast, with their ears plugged by the elite, the sailors below deck, like the later working class, labour away, taught to be afraid of nature and made deaf to what true art has to offer.

As Adorno notes, referencing Nietzsche, enlightenment has always been a tool for the great manipulators of government, such as the Roman Empire.[22] For Adorno, I suspect, Augustus would be best interpreted along Symean lines: the leader who plugged the ears of his people in order to prevent them from hearing the truth. Is that the most fruitful way of thinking about Augustus in relation to Adorno's theories? I suggest that mimesis offers a more sophisticated way of understanding how Augustus' achievements were based on a subtle interaction with the republican past, one which can help us understand why they chimed so well with wider Roman opinion.

2.1 Adorno and Mimesis

Adorno's concept of mimesis, deriving from the Greek term for 'imitation', differs in important respects from both modern usage and that of ancient philosophers. The OED defines mimesis as 'a figure of speech, whereby the words or actions of another are imitated' and 'the deliberate imitation of the behaviour of one group of people by another as a factor in social change'. Mimesis, therefore, is generally used now to indicate nothing more than a process of mimicry.

This simple understanding of mimesis in many ways reflects the ancient understanding. Mimesis was used to denote the act of representation in art. For Plato, the mimetic world was therefore inherently inferior to the real world it represented, since such imitation would always be of secondary value to the original. Worse, mimetic activity generated illusions which could deceive people and trick them into acting in ways which would deviate from the truth. For Plato, given that he sees the 'real' world as itself an image of an underlying world of truth, art is nothing better than a poor copy of a copy. Art is something inherently untrustworthy, far removed from the underlying truth, an inauthentic illusion that deceives its viewers into acting irrationally (Pla. *Rep.* 10).

Aristotle saw the relationship between art and imitation in more positive terms. Mimesis is seen as natural to humans, since they differ from other animals in that they are the most imitative of all and learn their earliest lessons by imitation. Moreover, Aristotle argued that humans are imbued with an instinct to enjoy

---

22 Adorno/Horkheimer 1987, 36

works of imitation.²³ Mimesis is therefore a normal means of human experience of the world, which enables individuals to learn about their environment in a useful way. Works of art, in this view, do not deceive anyone into thinking they are representations of reality, since viewers can understand the difference. The process of mimesis also changes that which is being represented in a work of art because it changes it in certain respects to make specific artistic points. Whereas Plato sought to exclude artists from his ideal city because their representations encouraged irrationality, Aristotle saw mimesis as an inescapable part of human existence, capable of being used for both good and bad ends.

Adorno's notion of mimesis starts from a similar premise to that of Aristotle. Mimicry, he argues, is a zoological necessity in that it enables animals to adapt to their environment and thereby escape detection by predators. Survival therefore depends upon an animal's ability to identify itself with other material, external to its self. In human pre-history, Adorno argues that this simple animal mimicry becomes an imitative capacity through which humans could make themselves similar to their surroundings and thereby understand their world. Through various acts of physical mimesis, as simple as a child imitating a windmill, the boundary between the self and the other becomes open and flexible. It is what the anthropologist, Michael Taussig, has called, the faculty to 'create second nature ... to copy, imitate, make models, explore difference, yield into and become Other'.²⁴ Adorno gives the example of a magician imitating demons, whereby an attempt is made to become like the other in order to ward off what is feared: copying something to take on the power of that something, or, as Taussig puts it, 'The wonder of mimesis lies in the copy drawing on the character and power of the original, to the point whereby the representation may even assume that character and that power'. Mimesis does not, therefore, seek to dominate nature, rather it coexists with and adapts to it. As Taussig has also argued, this idea of mimesis can be used to examine the way that people from one culture both adopt and distance the culture of another people.²⁵

In Dialectic of Enlightenment, Adorno outlines how this natural human practice of mimesis has been repressed in the Enlightenment process of dominating nature, first seen at work in the *Odyssey*. Mimesis, Adorno argues, has found refuge only in art, which provides modernity with 'a possibility to revise or neutralize the domination of nature'. This aesthetic mimesis succeeds in assimilating the

---

23 For an overview of the development of the concept of mimesis, see Durix 1998, esp. 45–77.
24 Taussig 1993, xiii.
25 Taussig also introduces the idea of alterity, the process by which people simultaneously maintain a distance from the other culture.

social reality in which it is produced without that context subsuming its meaning.[26] Art does not simply imitate reality. For Adorno, the kind of simple representation which Plato saw art as effecting – an art which sought to present society as it is or should be – was nothing other than propaganda. Such art, the kind produced by popular culture under capitalism, can offer enticing images of a unified society but it is in fact produced by a world that is riven by conflict and social division. By contrast, authentic art can use mimesis to resist the demands of capitalism by refusing to represent it. Adorno therefore sees mimetic art as being not only autonomous but oppositional to its social context: 'art becomes social by its opposition to society, and it occupies this position only as autonomous art'.[27] It serves as a 'movement against society'.[28] Clearly what a work of art 'says' is always in some sense imitative of its context, but true art need never express exactly what that reality is: it will always project a world of possibilities different from the status quo.

It is this essence of genuine freedom in mimetic art which Adorno argues makes its audience experience it differently from simple ideology or propaganda. The audience is engaged in something which has a life of its own, which disconcerts them and unsettles their normal view of the world. As they experience mimetic art, so the audience seeks to imitate it and move closer towards it. Rather than a hard border being set up between the viewer and the viewed, mimetic art establishes a permeable boundary that brings both sides closer together. It is a two-way process in which there exists 'the power of the copy to influence what it is a copy of'.[29] Yet, as well as containing such expressive and liberating implications, mimesis also contains a simultaneous element of repression, in that it compels the viewer away from his or her current stance towards the new ground created in the middle.

3 Augustus and Mimesis

The mimetic process can be used to understand the way in which Augustus' representation of the past successfully functioned to reunite Roman society, without recourse to ideas about his true power being 'veiled'. There are two key elements to this. Firstly, there was no simple sense of domination. Augustan art did not set

---

26 Adorno/Horkheimer 1987, 22; 24.
27 Adorno 1970, 225.
28 Ibid. 227.
29 Taussig 1993, 250.

out to dominate Rome's history and simply appropriate it for its own purposes. Rather, it sought to reconcile the present with the past, and place both in a reciprocally reconstitutive relationship that saw both being refashioned. This two-way process served to change the Roman understanding of the idea of republic in a way that no hard division seemed applicable between the Augustan present and the republican past. Secondly, Augustus' mimetic art created a certain freedom to engage with the past, in ways which served to engage its audience more fully, while at the same time using art to bring the viewer closer towards a new understanding of tradition. In doing so, his ideology established a strange mix of activity and passivity: giving and controlling but yielding also, especially to the 'correct' morality of the past. I want to examine how this process can be seen to have worked by looking at three distinct types of Augustan imagery concerning the past: the *Res Gestae* and his claim to have restored the republic (*respublica restituta*); the prima porta statue of Augustus; and Livy's *ab Urbe Condita*. I aim to show that Augustan historiography, broadly defined, can be seen to be engaging in a number of concrete ways with issues raised by Adorno's theories about a society's relationship with the past.

The *Res Gestae*, 'My Achievements', represents a first-hand account of what Augustus felt best summarised his reign. It deals with the first emperor's political offices and honours, including those he declined to hold, his lavish expenditure of his own money on various benefits for his soldiers and the people of Rome, his military victories, and his popularity. Near the end of the text, Augustus states, 'In my sixth and seventh consulships, when I had extinguished the flames of civil war, after receiving by universal consent the absolute control of affairs, I transferred the republic from my own control to the will of the senate and the Roman people' (*Res Gestae* 34.). While it is true that the phrase '*respublica restituta*' does not appear in official documents,[30] it was deployed on various Augustan coins and is reflected in Augustan writing, such as the history of Velleius Paterculus: 'validity was restored to the laws, authority to the courts, and dignity to the senate; the power of the magistrates was reduced to its former limits, with the sole exception that two were added to the eight existing praetors. The old traditional form of the republic was restored'.[31]

---

[30] Noted by Gruen 2005, 34.
[31] Vell. Pat. 2.89.3–4 *restituta vis legibus, iudiciis auctoritas, senatui maiestas, imperium magistratuum ad pristinum redactum modum, tantummodo octo praetoribus adlecti duo. Prisca illa et antiqua rei publicae forma revocata.*

It is easy to see all this as propaganda, which glossed over the bloodier side to his rule.[32] A con-trick perpetrated by a 'crook', as Cartledge called him, to dupe a gullible public into believing that this autocrat was somehow anything but that.[33] Modern literature describing the Augustan settlement is replete with the language of political trickery. To quote but one example, 'The settlement in 27 was in no meaningful sense a restoration of the Republic'.[34] I do not want to suggest that Augustus' power was not real but I do want to suggest that Adorno's thinking can shed light on how imperial imagery meant that there was no need for any veil: the reality of his power was all too obvious. What his imagery did was to set self-imposed limits on that power, provide a means by which it might be held accountable, and, above all, find a common ground by which it might become acceptable to a Roman audience.

The first thing such imagery achieved was to establish a mimetic relationship between the present and the past. Augustus needed to make his new style of autocratic rule palatable to a culture which had been traditional republican and anti-monarchic and he achieved this by making himself both similar and dissimilar to the preceding Republic. The first section of the *Res Gestae* works hard to emphasise Augustus' legitimacy and the republican offices and honours he held. But the first section also makes it brutally clear that the republic had failed and that it was only because Augustus had held sole power that he had been able to restore peace. It would never be enough simply to go back to the old style republic. Here it is worth noting that the term *restituta*, as used on his coins and in Augustan-inspired texts such as Velleius Paterculus, has, as in English, two different meanings. The first is a literal meaning of 'putting back in the same place', but there is second meaning of 'making as good as before'. As with a damaged antique, an act of restoration involves adding new material to blend in with the old in order to generate an appearance of originality. In a sense, what is created is the same, in a sense it is not. By using traditional republican imagery, we can see Augustus as freeing the present from the powerful grip of the past by copying it in a way that makes it clear that it could not be repeated. Rather than simply trying to appropriate the traditional language of republican government, he is emphasising that the republic has been both revived and improved upon by allowing those republican principles to operate within a framework that enabled them to function effectively. When Augustus' coins also proclaimed he had given

---

32 Eck 2003, 171.
33 Cartledge 1975, 31.
34 Gruen 2005, 34.

back the republic (*res publica reddita*), he did not say that he had returned it back in exactly the same form as before.

We can see another side of this mimetic process if we look at Augustan art. Perhaps the most famous example is the *Ara Pacis Augustae*. The altar harks back to the principles of the republican tradition but places these alongside stark reminders of the political realities of the day. Yes, the republic has been brought back, but it is the imperial family who provide the context within which this new republic operates. The peace, after all, is Augustan. The sophistication of this new kind of imperial imagery has been well studied, most notably by Zanker. As he argued, it is tempting from a modern perspective to see 'a propaganda machine at work' but that there was no such thing in Rome. Zanker's interest is in the new 'visual imagery' that the first emperor created and how the Romans, over time, bought into it. What he does not do, though, is explain why people were prepared to accept, even enthusiastically support, such ideology when, as many modern commentators have argued, it was a sham.[35] If it was simply a case of self-interest and survival in the face of a military dictatorship, we might expect to find cynicism and fatigue in the face of the repeated use of imperial imagery. Instead, many, perhaps most, seem to have believed, in part at least, that 'they lived in the best of all possible worlds in the best of all times'.[36]

The answer, perhaps, lies in the the widespread use of mimetic art. As Zanker and many others have amply demonstrated, Augustus never simply promoted propaganda. He allowed artists sufficient freedom for them to engage with the past in a genuinely creative way. Allowing such freedom was a core part of his political message: a practical level of individual freedom could be maintained and expressed within a context that did set some limits on that freedom. Ovid famously could write his *Ars Amatoria* at a time of Augustan moral legislation precisely because of this prescribed liberty. Even if it was this *carmen* that contributed to his exile, that did not take place until some years later and took an error, too, to bring it about. In the meantime Ovid was free to reject the past: 'Let ancient times please others. I congratulate myself that I wasn't born earlier' (*Ars amatoria* 3.121–2). Other texts, such as the *Aeneid*, do not simply toe the Augustan line. It was always possible to express nostalgia for the values of the republic while simultaneously supporting the *princeps* with enthusiasm. Clearly, it would be wrong to see all Augustan artistic life as fully oppositional to the context of its creation, as Adorno sees mimetic art as being, but it did retain a certain level of autonomy, sufficient to express gentle criticisms, to poke fun at the regime's

---

35 Zanker 1988, 3.
36 Ibid. 4.

moral aims, and to imagine worlds somewhat different from the status quo. It was this licence which allowed Augustan art to engage its audience more fully. The art had a life of its own but, like the viewers' own lives, that existence was played out on a more bounded stage than before.

It was not only the viewers and artists who had certain constraints set on them by the new Augustan regime. Augustan imagery's mimetic relationship with Rome's past also served to establish limits on the emperor's power. If we consider the Prima Porta statue of Augustus, for example, we find a subtle but clear expression of Augustus' re-establishment of Rome's military past combined with a statement of his divine links with the gods who recall Rome's mythical foundation. As Zanker shows, the entire work of art is designed to 'elevate the figure onto a higher plane'.[37] A simple historical event – the defeat of the Parthians and the recovery of the lost standards of Carrhae – is presented on the breastplate as the centre of the new relationship between heaven and earth. Through his divine ancestry, Augustus has restored proper order to the world: Pax has returned, Roman martial spirit has recovered from Crassus' shameful defeat, and Rome has become a land of plenty again, all of which will stand for as long as the sun and moon rise and fall. The mythical past not only lent legitimacy to the Augustan regime but it made clear that this was no temporary arrangement. Empire was now an eternal matter.

This moral stance is also reflected in the simple classicism of the statue. The Augustan regime, the message seems to be, was not about excess but restraint in all areas of life. But morality worked both ways. Setting oneself up as divine brought with it a whole set of expectations. Gods, like fathers, had a range of responsibilities to those who lived under their protection. Just as a father had to look after all aspects of his children's physical and moral well-being, so too the father was expected to live up to certain standards of behaviour if he was to maintain the traditions of the family's ancestors. This was clearly a message that was not lost on Augustus. His august image meant that he expected members of his own family to behave themselves and those who did not, like his daughter Julia, faced harsh penalties. The imperial family could not be seen to fall short of the ideal that images such as the Prima porta statue helped to create.

That contemporary morality was an issue for the Romans of this time is clear from the opening of Livy's *ab Urbe Condita*. He states that he has no interest in Rome's mythical past or whether the Roman people's father was none other than Mars (Livy 1.9.). Clearly this could have been interpreted as a statement of disinterest or even worse in the divine aspirations of the Augustan regime. But what

---

[37] Zanker 1988, 189–193.

interests Livy was 'life and morals', the ways in which empire was won by Rome's heroes, then the process by which, 'with the gradual relaxation of discipline, morals first gave way, as it were, then sank lower and lower, and finally began the downward plunge which has brought us to the present time, when we can endure neither our vices nor their cure'. Again, this could be interpreted as an indirect criticism of the Augustan regime and the degree to which it was symptomatic of Rome's decline. But, more obviously, Livy's emphasis on Rome's heroes of the past showed how 'wholesome and profitable' the study of history was, in that it made clear the principal lesson that would arrest Rome's decline: that Augustus was a modern hero cast from a traditional mould (Livy 1.10). The Romans had suffered in the late republic, a punishment they deserved because of their own immoral behaviour, but history showed the path to a new golden future.

Morality, for Livy, was a two-way street. The view that success had generated its own failure was a common enough theme among Roman authors, but in Livy we find a more positive message about the reversibility of this decline, a message which accorded with Augustus' own moral programme. *Virtus*, that potent mix of manliness and piety, would be rewarded. If Augustus failed, he too would be punished by the gods for Rome's continued immorality.

Augustus had no need to cloak the reality of his power. It was self-evident. As Ovid says, Augustus was the state (*res est publica Caesar*) (*Trist.* 4.4.13–16). We would be deluded if we did not recognise that there was a dark side to this power. As Dio later noted, it was at this time that truth became a victim of autocracy. Whereas previously, matters were reported accurately and regardless of the status of those involved, under Augustus 'most things that happened began to be kept secret and concealed' and those matters which were made public were 'distrusted because they could not be verified'. People suspected that 'everything is said and done with reference to the wishes of the men in power at the time and of their associates' (Dio 53.19). But Augustus did institute a range of self-imposed limitations on this power. One of the key components of his imperial imagery was that his power did not rest simply on brute force. Rather it reflected his authority, his auctoritas. Augustus' own high status reflected his moral standing and it had been granted to him by the senate and the Roman people because he was the best man for the job. In other words, the emperor was emperor because he deserved to be emperor because of his restoration of traditional republican morality in a form that made it fit for the modern age. This was not mere political spin. What was the republic in any case? A set of customs that no one could remember working? A system that had failed? It is tempting and easy from a modern perspective to set up the republic and the principate as polar opposites but for contemporaries who had lived through the violence of the civil wars perhaps the difference seemed far harder to discern. At any rate, the desire for peace may have left them open to the Augustan mimetic process whereby the present and the past were elided into one.

The Augustan state was still small by modern standards so perhaps it was also easy for those who wished to avoid direct contact with it to do so. The ubiquity of the imagery would doubtless have made regular indirect contact almost impossible. There was no escape from the imperial image: on coins, in the form of statues (by the fourth century Rome had 4,000 bronze statues of emperors, to say nothing of stone ones), and badly painted pictures, which are described as 'sitting on money-changers' tables, in stalls, in shops, hanging in the eaves, in entrance halls, in windows, in fact everywhere' (Fronto, *Letter to Caesar* 4.12). The importance of this imagery was that it established a two-way dialogue between the ruler and the ruled. To be sure, this was an asymmetric power relationship, but that did not mean the emperor's subjects had no influence. In one incident, a woman stopped the emperor Hadrian as he passed by her and asked him to hear her petition. When he said that he was too busy, she replied, 'Then stop being emperor'. She called out the emperor's claim to deliver just government and used his own imagery against him. Needless to say, he felt obliged to hear her complaint (Dio 69.6.3).[38]

The Augustan image made the emperor accountable to the Roman people. Clearly people had to be careful about what they said openly. But the imperial image proclaimed publicly the grounds on which an emperor could be judged. When taxes were too high or food in short supply, the ordinary people of the empire could vent their ire against the very imperial images that in other circumstance they were happy to revere. During one tax riot in Antioch in the late fourth century, for example, the crowd threw stones at the many painted pictures of the emperors that were hanging at various places in the city and jeered as they were smashed. The statues of the emperor and empress were then thrown down and dragged through the city and, 'as is usual on such occasions, the enraged multitude uttered every insult which passion could suggest' (Sozomen, *History of the Church* 7.23). Or they would even attack the emperor himself. During a grain shortage, Claudius was surrounded in the forum by an angry mob who hurled insults at him and pelted him with rock-hard crusts of bread. He was lucky to escape back to the imperial palace on the Palatine by a back door. It is also clear that the crowd were not out to harm him – they would have thrown stones and used weapons if so. It was like throwing eggs at a politician. Hitting the emperor

---

[38] For various versions of this tale, see Kelly 2004, 114 n. 1, which may itself show that it was a common tactic for the weak to adopt.

with bits of mouldy bread served to shame him into doing his duty by his people. It worked. Claudius went to great efforts to source grain for the city's population (Suet. *Claud.* 18).

It was also possible for Rome's upper classes to hold the emperor to account. Stories about previous emperors, as found in the writings of Tacitus and Suetonius, used the safe space provided by history to judge whether earlier rulers had successfully lived up to the claims of the imperial image. The result was twofold. Firstly, that both the current and future emperors could be gently encouraged to be 'good' rulers and deliver on their claims of moral governance. Second, that there was an implicit threat in such history: behave or face the same fate as befell Caligula, Nero, and Domitian: assassination, *damnatio* and certainly no apotheosis. However subtly and obliquely it had to be expressed, the message was stark. The problem, of course, was the imperial system's lack of controls on executive power. It was up to the individual emperor to decide whether he was to be bound by the imperial image since his power was such that he had carte blanche to express his dominance over Roman society by acting as he wished. The ruled had no way of enforcing their claims until it was too late and they had suffered perhaps years of oppression and the abuse of power. Even then, assassinations required plots and brought great personal risk to those involved. We are dealing here with 'weapons of the weak'.[39]

However unequal was the division of power in Roman society, Augustus succeeded in establishing a stable government after decades of political conflict and set up an imperial system that lasted for centuries. The idea that he achieved this by carrying out some kind of con-trick on the Roman people does too little justice both to the complexity of the Augustan system and the intelligence of his subjects. Augustus placed the past in a new kind of relationship with the present, establishing a process whereby both were changed and moved closer together. It worked because it set limits on all people's behaviour, even the emperor's. It worked because those limits were flexible and symbolic, rarely needing to be rigorously enforced. Above all, it worked because it restored the system of the past into a form that meant it could function effectively with Augustus as its enforcer. This imperial settlement developed a sophisticated system of mutually beneficial relationships between the various classes of Rome, which in many ways anticipated the modern culture that was to be so criticised by Adorno. Rome's past played a core role in the establishment of the ideology that supported this culture and, in its mutually reconstitutive relationship with the present, we can see a praxis that also looked forward to Adorno's theories on mimesis.

---

39 See Scott 1985.

Bibliography

Adorno, Theodore (1970), *Aesthetic Theory* (eds. Gretel Adorno and Rolf Tiedemann, trans. Robert Hullot-Kentor), Minneapolis.
Adorno, Theodore/Horkheimer, Max (1987), *Dialectic of Enlightenment: Philosophical Fragments* (edited by Gunzelin Schmid Noerr, trans. Edmund Jephcott), Stanford.
Adorno, Theodore (2003), "Reflections on Class Theory", in Rolf Tiedemann (ed.), *Can One Live After Auschwitz?*, Stanford, 93–110.
Briel, Holger/Kramer, Andreas (eds.) (2001), *In Practice: Adorno, critical theory and cultural studies*, Berlin.
Cartledge, Paul (1975), "The Second Thoughts of Augustus on the Res Publica in 28/7 B.C.", *Hermathena* 119, 30–40.
Comay, Rebecca (2000), "Adorno's Siren Song", *New German Critique* 81, 21–48.
Cooley, Alison E. (2009), *Res Gestae Divi Augusti: text, translation and commentary*, Cambridge.
Durix, Jean-Pierre (1998), *Mimesis, Genres and Post-Colonial Discourse: deconstructing Magic Realism*, New York.
Eck, Werner (2003), *The Age of Augustus*, Oxford.
Elder, Walter (2005), "Augustus and the Power of Tradition", in Karl Galinsky (ed.), *The Cambridge Companion to the Age of Augustus*, Cambridge, 13–32.
Galinsky, Karl (ed.) (1998), *Augustan Culture: an interpretative introduction*, Princeton, NJ.
Galinsky, Karl (ed.) (2005), *The Cambridge Companion to the Age of Augustus*, Cambridge.
Galinsky, Karl (2012), *Augustus: introduction to the life of an emperor*, Cambridge.
Gibson, Nigel C./Rubin, Andrew (eds) (2001), *Adorno: a critical reader*, Oxford.
Griffin, Jasper (2005), "Augustan Poetry and Augustanism" in Karl Galinsky (ed.), *The Cambridge Companion to the Age of Augustus*, Cambridge, 306–320.
Gruen, Erich S. (2005), "Augustus and the Making of the Principate" in Karl Galinsky (ed.), *The Cambridge Companion to the Age of Augustus*, Cambridge, 33–52.
Heberle, Renée J. (2006), *Feminist interpretations of Theodor Adorno*, Pennsylvania.
Horkheimer, Max (1987), *Gesammelte Schriften: Dialektik der Aufklärung und Schriften 1940–1950*, (ed. Gunzelin Schmid Noerr), Frankfurt.
Jarvis, Sion (1998), *Adorno: a critical introduction*, Cambridge.
Kelly, Christopher (2004), *Ruling the Later Roman Empire*, Cambridge, MA.
Levick, Barbara (2010), *Augustus: image and substance*, Harlow.
Müller-Doohm, Stefan (2009), *Adorno: a biography: an intellectual biography*, Cambridge.
O'Connor, Brian (2013), *Adorno*, London/New York, NY.
Schmidt, James (ed.) (2007), *Theodor Adorno*, Farnham.
Scott, James C. (1985), *Weapons of the Weak: everyday forms of peasant resistance*, New Haven, CT.
Syme, Ronald (1939), *The Roman Revolution*, Oxford.
Taussig, Michael (1993), *Mimesis and Alterity: a particular history of the senses*, London/New York, NY.
Tiedemann, Rolf (2003), *Can One Live After Auschwitz?: a philosophical reader*, Stanford, CA.
Wallace-Hadrill, Andrew (2008), *Rome's Cultural Revolution*, Cambridge.
Wilson, Ross (2007), *Theodor Adorno*, London/New York, NY.
Witkin, Robert W. (2003), *Adorno on Popular Culture*, London/New York, NY.

Zanker, Paul (1988), *The Power of Images in the Age of Augustus* (trans. Alan Shapiro), Ann Arbor, MI.

David Carr
Teleology and the Experience of History

History is the story of human progress. Or so many have thought. The teleological view of history reached the height of its influence in the work of Hegel, Marx, and early positivism, continued as the Whig interpretation of history in Britain, and then, after being attacked and rejected in many quarters, seems to reappear in Husserl's late work, in the 1930s. It surfaces once again in the 1990s in the work of Francis Fukuyama, and, more recently, in Niall Ferguson and Steven Pinker. In spite of seemingly being refuted again and again by facts and arguments, this idea seems unwilling to relinquish its hold on us. Why is this so? That's the question I want to consider in this paper. And in answer I want to suggest that something in the nature of our experience — our historical experience — inclines us toward this view. By analogy with Kant, I want to suggest that the idea of historical progress constitutes something like a transcendental illusion we find it hard to overcome.

I'll begin with a brief historical review of the teleological idea.

1 Teleology in History

Enlightenment thinkers believed that we could become masters and possessors not only of nature, as Descartes predicted, but also of ourselves. Human beings could take control of their own destiny and shake off the tyranny of ignorance, fear and superstition enshrined in religion and the divine right of kings. History is headed inexorably toward human emancipation.

The enlightenment idea was open-ended and somewhat vague on when and how human freedom would arrive. It was left to Hegel to work out the details. His famous and popular lectures on the philosophy of history, delivered several times at the University of Berlin in the 1820s, have become the classic statement of the teleological view of history. His account bears the traces of the Enlightenment view, but adds significant new elements. The "only" thought that philosophy brings to the study of history, he says, is that of reason —"that reason rules the world," and thus that world history like everything else can be seen as a rational or reasonable affair.[1] Reason not only sets the goal for history but also governs the realization of that goal. Hegel did not invent this idea, he reminds us; the idea

---
[1] Hegel 1988, 12.

that reason rules the world goes back to Anaxagoras, and it has also been expressed in the idea of divine providence. This too suggests a rational plan, God's plan, but such a plan is usually invoked when its features are not evident to us. Rather than take refuge in pious ignorance, however, Hegel believes that the rationality of providence can be known and explained. If we take seriously the idea of providence, the demonstration of its rationality would amount to a theodicy or "justification of God".[2] Thus rather than contrasting rational and religious views, as in the Enlightenment, Hegel wants to reconcile them.

The embodiment of reason is spirit (*Geist*), both as individuals and as peoples, whose nature is to be conscious and self-conscious, and whose actualization is to be autonomous and self-sufficient — that is, to be free. But this actualization is a temporal process, and that process is history. Spirit actualizes itself and achieves freedom through history, using human passions and intentions as its driving force; but the result of this process is often at odds with the actual intentions of those individuals and peoples who are thus used. This is where Hegel speaks of the "cunning of reason", since reason achieves ends of its own by using the ends of others.[3] In history, it is only when individuals and peoples organize themselves into states that freedom can finally be truly actualized. It is here, in law, the ethical life of the community and political order, not in the mere absence of constraint, that the "positive reality and satisfaction of freedom" are to be found.[4]

The actual course of history can be seen as the display of human perfectibility leading toward the realization of freedom. This pathway is not a smooth one, however, but consists in the spirit's "hard and endless struggle against itself." Spirit hides its own nature from itself, and is even "proud and full of enjoyment in this self-estrangement".[5] Individuals and peoples struggle against each other, and many morally good and virtuous people suffer unjustly. But history moves on a different plane, and here the acts of individuals, especially those of the great figures of history, are not to be judged by moral standards. It is the spirit of peoples, not individuals, that are the agents of history, but these, "progressing in a necessary series of stages, are themselves only phases of the one universal Spirit: through them, that World Spirit elevates and completes itself in history, into a self-comprehending totality".[6] Thus another feature of Hegel's view of historical

---

2 Ibid. 18.
3 Ibid. 35.
4 Ibid. 41.
5 Ibid. 59
6 Ibid. 82.

progress that departs from his Enlightenment predecessors is that of its dialectical character. It moves toward its goal through the struggle of opposing forces, and achieves it in ways that are indifferent to the actual desires and aims of individuals, great and small.

In several places Hegel presents in the broadest outlines the necessary stages through which the world spirit has passed on its path toward the realization of freedom. Like the sun, history rises in the east and sets in the west. In the ancient Oriental world only one — the emperor or tyrant — is free. In the Greek and Roman worlds only some persons are free. It was the "Germanic peoples, through Christianity, who came to the awareness that every human is free by virtue of being human".[7] The realization of freedom is the goal which gives meaning to what happens in history, and this realization takes place within history itself, not beyond it. Moreover, it has occurred or is occurring in "our world," "our time".[8]

Hegel was at the height of his influence when he gave these lectures, but not long after his death his philosophy fell on hard times. One of his detractors was Marx, who derided Hegel for overlooking the material conditions of human history. But Marx's "historical materialism," for all its differences with Hegel's idealism, retained the idea that history is advancing inexorably, and dialectically, toward human emancipation. Other thinkers of the time, such as the early positivists and socialists, shared this teleological view of history without endorsing the Hegelian or Marxian detail.

But other critics rejected the teleological view as a whole. The historians of the historical school, trying to create a discipline based on evidence, had their doubts about such untested generalizations. Dilthey and Nietzsche, among others, were deeply skeptical. The *grands récits* of the classical, 19th century philosophies of history gave way to the modest epistemologies of historical knowledge pursued by the neo-Kantians and the life-philosophers, who concerned themselves with the differences between the natural and the human sciences.

The First World War made the idea of historical progress less plausible than ever. Marx's teleological emancipation narrative was kept alive by the ideologues of the new Soviet Union, but this aspect of his theory was played down by Western Marxists. Hegel's Western triumphalism was hard to sustain when the war led to the collapse of the great European monarchies, and Oswald Spengler turned it on its head when he proclaimed the Decline of the West in 1918. Thus it is all the more remarkable that the founder of phenomenology, Edmund Husserl, seemed to revive the idea of historical teleology, and the primacy of Europe, in his late

---

7 Ibid. 21.
8 Hegel 1976, 524.

works of the mid-1930s, notably *The Crisis of European Sciences and Transcendental Phenomenology*.[9] To those who know his earlier work, this idea seems an incongruous innovation.

Let's recall the broad framework in which Husserl presents his new "Introduction to Phenomenological Philosophy" as it's called in the subtitle. Most striking are the words "Crisis" and "Europe" in the title. Of course, it was obvious that Europe was in crisis at that time. Even though in retrospect we can say that the Europeans of 1935 hadn't seen the half of it, there was plenty to justify this talk. Vienna and Prague were still outside the German Reich — that's why Husserl was still able to lecture there — but Hitler already had his eye on them, and rumblings of a "second world war," barely twenty years after the first, were already in the air.

But the "crisis" talk was not new to the 1930s. Charles Bambach points out that the term "*Krisis*" figured in the titles of several prominent earlier studies Husserl probably knew about. Bambach refers to the "crisis-mentality of Weimar" marked by "the style and signature of apocalypse".[10] For Europeans of Husserl's generation, it was the First World War that had brought on the crisis. Germans of the 1920s saw themselves ruled by a constitution imported from the west, while Bolshevism threatened from the east and fascism from the south. So the term "crisis" was a historical topos that belonged to the whole interwar period. But by 1935 fascism and anti-Semitism had arrived in Germany, and Europe seemed headed for the abyss.

Thus the talk of Europe's crisis is certainly topical, and the tone and emphasis here are so foreign to that of Husserl's earlier texts that one is inclined to suspect that they are merely window dressing, mean to draw in the reader. But that interpretation won't hold up, since Husserl obviously believes that the teleological and historical approach is integral to his presentation of phenomenology. As he says in his preface to original publication of the *Crisis*, his new work "makes the attempt, by way of a teleological-historical reflection upon the origins of our critical scientific and philosophical situation, to establish the unavoidable necessity of a transcendental-phenomenological reorientation of philosophy".[11]

What does it mean to philosophize about Europe in the way that Husserl does? Early in the *Crisis* Husserl raises the question of whether "Europe" is "merely an anthropological type, like 'China' or 'India'".[12] Well, why not? What

---

9 Husserl 1970.
10 Bambach 1995, 37n.
11 Husserl 1970, 3.
12 Ibid. 16.

more should it be? Of course, Europe is more than a merely geographical entity, as Husserl says, with its shifting boundaries and its colonial outposts, including North America. But couldn't we say the same of "China" and "India?" They too are certainly more than just geographical. We could even add that Europe is more than just anthropological — comprising language, culture, religion, etc.; it is also historical, exhibiting a continuity over time and embodying certain large-scale social and political transformations. But China and India likewise have their own histories. What is Husserl after?

What is at stake for Husserl is an idea of "humanity" that begins as Greek humanity, is renewed in the European Renaissance, and is the "breakthrough to what is essential to humanity as such".[13] European humanity bears within itself an absolute idea, and we who philosophize under this idea are "functionaries of mankind," acting on behalf not just of Europeans but of all human beings.[14] And tellingly, Husserl believes that what he calls "the spectacle of the Europeanization of all other civilizations bears witness to the rule of an absolute meaning, one which is proper to the sense rather than to a historical non-sense, of the world".[15]

These features of Husserl's late thought, together with what appears to be a condescending dismissal of China and India, seem to place him squarely in the camp of what would later come to known as Eurocentrism. How should we react to Husserl's views of Europe? Is he just expressing the prejudices of his generation and his class, leaving his philosophy intact? It is true that until this late stage in his career, Husserl has presented his philosophy without clothing it in the teleological-historical reflections that focus so intently on the "European" origins of philosophy. Perhaps Husserl thinks that since Europe is so clearly caught up in crisis, he needs to attack the European crisis by exploring its European roots. But Husserl devotes so much attention to the idea of Europe in these late writings that it is it is clear that much more is at stake.

Many readers have felt the influence of Hegel's philosophy of history in Husserl's late work, and those who know Husserl are surprised by this. Husserl had very little interest in and knowledge of Hegel's work, and was not concerned to pursue any similarities there might have been, including, of course, the important use of the term "phenomenology." Husserl's background was in 18th and 19th century empiricism and positivism, and in Kant and neo-Kantianism. By emphasizing reason and science rather than freedom, Husserl was perhaps closer to

---

13 Ibid. 15.
14 Ibid. 17.
15 Ibid. 16.

the Enlightenment and early positivist sense of history than he was to Hegel. But in the Enlightenment conception the reference to Europe was at most implicit, and here Husserl puts great emphasis on it.

If Husserl reveals an affinity with Hegel in these writings, this would reinforce the charge of Eurocentrism. If Kant is considered the thinker of the French revolution, Hegel is thought to be the guiding genius of European hegemonism, colonialism and the white man's burden. Husserl's apparent endorsement of Europeanization seems to confirm this. Hegel admitted that while freedom had arrived in Europe, slavery and despotism still survived in other parts of the world, and these would have to be eventually raised to European standards. Is this what Husserl means?

I must say that there is something bizarre and tragic about the aged Husserl, extolling the virtues of Europe on the eve of the second world conflagration in which Europe seemed to destroy itself once and for all. The Shoah revealed unspeakable evil at its heart, and its colonial empires, which for many had been proof of its moral superiority and world-civilizing historical destiny, began to fall apart, subject to rebellions by populations somehow not grateful for the blessings colonial rule had brought them. From this post-war perspective the idea of Europe as the pinnacle of civilization and the culmination of world history, seemed more than absurd.

One document of the period, which presents a root-and-branch deflation of the very idea of philosophy of history, is Karl Löwith's *Meaning in History* (1949). Löwith is an avowed Nietzschean and "pagan" who reads Nietzsche's doctrine of eternal return as an attempt to uproot the ideas of teleology and eschatology deeply rooted in Western thought. To me Löwith is the precursor of a general rejection of the teleological view of history in European post-war philosophy. French thinkers like Foucault and Lyotard, expressing their incredulity toward "grands récits," likewise take their inspiration from Nietzsche rather than Hegel and Marx.

It should be noted, however, that this rejection of teleology is to be found among the Germans and the French, i.e., the losers of World War II. History, as we know, is written by the winners, not the losers. What about the Americans and the Russians? We've already noted that the Marxist teleology of history is upheld by the official ideology of the Soviet Union. What about the Americans? The dominant analytic philosophy pretends not to be interested in the "speculative" philosophy of history, but the underlying neo-positivism of analytic philosophy keeps the idea of progress alive. For neo-positivism, as for Auguste Comte, modern science triumphs over mythology, theology and metaphysics. This is the teleology of history. But this belief in progress only expresses covertly, in the abstruse jargon of academic philosophy, the wide-spread American triumphalism in politics and the public mind. It was easy for the Americans to see themselves as the culmination and salvation of history, offering the form of government and civilization that the world has been yearning for, though sometimes without knowing it. The American victories of World War II — and World War I for that matter — seemed to confirm the American exceptionalism that had been alive since at least the days of Woodrow Wilson. As Americans reveled in their growing prosperity and the wonders of science, technology, and medicine, how could they doubt that history was the story of human progress, and that if other countries followed the lead of the United States, they too could share in these blessings?

Of course, against every exaltation of modern life a countervailing voice will be raised, claiming that there was a time, date unspecified, when we all ate healthful food and lived in harmony with nature. On this scenario technology and industrialization bring ruin and devastation, despoiling the environment and our own well-being in a downward spiral. This romantic revolt against the industrial age is as old as industrialization itself, and, like Spengler, simply flips the salvation narrative on its head. And it is always exposed to the obvious questions: would you really want to go back to the misguided medicine, abbreviated lifespans, and bad sanitation of the pre-industrial age? Nobody wins these arguments, but the champions of modernity generally prevail.

This is where Fukuyama comes in. In his 1993 book *The End of History and the Last Man* he resurrects the explicitly Hegelian narrative, now seen as the ultimate triumph of capitalism and liberal democracy. He admits that it was easy to lose faith in this scenario in the face of the horrible wars, genocides and the persistent Cold War of the 20th century. But with the collapse of Communism and the move toward democracy in many parts of the world, we can now see that these were only temporary adversaries now vanquished by the World spirit. The only danger is that we would all become bored with the benevolent new world order. In his more recent work Fukuyama has retreated significantly, limiting himself to touting the advantages of liberal democracy without predicting its triumph. But the progressivist interpretation of history, as part of the neoliberal view of capitalism, has recently been championed by Niall Ferguson, and Steven Pinker presents arguments for progress based primarily on advances in science.[16]

---

16 Ferguson 2018; Pinker 2018.

2 The Experience of History

At the beginning I suggested that the prevalence of the teleological view of history might be explained by reference to our experience of history. But I am not, like Pinker, claiming that there is empirical evidence for historical progress. My approach is quite different. Let me explain what I mean. I am distinguishing between the philosophical representation of history, on the one hand, and the actual experience of history on the other. The various teleological views I have discussed so far are representations of history. But now I want to ask, not how history is represented, but how it is experienced. Thus I am raising an explicitly phenomenological question. Phenomenology asks, of something like history, not what it is in itself, or even how we know it, but how it is given, how it enters our lives, how we encounter it directly. It is in this way that phenomenology differs from metaphysics and epistemology.

Is there a direct experience of history, a distinctively historical experience that differs from other experience? I think there is, but its relation to experience in general is a peculiar one. It is not a separate experience but an aspect of all experience, and we can reach it by building on what phenomenology teaches us. At first glance, this connection between experience and history might seem to involve a simple four-step progression. Experience is essentially temporal; experience is essentially intersubjective; history is intersubjective temporality; thus experience is essentially historical. But each of these steps, especially the third, needs elaboration, and this is what I propose in the following.

First, temporality: The temporal flow of consciousness is essential to the concept of subjectivity, and phenomenology, beginning with Husserl, has developed an account of consciousness that is unified while spanning past, present and future. Husserl's great accomplishment is his introduction of the notion of retention and the sharp distinction he makes between it and memory in the usual sense, which he calls "recollection" or sometimes "reproduction." What Husserl is trying to describe here is the experience of both the presentness of the present and the *continuity* of the present. Retention is definitely a consciousness of something past. Yet I am conscious of it *together with* the present and it makes the present possible.

Second, our experience is not in our heads but relates us to a world. Consciousness, as Husserl famously recognized, is not wrapped up in itself, but is always *of something*. As Sartre would later insist, interpreting Husserl, consciousness is entirely outside of itself, *in the world*. This is what the phenomenologists call *intentionality*.

The concept of subjectivity which emerges from this discussion is one that combines its temporality and its intentionality. Consciousness flows, and has its retentional-protentional structure. It is of the here-and-now, the present, but only because the present stands out from a kind of temporal field that encompasses past and future. And it is *of* the here-and-now in the sense that it relates intentionally to objects that are other than and outside itself.

The introduction of intentionality into the discussion of experience means that we cannot properly speak of experience without discussing *what* is intended, *as* it is intended. It is not just that we want to consider those "objects that are other than and outside" the intention; we *must* consider them of we want to understand experience. Husserl spoke of "temporal objects" as a special class of objects — things that take time or unfold in time, and must do so in order to be what they are, and to be experienced *as* what they are. The melody is one example, but so is the dancer's twirl, the tree's sway in the breeze, a conversation. But we have a perfectly good word to describe such "objects:" they are *events*. Things that don't take time, or just persist through time, like my pen, can be distinguished from events. Of course, my experience, even of my pen, is itself an event; that is, it unfolds in time, even if my pen just sits there. So, when we talk of experiencing an event, like hearing a melody, we must distinguish between the event of hearing and the event that is heard, the melody itself.

In sum, the experience of the here and now, is intentionally related to things and events as its "objects," in the broadest sense. But as *intentional* objects, things and events have *meaning* — and this leads us to the concept of *world*. This is one of those terms that have developed a special sense in the context of phenomenology, largely thanks to the work of Husserl and Heidegger. "World" can mean just the totality of what is, the universe, all the things that exist, and so on. The phenomenological understanding of world retains the sense of totality, but includes the idea of things and events *as intended*, that is, as having meaning — for consciousness, for someone, for human existence — meanings they have in relation to one another and in relation to the totality itself. Things and events added together may make up a universe, but things and events that have meaning for someone make up a world, at least in the phenomenological sense. This does not mean that these things and events, or their meanings, or the world itself, are "merely subjective." Indeed one of the meanings they have is, as we have seen, that they are other than or outside consciousness. In virtue of intentionality, experience relates itself to what is beyond itself. In this sense, the subject is in the world, and the world, as a complex of meaningful things and events, is as essential to it as intentionality itself.

The phenomenological account of time and subjectivity is initially tied to the first-person singular point of view. And yet this focus seems highly inappropriate for talking about history. History, it is fair to say, is not itself focused on individuals, but concerns the social world. If we are to find a connection between subjectivity and history, then consciousness is in some sense going to have to concern more than just the individual. This is where intersubjectivity comes in. We are going to have to talk about the experience of the social world, and, at the limit, about experience itself as something that occurs *socially*. The concept of subjectivity in modern philosophy came to prominence in response to epistemological concerns, and these were conceived in relation to the newly developing sciences of nature. The only *objects* of experience that were considered important, accordingly, were physical and natural objects. This focus on *things* meant that our encounter with other people was conceived in terms of our perception of their bodies as physical objects and led to the notorious problem of "other minds." But this gets it backwards. We experience persons as persons, their bodies as human bodies, not as physical objects. Thus our world is primarily, indeed overwhelmingly, a human and social world.

Once this human world moves to the center of our concern, and becomes more fully elaborated, we can return to the *temporality* of experience in relation to the social world and to social existence. The human world is a world not just of things but of events and processes, of actions and developments, which we experience as continuities thanks to the retentional-protentional structure. Like the natural world the human world is temporal, and we experience it as temporal continuity, but the temporality of the human world is different from that of the natural world.

Houses and streets, cities and their configurations, have a past which is given with them as horizon and background when we experience them in the present. Indeed, we can say the same thing of other people. This horizon of pastness is given in retention, and thanks to retention we have something like an experience of the past — but only as background for the present. Further, we can say that many of these objects, and many of these people, are older than we are — i.e. older than I, the particular subject of any given experience. In these cases the horizon of pastness reaches back into the time before our birth. Thus the depth and breadth of this past, receding into the indefinite, as horizon and background for the present, is always given in every experience of the human world. In this sense what is experienced is not limited to the lifetime of the experiencing subject.

Merging the phenomenological account of temporality with that of the social world we can say that the direct experience of persons, groups and other social entities, such as artifacts, buildings, streets, etc. bears its past along with it in the manner of retentional consciousness. To have an experience in this first sense is to be in the presence of an object that stands out from its temporal background. To experience an action or event is likewise to see it emerge from its antecedents. In each of these cases the retained past is part of what gives meaning to the present and makes it what it is. Each object and event, in other words, comes to us with its past attached. Without this past it would not only be meaningless, it could not even be an item in our experience. If it is true that our experience is in the present and connects us with the present, it is equally true that it gives an unmediated connection with the past.

To correctly describe and fully understand this relation to others, we need to introduce an indispensable new term, namely that of the group to which I and the others belong. It is precisely as fellow members of a group that others are encountered in this way, and so we need to explore what "group" means in this context, to understand how it exists, how far it extends, etc. What we have in mind here is not merely an objective collection of individuals, united by some common objective characteristic like size, shape, hair color or complexion, or geographical location. The relevant sense of group for our purposes is united from the inside, not from the outside. The word most often used to convey this sense of group is *community, Gemeinschaft*. These terms derive from the common or the shared, but this must be understood in a special way.

If the community makes possible a certain kind of encounter with others, how do I encounter the community itself? It too is not primarily an object standing over against me as something to be perceived or known, as if I were an anthropologist or sociologist. I relate to it rather in terms of membership, adherence or belonging. The sign of this relation is my use of the "we" to characterize the subject of certain experiences and actions. The possibility that the community can emerge as a "we"-subject affords a way of understanding not only the nature of the community but also the peculiar character of being with others that makes it up. Notice that we have not given up the first-person perspective here, but moved from the singular to the plural first-person.

Describing this plural subject phenomenologically involves reflecting on those occasions and experiences in which I identify myself with a group or community by enlisting, so to speak, in the "we." It happens when the experience or action in which I am engaged is attributed not just to me but to "us," when I take myself to be a participant in a collective action or experience. But the action or experience must be enduring or ongoing, and with it the existence of the collective subject, the "we." To say that we build a house is not equivalent to saying that I build a house, you build a house, she builds a house, etc. The common project is articulated into subtasks distributed among the participants such that the agent cannot be any of the members singly but only the group as such.

To say that I enlist in or participate in such collective endeavors or experiences is to say that I identify myself with the group in question, and this sense of "identifying oneself" deserves our attention. The identity of the subject of experience is not a given but constitutes itself over time as a sort of project, and I identify myself in relation to others. This is often taken to mean that I gain my identity in opposition to others, but it is also true that one asserts one's identity by joining with others.

Thus individuals identify themselves with groups that range from small and intimate to larger and more encompassing. But it must not be thought that these groups nest easily inside each other like a series of concentric circles. Groups criss-cross one another, and I identify myself sometimes more with one than another, depending on circumstances. Furthermore, participation in one may not always be compatible with participation in another. Family may conflict with profession, class with country, religion with civic duty, etc., to name only a few of the classic conflicts. These conflicts can be personal and psychological, "identity crises" in which the individual is torn between conflicting commitments and allegiances; and through the individuals involved the conflicts can be social as well, pitting groups against each other in collective action and enmity.

Much more could be said about various aspects and implications of the We-relation, but I want to turn now to its relevance to our topic. We have been looking for a connection between subjectivity and history that could be described as the experience of historical existence. I want to contend that it is in the experience of membership in communities that time is genuinely historical for us. As a member of a community I become part of a We-subject with an experience of time that extends back before my birth and can continue even after my death. Since the We is experienced as genuinely subjective, it has the same sort of temporality as the I-subject. That is, it is not just an entity persisting in time, or a series of nows, but a occupies a prospective-retrospective temporal field encompassing past and future. Just as we attribute agency and experience to the we-subject, so we can speak of its expectations and its memories. History is sometimes spoken of as "society's memory," the manner in which a community retains its past such that the past plays an enduring role in the life of the present. To put it another way: just as the present is for the I-subject the vantage point which gives access to a temporal field encompassing past and future; likewise, for the we-subject, the present similarly functions as a vantage-point. But the field which is opened up in this case is much broader. It is to this field that I gain access in virtue of my membership and participation in a community.

One thing to be emphasized about our account of subjectivity and history is that it remains anchored, like the concept of experience itself, firmly in the present, the here-and-now. But one great advantage of the phenomenological approach to temporality, on which we have drawn extensively, is that it shows there can be no experience of the present, and no presence as experienced, without its horizon or background of past — and future. The "here-and-now" is possible only as emerging from the past and anticipating the future. This is true of the flow of our experience itself, and it is true of the meaningful events, objects, persons and other entities that occur around us and make up our world.

What we have been trying to describe here is what the German philosophers called the *Geschichtlichkeit*, or historicity, of human existence. Dilthey (1970) wrote that "we are historical beings first, before we are observers [*Betrachter*] of history, and only because we are the former do we become the latter...The historical world is always there, and the individual not only observes it from the outside but is intertwined with it [*in sie verwebt*]".[17] Dilthey, Husserl, Heidegger and others who used this term, in keeping with the historicist tradition, thought of historicity as something like an essential human trait, something bound to subjectivity itself. But we usually identify historicity with the manner in which the past plays a role in the present. What my analysis shows, I think, is that it is primarily as members of communities of various sorts that we experience the reality of the past in our present lives. It is here that such terms as "tradition," "inheritance," "legacy" come into play. In the agency of the "we" the past is not just passively given; we take it over or, as Heidegger put it, we "hand down" to ourselves the legacy of the past.[18] Communal existence is active in many ways, but a constant feature of its activity is the manner in which it appropriates its past. That this is an activity is evident from the varying forms this takes. We select from the past what we wish to take over and neglect what we wish to forget. Indeed, remembering and forgetting are central activities by which communities constitute themselves. Remembering leads to commemoration and memorialization, in which we celebrate our heroes and achievements in monuments and popular songs on national holidays. The silence of forgetting can seek to evade responsibility for evils such as slavery or genocide; but it can in some cases have the beneficial effect of overcoming past resentments and grievances. Some communities remember too little; others remember too much.

Let us summarize the results of our account of historicity. We exist historically by virtue of our participation in communities that predate and outlive our

---

17 Dilthey 1970, 346.
18 Heidegger 1957, 383.

individual lives. Through the we-relation historical reality enters directly into our lived experience and becomes part of our identity. Our membership gives us access to a past, a tradition, and a temporal span that it not so much something we know about as something that is part of us. This is the primary sense in which we are, in Dilthey's sense, historical beings before we are observers of history; this is the sense in which we are "intertwined" with history.

Now we come back to our original question: how does teleology fit into this scheme? Clearly we do not experience time as a series of nows, like the ticking of the clock, or like a series of still snapshots succeeding one another. Rather, time as experienced is better described as a complex structure of mutually illuminating or adumbrating horizons. The foreground-background structure is essential for understanding this phenomenon. The present stands out from and gets its sense from the background of past from which it emerges. It is what it is because it has, not just a past, but this particular past. But likewise this past gets its sense from being the past of this particular present. Thinking of the present as a dimensionless instant is a product of abstract thought. Attention to the experience of time reveals the present as a kind of fullness adumbrated by the past. The present is an event. In objective terms an event can last a split second or a year. What counts is that it achieves a contour that distinguishes itself from what went before. Its content is always changing as it itself now belongs to the past. So it enlarges the past even as it emerges from the past.

Its content is derived from the future. It gets it meaning from the past but also from the future. So the present has a double figure-background structure: the horizon of the past and the horizon of the future. To think of the future as empty or undetermined is again a product of abstract thought. In experience the future is, like the past, always full and particular, and present and future give each other meaning. The future differs from the past in that it derives its peculiarity either from our passive expectations or our plans. It also differs, of course, in that either of these can be disappointed. But the meaning of the present is always determined by our plans and expectations. It is oriented toward these plans and expectations, it is directed toward them. But this structure also determines the past, which is a past that leads up to a present oriented towards a future.

We can call this temporal structure a teleological structure in that the whole complex of mutually determining meanings is oriented toward the fulfilment of our expectations and plans. This is why Heidegger thought that futurity had priority among the dimensions of temporality. In a sense the whole structure of meaning seems to emanate from the future. In this sense the present seems always a crisis or turning point between past and future, always on alert against the possibility that expectations and plans may be disappointed or thwarted.

If my previous analysis of the plural subject is valid, then this whole structure can be discerned on the level of social experience as well as individual experience. As individuals we exist in a social or communal present defined by its past and future, which are likewise social and communal. This past gets its meaning from its relation to a present defined by it orientation to a future of plans and expectations. What is important about the past is what prefigures the present, leads up to it. Our experience of history, our historicity, is one of a social past that gives meaning to the present as oriented to the future. As for the first-person singular, so for the first person plural, past and present, now in the social sense, make up a complex meaning-structure which is teleological in character.

3 Conclusion: Teleology and "Transcendental Illusion"

As I indicated at the outset, I see certain parallels here to an aspect of Kant's "transcendental dialectic" in the *Critique of Pure Reason*. For Kant, it was just as important to explain why certain metaphysical questions are asked as to show why they cannot be answered. He claimed that our reason demands a certain kind of satisfaction that can only be provided by the ideas of God, freedom and immortality. "There are fundamental rules and maxims for the employment of our reason" which "have all the appearance of being objective principles. We therefore take the subjective necessity of a connection of our concepts, which is to the advantage of the understanding, for an objective necessity in the determination of things in themselves. This is an *illusion* which can no more be prevented ... than the astronomer can prevent the moon from appearing larger at its rising, although he is not deceived by this illusion".[19] And when Kant speaks of teleological reason directly, in the *Critique of Judgment*, he likewise ascribes to it a "natural dialectic" and an "unavoidable illusion, which one can unmask and dissolve through critique, so that it not deceive us." Again this dialectic of illusion "has its ground in the nature of our faculty of knowledge".[20]

Here, of course, Kant is dealing with teleology in nature. But he says something very similar about history in his 1963 essay on the "Idea for a Universal History from a Cosmopolitan Point of view". Does human history reveal progress? Kant won't assert this outright, but he thinks that this idea is the only way we can

---

19 Kant 1959, a297, b354.
20 Ibid. 312–313.

make sense of history. Only this idea "permits us to hope" that history can be freed from its apparent moral chaos. Kant's philosophy of history belongs to his practical, not to his theoretical philosophy, since to succumb to our tendency to indulge in teleological judgment would be to submit to a dialectic of illusion.

So perhaps this is the answer to our question about the staying power of the idea of teleology in history. Perhaps our sense of history calls for the kind of wholeness and closure that the classical philosophies of history sought to provide. We want history as a whole to "make sense"— that is, we want it to form a large-scale narrative with a beginning, a middle and an end. Given the temporality of our experience, it seems a natural illusion that we view the past as a series of steps preparing the way for the present. Or alternatively, in a more Marxist perspective, the present is experienced as a decisive turning point or crisis in relation to an immanent goal, calling for immediate action. In either case, history has a direction, an orientation toward some temporal fulfilment, one in which we are important participants. Teleology is "transcendental" in the sense that it is a condition of our temporal experience of the world. But it is an illusion nonetheless.

Bibliography

Bambach, Charles (1995), *Heidegger, Dilthey and Crisis of Historicism*, Ithaca.
Dilthey, Wilhelm (1970), *Der Aufbau der geschichtlichen Welt in den Geisteswissenschaften*, Frankfurt.
Ferguson, Niall (2018), *The Square and the Tower: Networks and Power from the Freemasons to Facebook*, New York.
Fukuyama, Francis (1992), *The End of History and the Last Man*, New York.
Heidegger, Martin (1957), *Sein und Zeit*, Tübingen.
Hegel, G.W.F. (1976), *Vorlesungen über die Philosophie der Geschichte*, Frankfurt.
Hegel, G.W.F. (1988), *Introduction to the Philosophy of History*. Tr. Leo Rauch, Indianapolis.
Husserl, Edmund (1970), *The Crisis of European Sciences and Transcendental Phenomenology*, Tr. D. Carr, Evanston.
Kant, Immanuel (1956), *Kritik der reinen Vernunft*, Hamburg.
Kant, Immanuel (1959), *Kritik der Urteilskraft*, Hamburg.
Kant, Immanuel (1963), *On History*. Ed. L.W. Beck, New York: Macmillan.
Löwith, Karl (1949), *Meaning in History*, Chicago: University of Chicago Press.
Pinker, Steven (2018), *Enlightenment Now: The Case for Reason, Science, Humanism and Progress*, Viking.

Aaron Turner
The Limits of Progress and the Modern Problem of Historical Meaning

1 Introduction

The historian produces history. The question of what history *is* has dominated western thought since at least antiquity. Traditionally, history is produced when the historian sets into relief those aspects of the past that necessarily contribute to an explanation of the *why* of something. In modern historiography, since at least Ranke, the relation of truth and reason coexist within propositional statements about the past. The principle of reason that guides historical enquiry asks why some state of affairs is and why it is necessarily the way it is. Historiography, as both the writing of history and the methodological framework that facilitates the writing of history, is employed toward determining the true reason and, in turn, the correct explanation of some state of affairs. Where the development of the philosophy of history from antiquity to modernity is typically characterised in terms of progress, the tendency in the progress of historiography is toward greater and greater accuracy in the representation and explanation of past events. In search of propositions grounded in definitive truth, it was perhaps inevitable that history would appropriate the measures and methods of the natural sciences in order to legitimate its enterprise.

The history of the philosophy of history since Aristotle represents a conflict between two extreme doctrines: positivism and historicism. Positivism is the attempt to ground all explanations of social, cultural, and historical phenomena according to natural scientific (metaphysical) modes of universally valid truth. Positive history, then, represents the quest for universal laws of history that facilitate the foundation of historical explanation on the basis of absolute truth. Historicism pertains to the understanding that reality itself is fundamentally historical and that truth is relative to the particular historical epoch. Historicism represents the attempt of historical enquiry to emancipate itself from the supervision of metaphysics and the methodologies of the natural sciences. Where the natural sciences seek to generalise, and through generalisation exclude the particular as inessential and identify truths of universal validity, historicism aims precisely at individualisation. Through historicism, reality becomes historical through its individuality and uniqueness. Historicism, then, pertains to relativise truth according to the given epoch (itself unverifiable in terms of length and content).

The decline of both positivism and historicism within the philosophy of history occurred in the mid-20th Century when the insufficiency of both for the task of genuine historical enquiry became clear. The transformation of historicism in the mid-20th Century into pure narrativism radicalised its relativistic truth-conditions and severed historical enquiry from its relationship to past reality itself. The philosophical 'linguistic turn', initiated by Ludwig Wittgenstein and Martin Heidegger, was transposed to the sphere of the philosophy of history by Hayden White, Frank Ankersmit, Louis Mink, among others. Historical narrative, reduced to the definition of 'explanation sketch' by Carl Hempel in the 1940s, became fertile ground for all manner of linguistic and literary interpretative methods. Meanwhile, the advancement of both the social sciences in the mid-20th Century and the diversification of the particular sciences in the late 20th Century led to the realignment of the philosophy of history to the methodological frameworks of scientific enquiry and facilitated the rise of what might now be called the philosophy of scientific historiography.

In this chapter it is argued that both narrativism and the philosophy of scientific historiography, defined in the context of their shift away from the doctrines of, respectively, historicism and positivism, amount to nothing more than the perpetuation of the fundamental principles of truth that guided the initial determination of their precursors. Since the awakening of the modern historical consciousness during the enlightenment the problem of historical meaning has lain dormant throughout the development of the modern philosophy of history. This chapter serves to prepare the way for a reconsideration of the classical historiography as a comportment toward historical meaning and the mode of truth that it entails.

2 The Emergence of Historical Consciousness and the Rise of Historicism

The awakening of modern historical consciousness occurred largely as a result of the Enlightenment's comprehension of an epochal shift away from both antiquity and the middle-ages. Essentially, historical consciousness emerged through the establishment of the concept of culture in western thought in the 18th Century. Fundamentally, culture is the *historical* and the provenance of historical consciousness is *the cultural*. The cultural and the historical are synonymous in the Enlightenment in that there is an equivocation between 'a people without culture' and 'a people without history'. The period of Enlightenment that characterises the

18th Century is itself not a historical category but perceives itself as the perfection of history as civilisation emerged from out of barbarism and socio-political disorder. Historical consciousness, in this context, pertains to a "worldview". A historical worldview is indicative of a historical knowing that produces a complete overview of human affairs. History becomes universal history. While the concept of universal history extends back to antiquity, most famously to Plato, Aristotle, and Polybius, its re-emergence in the Enlightenment looks beyond cycles of generation and decay toward the perfection of history. It looks more broadly toward the solidarity of humankind and identifies this fundamental meaning of human existence as the objective of enlightenment.

Opposition to this teleological conception of the historical process began with Giambattista Vico, who stands on the frontier separating antiquity and modernity. His concept of universal history sustains both the ancient notion of the cyclical and the medieval jurisdiction of the divine but the development of his thought, which culminates in his most significant work, *La Scienza Nuovo* (1725), represents one of the most significant contributions to the modern philosophy of history. Universalism, for Vico, involves grasping common features that make history intelligible. He calls his 'new science' "a rational civil theology of divine providence".[1] Divine providence in this context excludes the possibility of the divine directly influencing human affairs. It rather promotes the agency of God in directing the broader historical processes so that humanity is guided toward the realisation of God's plan. For Vico, history as a science identifies universal patterns of change within the historical process.

> Not the particular history in time of the laws and deeds of the Romans or the Greeks, but the ideal eternal history of the eternal laws which are instanced by the deeds of all nations in their rise, progress, maturity, decadence, and dissolution, even if there were infinite worlds being born from time to time throughout eternity.[2]

From his metahistorical perspective, Vico develops a cyclical understanding of history whereby the preconditions of a civilisation's decline are intrinsic elements within the process of its generation.

As early as 1710, Vico had recognised the possibility of a human science distinct from the measures and methodologies of the natural sciences. Vico opposed the traditional Cartesian notion of truth that dominated metaphysical thought. For Vico, the universal, scientific methods of the natural sciences were not

---

[1] Vico, *NS* 2, 342, 385.
[2] *NS* 1096.

equipped to derive truths relative to certain cultures of diverse character. Vico's revolutionary understanding of pluralism represents the inception of historicism.

Vico's confrontation with Cartesian truth laid the groundwork for Johann Gottfried Herder's all-encompassing assault on the traditional concept of a universal, standardised mode truth that enabled his contemporaries to observe the course of history as a unified whole embodying the cultivation of humanity in its progression towards the enlightenment of the 18th Century. Through Herder, historical consciousness arrived at a critical and decisive insight. Herder was deeply influenced by Immanuel Kant, who acted as mentor to Herder during their time at Königsberg, but his understanding of universal history was fundamentally divergent from Kant's. For Kant, history pertains to a *telos* of moral perfection that is accomplished through humanity's pursuit of freedom under law. Herder, though, rejected the schematically linear progress of history that develops in stages from out of barbarism toward enlightened rationality. He identified, conversely, within historical reality the irrational divergence of normative standards and truths across different cultures and epochs. All of David Hume, Voltaire, Jean le Rond d'Alembert, Isaak Iselin, and Jean-Jacques Rousseau, who each developed to varying degrees an understanding of the present age as 'the highest peak of humanity', fell under the critical gaze of Herder's historicism.

While Vico and Herder, as well as Friedrich Schleiermacher, who, similarly recognised the fundamental relativity of cultural and epochal truths that divested history of its universalism, were highly influential figures in the 19th Century, it was the impact of Kant's three *Critiques* that would be most strongly impact proceedings. Kant's rejection of British Empiricism, particularly John Locke and Hume, was based on its incapacity to ground the apodictic character of universality that Kant conceived as the fundamental ground of normative truth. Kant, identifying within consciousness itself a pure logic of transcendental understanding, turned philosophy into epistemology. Through his 'Copernican revolution', which consisted of reversing the traditional Cartesian understanding that the mind should accommodate itself to the object, Kant effected one of the most significant paradigm shifts in the history of western philosophy. Through the 'Copernican dictum', Kant laid the groundwork for a German Idealism delivered through Friedrich Schelling, Johann Gottlieb Fichte, and most significantly, Georg Wilhelm Friedrich Hegel. Furthermore, by placing the problem of knowledge on the constitution of a world by a human subject, Kant provided a broader framework for anthropological studies and, ultimately, facilitated the development of the human sciences in the late 19th Century.

Where Fichte and Schelling continued Kantian metaphysics under the banner of German Idealism to varying successes, it was Hegel who radicalised its fundamental principles. German Idealism dominated western thought for the first half of the 19th Century. Its reformulation through Hegel fulfilled its directive but laid the foundations of its inevitable decline. This decline coincided with the gradual development of specialised disciplines grounded in empirical research. It is at this critical juncture that the manifold complexities of historical thought began to unfold. Under the auspices of a 'naturalistic worldview', whereby the principles of the natural sciences revealed the machinations of reality as a totality, theories of historical explanation began to systematise themselves according to these extra-empirical principles. The scientification of historiography had, since before even Vico and Herder, dominated historical discourse. The monumental advances the natural sciences underwent in the 19th Century propagated similar advancements in historical thought, owing primarily to the concept of absolute truth that enabled the natural sciences to exercise authority. The bifurcation of empirical historical research in the mid-19th Century between Rankean inductive empiricism and neo-Kantian epistemology renewed historicism's conflict with the ubiquitous expansion of positivism.

Following Herder and Schleiermacher, Wilhelm van Humboldt developed a concept of historical methodology that would lay the foundations of what become known as scientific historiography. Humboldt directed historical research away from the metaphysical speculative methodologies of the natural sciences toward an empirical reality distinct from the laws and processes of the natural world. Subsequently, philological, textual criticism became the benchmark of Barthold Georg Niebuhr's critical method of historical understanding. Between them, Humboldt and Niebuhr facilitated the emergence of a new mode of historical research: inductive textual criticism.

The next step, one of the most significant in the history of the philosophy of history, was taken by Leopold von Ranke. He articulated an understanding of textual, documentary criticism on the grounds that the foundation of history, *contra* Hegel, could not be constructed according to *a priori* principles like progress or reason. Rather, Ranke determined that owing to the individual richness and particular properties of any given age (*Zeitalter*), its 'guiding tendencies' must be deduced from exact and rigorous archival research. Through the reconstruction of history *wie es eigentlich gewesen*, normative standards of truth relative to the given *Zeitalter* are revealed. Ranke maintained through the elucidation of world history according to its principle parts the notion of universal history. He was one of the most prominent voices of the 19th Century in calling for historical enquiry to emancipate itself from the mechanistic methods of the natural sciences.

Ranke's assertion that historiography could adequately re-present the past 'as it really happened' became a fundamental principle of historical writing until its transition into narrativism in the mid-20th Century.

3 Historicism and Narrativism

The 'linguistic turn' of the mid-20th Century, initiated by Martin Heidegger and Ludwig Wittgenstein and transposed to the sphere of the philosophy of history by the likes of Hayden White, Arthur Danto, Richard Rorty, and Louis Mink, significantly altered the landscape of historiographical interpretation. The linguistic turn arose from both Wittgenstein's and Heidegger's conception of language as the only possible platform upon which an understanding of truth and reality can be founded. Through White's seminal work, *Metahistory* (1973), the postmodern challenge breached traditional historiography. White, challenging the views of Hegel, Nietzsche, and Croce that history operates fundamentally differently to literature, developed a rhetorical theory of historical explanation that subordinated the traditional '*wie es eigentlich gewesen*' character of history to the invocation of meaning summoned through narrative, literary, and aesthetic tropes. As Iggers wrote of this challenge, "The basic idea of postmodern theory of historiography is the denial that historical writing refers to an actual historical past".[3] History, a product of creative forces and devoid of any actual relation to the past itself, fell under the auspices of literary theory. Naturally, the traditional format for documenting history, narrative, was particularly scrutinised. The possibility of narrative as a vehicle for historical explanation has since Ranke been questioned owing primarily to its seemingly arbitrary capacity to reduce historical events to a single chain of causes and consequences.

The linguistic turn allowed for the exculpation of this format, and Arthur Danto's defence of historical narrative was highly significant. Danto identifies the perfect being for the task historical enquiry: the Ideal Chronicler. According to Danto:

> [The ideal chronicler] knows whatever happens the moment it happens, even in other minds. He is also to have the gift of instantaneous transcription: everything that happens across the whole forward rim of the Past is set down by him, as it happens, the way it happens.[4]

---

[3] Iggers 1997, 118.
[4] Danto 2007, 149.

The Ideal Chronicler accomplishes the impossible Rankean task of presenting the past *wie es eigentlich gewesen*. The incalculable and limitless multiplicity that constitutes historical reality is transcribed and archived *ad infinitum*. The problem of history is solved.

Danto immediately clarifies and diminishes the activity of the Ideal Chronicler by suggesting that, for historical purposes, an absolute and inexhaustible account of everything that has ever happened *is not enough*.

> There is a class of descriptions of any event under which the event cannot be witnessed, and these descriptions are necessarily and systematically excluded from the Ideal Chronicle. The whole truth concerning an event can only be known after, and sometimes only long after the event itself has taken place, and this part of the story historians alone can tell. It is something even the best sort of witness cannot know. What we deliberately neglected to equip the Ideal Chronicler with was knowledge of the future.[5]

For Danto, the function of the historian resides in the capacity to identify meaning or significance within historical events but only through retrospection. He develops the concept of 'narrative sentences', the general characteristic of which is it describes an event with reference to later events. A narrative sentence concerns the present but refers to the actual subsequent course of events.[6] The sentence 'the Thirty Years War began 1618' concerns the beginning of the war and could not be described as such prior to 1948. Such a statement refers to two distinct and time-separated events. William Dray remarks that "it is a judgement which could be regarded as typically historical, since it introduces a kind of retrospective intelligibility ... it clearly does this by *connecting* facts or events at different times".[7] The principle of selection of events that constitute the narrative is grounded in the realisation of the significance or meaning the historian identifies as necessitating the composition of the narrative in the first place. The narrative is structured toward elucidating the historical meaning that the historian recognises.[8] In forming a narrative, then, the historian sets into relief those historically meaningful particularities while omitting the meaningless differences.

---

5 Danto 2007, 151.
6 Ibid. 165–180.
7 Dray 1971, 159.
8 Cf. Carr 1986, 29: "The counterpart of the chronicler at the level of small-scale events would be the radio announcer giving us a live description of a baseball game: 'There's the pitch ... the batter swings ... line drive to centre-field!' etc. The story of the game, by contrast, is told afterwards and in full knowledge of who won. It will mention only the most important events, especially those that contributed to scoring points and thus to the outcome. All else will be eliminated, except perhaps for touches of human interest or comic relief".

Danto evinces an understanding of relativistic truth similar to that pertaining to historicism. He argues that narrative sentences indicate a mode of truth contingent on the *intensional* meaning and context that the historian imbues within them. Such meaning or significance is not encountered by the people whom the narrative sentence is about. As Ankersmit remarks, "People living in a certain historical epoch experience their world directly, that is to say, in the light of the beliefs they hold to be true".[9] It is the purpose of the historian to imbue such beliefs with meaning and through such intension to construct a representation of this world.

> And something of the same sort is true for the historical period considered as an entity. It is a period solely from the perspective of the historian, who sees it from without; for those who lived in the period it would be just the way life was lived. And asked, afterwards, what is was like to have lived then, they may answer from the outside, from the historian's perspective. From the inside there is no answer to be given; it was simply the way things were. So when the members of a period can give an answer in terms satisfactory to the historian, the period will have exposed its outward surface and in a sense be over, as a period.[10]

For Danto, then, only through the historian's retrospection can a historical event be understood. The full significance of the event is unknown to its participants, who may act with forethought to bring about the occasion of the event, or of course to prevent its occurrence and thus producing the realisation of a completely different event, but ultimately the actor is oblivious to the full significance of the event in its historical context.

The gift of hindsight that Danto bestows upon the Ideal Chronicler and his determination of 'narrative sentences' signalled a profound development in the philosophy of narrativism. The process of the configuration of narratives grounded in hindsight allows for historical explanations to be proceed backwards from a definitive endpoint in search of the origins and circumstances that led to its realisation. Paul Ricœur, in particular, recognised the importance of Danto's thesis. He argued that in such 'retrodiction' we begin "from the fact that something has happened, we infer, backward through time, that the antecedent necessary condition must have occurred and we look for its traces in the present".[11] For Ricœur, the understanding of history as literature allowed for the cultivation of causal explanations distinct from scientific equivalents. He does, though, differentiate between 'necessary' causes and 'sufficient' causes, whereby

---

9 Ankersmit 2009, 203.
10 Danto 2007, 183.
11 Ricœur 1984, 135.

the former signifies why-did explanations and the latter indicates how-possible explanations.

> We respond to the question "Why did such a state necessarily happen?" in terms of a sufficient condition. On the other hand, we respond to the question "How was it possible for such a state to occur?" in terms of a necessary, but not sufficient, condition.[12]

In Ricœur's estimation of both necessary and sufficient causes, the element of prediction that presupposes scientific causal explanations remains intact. Ricœur, more radical than any of his contemporaries, seemingly aimed at conflating both history-as-literature and history-as-science. Such views, though, alienate Ricœur from the emerging doctrine of narrativism propagated by the likes of Mink, White, and Ankersmit.

Where the concept of history-as-literature has given way to numerous developments within the philosophy of historiography, such as narratology (Todorov, Barthes, Genette, etc.) and experientiality (Carr, Grethlein), the recent emergence of 'postnarrativism' represents the next radical step. Conforming to the distinction between history as the past itself and historiography established by the linguistic turn, Jouni-Matti Kuukkanen predicates postnarrativism on the definition of historiography as "the philosophical study of the results of inquiries about history, including history writing, the investigation of evidence and other epistemic questions (that may precede writing) as well as the central concepts and other structuring elements of historiographical presentation".[13] While Kuukkanen adheres to the core narrativist principles of constructivism and anti-realism, he questions the truth-claims of historiographical theses.

> There is a *morphological* or *structural* difference between the historian's presentation and historical reality, which explains why any idea of copying or matching between the two is fundamentally misconceived. One simply cannot make two structurally totally different entities correspond with each other. Elephants cannot be made to correspond with butterflies due to the obvious structural difficulties. The historian's narrative is verbal and textual, while historical reality is non-narrative and non-verbal in nature.[14]

Ultimately, Kuukkanen's objective is to demonstrate the incapacity of historians to colligate concepts, that is, to cluster events together under nominal headings such as the Renaissance or the Classical period. What is clear, though, is that the

---

12 Ibid. 135.
13 Kuukkanen 2015, 6.
14 Ibid. 42.

concerns of narrativism resonate closely to the concerns of the modern philosophy of scientific historiography.

4 Positive History

The methodological dogmatism of the natural sciences dominated historical enquiry until the awakening of historical consciousness in the 18th Century. Since at least Plato and Aristotle and until the end of the 19th Century, the classification of the sciences in western thought had undergone constant revision. Plato's tripartite division of dialectics, physics, and ethics survived Aristotle's system of formal logic and carried on into Leibniz' system, which established physics, moral sciences, and logic as the 'three great provinces' of science. Descartes' dichotomy between the physical and the spiritual — between the inner workings of the mind and the external, physical world — eventually became the metaphysical grounding for all sciences. By the 19th Century, the division between the natural sciences (*Naturwissenschaften*) and the human sciences (*Geisteswissenschaften*) prevailed over western thought. Until the neo-Kantian development of the historical sciences in the 19th Century the mode of truth that predominated over historical enquiry pertained to the absolute truth of *Naturwissenschaften*. Such truth has the character of universal validity. How could history, whose domain encompasses the boundless realm of particularity and uniqueness, possibly aspire to such determinations? That such a doctrine of truth dominated western thought since at least Plato rendered the mission of *Naturwissenschaften* as superior to that of *Geisteswissenschaften*. The insecure status of history was founded initially on Aristotle's denouncement of historical enquiry as the domain of the particular (ἡ δ' ἱστορία τὰ καθ' ἕκαστον λέγει) (*Poetics* 1451b.5–9).

The understanding of general laws that drive the historical process extend back at least as far as Vico. Through Montesquieu, Comte, Herder, Hegel, Marx, and Spengler, the idea of historical laws has been a central feature of historiographical explanation. Ultimately, the identification of such laws laid bare the *truth* of the causal mechanisms of history and thus enabled the possibility of producing universally valid statements about the past. By the end of the 1960s, the idea of laws in history had all but been extinguished. Where philosophers such as Karl Popper and Isaiah Berlin condemned the notion of historical determinism, the philosophy of history dissociated itself from the natural sciences and embraced the linguistic turn. Until the late 20th Century, the fundamental mission of the natural sciences was to determine the universal laws from which deductions can be made regarding any specific event. For the methodologies produced by causal theorists such as Hempel, Popper, and Oppenheim, the historical particular was utterly redundant.

Where Carl Hempel's reduction of the historical particular seemingly plunged history into yet another identity crisis as it struggled to establish and maintain itself as a science, already between the 1940s and 1960s philosophers of history were questioning the reducibility of historical events to general laws of history. This represented a shift away from the laws of Newtonian determinism and Marxist doctrines of dialectical materialism. The philosophy of scientific historiography stagnated somewhat until the 1990s. The issue though, according to Laudan, was the philosophy of history's intransigence against moving with the times.

> Philosophers of history ... failed to keep pace with change in cognate disciplines ... [and] have not incorporated the results of the extensive research on theory of explanation carried out since Hempel's pioneering work, research that might significantly alter their analysis of history.[15]

While the philosophy of science moved on to consider questions of validity within reconstructions of natural phenomena, the philosophy of history continued to toil in its concerns for forms of explanations. It was this stagnation of thought within the philosophy of scientific historiography that led to its decline within mainstream philosophy. its re-emergence and subsequent development, contiguous with the philosophy of science's accelerated interest in the particularity of dynamic and nonlinear complex systems, produced novel determinations of abstract concepts such as necessity, contingency, teleology, colligation, probability, and causation (processual, exceptional, conditional, etc.).

The rise of the philosophy of scientific historiography occurred in part due to the modern developments of the social and theoretical sciences but also in part as a response to the authority that the philosophy of language now exercised over historical enquiry. Aviezer Tucker, a strong advocate of scientific historiography, calls for the removal of linguistic-based philosophy within historiographical discourse. His book, he asserts, "calls for the liberation of the philosophy of historiography from imperialist ambitions of partisans of other philosophical debates".[16] Following Peter Kosso's suggestion that the relation between evidence and historiography is not distinct from the relation between evidence and theory in the sciences,[17] Tucker argues:

---

15 Laudan 1992, 55–67.
16 Tucker 2004, 8.
17 Kosso 1992, 21–36.

> A misleading analogy between historiographic descriptions of past events and scientific descriptions of evidence led to the common mistake that since historians cannot observe historical events, knowledge of history can never be scientific. Yet, descriptions of historical events in historiography are as theoretical as descriptions of electrons are in physical theory.[18]

What remains problematic in the philosophy of scientific historiography, however, are those same issues that prefigured the identity crisis of history between its systematisation of historiographical method of the mid-19th Century and its characterisation as literature subject to literary methods a century later.

Nietzsche once wrote, "It is not the victory of science that distinguishes our 19th Century, but the victory of scientific method over science" (*Will to Power*, 466). Such could be said about modern scientific historiography. The development of the social sciences and the reformation of the natural sciences in latter half of the 20th Century coalesced to breathe new life into the philosophy of history over the past thirty years. Transposing the reduction of human motivation from laws governed by a static, a-historical human nature to abstract conceptual schematics, though, offers little in the way of genuine historical enquiry. Tucker argues against the claims of prominent historical thinkers such as Dilthey, Collingwood, Gadamer, Apel, Berlin, and Habermas, who concur that, in Berlin's words, "to say of history that it should approximate to the condition of a science is to ask it to contradict its essence".[19] Tucker retorts that he is "not acquainted with the essences of historiography or history and [doubts] there are any".[20] For Tucker, knowledge of the past has been expanded through the discoveries of scientific historiography.

> When historians reach an uncoerced, uniquely heterogeneous and large consensus on historiography, the best explanation is that they possess knowledge of the past. When one historiographic common cause hypothesis is clearly superior to all its alternatives, when it increases the likelihood of a broad scope of evidence, it generates a sufficient degree of belief in it, similar to that we have in everyday facts.[21]

Such historical knowledge, however, is still predicated on an empirical principle of systematisation, namely, the establishment of facts whose authority relies on questionable 'truth-conditions', abstract concepts, and definitive modes of

---

18 Tucker 2004, 8.
19 Berlin 1960, 31.
20 Tucker 2004, 210.
21 Tucker 2004, 257.

knowledge. Ultimately, the foundations of the philosophy of scientific historiography in the 21st Century are laid on the same principles that grounded history's turn to scientific methodology in the late 19th Century.

Despite its self-proclaimed 'progress', history in its modern scientific sense, encompassing both the 19th century scientification of history according to the universal laws of the natural sciences and the current reliance on complex systems theory to justify the application of abstract concepts to historical events, amounts to nothing more than a calculative reckoning. In both history-as-science and modern scientific historiography, historical enquiry is characterised as an explanation of the past conforming to the universal process of cause and effect. The problem of historical meaning is the problem of historical truth. Therefore by admitting that

5 Classical Historiography

The development of scientific historiography from the 19th Century onwards and the implication of 'progress' that defined its attachment to universal values of truth rendered ancient historiography obsolete within the modern philosophy of history. Following the linguistic turn, however, ancient historians, buoyed by the possibilities that modern literary criticism offered to the study of classical historiography, embraced this new development. One of the most successful models pertaining to the interpretation of ancient historical writing was narratology, developed primarily by Genette, Barthes, and Todorov. Toward the end of the 20th Century narratology began to dominate classical scholarship through the likes of de Jong, Hornblower, and Rood.

One of the most controversial developments in the history of classical scholarship occurred on account of this new linguistic trend. Anthony Woodman's 1988 study, *Rhetoric in Classical Historiography*, attempted to reclassify ancient historiography by undermining its core principle of truth. He wrote:

> Historiography was regarded by the ancients as not essentially different from poetry: each was a branch of rhetoric, and therefore historiography, like poetry, employs the concepts associated with, and relies upon the expectations generated by, a rhetorical genre.[22]

---

[22] Woodman 1988, x.

For Woodman, as well as Wiseman,[23] rhetorical education superseded the seeking of truth that traditionally characterised the fundamental aim of ancient historiography.[24] Ernst Badian summarised the sentiment when he wrote that "Thucydides' method of presentation is more like that of the journalist than like that of the historian" owing to the fact that Thucydides "edited" his material and only what he deemed "fit to print" was recorded.[25]

The charge against ancient historiography as 'journalistic' or 'not essentially different from poetry' was strongly contested by J.E Lendon, who launched a strong invective against the emerging conception of ancient historiography as literature.

> Wiseman and Woodman freed the study of ancient historical texts from the mortification of being a discipline ancillary to history, like the study of ancient inscriptions. No longer would the humble historiographer supply Hamburger Helper at the historians' barbecue. The Latin historians were made available to "real" classicists and their literary methods; Wiseman and Woodman's conclusions fitted too with Hayden White's fashionable reduction of history to a function of literature ... young classicists [following Wiseman and Woodman] saw in the literary study of historians a road to lofty elevation.[26]

Lendon attempts in his essay to ground the concept of historical truth within the relationship between historian and reader. Quoting Quintillian, who wrote "history is written for telling, not proving" (*Inst.* 10.1.31), Lendon suggests that the purpose of the ancient historians is to "relate a series of events without telling his reader where he got the information about them, or stopping to say why his reader should believe him: a convention that only works if the reader already accepts that the truthfulness of what he is being told is pre-emptively vouched for by the genre of the work he is reading".[27]

Like the modern idea of history, the treatment of classical historiography, as evidenced through the case of Lendon vs. Woodman, remains locked in an identity crisis. Where the problem of historical meaning is the problem of historical truth, and where all of historicism, positivism, narrativism, and the philosophy of scientific historiography have failed to identify the essence of historical truth, either by paving over it with endless methodologies or by relativising it into oblivion, retroactive applications of such approaches have collaterally concealed the

---

23 Wiseman 1979.
24 Cf. Master 2016, 18: "In Woodman's reading, plausibility, not veracity, was ancient historiography's guiding principle".
25 Badian 1993, 127. Cf. Hunter (1973), who titles her monograph *Thucydides: the Artful Reporter*.
26 Lendon ('Historians without History: Against Roman Historiography', 56–57).
27 Ibid, 55.

possibility of an ancient engagement with historical meaning. What other avenues remain open?

6 The Essence of Historicity

Having outlined broadly the general trajectory of historical thought from its origins in modern historical consciousness to its current situation within the domains of narrativism and the philosophy of scientific historiography, as well as the trend of modern approaches to classical historiography symptomatic of these developments, it would be worth considering, before a brief engagement with Thucydides, the character of 'historicity' that emerged in 19th Century Germany.

The decline of German Idealism in the mid-19th Century signalled the gradual deterioration of metaphysical thought in western philosophy. The shift of the natural sciences away from metaphysics was epitomised by predominance of a new 'naturalistic world-view' in the 1860s and 1870s that sought to explain all natural processes according to the construction of laws. It was this development that culminated in Hempel's *coup de grâce* of the historical particular in the 1940s. Against the rise of scientific, law-based historical understanding stood the neo-Kantian doctrine of German Historism. Following Aristotle's broad exclusion of history from his theory of knowledge, the development of the history of philosophy as the metaphysical pursuit of the fundamental principle of reason has largely been conducted ahistorically. Hegel, though, disagreed with Kant's conception of reason as ahistorical and held that, in fact, history is rational and thus, in opposition to his philosophical predecessors, cognisable. Even Augustine, who conceived of history as eschatological, thought it was not cognisable as to know history would be to know the mind of God. For Hegel, if human action, as goal-orientated in the Aristotelian sense, is rational, then it follows that history, which is the record of human action, is also rational and therefore cognisable. Like Hegel, Dilthey attempted to overcome Kant's ahistorical view of reason. In developing his critique of historical reason, Dilthey grounds the principle of reason in life itself and, like Hegel, understands people as intentional beings. He takes experience (*Erlebnis*) as the foundation of objective knowledge within in the social sciences and therefore grounds historical knowledge not in scientific method but in lived experience. For Dilthey, the human being itself is historical and understands itself according to its own historicity, and thus a comprehension of historical reason can only be attained through hermeneutical enquiry.

While hermeneutics initially stood, as for Augustine and Luther, as the means of interpreting holy texts, Friedrich Schleiermacher became the first to systematise hermeneutics as a universal and scientific theory of understanding. While historiographers such as Ranke and Humboldt appropriated Schleiermacher's hermeneutics to serve their own new brand of source criticism, Dilthey identified in it a new possibility for the emerging human sciences. Through Schleiermacher, Dilthey developed a model of hermeneutics that sought to interpret experience through 'recorded expression', which extended from written texts to artefacts, painting, etc. Dilthey attempted to develop a hermeneutic methodology that grasps the experience of others through analogy with self-experience, which itself is understood historically.

> We are mainly aware of the inner life of others only through the impact of our gestures, sounds, and acts on our senses. We have to reconstruct the inner source of the signs which strike our senses. Everything: material, structure, even the most individual features of this reconstruction, have to be supplied by transferring them from our own lives.[28]

For Dilthey, what is given to us in our consciousness is the totality of our being, and thus it is only through self-consciousness that we can begin to understand the experience, and thus the reason, of others.

It was precisely through the fundamental character of Dilthey's methodology, though, that his successors would expose the inadequacies of his philosophy of history. For both Heidegger and Gadamer, Dilthey's hermeneutic methodology upheld the prevailing Cartesian tradition of scientific knowledge that is simply incompatible with what Heidegger calls 'facticity'. That is, the factical existence of *Dasein* (there-being) as "*there* for itself in the 'how' of its ownmost being".[29] Like Dilthey, Heidegger emphasises the temporal particularity of the human being. Unlike Dilthey, Heidegger develops a hermeneutics that is the *self-interpretation* of *Dasein* in its own facticity. For Heidegger, modern historical thinking had become trapped within the confines of its own methodological rules. He distinguished between historical reflection on the one hand and historiographical consideration on the other.

The points of view of historiography toward the past are very arbitrary, and insofar as historiography as a science is concerned, they are chosen and evaluated primarily according to whether, and how far, they promote new historiographical cognitions, i.e., insofar as they enhance the progress of the science... Historiography is bound by past facts, interpreted in a certain way each time; historical reflection, however, is bound by that happening on the basis of which facts can arise and can be in the first place. Historical reflection is subject to a

---

[28] Dilthey [1900] 1976, 261.
[29] Heidegger 2008, 5.

higher and more rigorous law than historiography is, although it might seem, judging by appearances, that the reverse obtains.[30]

Fundamentally, Heidegger sought to deconstruct the enduring fallacy of the possibility of a historical science that dominated 19th Century thought and culminated in Dilthey's hermeneutic method, which was later advanced beyond recognition by Windelband and Rickert. For Heidegger, authentic historical thinking must transcend the basic assumption that the historical process obeys logical patterns that are themselves accessible through an empirically verifiable procedure. Heidegger's project was to overcome the traditional subject-object dichotomy that had endured since the inception of Platonic metaphysics by developing a new hermeneutical mode of disclosing being within the context of its own historicity.[31]

While Heidegger was by no means a philosopher of history in the traditional sense, his early criticisms of Dilthey and the German Historist tradition as well as the development of his own hermeneutics of facticity had a profound effect on the growth of historical thinking in the 20th Century. The philosophical hermeneutics of Hans-Georg Gadamer, who attended Heidegger's lectures on the hermeneutics of facticity in 1923 and was deeply influenced by Heidegger's historical ontology, is one such consequence. For Gadamer, true method is the "action of the thing itself".[32] It is not an arbitrary system of rules and procedures arranged in order to elucidate the content of something or another. For Gadamer, hermeneutics was not a theoretical enterprise, but practical. He said that "what I taught above all was hermeneutic praxis. Hermeneutics is above all a practice, the art of understanding and of making something understood to someone else".[33] In this sense, Gadamer' comprehension of the understanding is fundamentally dialogical and therefore structured by language. Gadamer completes the ontological turn of hermeneutics that Heidegger initiated by establishing in the place of traditional historicism a historically conscious hermeneutic grounded in both 'prejudice' and 'tradition'.

However, where hermeneutics had once firmly stood as the ground of interpretative methodologies, the ontological turn led by Heidegger and Gadamer left its foundations in ruin. For Paul Ricœur, the development of this ontological her-

---

30 Heidegger 1994, 46.
31 On Heidegger's concept of nihilism as the fulfilment of metaphysics through the culmination of Platonic idealism within Nietzsche's 'revaluation of all values', see Turner 2019, 369–394.
32 Gadamer 1990, 459.
33 Gadamer 2007, 21.

meneutics was a double-edged sword. On the one hand, the emergence of a hermeneutics of existence itself was highly instructive, but on the other hand, Heidegger and Gadamer had severed hermeneutics from its capacity to ground genuine historical inquiry.[34] In the wake of both Hempel's destruction of the historical particular and the demise of historicism at the hands of Heidegger and Gadamer, one of the major focuses of the philosophy of history was the capacity of narrative to adequately explain history. The growth of narrativism took on this responsibility, but where narrativism severs historical enquiry from past reality, and where ontological hermeneutics detaches itself from the possibility of conducting historiographical enquires, the problem of historical meaning endures.

7 Thucydides and the Problem of Historical Meaning

An extended investigation of ancient historical truth falls outside the jurisdiction and office of this chapter. What follows, though, is a contextualisation of Thucydides in terms of the current status of historical thought. In short, how can a reading of Thucydides expose the inherent flaws of the modern philosophy of history and to what extent can a study of ancient historiography *on its own terms* comport modern historical thinkers toward more fruitful avenues of enquiry.

Thucydides' self-presentation throughout the narrative suggests that he identifies his own vocation as being in line with that of Danto's Ideal Chronicler. He qualifies his "gift of instantaneous transcription" with the contention that he began documenting the Peloponnesian War "when they first took up arms, believing that it would be great and memorable above any previous war" (1.1.1). The narrative itself proceeds according to an annalistic structure, which gives the impression that each division is being composed as the war progresses. Pertaining to the Ideal Chronicler's precise explanation of 'what happens, the *way* it happens', Thucydides is equal to the task.

> Of the events of the war I have not ventured to speak from any chance information, nor according to any notion of my own; I have described nothing but what I either saw myself, or learned from others of whom I made the most careful and particular enquiry (1.22.2–4).

---

[34] Ricœur 1984.

Even regarding the Ideal Chronicler's preternatural ability to penetrate 'other minds', Thucydides is similarly prescient. Through logical inference he is able to "put into the mouth of each speaker the sentiments proper to the occasion, expressed as I thought he would be likely to express them, while at the same time I endeavoured, as nearly as I could, to give the general purport of what was actually said" (1.22.1). Thucydides, then, presents himself as an ideal chronicler, as a pursuant of truth and accuracy, as an objective witness of historical events, as they occur, whose sole purpose is documentation and elucidation.

While Thucydides' narrative of the war is entirely diachronic, notwithstanding the various historical digressions that frequent the account, he does betray at times his knowledge of the war's eventual conclusion. For instance, section 2.65, to which the subject passage of this essay belongs, is entirely devoted to outlining the nature of the cause of the Athenian defeat. Elsewhere he states that the war lasted twenty-seven years until "the destruction of the Athenian empire and the taking of Piraeus and the Long Walls by the Lacedaemonians and their allies" (5.26.1). It could be asked, to what extent is the shape of Thucydides' narrative determined by his fore knowledge of its ultimate conclusion? Are specific events selected and emphasised in order to demonstrate the significance of their contribution to this outcome? According to Danto's concept of the Ideal Chronicler, it is precisely this service which such knowledge commissions. To reiterate Carr's baseball analogy that is fully quoted above, "The story of the game, by contrast, is told afterwards and in full knowledge of who won. It will mention only the most important events, especially those that contributed ... to the outcome".[35]

In the case of Thucydides, the most 'important events' are relatively easy to pinpoint in the narrative. If a war is the sum of the battles that constitute it, then Thucydides' narrative of the Peloponnesian War definitively highlights the various battles that led to Spartan victory. The naval conquest of the Spartans over the Athenians at Aegospotami could well be considered the decisive battle as it resulted in the blockade of the Piraeus and, consequently, the Athenian surrender. Of course, this event took place after Thucydides' narrative broke off in 411, but Thucydides was obviously aware of it. Had Thucydides completed his narrative, it would not have been surprising to see the following narrative sentence conclude his account of the battle: 'The Athenian defeat at Aegospotami resulted in Athens eventual surrender to the Spartans'. Such a scenario might well be predicted but this statement could not have been uttered at the time precisely because nobody knew that the Spartans would blockade the city and starve the

---

35 See n. 8.

Athenians into submission. It is a narrative sentence because it forms a connection between two time-separated events. The connection speaks for itself. The function of the historian is to explicate it. For Danto, though, this explication represents the limit of the historian. Even with knowledge of the future, the historian is unable to produce an *understanding* of events, only an explanation.

How does Thucydides stand in relation to both positivism and the more recent philosophy of scientific historiography? Where Danto introduced the idea of an Ideal Chronicler armed with retrospection through which a meaningful narrative could be carved into relief from the chaos of an infinite multitude of past realities, in the domain of positivism, Pierre-Simon Laplace, considering the nature of inductive reasoning and probabilities, identified his own ideal entity for the purpose of scientific enquiry. He writes:

> We ought then to regard the present state of the universe as the effect of its anterior state and as the cause of the one which is to follow. Given for one instant an intelligence which could comprehend all the forces by which nature is animated and the respective situation of the beings who compose it — an intelligence sufficiently vast to submit these data to analysis — it would embrace in the same formula the movements of the greatest bodies of the universe and those of the lightest atom; for it, nothing would be uncertain and the future, as the past, would be present to its eyes.[36]

Laplace's Demon represents the ideal scientist. Until the late 20th Century, the fundamental mission of the natural sciences was to determine the universal laws from which deductions can be made regarding any specific event. Laplace's Demon is equipped with a functional understanding of these universal laws. If transposed to the sphere of the historical, Laplace's Demon produces judgments grounded in the principle of reason that guides historical enquiry, which asks why some state of affairs is and why it is necessarily the way it is. Following Aristotle's priority of σοφία over φρόνησις, the relation of truth and necessity became *the* fundamental principle underlying scientific, and consequently historical, understanding and explanation. For the methodologies produced by causal theorists such as Hempel, Popper, and Oppenheim, for whom the historical particular was utterly redundant, Laplace's Demon represents the supreme being. Both in regards the underlying knowledge of the laws of a fixed and constant human nature and the various causal mechanisms that constitute modern complex systems theories.

---

[36] Laplace [1814] 1902, 4.

To what extent does Thucydides demonstrate similar tendencies to Laplace's Demon? In the above quote, Laplace emphasises the omniscience of the supratemporal being: "nothing would be uncertain and the future, as the past, would be present to its eyes". For this vast intelligence, particularity is a *quantité négligeable*. What is 'present to its eyes' are the universal mechanics that govern and determine nature or, in a historical context, the various causal mechanisms that bring about historical change. Thucydides defines his *History* as "a true picture of the events which have happened, and of the like events which may be expected to happen hereafter in the order of human things (τὸ ἀνθρώπινον)" (1.22.4). Thucydides and his speakers frequently refer to an underlying human nature (ἀνθρώπεια φύσις) that resides beneath the thinly veiled façade of social relations (Cf. 1.76.4; 2.50.1; 3.82.2; 84.2). At 1.22.4, Thucydides' concern is not simply the demonstration of events that constitute the Peloponnesian War but the probability of similar future events based on the universal human condition. In the following passage, Thucydides differentiates between the 'publicly alleged reasons' (φανερὸν λεγόμεναι αἰτίαι) that led to the outbreak of the war and the 'truest cause' (ἀληθεστάτη πρόφασις) of the war (1.23.6). While the former concerns the various disputes and events that precipitated the conflict, the latter outlines the underlying mechanism that prompted Spartan hostilities.

> The truest cause (ἀληθεστάτην πρόφασιν), though least spoken, I believe to have been the growth of Athenian power (τοὺς Ἀθηναίους μεγάλους γιγνομένους), which, exciting fear (φόβον παρέχοντας) in the Spartans, necessitated them to war (ἀναγκάσαι ἐς τὸ πολεμεῖν) (1.23.6).

It seems entirely likely that the mechanism that Thucydides describes here pertains to the structure of τὸ ἀνθρώπινον that he signals in the previous passage. Armed with this knowledge of the universal structure of human nature, nothing would be uncertain and the future, as the past, would be present to Thucydides' eyes.

According to this brief assessment, Thucydides comports himself to the fundamental principles of both Danto's Ideal Chronicler and Laplace's demon. On the one hand, Thucydides identifies his task as conveying the events of the war in their entirety as they really happened. On the other hand, he lays claims to understanding the universal character of the human condition that, he asserts, drives the historical process. That is, Thucydides lays claims to understanding the underlying metaphysical structure of history itself. Could it then be argued that Thucydides, invoking both the Ideal Chronicler and Laplace's Demon, develops a historical understanding of the Peloponnesian War by retrospectively analysing the major events of the war according to an innate comprehension of human nature, thus documenting the cause and course of the war according to the laws of ἀνθρώπεια φύσις that direct it?

Thucydides provides a counterfactual statement within the *History* that fortuitously provides the grounds for such an assessment.

> τοσοῦτον τῷ Περικλεῖ ἐπερίσσευσε τότε ἀφ' ὧν αὐτὸς προέγνω καὶ πάνυ ἂν ῥᾳδίως περιγενέσθαι τὴν πόλιν Πελοποννησίων αὐτῶν τῷ πολέμῳ (2.65.13).

So that at the time Pericles was more than justified in the conviction at which his foresight had arrived, that the Athenians would win an easy victory over the unaided forces of the Peloponnesians.

This is a narrative sentence in the full Dantonian sense. It concerns not only the past moment of Pericles' foresight that is articulated at 2.13 but also the future moment of Athens' defeat in the war in 404. Explicitly, Thucydides asserts that Pericles predicted an easy Athenian victory over the unaided force of the Spartans based on his assessment of both Athenian and Spartan resources. Implicitly, Thucydides confirms that the Athenians will eventually lose the war. This sentence, then, refers forward to Athens' defeat and refers back to Thucydides' presentation of Pericles' initial sentiments regarding the war and its course. In the Spring of 431, at the outset of the Peloponnesian War, Pericles advised his compatriots that if they "refrain from engaging the Spartans in battle" (μάχην μὴ ἐπεξιέναι) and if they "prepare their fleet" (τὸ ναυτικόν ἐξαρτύεσθαι) and if they "keep their allies close to hand" (τά τε τῶν ξυμμάχων διὰ χειρὸς ἔχειν) they would "win through in the war" (περιέσεσθαι τῷ πολέμῳ) (2.13.2–9).

The sentence as a counterfactual essentially says, '*if* the Athenians had adhered to Pericles' defensive war strategy, they *would have* won the Peloponnesian War'. The narrative of the war, then, could be construed as essentially an antithesis of this counterfactual. It is a sequence of facts that demonstrates the *why* of the Athenian defeat in relation to the *what-might-have-been*. As a narrative sentence, the counterfactual is comprised of two events. The second event is the implied Athenian defeat that eventually occurs. Though Thucydides explicitly professes to be documenting the war as it progresses, his various confessions of knowing the outcome of the war throughout the narrative suggest that his explanation is conceivably directed toward elucidating the most prominent events that contributed to this outcome.

The significance of the counterfactual lies in the αὐτῶν, which implies that the Athenians would have won the war had the Persians never got involved. Thucydides' task as historian is to elucidate those events that contribute to the eventual *aiding* of the Spartans, which arrives in the form of Persian wealth that allows the Spartans to build a navy. This broadly characterises the retrospective knowledge that Danto identifies as missing from the Ideal Chronicler. The first event is Pericles' initial war strategy. If the Athenians adhere to the war strategy, they will win the war. They do not and so they do not. The essential question of the *History*, then, is what precipitated the Athenian defeat? Thucydides blames Pericles' successors:

> For [Pericles] had told the Athenians that if they would be patient and would attend to their navy, and not seek to enlarge their dominion while the war was going on, nor imperil the existence of the city, they would be victorious; but they did all that he told them not to do, and in matters which seemingly had nothing to do with the war, from motives of private ambition and private interest they adopted a policy which had disastrous effects in respect both of themselves and of their allies; their measures, had they been successful, would only have brought honour and profit to individuals, and, when unsuccessful, crippled the city in the conduct of the war (2.65.7).

Thucydides proceeds to attribute the deviation from Pericles' war strategy to what he perceives to be a deterioration of Athenian political leadership after the death of Pericles (2.65.8–12). It is precisely then that Thucydides reveals the counterfactual (2.65.13). To summarise Thucydides' stance, then: the Athenians, following Pericles' war strategy, *should* win the war. The political leadership that succeeds Pericles deteriorates to the extent that motives of private ambition contribute to derailing the Athenians from Pericles' war strategy.[37]

While the cause of the Athens' defeat in the Peloponnesian War as the deterioration of Athenian leadership is well-acknowledged in modern scholarship (most likely because Thucydides explicitly says so in 2.65), the nature of this deterioration has not been sufficiently addressed. In his summation of Thucydides' understanding of Athens' defeat, Ober writes:

> Thucydides' socio-political analysis suggests that when Athens took the road of modernity, Athenian performance (i.e. capacity to flourish as a *polis* and grow into an empire) became dependent upon the reflexive interaction of a technology of power with political institutions and culture, and with the impulses of human nature. Without Periclean leadership, the political side of the Athenian equation did not remain in a positively reflexive relationship with the other elements of the system. *Absent the appropriate agents* to give it rational direction, the system became unbalanced. Blind structures (both institutional and ideological) overweighed rational human agency. Human selfishness was uncoupled from the recognition that individual flourishing required collective efforts. Warranted trust in the

---

[37] Cf. Turner (2018, 239–254), where the concept of Groupthink is discussed in relation to the deterioration of Athenian democratic decision-making processes.

system declined, and with it the capacity to take rational risks. And thus, virtually inevitably, catastrophic mistakes were made, and despite the great resources that had led Pericles to predict victory, Athens lost the war.[38]

It is precisely the 'absence of appropriate agents' within the Athenian political infrastructure that has yet to be substantially worked out. For Connor, "the nature of that standing [of Pericles' leadership traits] becomes clear by the contrast to his successors, whose obsession with private advancement and gain drove them to the flattery of the masses and made them followers rather than leaders".[39] But why is there a sudden obsession with private advancement and gain in the countenance of the successors? Is it purely chance? Balot suggests it's a possibility. He discusses the inherently "addle-brained and greedy" nature of the Athenian Assembly and wonders how the Athenians achieved such success in the fifth century:

> To this question, Thucydides offered an interesting answer: that (somehow) outstanding leaders rose to the summit of politics and led the people, willy-nilly, to do the right thing for the city ... Athens' success does not undermine Thucydides' criticisms of democracy as a system because the system itself cannot guarantee that a new Pericles will arise or even be recognised as an outstanding leader ... Athens' post-Periclean leaders tended to be selfish, unpatriotic, and more concerned to outdo their political rivals than to advise the city well.[40]

Accusations such as 'human selfishness' (Ober), 'obsession with private advancement' (Connor), and 'selfish, unpatriotic, and more concerned to outdo their political rivals than to advise the city well' (Balot) are typically directed toward Thucydides' concept of human nature. Thucydides alludes to human nature infrequently but its agency is a pervasive force throughout the narrative. He develops an almost Nietzschean conception of historical recurrence through his assessment of human nature.

> But if he who desires to have before his eyes a true picture of the events which have happened, and of the like events which may be expected to happen hereafter in the order of human things (τὸ ἀνθρώπινον), shall pronounce what I have written to be useful (1.22.4).

---

38 Ober 2006, 153 — my italics. Consider also, Foster 2010, 216: "In sum, Pericles' leadership of the assembly and correct knowledge of Athenian resources was to be preferred to the selfish quarrels and mistakes of his successors".
39 Connor 1984, 61.
40 Balot 2008, 131 — my italics.

Does history, for Thucydides, follows a programmatic schema according to fixed characteristics of human nature? Crane certainly thinks so:

> Nowhere in the exact sciences does any thinker take a greater leap in the direction of reductive analysis than Thucydides. Operating without any mathematical models and with only the most rudimentary numerical measures, Thucydides applies a small but powerful set of rules to human events and, in so doing, transformed his understanding of events. Two ideas play a particularly crucial role. First, the powerful naturally dominate the weak, and, second, essential human nature —"the human thing," as Marc Cogan has neatly rendered it — remains the same in all cultures and at all times. Thucydides did not discover these ... but, for better or for worse, he perfected them as an analytical tool and refined them to an unprecedented and still unsurpassed degree. Much of the *History* is devoted to working out these ideas, and Thucydides' Athenians are, in some sense, his avatars, testing these principles against the different situations that crop up during the course of the war.[41]

For Crane, then, Thucydides' *History* constitutes an exercise in exposing the fixed characteristics of human nature against the various conditions that prolonged warfare exacts upon the human condition.

In the broader context of this chapter concerning the correct determination of history as a rendering of the past, Thucydides' elucidation of a seemingly fixed human nature as the fundamental ground of history seemingly fits the profile of both the Ideal Chronicler and Laplace's Demon. In the case of the former, Thucydides' retrospective understanding of Athens' defeat in the war facilitates the formation of a narrative that highlights the various events of the war that contributed most significantly to its conclusion. In the case of the latter, Thucydides identifies the seemingly ineluctable, constant, and universal laws of human nature that drive the historical process. If the particulars that Thucydides derives from his explicit historiographical methods — eye-witness testimonies, evidence, what he saw himself, etc. (1.21–22) — form a Hempelian 'explanation sketch' then the identification of these laws of human nature provide the principles that connect the various particulars and thus produce a valid, scientific explanation. What is problematic in the case of the retrospective understanding is the lack of any such principle that enables the narrativisation of key events. If, however, the principle is precisely the same as that which guides the scientific understanding of history then the historical meaning that the Ideal Chronicler serves to elucidate is the universality of human nature itself. In both cases, then, owing to the fixed

---

41 Crane 1998, 13. See also, Rabinow 2009, 72: "Thucydides is seeking to understand what happened in this long war ... in his presentation of the materials of the war, takes as his object public deliberation and makes it available as an object to ponder, consider, debate". Cf. Thomas 2006, 87.

a-historical properties of human nature, history is entirely deterministic. In the case of history-as-literature, within the narrative, as the self-enclosed delimitation of unique historical processes, the Peloponnesian War is deterministic to the extent that the narrative is entirely directed toward a single end: Athens' defeat. In the case of history-as-science, the narrative demonstrates the necessity of the particular end by elucidating the universal laws that compel its realisation. How, then, does the contingency of Thucydides' counterfactual at 2.65.13, which says the Athenians *would* have won the war had they followed Pericles' strategy, stand in relation to the necessity of Athens' inevitable defeat according to the laws of human nature?

What problematises readings of Thucydides' *History* in the context of an explanation of the war according to fixed and constant laws of human nature is that the humans that inhabit Thucydides' narrative seldom, if ever, act in full compliance to the natural laws that apparently govern their actions. For Thucydides, in the context of complex systems theory, historical processes simply do not allow for a concatenation of abstract concepts such as necessity and contingency. Such concepts, at most, allow for explanation. It could be argued that the Spartans winning the Peloponnesian War was contingent on the deterioration of Athenian political leadership, but such an explanation would be empty and obvious. It does not provide for an *understanding* of history precisely because the manifold *reasons* for the victory could not be reduced to a formula pertaining to necessary or contingent causal mechanisms.

The problem of the philosophy of scientific historiography is its essential reliance on degrees of probability that themselves lend weight to the various abstract causal mechanisms. It is precisely the science of *probability* that determines all historical concepts of causality. Bevir articulates the difference between natural and historical explanations thusly:

> Natural scientists explain things using law-like generalizations which postulate physical connections. Historians of ideas explain things primarily in rational terms by highlighting conditional connections.[42]

Conditional connections that allow for historical explanation are understood according to the 'degrees of sensitivity' between the probability of a historical event occasioning in a certain way and the initial conditions that facilitate the particular occasion. The difference between necessity and contingency, then, revolves around the theoretical application of probability. In this way, the philosophy of

---

[42] Bevir 1999, 254.

scientific historiography is manifestly a reworking of positivism's pursuit of historical prediction.

The didactic principle that underlies the modern understanding of ancient historiography is often grounded in this scientific concept of prediction. This might anachronistically be applied to Thucydides' understanding of historical recurrence at 1.22.4. But for Thucydides, as for Polybius 300 years later, the notion of historical recurrence is not supposed to send scientific historiographers off searching for antecedent conditions to draw out probability theories grounded in necessity and contingency. Thucydides points to τὸ ἀνθρώπινον – the human thing – as a grounds for understanding the universality of history. Such universality is not akin to general laws that govern human behaviour and render historical processes deterministic. Rather, through historical understanding, Thucydides aims at getting human beings to confront and come to terms with their own activity. For Thucydides, history is the disclosing of truth and reason that lies not in correct propositional statements about the past but within the fundamental structure of τὸ ἀνθρώπινον. Only through hermeneutical analysis of the historicity of τὸ ἀνθρώπινον can the essence of history be disclosed. The piling up of methodologies and approximation of history to the physical and theoretical sciences, as well to the linguistic structures of literature, serves only to conceal further and further still the essence of history. It is toward a revaluation of ancient historiography through the devaluation of the modern concept of history that future research must proceed.

Bibliography

Ankersmit, Frank R. (2009), "Narrative and Interpretation", in Aviezer Tucker (ed.), *A Companion to the Philosophy of History and Historiography*, Malden, MA, 199–208.
Badian, Ernst (1993), *From Plataea to Potidaea: Studies in the History and Historiography of the Pentecontaetia*, Baltimore, MD.
Balot, Ryan K. (2008), *Greek Political Thought*, Malden, MA.
Berlin, Isaiah (1960), "History and Theory: The Concept of Scientific History", *History and Theory* 1, 1–31.
Bevir, Mark (1999), *The Logic of the History of Ideas*, Cambridge.
Carr, David (1986), *Time, Narrative, and History*, Indianapolis, IN.
Connor, W. Robert (1984), *Thucydides*, Princeton, NJ.
Crane, Gregory (1998), *Thucydides and the Ancient Simplicity: The Limits of Political Realism*, Berkeley, CA.
Danto, Arthur (2007), *Narration and Knowledge*, New York, NY.
Dilthey, Wilhelm [1900] (1976), *Selected writings of W. Dilthey* (Trans. H.P. Rickman), Cambridge.

Dray, William Herbert (1971), "On the Nature and Role of Narrative in Historiography", *History and Theory* 10, 153–171.
Foster, Edith (2010), *Thucydides, Pericles, and Periclean Imperialism*, New York, NY.
Gadamer, Hans-Georg (2007), "Autobiographical Reflections", in Richard E. Palmer (ed.), *The Gadamer Reader*, Evanston, IL., 3–41.
Gadamer, Hans-Georg [1960] (2013), *Truth and Method*, London.
Heidegger, Martin (1994), *Basic Questions of Philosophy* (trans. Richard Rojcewicz/Andre Schuwer), Indianapolis, IN.
Heidegger, Martin (2008), *Ontology: The Hermeneutics of Facticity* (trans. John van Buren), Indianapolis, IN.
Hunter, Virginia (1973), *Thucydides: the Artful Reporter*, Toronto.
Iggers, Georg (1997), *Historiography in the Twentieth Century: From Scientific Objectivity to the Postmodern Challenge*, Middleton, CT.
Kosso, Peter (1992), "Observation of the Past", *History and Theory* 31, 21–36.
Kuukkanen, Jouni-Matti (2015), *Postnarrativist Philosophy of Historiography*, Basingstoke.
Laplace, Pierre Simon [1814] (1902), *A Philosophical Essay on Probabilities* (trans. Frederick Wilson Truscott/Frederick Lincoln Emory), London.
Laudan, Rachel (1992), "What's so Special about the Past?" in Matthew H. Nitecki/Doris V. Nitecki (eds), *History and Evolution*, Albany, NY, 55–67.
Lendon, J.E. (2002), "Historians without History: Against Roman Historiography", in Andrew Feldherr (ed.), *The Cambridge Companion to the Roman Historians*, Cambridge, 41–62.
Master, Jonathan (2016), *Provincial Soldiers and Imperial Instability in the Histories of Tacitus*, Ann Arbor, MI.
Ober, Josiah (2006), "Thucydides and the Invention of Political Science" in Antonios Rengakos/Antonis Tsakmakis (eds), *Brill's Companion to Thucydides*, Leiden, 131–160.
Rabinow, Paul (2009), *Marking Time: On the Anthropology of the Contemporary*, Princeton, NJ.
Ricœur, Paul (1984), *Time and Narrative*, Chicago, IL.
Thomas, Rosalind (2006), "Thucydides' Intellectual Milieu and the Plague", in Antonios Rengakos/Antonis Tsakmakis (eds), *Brill's Companion to Thucydides*, Leiden, 87–108.
Tucker, Aviezer (2004), *Our Knowledge of the Past*, Cambridge.
Turner, Aaron (2018), "Thucydides, Groupthink, and the Sicilian Expedition Fiasco", in Jeroen Lauwers/Hedwig Schwall/Jan Opsomer (eds), *Psychology and the Classics: a Dialogue of Disciplines*, Berlin, 239–254.
Turner, Aaron (2019), "Being as Value: The Essence of Nihilism between Dostoevsky and Heidegger", *Clio: A Journal of Literature, History, and the Philosophy of History*, 369–394.
Wiseman, T.P. (1979), *Clio's Cosmetics*, Oxford.
Woodman, Anthony (1988), *Rhetoric in Classical Historiography*, London.

Neville Morley
Thucydides and the Historiography of the Future

> I shall be content if those wishing to know the truth about the things which happened, and which, people being as they are, will happen again in the same or similar manner, will judge my work to be useful.
>
> Thucydides 1.22

> Knowledge of the past is treasured at all times only in the service of the future and the present, not for the weakening of the present or the uprooting of a vigorous future.
>
> Friedrich Nietzsche, 'Zum Nutzen und Nachtheil der Historie für das Leben' (1874), 271.

What is, or should be, the goal of historical research and writing? How can knowledge of the past be made useful or productive? As the title suggests, the aim of this chapter is to develop a dialogue between Thucydides and Nietzsche, or at any rate to juxtapose their ideas and explore the consequences, in relation to historiography and the possible meanings of the past. Nietzsche's admiration for Thucydides is now a well-established element of Thucydidean reception, above all when he presented him as the perfect embodiment of 'realist culture' in opposition to the deception and cowardice of Platonism, an interpretation whose influence on twentieth-century readings is increasingly recognised.[1] Here, however, I want to focus on a much earlier piece in which Nietzsche nowhere mentioned Thucydides, but which raises important questions about the nature, purpose and reception of Thucydides' work, and where, I suggest, his presence can be surmised throughout: the second *Untimely Meditation* from 1874, 'On the uses and disadvantages of history for life'.

There are three dimensions to the dialogue that I want to establish. The first and most straightforward involves reading key aspects of Thucydides' work through the framework of ideas which Nietzsche developed to characterise historiography, and especially of his own age; above all, considering how far Thucydidean historiography conforms to one or other of the different categories of historical thinking identified in the essay.[2] This is an exercise in self-conscious

---

[1] Nietzsche 1889, 156. On Nietzsche, Thucydides and 'realism' see e.g. Zumbrunnen 2015 and Morley 2018.
[2] For a more conventional reading of Thucydidean historiography, see Greenwood 2006.

anachronism; we can read Thucydides in Nietzschean terms, without for a moment implying that this was his deliberate intent. The enterprise can to some extent be defended on the grounds that Nietzsche identified parallels between the saturation of his own age with history and the fact that the Greeks were the first to experience a fully historical culture; we might then might surmise the existence of parallels in ancient and modern desire for and modes of engaging with the past, even if the end results were (as he argued) quite different.[3] However, it seems more likely that the *contrasts* between Nietzsche's account of modern historical drives and Thucydides' ideas (or at least a plausible reading of them) will be most illuminating – and that this is the intended outcome of his reflections, rather than revealing flaws in his supposedly would-be universal framework of interpretation.

Secondly, we can reverse the perspective, and evaluate Nietzsche's ideas in terms of their resemblance to Thucydides' claims about how and why he wrote his work. This includes the possibility that Nietzsche's ideas were significantly influenced by his reading of the Greek text, which he had studied, together with a range of relevant contemporary scholarship including Wilhelm Roscher's *Leben, Werk und Zeitalter des Thukydides* and Friedrich Creuzer's *Die historische Kunst der Griechen*, in the late 1860s, while developing an outline for a new course on the beginnings of Greek historiography.[4] Thucydides can become a Nietzschean only in retrospect, whereas Nietzsche might indeed be a thorough-going Thucydidean, and not only on those occasions in his later works where he chose to present himself as such. Of course, in the absence of any direct references or citations of Thucydides in the essay, this can only be a matter of speculation on the basis of identifying possible parallels in thought and expression – but some of these are suggestive, as seen in the emphasis that both authors place on historiography being concerned with more than just knowledge of the past as an end in itself.

The third element of this brief discussion applies Nietzsche's historiographical framework to contemporary receptions of Thucydides and debates about his significance. As James Porter has observed in the case of the other philological writings, Nietzsche's accounts of antiquity generally tell us far more about his own ideas about modernity than they do about the ancient past, and are better understood as a form of cultural critique, including the critique of how others imagine and represent classical antiquity in their own image.[5] We might imagine,

---

[3] Nietzsche 1874, 333–4; foreshadowed at 271.
[4] Hennis 2003, 36; Emden 2008, 49.
[5] Porter 2000, 5.

therefore, that he would be at least as concerned with contemporary readers' (mis)readings and (mis)appropriations of Thucydides as with his own ideas about Thucydides' work – but in any case, his claims about the different ways in which the past is interpreted and represented can be applied to modern accounts of Thucydides, regardless of whether that was Nietzsche's intention, in order to explore Thucydidean reception from a new perspective.

1 Monuments, Data, Judgements

Nietzsche's essay opens by establishing that the historical sense is an essential part of being human. The ignorance of animals who live contentedly fettered to the moment may seem enviable, a kind of lost paradise or return to childhood, as it brings happiness at least in the negative sense of not being tormented by thoughts of the past or fear of the future, but it is beyond human reach except through the ultimate forgetting of death. But it remains the case, Nietzsche argued, that a certain amount of forgetting is essential for life; 'a man who wanted to feel everything historically through and through would be like someone who was forcibly deprived of sleep', and there is a degree of insomnia, of constant reflection and of historical sense which is harmful and ultimately fatal to ordinary beings.[6] One might, through an excess of history, attain a *suprahistorical* perspective, in which one recognises the pointlessness of existence, the blindness and injustice on which all human action depends, and sees that there is no real difference between past and present – but that perspective too is hostile to life, since it destroys any temptation to go on living or take part in events. What matters for ordinary people is the balance between knowing and forgetting, between the historical and the unhistorical; accepting historical knowledge as part of being human, while staying on the right side of the boundary where an excess of history allows the past to become 'the gravedigger of the present'.[7] If history and the historical sense are unavoidable, especially for Europeans, they should at least be employed better for the purpose of life.[8]

---

6 Nietzsche 1874, 250.
7 Ibid., 251.
8 Ibid., 256–7.

Nietzsche identified three ways in which life needs the service of history, pertaining to three different aspects of human existence: acting and striving, preserving and revering, and suffering and in need of deliverance.⁹ This gives rise to a trio of historical varieties, the monumental, the antiquarian and the critical — ideas which apply equally to the motives of production and appetites for consumption of history. Monumental history desires and provides models, teachers and comforters. It shows that greatness was once possible and so may be possible again, banishing doubt and resignation in the face of the present, and it acts as a stimulus, presenting the past as worthy of imitation. Antiquarian history seeks and offers comfort and certainty, 'the contentment of the tree in its roots', knowing and revering one's origins and the origins of the community or nation. Critical history, in contrast to both these approaches and in active opposition to them, seeks to identify those parts of the past that weigh us down, so that they can be scrupulously examined and finally condemned. Each of these varieties of history serves the cause of life; each of them, Nietzsche argued, can easily be taken to excess and lose touch with the true purpose of engaging with the past, and so become a danger.

How does Thucydides' work compare with these ideas? Certainly he did not share Nietzsche's concern with the problems of the excess of the historical; rather, he disparaged *hoi polloi* who fail to enquire properly into the past but simply accept the first story they hear (1.20), and writers who narrate past events with a view to entertainment rather than truth (1.21), both of which might be regarded as a necessary (or at least desirable) form of 'forgetting'. However, Thucydides' project was certainly not study of the past for its own sake. Rather, his stated criterion for the success of his history was that a reader, or the right kind of reader, should find it useful for understanding present and future events — exactly as Nietzsche, perhaps deliberately echoing him, had insisted: 'Knowledge of the past is treasured at all times only in the service of the future and the present'.¹⁰ Far more almost any historian who has come after him, Thucydides devoted himself and his work to the service of present and future Life rather than the dead past.

Modern interpreters of Thucydides have argued extensively about *how* Thucydides intended his readers to find the work useful — that is, what kinds of knowledge or understanding they should draw from it, and how (or whether) they should put it into action.¹¹ Nietzsche's template of the three kinds of history offers

---

9 Ibid., 258.
10 Ibid., 271.
11 Morley 2014, 139–64.

a different perspective on this question – if only in negative terms. There is little in Thucydides' account that matches the 'monumental' conception – that seems far closer to Herodotus' stated goal in writing, 'in order that in this way the memory of the past may not be blotted out from among men by time, and that great and marvellous deeds done by Greeks and foreigners and especially the reason why they warred against each other may not lack renown' (1.1.0). Thucydides explicitly criticised the most prominent example of a monumental conception in classical Athens, the story of the Tyrannicides, by pointing out the extent to which its inspirational effect depended on the distortion of the past. Further, while less explicitly targeted at versions of past events intended to inspire and stimulate people, his critique of the reasons why other accounts of the past cannot be trusted – the tendency to project present assumptions back onto the past, as in the case of Mycenae (1.10); the influence of partiality, forgetfulness, and romanticism on people's accounts, and a preference for harmony and the illusion of completeness over harsh complexity (1.22) – runs in parallel with Nietzsche's criticism of the monumental approach: 'How much difference must be overlooked, if it is to have that powerful effect, how violently must the individuality of the past be squeezed into a general form, and all its sharp corners and outlines broken off for the sake of conformity'.[12] Finally, we might simply note how little of Thucydides' account offers heroic examples for celebration or imitation – one might see here an echo of one of Dionysius of Halicarnassus' complaints about his unedifying and unworthy depiction of the Athenians at Melos (*Thucydides* 38–40) – unless one breaks the narrative apart and discards the awkward elements, in order to establish Pericles as a model leader. The Thucydidean past is offered not as an inspiration but as an awful warning from which we should learn.

An insistence on the need for accuracy, even at the expense of good writing, entertainment or improving moral purpose, might seem to take Thucydides closer to Nietzsche's conception antiquarian history. However, as noted above, his work was certainly not dedicated to chronicling past events for their own sake – let alone a 'a restless scrabbling together of everything that has ever existed' – and as critics since Dionysius have noted, his account is neither complete nor straightforward, but uneven in its coverage and carefully constructed to offer Thucydides' version of the war rather than 'the' war.[13] To this point we can add the striking resemblance of Nietzsche's antiquarian historian to the portrait of the 'historical artisan' offered by Wilhelm Roscher in his 1842 analysis of Thucydides

---

12 Nietzsche 1874, 261–2.
13 Ibid., 268.

as a historical writer.¹⁴ Thucydides, Roscher claimed, is the true historian, developing a proper understanding of the past, in contrast to someone who 'remains confined in the simple collection of material... What the sources have to say, he passes reliably on to us; but never anything further or deeper'.¹⁵ Nietzsche's account of the antiquarian is more damning and dramatic, complaining of 'the stench of must and mould', the decay of any creative spirit and the insatiable thirst for antiquity, 'even the dust of bibliographical quisquilian', but it offers the same contrast between understanding the past and merely compiling and preserving it as an end in itself.¹⁶

This leaves us with critical historiography. On the one hand, if Nietzsche intended his trio of historical types to cover all eventualities, or we take them as such for the sake of argument, then this is the only viable option. Thucydides depicted a past that is indeed worthy of condemnation, as Nietzsche suggested: a succession of human errors, crimes, violence and injustice. On the other hand, there is the notable absence of actual condemnation in his text, the often-remarked absence of explicit authorial judgements.¹⁷ Of course Thucydides could present individuals and events as manifestly culpable without overtly condemning them in his own words (Cleon, and the fate of the Plataeans, are two examples that come to mind), but he does this without showing partisanship for either side. The overall spirit of his work seems to come closer to what Nietzsche identified as the main danger with critical history, the fact that *all* history is worthy of condemnation: 'because so it is with human affairs ['mit den menschlichen Dingen' – echoes here of Thucydides' *kata to anthrōpinon*, 'the human thing', as the explanation for the repetitiveness of events?] that human violence and weakness are always powerful forces'.¹⁸ The critical historian scrutinises, judges and condemns specific elements of the past, chosen for self-serving reasons, and if he realises that these judgements could apply to the whole past, to all his roots, he risks losing his own nature. Thucydides chose his subject matter because of its perceived importance; he revealed the threads of human violence, folly and weakness that run through it — and by implication through human history as a whole — but without losing himself.¹⁹

---

14 Morley 2012.
15 Roscher 1842, 11–12.
16 Nietzsche 1874, 268.
17 Cf. Morley 2014, 79–91 on accounts of Thucydides' impartiality.
18 Nietzsche 1874, 269.
19 Cf. Nietzsche 1875, 5[58]: 'Whoever does not understand how brutal and senseless history is will never understand the drive to make history intelligible.'

2 Transcending History

It requires, Nietzsche argued, a great deal of strength to be able to live and to forget how far living and injustice are one and the same (echoes of Melos?).[20] Those who serve life by judging and destroying the past are both dangerous and endangered, since it is never possible to escape the past completely: 'because we are the product of earlier generations, we also the product of their aberrations, passions and errors, and their crimes; it is not possible to free oneself completely from this chain.[21] But Thucydides did not forget this, or pretend to transcend history; he is fully implicated in events — we see his own failure, treated as dispassionately as every other human misjudgement in his account — and the point of his endeavour was not to destroy the past but to learn from it. His recognition of 'the essential conditions of all events', the blindness and injustice of human action throughout history, comes close to Nietzsche's characterisation of the 'suprahistorical' perspective — but Thucydides did not fall into the temptation of despair or indifference in the face of this insight, since he continued to insist on the possibility of understanding as the basis for action in the present and future.

Instead, Thucydides better fits Nietzsche's idea of the historical man, which is presented as one possibility within the wider field of the suprahistorical:

> We will call them the historical men: looking into the past drives them towards the future, fires up their courage to continue to hold on to life and kindles the hope that justice will still be done and that happiness lies behind the hill towards which they are advancing. These historical men believe that the meaning of existence will come more and more to light in the course of its *process*, they look backwards only so that, through consideration of the process so far, they can learn to understand the present and to desire the future more fiercely; they have no idea how unhistorically they think and act, despite all their history, nor how their preoccupation with history stands in the service, not of pure knowledge, but of life.[22]

It seems fair to suggest that Thucydides was conscious of acting unhistorically, stepping outside his own time and its assumptions in order to achieve a better understanding of events that could serve times to come. How far he retained hope in future justice and happiness remains uncertain — hope, after all, appears as 'a great comfort in danger' and the basis for numerous unwise decisions in his account. Nevertheless, the idea that meaning emerges in the process of history, the

---

20 Nietzsche 1874, 269.
21 Ibid., 270.
22 Ibid., 255.

succession of events, perfectly sums up the basic method of his narrative; and he himself stated that the goal of the enterprise was usefulness, not pure knowledge. Such an attitude, Nietzsche argued, offers the possibility of overcoming rather than destroying the past, so that it no longer has power — but without thereby abandoning the world of history and action:

> A historical phenomenon, purely and completely grasped and resolved into a phenomenon of knowledge, is, for whoever has grasped it, dead: for he has recognised in it the delusion, the injustice, the blind passion and in general the whole earthly darkening horizon of that phenomenon and at the same time the historical power within it. This power has now become, over him who knows, impotent; if perhaps not yet over him as a living being.[23]

If we imagine we see an image of Thucydides behind these ideas, then one implication is that he transcended not only the past but the category of 'historian'. As Nietzsche argued in his later comments, Thucydides grasped the truth about historical phenomena and about reality as a whole, he had the courage the face that truth rather than retreating into the comforting world of the ideal, and he sought to teach that understanding to others. In contrast to the moderns, Nietzsche claimed, the Greeks kept a tenacious hold of their unhistorical sense, and so avoided being destroyed by an excess of the past.[24] Their culture was for centuries a chaos of foreign ideas, throwing their own traditions and roots into question — is this an echo of Herodotean historiography, setting Greek history within a colourful maelstrom of foreign ideas and practices, and raising the unsettling idea that 'custom is king'? — but they held fast to the Delphic principle of knowing themselves and so organised the chaos.[25] Thucydides, praised by Nietzsche later as an exemplar of the healthy instincts of the pre-Socratic Greeks in their engagement with the world, is at the very least a representative of their mastery of history; his work might indeed be seen as one of the actual means by which they made sense of the chaos of events and understood their own nature. 'History can be endured only by strong personalities, it completely extinguishes the weak'.[26]

If the idea that Thucydides, or an idealised image of Thucydides, lies behind Nietzsche's critique of existing forms of history has any plausibility, then this might perhaps explain the vehemence of his attack on the idea of history as science that plays a central role in his discussion of modern historical culture in the

---

23 Ibid., 257.
24 Ibid., 273–4.
25 Ibid., 333.
26 Ibid., 283.

second part of his essay.²⁷ The demand that history should be a science, he argued, is modernity's fundamental error: 'Now life no longer reigns alone and sets limits on knowledge of the past; but all the barriers have been torn down, and everything that every was is dumped upon humanity'.²⁸

Within the barrage of denunciations and laments about the state of modern German culture, we can identify three which bear directly on ideas of historiography. Firstly, 'history as science' has no sense of priorities or purpose, but knowledge of any kind is regarded as equally valuable: 'Knowledge, consumed in excess without any hunger and even contrary to one's needs'.²⁹ Secondly, the accumulation of such masses of information supports misconceived ideas about the superiority of the modern age — 'though this surfeit, an age develops the idea that it possesses the rarest of virtues, justice, to a higher degree than any other era'.³⁰ This goes hand in hand with the idea of historical objectivity, claimed as a distinctly modern achievement, which is in fact merely the naïve elevation of present-day knowledge and assumptions above every other mode of understanding, and which implies that the best person to study the past is someone to whom it means nothing.³¹ This characterisation overall bears a significant relationship to the decadent form of antiquarianism, the relentless accumulation of information about the past, so that modern culture loses any sense of its own nature but becomes a mere walking encyclopaedia. The distinctive modern claim is that the possession of such masses of data will automatically result in a better understanding of the world; and Nietzsche's greatest contempt is reserved for the nature of the knowledge that is produced by 'scientific history', general laws and principles about human behaviour.

> It seems to me that such historians ... cease to teach as soon as they become general and then exhibit their sense of weakness in obscurities. In other sciences the generalisations are the most important thing, insofar as they contain the laws; but if such [historical] statements as those quoted want to be taken as laws, then it would be objected, that the work of the history-writer is a waste of time; because whatever truth remains in such sentences, after the removal of the dark unresolvable residue of which we spoke — that is already known and indeed trivial; because it will be obvious to anyone with the smallest amount of experience.³²

---

27 Discussed by Zumbrunnen 2002.
28 Nietzsche 1874, 271–2.
29 Ibid., 272.
30 Ibid., 279.
31 Ibid., 285–7, 293.
32 Ibid., 291–2.

The relevance of Thucydides to this discussion is that, alone among pre-modern historians, he was claimed as a predecessor and inspiration by 19th-century proponents of 'Geschichte als Wissenschaft'.[33] This reading relied primarily on his methodological statements at the beginning of Book 1, interpreting these as anticipations of modern precepts: critical analysis of evidence, objectivity (the new way of characterising what earlier readers had labelled 'impartiality') and the rejection of the idea of history as art, exemplified by his disparagement of works written as 'performance pieces'. In addition, however, some of these interpreters saw in Thucydides a new idea — or rather, a modern idea prefigured — of the kind of knowledge and understanding that history could offer, to match its rivals in the natural and social sciences.

> He conceives of history not only as the new science of facts, but as a new science which, attaching itself to events, discerns in them the secret combinations, determines in them the laws and recognises in them the effects of intelligence.[34]

This offered a new way of understanding Thucydides' claim that his work would be useful: he had intended all along to identify through his study of past events the kinds of general principles of human nature that 19th-century historians now realised were required. The fact that his account contained no such statements of general principles — as Thomas Hobbes had observed two and a half centuries earlier — was of no great import.

From a Nietzschean perspective, such a reading was absurd: it reduced the depth and detail of Thucydides' account, and the underlying principle that understanding would develop in the course of events, to a clumsy vehicle for presenting banalities as universal laws. It disparaged the artistic elements of engagement with the past; not invariably, as Roscher's version of Thucydides as a proponent of scientific history insisted on the necessity of creative and literary skill to present scientific findings in an effective and persuasive manner, but the majority of 19th-century Thucydideans emphasised his disparagement of history written as entertainment and history exaggerated by the poets, and managed to overlook or negotiate the way around the obvious problem presented by his comments on the composition of the speeches. In terms of Nietzsche's typology of history, this modern reading of Thucydides epitomises the monumental, to be set alongside the 'antiquarianism' of philological readings: Thucydides is claimed as a heroic predecessor, and his example is offered for imitation and reverence —

---

33 Morley 2014, 59–69. Zumbrunnen 2002 discusses this tradition of Thucydidean reception, but focuses solely on 20th-century readings rather than those contemporary with Nietzsche.
34 Girard 1860, 11. I have not been able to establish whether Nietzsche knew of Girard's essay.

but at the expense of distorting or even destroying the reality of the past, knocking off its rough edges (that is, elements of Thucydidean historiography that do not fit or even contradict modern assumptions). Modern Thucydideans might, perhaps, experience the anxiety of being epigones, and of being unable to match the greatness of past achievements (cf. Roscher's insistence in his preface that a historian like Thucydides can only be born, not educated), but for the most part their engagement with the past simply bolsters their own sense of superiority, just as the universal historian now finds traces of himself in primeval slime, congratulates himself on being capable of tracing such a course of development, and thinks of himself as nature perfected.[35]

'Overproud European of the nineteenth century, you are raving!'[36] Such historiography is not a perfection of Thucydides' work, but the destruction of it; it has none of his understanding of the true nature of reality and the human thing, but generates only banal truisms and the belief that the past should be studied only by someone with no emotional connection to it will do nothing to save humanity from an excess of history.

> What is needed instead above all is a great artistic power, a creative overview, a loving immersion in the empirical data, further development of given types — and of course objectivity is also required, but as a positive quality.[37]

3 Confronting Ancient and Modern Historiography

Nietzsche had little interest in 'reconciling' ancient and modern conceptions of and responses to history. On the contrary, he constantly emphasised the differences between them, above all at the cultural level, and invariably to the benefit of the ancients. As he remarked at the end of the Introduction to his essay,

> I do not know what meaning classical studies would have in our time if not that of working in their untimeliness — that is to say, against our time and thereby on our time and, let us hope, for the benefit of a time to come.[38]

The different modern approaches to historiography are implicitly contrasted with a true, life-affirming historiography that does not merely draw on the past but

---

[35] Roscher 1842, xi. Nietzsche 1874, 312–13.
[36] Nietzsche 1874, 313.
[37] Ibid., 292.
[38] Ibid., 247.

helps people overcome it and remove its power over them — a historiography that bears a significant resemblance to that of Thucydides. The dominance of modern culture by an unbridled sense for history is explicitly contrasted with the ability of the Greeks to remain true to themselves despite their invention of history as a form of knowledge. Above all, Nietzsche decried the attempts of the moderns to present themselves as the heirs or culmination of Thucydidean understanding, as the perfecters of historiography, where in fact for all their reverence they had radically misunderstood its true nature, and so would be incapable of echoing its achievements.

Thucydides assumed the existence of 'the human thing' as the source of a basic continuity or similarity between past, present and future, such that true knowledge of the former can illuminate and serve other times. Nietzsche for the most part insisted on discontinuity and untimeliness as the basis of understanding, but this was presented largely in opposition to the universalising claims of nineteenth-century knowledge. He shared a sense with the Greeks — or at least claimed to identify this already in classical Greece — of the timeless nature of 'human things' as an endless succession of injustice and violence, with no justificatory meaning beyond the fact that this is how life is; and this had the effect of establishing Thucydides, at least for his own purposes, as a model for the historiography of the future that radically contrasted with the way he was understood by contemporary historians.

Bibliography

Emden, Christian J. (2008), *Friedrich Nietzsche and the Politics of History*, Cambridge.
Girard, Jules (1860), *Essai sur Thucydide*, Paris.
Greenwood, Emily (2006), *Thucydides and the Shaping of History*, London.
Hennis, Wilhelm (2003), *Max Weber und Thukydides: Nachträge zur Biographie des Werks*, Tübingen.
Morley, Neville (2012), 'Thucydides, history and historicism in Wilhelm Roscher', in Katherine Harloe/Neville Morley (eds), *Thucydides and the Modern world: reception, reinterpretation and influence from the Renaissance to the present*, Cambridge, 115–39.
Morley, Neville (2014), *Thucydides and the Idea of History*, London.
Morley, Neville (2018), 'Thucydides: the origins of political realism?', in Myles Hollingsworth/Robert Schuett (eds), *The Edinburgh Companion to Political Realism*, Edinburgh, 111–123.
Muhlack, Ulrich (2011), 'Herodotus and Thucydides in the view of nineteenth-century German historians', in Alexandra Lianeri (ed.), *The Western Time of Ancient History: historiographical encounters with the Greek and Roman pasts*, Cambridge, 179–209.
Murari Pires, Francisco (2006), 'Thucydidean modernities', in Antonios Rengakos/Antonis Tsakmakis (eds), *Brill's Companion to Thucydides*, Leiden, 811–37.

Nietzsche, Friedrich (1874), 'Vom Nutzen und Nachtheil der Historie für das Leben', *Unzeitgemässe Betrachtungen II*, in Nietzsche, *Sämtliche Werke: Kritischen Studienausgabe* I, eds. Giorgio Colli/Mazzino Montinari, Berlin (2nd edn 1988).

Nietzsche, Friedrich (1875), 'Wir Philologen' [unpublished notes], in: Nietzsche, *Werke* IV.1, eds. Giorgio Colli/Mazzino Montinari, Berlin (1967).

Nietzsche, Friedrich (1889), *Götzen-Dämmerung, oder Wie man mit dem Hammer philosophirt*, in: Nietzsche, *Sämtliche Werke: Kritischen Studienausgabe* VI, eds. Giorgio Colli/Mazzino Montinari, Berlin (1988).

Porter, James I. (2000), *Nietzsche and the Philology of the Future*, Stanford.

Roscher, Wilhelm (1842), *Leben, Werk und Zeitalter des Thukydides*, Göttingen.

Zumbrunnen, John (2002), 'Courage in the face of reality: Nietzsche's admiration for Thucydides', *Polity* 35, 237–63.

Zumbrunnen, John (2015), 'Realism, constructivism, and democracy in the *History*', in Christine Lee/Neville Morley (eds), *A Handbook to the Reception of Thucydides*, Malden MA, 296–312.

List of Contributors

David Carr – Emory University

Katherine Clarke – University of Oxford

Jonas Grethlein – Heidelberg University

François Hartog – École des hautes études en sciences sociales

Laurence Paul Hemming – Lancaster University

Ahuvia Kahane – Trinity College Dublin

Duncan F. Kennedy – University of Bristol

Inger N.I. Kuin – University of Virginia

Alexander Meeus – University of Mannheim

Neville Morley – University of Exeter

Aske Damtoft Poulsen – University of Bristol

Jerry Toner – University of Cambridge

Salvatore Tufano – Sapienza University of Rome

Aaron Turner – Royal Holloway, University of London

Index

Aeschylus 69
Ammianus Marcellinus 104, 108, 112
Appian 214
Aristophanes 69, 203
Aristotle 4, 5, 11, 14, 15, 16, 17, 18, 19, 22, 25, 26, 27, 29, 32, 33, 34, 35, 36, 38, 40, 47, 48, 52, 54, 56, 61, 62, 71, 80, 86, 124, 129, 130, 131, 132, 133, 140, 144, 145, 168, 195, 245, 247, 266, 286, 298, 299, 327, 329, 336, 341
Arrian 87

Carr, Edward Hallett 137
Cassius Dio 188
Cicero 15, 17, 18, 20, 22, 91, 93, 94, 95, 196, 212
Colligation 335
Common Cause Theory 338
Consciousness, Historical 1, 3, 4, 7, 225, 282, 283, 328, 329, 336, 341
Constructivism 335
Contingency, Historical 3, 152, 337, 352, 353
Counterfactualism 156, 165, 348, 352
Croce, Benedetto 2, 332

Danto, Arthur 2, 332, 333, 334, 346, 349
Deleuze, Gilles 31
Demosthenes (orator) 212
Descartes, René 67, 311, 336
Dilthey, Wilhelm 1, 3, 313, 323, 338, 341, 342, 343
Diodorus Siculus 6, 89, 91, 96, 98, 100, 101, 110, 113, 114, 116, 185, 186, 189, 190, 191, 192, 193, 194, 195, 196, 197
Dionysius of Halicarnassus 191, 195, 359

Emplotment 2, 143, 209
Ephorus 104, 189, 190
Epistemology 23, 52, 59, 84, 85, 86, 90, 94, 117, 118, 318, 330
Euripides 70
Experientiality 6, 149, 150, 151, 153, 154, 166, 168, 171, 176, 335

Foucault, Michel 31, 142, 238, 239, 255, 316
Fukuyama, Francis 58, 123, 311, 317

Gadamer, Hans-Georg 125, 126, 338, 342, 343, 344

Habermas, Jürgen 128, 338
Hecataeus 4, 104, 190
Hegel, Georg Wilhelm Friedrich 1, 2, 27, 28, 32, 33, 38, 40, 50, 126, 311, 312, 313, 315, 316, 317, 326, 330, 331, 332, 336, 341
Heidegger, Martin 1, 4, 25, 27, 28, 29, 30, 31, 33, 35, 36, 37, 38, 39, 40, 41, 54, 57, 60, 61, 62, 67, 78, 142, 319, 323, 324, 326, 328, 332, 342, 343, 344, 354
Hempel, Carl 1, 127, 328, 337, 346
Herder, Johann Gottfried 1, 330, 331
Herodotus 6, 7, 11, 12, 13, 14, 18, 19, 20, 21, 23, 38, 44, 50, 51, 52, 57, 63, 64, 65, 66, 67, 68, 69, 70, 71, 72, 77, 78, 79, 80, 87, 88, 93, 96, 103, 104, 110, 119, 120, 131, 134, 144, 145, 179, 181, 187, 190, 191, 192, 199, 200, 201, 202, 203, 204, 205, 206, 228, 235, 256, 264, 267, 278, 269, 270, 271, 272, 273, 277, 278, 281, 282, 283, 286, 287, 288, 289, 359, 366
Hieronymus 97, 106, 191
Historicism 1, 3, 123, 124, 125, 126, 127, 130, 145, 276, 279, 289, 326, 327, 328, 330, 331, 332, 334, 340, 343, 344, 366
Hobbes, Thomas 26, 137, 364
Homer 11, 13, 15, 21, 78, 102, 179, 235, 278, 293

Kant, Immanuel 1, 311, 315, 316, 325, 330
Koselleck, Reinhart 48, 126, 129, 136

Laws, Historical 93, 94, 124, 126, 127, 129, 141, 327, 329, 331, 336, 337, 338, 339, 341, 346, 351, 352, 353, 363, 364
Linguistic Turn 2, 143, 192, 209, 328, 332, 336, 339

Livy 156, 159, 161, 178, 186, 194, 304, 305
Lucian 15, 19, 20, 21, 22, 23, 87, 95, 98, 109, 110, 111, 116, 198

Machiavelli, Niccoló 137
Marx, Karl 27, 33, 255, 275, 292, 311, 313, 316, 336
Marxism 274, 313, 316, 326, 337
Mimesis 7, 14, 97, 98, 99, 101, 102, 116, 131, 132, 191, 193, 194, 195, 198, 199, 202, 203, 291, 295, 298, 299, 300, 307
Momigliano, Arnaldo 15, 84, 196
Myth 115, 140, 189, 265, 296, 297

Narratology 2, 209, 268, 270, 335, 339
Necessity, Historical 3, 50, 56, 57, 58, 131, 152, 244, 325, 337, 346, 352, 353
Nietzsche, Friedrich 2, 8, 32, 37, 41, 276, 298, 313, 316, 332, 338, 343, 350, 355, 356, 357, 358, 359, 360, 361, 362, 363, 364, 365, 366

Parmenides 62, 63, 64, 70, 71
Pausanias 216, 273
Pindar 38, 241, 265
Plato 4, 15, 17, 38, 44, 48, 53, 54, 55, 57, 60, 61, 63, 64, 65, 66, 69, 70, 71, 72, 73, 75, 77, 78, 79, 80, 86, 113, 122, 131, 132, 218, 235, 245, 247, 249, 252, 253, 255, 257, 258, 259, 265, 266, 298, 299, 300, 329, 336, 343, 355
Pliny the Elder 267
Pliny the Younger 186, 267
Plutarch 6, 14, 37, 40, 87, 93, 95, 120, 121, 197, 207, 208, 209, 210, 211, 212, 213, 214, 215, 216, 217, 218, 219, 220, 221, 222, 223, 224, 225, 226, 227, 228, 229, 265
Polybius 14, 16, 17, 18, 87, 89, 93, 96, 97, 99, 100, 103, 105, 106, 107, 110, 112, 114, 119, 120, 121, 122, 168, 181, 190, 191, 192, 193, 194, 198, 200, 205, 289, 329, 353
Positivism 1, 3, 84, 124, 255, 311, 315, 316, 327, 328, 331, 340, 346
Postnarrativism 335
Probability 131, 132, 347, 352, 353

Ranke, Leopold von 1, 19, 23, 124, 126, 141, 276, 278, 327, 331, 332
Representation, Historical 5, 6, 7, 68, 69, 101, 102, 116, 131, 141, 143, 183, 192, 194, 195, 196, 197, 199, 202, 203, 298, 300, 318, 327
Ricœur, Paul 14, 151, 334, 335, 343

Sallust 109, 114
Sophocles 56, 57
Suetonius 104, 291

Tacitus 2, 6, 91, 96, 149, 150, 153, 156, 157, 158, 162, 165, 166, 168, 169, 170, 171, 172, 173, 177, 178, 179, 180, 181, 182, 183, 186, 187, 188, 189, 190, 193, 194, 202, 204, 205, 254, 255, 307, 354
Teleology, Historical 3, 6, 58, 149, 150, 151, 152, 153, 155, 156, 157, 166, 176, 177, 312, 313, 316, 324, 325, 326, 337
Theopompus 101, 107, 110, 112
Thucydides 2, 5, 6, 8, 12, 13, 14, 18, 20, 21, 22, 23, 49, 58, 83, 85, 87, 88, 93, 94, 95, 96, 97, 98, 102, 103, 104, 109, 110, 113, 120, 121, 122, 124, 129, 130, 131, 133, 134, 135, 136, 137, 138, 139, 140, 141, 143, 144, 145, 146, 153, 178, 179, 185, 186, 189, 197, 205, 206, 210, 231. 232, 233, 235, 236, 237, 238, 239, 241, 242, 243, 244, 245, 246, 247, 248, 249, 250, 251, 252, 256, 257, 258, 259, 260, 264, 267, 276, 277, 278, 279, 283, 284, 285, 286, 288, 289, 340, 341, 344, 345, 346, 347, 348, 349, 350, 351, 352, 353, 354, 355, 356, 357, 358, 359, 360, 361, 362, 364, 365, 366, 367
Timaeus 97, 91, 92, 97, 103, 105, 106, 107, 110, 112, 190, 191

Vico, Giambattista 7, 329, 330
Virgil 58, 174, 266

White, Hayden 2, 5, 11, 153, 196, 209, 328, 332, 335

Xenophon 14, 20, 21, 23, 95

www.ingramcontent.com/pod-product-compliance
Lightning Source LLC
Chambersburg PA
CBHW031845220426
43663CB00006B/508